# Lecture Notes in Computer Science    3928

*Commenced Publication in 1973*
Founding and Former Series Editors:
Gerhard Goos, Juris Hartmanis, and Jan van Leeuwen

Josep Domingo-Ferrer    Joachim Posegga
Daniel Schreckling (Eds.)

# Smart Card Research and Advanced Applications

7th IFIP WG 8.8/11.2 International Conference, CARDIS 2006
Tarragona, Spain, April 19-21, 2006
Proceedings

 Springer

Volume Editors

Josep Domingo-Ferrer
Universitat Rovira i Virgili, Departament d'Enginyeria Informatica i Matematiques,
Av. Paisos Catalans 26, 43007 Tarragona, Catalonia, Spain
E-mail: josep.domingo@urv.net

Joachim Posegga
Daniel Schreckling
Universität Hamburg
Arbeitsbereich Sicherheit in Verteilten Systemen (SVS)
Fachbereich Informatik
Vogt-Kölln-Str. 30, 22527 Hamburg, Germany
E-mail: {posegga,schreckling}@informatik.uni-hamburg.de

Library of Congress Control Number: 2006922624

CR Subject Classification (1998): E.3, K.6.5, C.3, D.4.6, K.4.1, E.4, C.2

LNCS Sublibrary: SL 4 – Security and Cryptology

ISSN        0302-9743
ISBN-10     3-540-33311-8 Springer Berlin Heidelberg New York
ISBN-13     978-3-540-33311-1 Springer Berlin Heidelberg New York

Springer is a part of Springer Science+Business Media

springer.com

© 2006 IFIP International Federation for Information Processing, Hofstr. 3, A-2361 Laxenburg, Austria
Printed in Germany

Typesetting: Camera-ready by author, data conversion by Scientific Publishing Services, Chennai, India
Printed on acid-free paper      SPIN: 11733447      06/3142      5 4 3 2 1 0

# Preface

Smart cards are an established security research area with a very unique property: it integrates numerous subfields of IT Security, which often appear scattered and only loosely connected. Smart card research unites them by providing a common goal: advancing the state of the art of designing and deploying small tokens to increase the security in Information Technology.

CARDIS has a tradition of more than one decade, and has established itself as the premier conference for research results in smart card technology. As smart card research is unique, so is CARDIS; the conference successfully attracts academic and industrial researchers without compromising in either way. CARDIS accommodates applied research results as well as theoretical contributions that might or might not become practically relevant. The key to making such a mixture attractive to both academia and industry is simple: quality of contributions and relevance to the overall subject.

This year's CARDIS made it easy to continue this tradition: we received 76 papers, nearly all of them relevant to the focus of CARDIS and presenting high-quality research results. The Program Committee worked hard on selecting the best 25 papers to be presented at the conference.

We are very grateful to the members of the Program Committee and the additional referees for generously spending their time on the difficult task of assessing the value of submitted papers. Daniel Schreckling provided invaluable assistance in handling submissions, managing review reports and editing the proceedings. The assistance of Jordi Castellà in handling practical aspects of the conference preparation is also greatly appreciated.

Financial support by the following organizations is gratefully acknowledged: IEEE Spain Section, Rovira i Virgili University (ETSE, DEIM) and Spain's Ministry of Science and Education.

Finally, we would also like to thank all those who have submitted papers to IFIP CARDIS 2006, and encourage them to stay with CARDIS in subsequent years. The authors of the accepted papers certainly deserve the highest respect, since it is they who wrote this book.

January 2006

Josep Domingo-Ferrer
Joachim Posegga

# Organization

CARDIS 2006 was organized by the Universitat Rovira i Virgili, Catalonia, Spain.

## Conference Organization

Conference General Chair
    Josep Domingo-Ferrer
      (Universitat Rovira i Virgili, Catalonia, Spain)

Program Committee Chair
    Joachim Posegga
      (University of Hamburg, Germany)

Advisory Committee
    José A. Delgado-Penín
      (IEEE Spain Section Chair, Spain)

## Program Committee

Boris Balacheff
(Hewlett-Packard Labs, UK)
Bertrand du Castel
(Axalto, USA)
Josep Domingo-Ferrer
(Universitat Rovira i Virgili, Catalonia, Spain)
Dieter Gollmann
(TU Hamburg-Harburg, Germany)
Louis Guillou
(France Télécom, France)
Pieter Hartel
(University of Twente, Netherlands)
Peter Honeyman
(University of Michigan, USA)
Dirk Husemann
(IBM Research, Switzerland)
Eduardo de Jong
(Sun Microsystems, USA)
Jean-Louis Lanet
(Gemplus Labs, France)

Javier Lopez
(University of Malaga, Spain)
Bernd Meyer
(Siemens AG, Germany)
Mike Montgomery
(Axalto, USA)
Pierre Paradinas
(CNAM, France)
Jean-Jacques Quisquater
(Université Catholique de Louvain, Belgium)
Francesc Sebé
(Universitat Rovira i Virgili, Catalonia, Spain)
François-Xavier Standaert
(Université Catholique de Louvain, Belgium)
Jean-Jacques Vandewalle
(Gemplus Labs, France)

# Additional Referees

A. Ali
V. Benjumea
D. Bolzoni
E. Brier
R. Brinkman
I. Buhan
M. Casassa-Mont
J. Castellà-Roca
J. Cederquist
L. Chen
M. Ciet
R. Corin
M. Czenko
M. Dekker
G.M. de Dormale

J.B. Fischer
C. Fontaine
P. Girard
B. Gonzalvo
D. Gross-Amblard
H. Handschuh
K. Harrisson
Z. HuanGuo
M. Johns
M. Joye
A. Kargl
K. Lu
F. Macé
A. Maña
W. Mao

A. Martínez-Ballesté
A. Muñoz E. Peeters
H.C. Pöhls
E. Prouff
R. Roman
A. Saptawijaya
D. Schreckling
J. Seedorf
D. Simplot-Ryl
A. Solanas
A. Viejo-Galicia
L.Y. Wei
A. Zych

# Table of Contents

## Smart Card Networking

## Cryptographic Protocols

## RFID Security

## Formal Methods

# Design, Installation and Execution of a Security Agent for Mobile Stations

William G. Sirett*, John A. MacDonald**,
Keith Mayes, and Konstantinos Markantonakis

Smart Card Centre, Information Security Group,
Royal Holloway, University of London,
Egham, TW20 0EX, England
{w.g.sirett, k.markantonakis, keith.mayes}@rhul.ac.uk,
john@madgo.com

**Abstract.** In this paper we present a methodology and protocol for establishing a security context between a Mobile Operator's application server and a GSM/UMTS SIM card. The methodology assumes that the already issued Mobile Station is capable but unprepared. The proposed scheme creates a secure entity within the Mobile Station "Over The Air" (OTA). This secure entity can then be used for subsequent SIM authentications enabling m-Commerce, DRM or web service applications. To validate our proposal we have developed a proof of concept model to install and execute the security context using readily available J2ME, Java Card, J2SE and J2EE platforms, with the KToolBar MIDP2.0 emulator tool from Sun, and a Gemplus Java Card.

**Keywords:** Mobile Station, Security Agent, Application Deployment, Smart Card, GSM, Security Protocol, JSR177, MIDP2.0.

## 1 Introduction

The GSM network offers a wide scope of applications and benefits for mobile operators. The merits of a Mobile Station capable of implementing a *Security Agent* are well documented in the literature [17, 18]. In this paper we consider the deployment of a *Security Agent* that is comprised of two components: a device application executing resource-intensive tasks, and a secure entity application responsible for secure functionality. The secure entity is a tamper resistant [5] entity and in the case of this work is a GSM/UMTS SIM card. For some time the GSM network has allowed for "Over The Air" (OTA) SIM application installation with limited bandwidth capacity. To install these applications utilising a high bandwidth channel and a non-GSM specified protocol currently demands trust/keys being provided to the Mobile Device. This work considers the Mobile Device to be hostile. This raises a need for the same high bandwidth OTA functionality to be available whilst protecting against malicious equipment.

---

\* This work was supported by sponsorship funding from the Smart Card Centre founded by Vodafone and G&D.

\*\* This work was supported by sponsorship funding from Telefonica Móviles, España.

J. Domingo-Ferrer, J. Posegga, and D. Schreckling (Eds.): CARDIS 2006, LNCS 3928, pp. 1–15, 2006.

This work establishes a security context between a Mobile Operator Application and Mobile Station and proposes an authenticated key establishment protocol. By establishing session keys independent of the network security keys, we can provide integrity, authentication and confidentially at the application layer. In the GSM/3GPP mobile architecture [24], the user security context resides in two locations, the network HLR and the Operator issued tamper resistant SIM card. The Mobile Operator generally has much less control over the Mobile device than the SIM. Consequently they are more reluctant to load sensitive components or data into the device. This motivates the division of the *Security Agent* between the device and the SIM, where the SIM is responsible for particularly sensitive components. We propose a scenario where the Mobile Operator Application server communicates with the device resident component of the *Security Agent*. This subsequently uses the security services provided by the secure entity to establish authenticated keys.

In section 2 we review the design requirements for a *Security Agent* deployed on a GSM/3GPP Mobile Station. In section 3 we review our proposed authenticated key establishment scheme. A protocol for wireless installation of the *Security Agent* to a compatible but remote and unprepared Mobile Station (colloquially termed "OTA" and "backward compatible field installation") is detailed in section 4, whilst the protocol used to establish session integrity and confidentiality keys is presented in section 5. Finally, in section 6, we describe the Proof of Concept model constructed using readily available components and open source development tool kits and provide concluding remarks in section 7.

## 2    Design Requirements

A critical requirement is for a backward compatible field installable *Security Agent* designed to provide an authentication service using SIM based credentials. It is required to be executable on a significant proportion of globally standardised and deployed Mobile Stations. The design of our proposed *Security Agent* uses four widely adopted technologies and standards:

- ETSI TS03.48 Security Mechanism [1];
- SIM Application Toolkit (SAT) [12];
- MIDP2.0 J2ME Runtime Environment [15];
- UICC Java Card SIM cards [3].

### 2.1    ETSI TS03.48 Security Mechanism

ETSI TS03.48 [1] specifies a mechanism for providing end to end security for any Short Message Service (SMS) going to or from the SIM card. SMS messages contain a maximum of 140 bytes. SMS messages are sent in accordance with the SUBMIT_SMS format, and received with the SMS_DELIVER format. Translation from one format to the other is performed by the Short Message Service Centre (SMSC), an active component of the network. In an output SUBMIT_SMS packet, the 40 bytes of User Data are complemented by a 13 byte *Mandatory Header* and an optional variable length *User Data Header*.

– The *Mandatory Header* includes the Data Coding Scheme byte which specifies how the data is encoded, and the Protocol Identifier byte which specifies
how the receiving mobile should process the message. One of these values,
$0xF7$, specifies that the device should pass the whole packet to the SIM
card.

– The *User Data Header* comprises a concatenation of tag, length and value
(TLV) fields which describe the optional features that should be applied to
the attached 140 bytes of user data. Of interest to our proposal are tag values
$0x00$ and $0x70$, meaning Concatenated SMS and SAT Security respectively.

  • The concatenated SMS tag allows up to 255 SMSs to be concatenated.
  It is reported [13] that most operators limit this to approximately five,
  because of uncertain and indeterminate device operation when receiving larger numbers of SMS messages to be concatenated. Five messages
  represents a total payload of 5x140 = 700 bytes [18].

  • The presence of the SAT Security tag ($0x70$) indicates that the message
  contains an additional header, the *Command Header*, prior to the *User
  Data Header*. This comprises of 9 fields which define how the User Data
  is secured by:

    * specifying the cryptographic functions,
    * providing a replay protection counter,
    * quoting the sender's cryptographic integrity value for the secured
      *User Data Header*.

Through the use of this SAT Security mechanism it is possible to provide
confidentiality and integrity services for up to 700 bytes of user data, when the
data is sent between the Mobile Operator application server and the SIM card.
Performance and payload are limited and applications are restricted.

## 2.2   SIM Application Toolkit

The SAT API allows an application on the SIM card to be informed of events
by, and to issue commands to, the host mobile device. When an information
flow is initiated to the SIM application, it is termed an event download, and
when an information flow is initiated from the SIM application it is termed
a proactive command. Using the proactive command SET_UP_EVENT_LIST,
the SIM application can register to be informed of a number of events via the
ISO/IEC 7816-4 ENVELOPE APDU command [8]. Of relevance to this paper
is the SMS_PP or CELL_BROADCAST event, which downloads the contents of
the received SMS to the SIM application as a compound TLV in the data field of
an ENVELOPE APDU [13]. The SIM application's response to the ENVELOPE
command is then returned to the sender in a response packet.

## 2.3   MIDP2.0 J2ME Runtime Environment

A Java application that runs on a Mobile Information Device Profile (MIDP)
2.0 device is known as a MIDlet and may be installed within a certain domain if

it complies with the domain-specific access control requirements [6]. There are 4 domains specified for GSM compliant devices:

- Untrusted,
- Trusted 3rd Party,
- Mobile Operator,
- Manufacturer.

A Domain Protection Root Certificate (DPRC) controls MIDlet access to a domain. The DPRC must be made available at a specified location in the SIM application [15]. The MExE [2] security framework, when making an access control decision relies on signature verification of the signed MIDlet using the public key contained within the DPRC. Successful verification of the digital signature allows the MIDlet to be installed into the appropriate domain of the device.

Any MIDlet within a domain enjoys a set of unique permissions provided by that domain. The permission model allows these installed MIDlets access to restricted and sensitive APIs. The Security and Trust Services API [16] specifies that access to three of the four defined packages is limited to MIDlets located within the operator domain. These packages are:

- SATSA-APDU
- SATSA-JCRMI
- SATSA-PKI

These provide the ability for MIDlets to access trusted elements (i.e. a SIM card) using APDU communication, invoke a method of a remote Java Card object and provide support for digital signatures and credential management. It is worth nothing the value of being able to process cryptographic functions upon the device, as well as the smart card, as the card is a constricted environment [19].

## 2.4   UICC Java Card SIM Cards

The Global Platform specification [10] is the industry standard interface for downloading applications and is the most important international specification for application management in multi-application smart cards [11, 21]. This standard allows card issuers to securely manage third party applications independently of the operating system provider. Mobile Operator are increasingly deploying UICC [3] Java Cards, where the SIM application [4] is just one of the possible java applications [9] that the card is capable of running. Java applications that run on smart cards are known as Applets. A Card Manager is responsible for ensuring that new Applets are integrity checked and their source authenticated prior to installation. This security service uses a secret key, $K_{CI}$ that is embedded in the smart card prior to issue and termed the Card Issuer Key. Although a UICC SIM card can execute multiple Applets from different providers, the Card Manager application will be owned by the Mobile Operator who actually owns and issued the physical card.

## 3 The Proposed Scheme

Consider the scenario of having the requirement to remotely deploy our *Security Agent* to Mobile Stations in the field. The device is capable but unprepared; this section introduces the proposed scheme to install the *Security Agent*. This is again described as a protocol in section 4 and is represented in Fig. 1. The scheme is preparation for the execution protocol, detailed in section 5 that establishes session keys for future communication.

1. A small SAT application is securely installed OTA to the SIM using the TS03.48 mechanism.
2. The SAT application uses the proactive command SET_UP_EVENT_LIST to register to be informed, via the ISO/IEC 7816-4 ENVELOPE APDU command [8], when a SMS_PP or CELL_BROADCAST event occurs.
3. A corresponding SMS_PP or CELL_BROADCAST is sent to the device. The DPRC is contained within the payload of a of the concatenated SMS messages.
4. The device transfers the payload to the SAT application as a compound TLV in the data field of an ENVELOPE APDU command. The DPRC is stored in the appropriate location of the UICC SIM Card [15].
5. The SAT application retrieves the SIM's unique identifier, and returns it to the device as the response to the ENVELOPE command.
6. The unique identifier is then returned to the Mobile Operator application server. This acts as a proof of delivery of the DPRC and enables the Mobile Operator application server to reference the card's secret key $K_{CI}$ and commence the MIDlet preparation and download process.
7. Using the SIM's unique identifier, the Mobile Operator constructs the appropriate *Security Agent* MIDlet containing the relevant install commands and

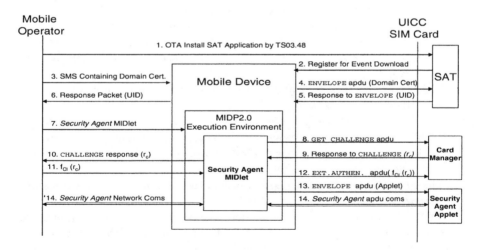

**Fig. 1.** Installation Scheme

byte code for the *Security Agent* Applet. The Applet byte code is encrypted and digested with the card issuer key $K_{CI}$ and packaged within the MIDlet JAR file.

The MIDlet must be prepared for the secure MIDlet installation procedure defined by J2ME MIDP2.0 and implements a second security context between server and device. The server generates a RSA X.509(v3) certificate or requests one from a Certificate Authority (CA). The certificate is inserted into the application descriptor of the MIDlet application. The path of the descriptor holds all certificates necessary to validate the application except the root certificate. The DPRC resides on the smart card and is called into play during MIDlet installation. Finally, the signature of the JAR file (format used to distribute MIDlets) is generated with the private key of the RSA certificate according to the EMSA-PKCS-v1.5 encoding method of PCKS#1 version 2.0 standard. This signature is then inserted into the application descriptor, the MIDlet is considered prepared and delivered to the device.

The J2ME JRE must authenticate the MIDlet application for installation into a secure domain. First the certificate is retrieved from the application descriptor and validated against the DPRC held upon the smart card. The JRE then verifies the MIDlet JAR file; by taking the public key from the verified signer certificate along with a fresh SHA-1 digest of the JAR file and comparing it to signature defined in the application descriptor. The JRE can install the MIDlet into the Operator domain of the MIDP2.0 runtime environment.

8. The *Security Agent* MIDlet is installed in the Operator domain of the user device with full access to JSR 177 APIs. This allows APDU commands to be issued to SIM card. The *Security Agent* MIDlet executes its Applet installation routine. The MIDlet starts by using the **SELECT** command to initiate communication with the SIM Card Manager. Once the Card Manager application is selected the MIDlet then issues a **GET CHALLENGE** command.

9. Before the Card Manager will accept installation of an Applet onto the SIM Card, it must first authenticate the source of the Applet. It does this by responding to the **GET CHALLENGE** with a random number $r_C$.

10. The MIDlet is not in possession of the secret $K_{CI}$ required to prove a trusted source for a new Applet, so the challenge response $r_C$ must be sent back to the Server.

11. The Server encrypts $K_{CI}$ and $r_C$ with $K_{CI}$ and returns the byte string to the MIDlet.

12. The MIDlet authenticates the source of the applet using the **EXTERNAL AUTHENTICATE** command providing the encrypted response to the random challenge $r_C$. The Card Manager, also in possession of $K_{CI}$, authenticates the source of the Applet and allows the applet installation process to continue.

13. The *Security Agent* MIDlet now transfers the encrypted and integrity protected byte code of the *Security Agent* Applet to the SIM card via the **ENVELOPE** command. At no point does the MIDlet have any knowledge of the key $K_{CI}$ as it acts as a delivery mechanism between SIM and Server for predefined parcels of bytes. The integrity and confidentiality of the applet code and the long term secret $K_{CI}$ is assured. Subsequent to the download-

ing of the byte code to the card, the same Card Manager using, the Global Platform specified Data Authentication Pattern (DAP) verifies the integrity of the received byte code. Verification allows the byte code to be decrypted. A *Security Agent* applet instance is created and registered with the Java Card runtime environment.

Contained within the *Security Agent* Applet byte code is a long term *Security Agent* symmetric key $K_{SC}$ used for mutual authentication and establishment of secure session keys for subsequent execution of a *Security Agent* controlled authenticated key establishment process (Section 5).

14. APDU communication between the MIDlet and Applet components of the *Security Agent* can now proceed under J2ME application control. Communication between the Application Server and the J2ME environment may use any of the supported network protocols such as http or https for security services.

## 4 Installation Protocol

Our protocol uses both symmetric and asymmetric cryptographic techniques [20] to provide the authentication and integrity services required. The specific algorithms involved are either defined by the standards or rely on what the individual smart card supports.

Throughout this discussion we will use the following notation:

$$S = \text{Server}$$
$$M = \text{MIDlet}$$
$$C = \text{SIM card}$$

where:

$$K_{CI} = \text{Shared secret between Server and SIM pre-issuance}$$
$$K_{SC} = \text{Shared secret between Server and SIM post-installation}$$
$$\text{Cert}_{DPRC} = \text{Domain Protection Root Certification}$$
$$PK = \text{Public key of Cert}_{DPRC}$$
$$\epsilon_K(D) = \text{Symmetric encryption of data D using key } K$$
$$S_K(D) = \text{Signature computed on data D using key } K$$
$$\text{MAC}_K(D) = \text{MAC computed on data D using secret key } K$$
$$r_E = \text{Random nonce generated by entity E (S, C or M)}$$
$$i_E = \text{Identifier of entity E (S, C or M)}$$
$$CK = \text{Cipher Key}$$
$$IK = \text{Integrity Key}$$
$$\text{APDU}() = \text{APDU command from MIDlet to SIM card}$$
$$\text{SAT}() = \text{GSM SAT communication mechanism}$$
$$\text{SMS}() = \text{SMS communication mechanism}$$

**PHASE 1.** *Install the MIDlet into the Operator Domain.*

$$S \to C : \ SAT(MAC\_ID) \tag{1}$$

$$S \to C : \ SAT(SAT \ Applet \ Install \ code) \tag{2}$$

$$S \to M : \ SMS(Cert_{DPRC}) \tag{3}$$

$$M \to C : \ APDU(\text{ENVELOPE}: \ Cert_{DPRC}) \tag{4}$$

$$C \to M : \ APDU(\text{ENVELOPE}: \ UID) \tag{5}$$

$$M \to S : \ SMS(UID) \tag{6}$$

$$S \to M : \ S_{PK}(MIDlet) \| (MIDlet) \tag{7}$$

Our protocol has been designed on the assumption that the device and SIM card are preissued and in the field, and although they are both capable, neither are prepared nor contain preinstalled application code to create the desired secure high bandwidth channel. The first step is to therefore prepare the SIM card so that the MIDlet can be installed within the Operator domain of the J2ME device. It is assumed, however, that the device is operational on the Operators network (i.e. user authentication and sign on to the network has successfully been performed by the AUTHENTICATE [4] and subsequent functions of the 3GPP challenge response mechanism [24]). Although messages (1) through to (3) are unidirectional from the Server to the SIM card or mobile, we have presented them as 3 individual protocol messages. This is because they are transferred using GSM standard 03.48 and are most likely sent as 3 independent SMS messages. Protocol messages (1) provides the SIM card with the identifier specifying which GSM standard 03.48 MAC algorithm will be used to confirm integrity and data origin throughout the protocol sequence. Message (2) provides the SAT code be installed upon the card, whilst message (3) provides the root certificate of the device J2ME Operator domain. The payload of these messages are stored in the SIM card. The role of the SAT code is to discover the card's unique identifier (UID). By the means of the same mechanism the UID of the SIM card and $r_C$ is securely sent back to the Server. This information is used to find the related $K_{CI}$, this key is used to encrypt and sign the *Security Agent* Applet byte code that is embedded and readied for delivery as part of the integral code that comprises the MIDlet.

Upon receipt of protocol message (7), the MExE [2] J2ME implementation on the client will verify the signature using the root certificate on Cert$_{DPRC}$ previously stored into the SIM card via message (3). Valid verification provides data origin authentication and integrity of the MIDlet JAD and JAR files received. The *Security Agent* MIDlet is now installed OTA in the Operator domain of the J2ME MIDP2.0 compliant implementation of the client device, with full permissions to utilise SATSA-APDU and SATSA-PKI packages defined by JSR 177.

**PHASE 2.** *Install the Applet into the SIM card*

$$M \to C : \ APDU(\text{SELECT}: \ AID_{CM}) \tag{8}$$

$$M \to C : \ APDU(\text{GET CHALLENGE}) \tag{9}$$

$$C \rightarrow M : \text{APDU}(r_C) \tag{10}$$

$$M \rightarrow S : \text{SMS}(r_C) \tag{11}$$

$$S \rightarrow M : \text{SMS}(\epsilon_{K_{CI}}(K_{CI}\|r_C)) \tag{12}$$

$$M \rightarrow C : \text{APDU}(\text{EXTERNAL AUTHENTICATE: } \epsilon_{K_{CI}}(K_{CI}\|r_C) \tag{13}$$

$$M \rightarrow C : \text{APDU}(\text{MAC}_{K_{CI}}(\text{Applet})\|\epsilon_{K_{CI}}(\text{APPLET})) \tag{14}$$

$$M \rightarrow C : \text{APDU}(\text{INSTALL}(\text{Install}): \text{AID}_{SA}) \tag{15}$$

$$M \rightarrow C : \text{APDU}(\text{INSTALL}(\text{Selectable}): \text{AID}_{SA}) \tag{16}$$

The MIDlet, now securely stored OTA in the device, carried an array of byte codes (see appendix 2). These byte codes represent an encrypted and signed CAP file from the Server using the shared secret between the SIM and Server, $K_{CI}$. The process of verifying the MIDlet during download and installation, using $\text{Cert}_{DPRC}$, has already verified the integrity of these byte codes as well as the MIDlet application. The steps (8) to (16) outline the process going on between device and card but the untrusted device would have no knowledge of what is being sent as it is protected by a secret that it is not privy to.

Step (8) sends the SELECT command to the card to communicate with the Card Manager on the SIM operating system that will handle the authentication of the card acceptance device. This authentication process is represented by steps (9) to (13), it begin with collecting a challenge, random number, from the card using the GET CHALLENGE commands. This challenge is packaged in an SMS, step (11), and sent back to the Server. The Server using its shared secret $K_{CI}$, encrypts the number along with the key itself and sends it back to the MIDlet (12). The final authentication is performed by the Global Platform EXTERNAL AUTHENTICATE command which holds the encrypted challenge response (13). $\text{AID}_{SA}$ refers to the unique application identifier of the *Security Agent* Applet. Once authenticated, steps (14) through (16) show the encrypted and signed download of *Security Agent* Applet to card, it's subsequent installation and final completion of the process allowing it to be selected by any Operator Domain located MIDlets.

The MIDlet pseudo code to generate this secure authentication, download and installation of *Security Agent* Applet to SIM from an untrusted device is presented in appendix 1.

## 5   Execution Protocol

At some time later, i.e. after the http session of PHASE 2 has closed, the Operator may choose to download bulk data securely from the Server to the SIM card. Before this can begin both endpoints must verify the identity of the other with a mutual entity authentication protocol. We take our authentication protocol from the ISO/IEC 9798 standard [14], deriving session keys for data origin authentication, data integrity and data confidentiality as part of our authenticated key establishment protocol. The choice of protocol is heavily influenced by the parameters and characteristics of our mobile environment. For similar reasons, as stated previously, authentication via symmetric cryptography is preferred, and a MAC based approach limits the amount of network traffic required to a minimum. The choice is further restricted owing to the time-less nature of the SIM card [21]. Only three possible sources of time are available; an internal clock, a remote server or a neighbouring device [22] and there are no other alternatives. To have an internal time keeper would require at least a portion of the card chip to have a source of permanent power [7]. Although it is, of course, possible for the SIM card to obtain a measure of time from the client device via the TIMER MANAGEMENT proactive command and TIMER EXPIRATION event download of the SAT API. The client device is, as stated previously, likely to be untrusted by Operators for any function concerning the communication of potentially network critical information, and cannot be used as a source of time for confirming message freshness. In consequence message timeliness, to protect against replay attacks, must be achieved with either logical time stamps or nounces. In conclusion, therefore we have adopted the three-pass mutual authentication protocol using MACs and nounces as specified in ISO/IEC 9798-4 clause 5.2.2.

**PHASE 3.** *Perform mutual entity authentication*

$$S \rightarrow M : \text{start MIDlet with push registry} \tag{17}$$

$$M \rightarrow C : \text{APDU(select Applet)} \tag{18}$$

$$C \rightarrow M : \text{APDU}(r_C) \tag{19}$$

$$M \rightarrow S : r_C \tag{20}$$

$$S \rightarrow M : i_S \| i_C \| r_C \| r_S \| \text{MAC}_{K_{SC}}(i_S \| i_C \| r_C \| r_S) \tag{21}$$

$$M \rightarrow C : \text{APDU}(i_S \| i_C \| r_C \| r_S \| \text{MAC}_{K_{SC}}(i_S \| i_C \| r_C \| r_S)) \tag{22}$$

$$C \rightarrow M : \text{APDU}(i_C \| r_S \| \text{MAC}_{K_{SC}}(i_C \| r_S)) \tag{23}$$

$$M \rightarrow S : i_C \| r_S \| \text{MAC}_{K_{SC}}(r_S \| r_C) \tag{24}$$

Once again this step starts with an invocation of the push registry via message (17) and the device MIDlet *Security Agent* loaded in (7) selecting the SIM Applet loaded following message (16). The SIM card Applet generates a random nounce $r_C$, stores it, and supplies it to the MIDlet (19) where it is passed on (without storing) to the Server (20). Server generates nounce $r_S$, stores it together with received nounce $r_C$ and responds with (21). Again this is passed through the MIDlet to the SIM card Applet via an APDU, message (22). Upon receipt the SIM card Applet verifies that the received $r_C$ is the same as the one sent in (19) and that the identifiers are correct (note the UID could be used for $i_C$ and a parameter of certificate Cert$_{DPRC}$ supplied to the SIM card via message (3) used for $i_S$). The SIM card Applet then recalculates the MAC and if correct accepts the Server. Now that the Server is authenticated to the SIM card Applet, then Applet responds with message (23) via the MIDlet, which again passes it straight through to the Server in message (24). When Server receives message (24) it checks that the received value $r_S$ is indeed the one sent in (21) and that the SIM card identifier $i_B$ is correct. After confirming the MAC calculation the

Server can then accept the SIM card Applet as valid. Following the mutual entity authentication of STEP 3, both Server and SIM card will establish Integrity $IK$ and Confidentiality $CK$ keys to protect the subsequent bulk data exchange between the Server and the SIM Card.

**PHASE 4.** *Set up session keys to protect the content to be downloaded*

$$CK = f1_{K_{SC}}(r_S \| r_C) \qquad (25)$$
$$IK = f2_{K_{SC}}(r_S \| r_C) \qquad (26)$$

Both Server and SIM card Applet will contain identical functions $f1$ and $f2$ to calculate the session cipher and integrity keys using the protocol nounces $r_S$ and $r_C$ and the long term shared secret $K_{SC}$. Now that session keys have been established the bulk data may be transferred to the SIM card encrypted for confidentiality with $CK$ and concatenated with a MAC using $IK$ for data origin authentication and integrity as necessary for the data being transferred.

## 6   Proof of Concept Model

To validate our proposal we constructed a proof of concept model, based on readily available open source tools; it comprised of:

- *Server:*
  A J2EE Servlet web application performed the Mobile Operator function and was packaged as a Web Application Archive (WAR) file for easy deployment on a Tomcat Apache Web Server.
- *Mobile Device:*
  The J2ME Client was emulated by the Wireless KToolbar [23] from Sun Microsystems and run our *Security Agent* MIDP 2.0 MIDlet on the reference J2ME implementation.
- *SIM card:*
  The SIM card *Security Agent* function was provided by a Gemplus GemXpresso smart card. This was a Java Card and adhered to a number of industry standards such as Global Platform and had on-card cryptographic capability. The equipment used to connect the card to the test-bed was a USB card reader and Gemplus RAD3 development environment was used in early tests to load *Security Agent* Applets. This could have been just as easily realised using a variety of different platforms, notably G&D development hardware and tools.

The demonstration environment for our model was implemented in J2SE. J2SE provides the necessary Java Swing classes for monitoring the various use case applications being tested. The model is designed so that each phase of a specific use case is initiated manually and monitored by visual feedback through the use of J2SE's GUI `LayoutManager` class and `ActionListener` interface.

There are different technologies involved in this scenario and as such only some aspects of the system could be placed within the scope of the practical work undertaken. The SAT application download process is well document and involves access to SMS generation so this was omitted. The MIDlet could be constructed and the communication between the server and MIDlet over a secure channel was considered within the scope of this work and practically demonstrated using a secure HTTP link between a web server and mobile device. Both entities employed Java based technologies and demonstrated a secure channel based upon mutual authentication with a shared secret. The cryptographic functionality involved could not be performed by the MIDlet as the SATSA-PKI and SATSA-CRYPTO packages are provided by the JSR-177 and at the time of investigation was unavailable. Our approach was to separate out this functionality to a J2SE application that would communicate with the MIDlet and in turn generate APDU commands to the smart card whilst perform any cryptographic functions required. This allowed the JSR-177 to be effectively modelled with only a moderate increase in complexity. The J2SE JSR-177 proxy used the Open Card Framework (OCF) to create a connection to the smart card and build command and response APDU for exchanges in data.

## 7   Conclusion

In this work we introduce a methodology, discuss the component technologies and define a protocol for establishing a security context between a Mobile Operator application and SIM card. A solution is proposed to establish a *Security Agent* on an untrusted mobile device and trusted SIM card using "Over The Air" (OTA) techniques. A proof of concept demonstration capability is implemented with example java source code presented.

This work creates confidentiality and integrity session keys, $CK$ and $IK$ respectively. These are independent off all network security keys and therefore eligible to protect unrelated data, e.g. value added applications. The extension of trust from inherent network related credentials, to independent credentials used solely for providing security services to post-purchase applications, is an important step towards fulfilling the true potential of the mobile station field base by executing a new generation of secure applications.

## Acknowledgements

We would like to extend appreciation to Chris Mitchell for early guidance and participation. Additionally, thanks to Jennifer Squire for patience whilst proof reading drafts.

## References

1. 3GPP TS 03.48. *Technical Specification Group Terminals; Security Mechanisms for the SIM Application Toolkit; stage 2.* http://www.3gpp.org, 2001.
2. 3GPP TS 23.057. *Technical Specification Group Terminals; Mobile Execution Environment (MExE); Functional description; Stage 2.* http://www.3gpp.org, 2003.

3. 3GPP TS 31.101. *Technical Specification Group Terminals; UICC-terminal interface; Physical and logical characteristics*. http://www.3gpp.org, 2003.
4. 3GPP TS 31.102. *Technical Specification Group Terminals; Characteristics of the USIM application*. http://www.3gpp.org, 2003.
5. R. Anderson and M. Kuhn. Tamper resistance - a cautionary note. In *The Second USENIX Workshop on Electronic Commerce Proceedings, Oakland, California*, pages 1–11. USENIX Association, November 1996. http://citeseer.ist.psu.edu/400120.html.
6. C. Block and A. C. Wagner. *MIDP 2.0 Style Guide*. The Java Series. Addison-Wesley, London, 2003.
7. V. Cordonnier, A. Watson, and S. Nemchenko. Time as an aid to improving security in smart cards. In *7th Annual Working Conference on Information Security Management and Small Systems Security*, pages 131–144. Kluwer Academic Press, London, 1999. Amsterdam, The Netherlands.
8. ETSI TS 100 977. *Digital cellular telecommunications system(Phase 2+); Specification of the Subscriber Identity Module - Mobile Equipment (SIM-ME) Interface*. ETSI, http://www.etsi.org, 2000.
9. ETSI TS 101 476. *Digital cellular telecommunication system (Phase 2+); Subscriber Identity Module Application Programming Interface (SIM API); SIM API for Java Card; Stage 2 (GSM 03.19)*. ETSI, http://www.etsi.org, 2000.
10. Global Platform. *Card Specification v2.1.1*. http://www.globalplatform.org, 2003.
11. GSM 03.19, Version 8.2.0. *Digital Cellular Telecommunications System (Phase 2+); Subscriber Identity Module Application Programming Interface (SIM API); AIM API for Java Card; Stage 2*. ETSI, http://www.etsi.org, 2001.
12. GSM 11.14. *Digital cellular telecomunnications system (Phase2+); Specification of the SIM Application Toolkit for the Subscriber Identity Module-Mobile Equipment (SIM-ME) interface*. ETSI, http://www.etsi.org, 2001.
13. S. B. Guthery and M. J. Cronin. *Mobile Application Development with SMS & the SIM Toolkit; Building Smart Phone Applications*. McGraw-Hill, 2002.
14. ISO/IEC 9798-4. *Information technology - Security Techniques - Entity Authentication - Part 4: Mechanisms using a cryptographic check function 2nd ed.*, http://www.iso.org, 2nd edition, 1999.
15. JSR-118 JCP. *Mobile Information Device Profile, v2.0 (JSR-118)*. Sun Microsystems, http://java.sun.com, 2002.
16. JSR-177 JCP. *Security & Trust Services API (SATSA) (JSR-177)*. Sun Microsystems, http://java.sun.com, 2004.
17. J. A. MacDonald and C. J. Mitchell. Using the GSM/UMTS SIM to secure web services. In *2nd IEEE International Workshop on Mobile Commerce & Services (WMCS)*. IEEE, IEEE Computer Society Press, July 2005. Munich, Germany.
18. J. A. MacDonald, W. G. Sirett, and C. J. Mitchell. Overcoming channel bandwidth constraints in secure SIM applications. In R. Sasaki, S. Qing, E. Okamoto, and H. Yoshiura, editors, *20th IFIP International Information Security Conference (SEC 2005) - Small Systems Security and Smart cards,*, volume 181 of *IFIP International Federation for Information Processing*. Springer Science and Business Media, May 2005. Chiba, Japan.
19. K. Markantonakis. Is the performance of the cryptographic functions the real bottleneck? In M. Dupuy and P. Paradinas, editors, *Trusted Information: The New Decade Challenge*, IFIP TC11 16th International Conference on Information Security (IFIP/SEC'01) June 11-13, pages 77–92. Kluwer Academic Publishers, 2001. Paris, France.

20. F. Piper and S. Murphy. *Cryptography - A Very Short Introduction*. Oxford University Press, 2002.
21. W. Rankl and W. Effing. *Smart Card Handbook*. John Wiley & Sons, Ltd, 3rd edition, 2003.
22. L. Rousseau. Secure time in a portable device. *Proceedings of 3rd Gemplus Developer Conference, Paris, France*, 2001. Gemplus.
23. Sun Wireless Toolkit. *Wireless Toolkit, Version 2.1,*. Sun Microsystems, http://java.sun.com/products/j2mewtoolkit, 2004.
24. M. Walker and T. Wright. *GSM and UMTS : The creation of global mobile communications*. John Wiley & Sons, Ltd., 2002.

# A    Appendix 1 – Psuedo Java Code

This pseudo code is intended to be a demonstration of the proposed method of embedding encrypted *Security Agent* Applet code within the body of the *Security Agent* MIDlet. The MIDlet can call the Install method of a packaged class called Secure_Applet and undertake the selection of the *Card Manager*, authentication of shared secret, downloading of CAP file, its installation and finalisation without actually exposing the underlying Operator secret to the MIDlet. The *Security Agent* Applet is encrypted within the MIDlet and its integrity is checked on-card during installation.

The following code is not intended to be a literal but uses Java based concepts to express the intention of the proposal. The aim is to illustrate the declaration of a two dimensional array; a primary array holding arrays of 255 bytes representing APDU commands. The concept is that these APDUs can be declared by the Server during preparation of the MIDlet and therefore the device would not have the opportunity to alter or access the information. The only function the device or MIDlet must perform is the act of sending the APDUs to the device.

```
1   public class Secure_Applet{
2     //-- ISO7816 offsets
3     private bINS  = ISO7816.OFFSET_INS;
4     private bCLA  = ISO7816.OFFSET_CLA;
5     private bP1   = ISO7816.OFFSET_P1;
6     private bP2   = ISO7816.OFFSET_P2
7     private bLC   = ISO1716.OFFSET_LC;
8     private bData = IS07816.OFFSET_CDATA;
9
10    //--array of APDU byte codes
11    private byte[9][255] baAC
12        //-- select AID
13        = {00 A4 04 00 07 A0 00 00 00 18 43 4D},
14
15        //-- External Authenticate
16        {84 82 03 00 10 40 2F 82 CE 30 2C F5 78 F7 F7 60 32 0B 5A 4F 0E},
17
18        //-- First APDU of CAP file load
19        {84 E6 02 00 20 39 B0 DB 15 04 8D 75 BC 8D 71 46 83 52 A8 E2 D2
20        7D 48 32 25 AD DF DC 44 E2 28 55 2D 83 31 8B 34 00},
21
22        //-- following data packets
23        {84 E8 00 00 D8 B0 23 9E 36 52 BF 40 03 A1 F1 43 D8 3D 6A F8 93
24        //--consider full 255 byte apdu data array
25        71 0C 6D B3 41 56 B8 09 84 71 7C},
26        {...},{...},{...},{...},{...},{...};
27
28    public installSecureApplet() {
29      try {
30        //-- create card service and connect
31        //-- send all APDU commands confirming
32        //-- for length of parent array  loop
33        for (int x=0; x<baAB.length; x++){
34            //-- build APDU object using array and offsets
35            cmdAPDU = new ISOCommandAPDU(
36                baAC[x][bINS], baAC[x][bCLA], baAC[x][bP1],
37        baAC[x][bP2], baAC[x][bData]);
38            //-- send APDU and catch response.
39            resAPDU = service.sendCommandAPDU(cmdAPDU);
40            if(Integer.toHexString(resAPDU.sw()) != "90_00"){
41                break:}}}
42    //--catch errors and close down all objects}}
```

**Listing 1.1.** Psuedo MIDlet code

# Towards a Secure and Practical Multifunctional Smart Card

Idir Bakdi

Lehrstuhl für Wirtschaftsinformatik II,
Universität Regensburg, 93040 Regensburg, Germany
idir.bakdi@wiwi.uni-regensburg.de

**Abstract.** One of the most promising features of smart card technology is its potential to serve several applications using a single hardware
token. Existing multifunctional smart cards, however, are either simple
and suffer from serious limitations or they have a high complexity that
is not justified for most applications. This paper describes a new scheme
permitting different applications to flexibly share a hardware token. The
proposed solution supports off-line transactions as well as post-issuance
loading. Each application can load one or more "virtual tokens" (remotely) into a common smart card. Despite its simplicity, the scheme
guarantees the authenticity and integrity of virtual tokens and prevents
their duplication. Moreover, it protects the privacy of card holders by
providing a possibility to use pseudonymous identities that cannot be
linked to one another.

**Keywords:** Multifunctional smart card; secure hardware token; privacy.

## 1   Introduction

Nowadays, we all carry a lot of tokens in our pockets. These are keys, magnetic
stripe cards, smart cards, tickets, etc. Each application has to implement its own
infrastructure to issue and subsequently use these tokens. From an ergonomic as
well as from an economic point of view, it would be beneficial to virtualize all
those tokens, i.e. to convert them into digital files that can be loaded onto a single
medium. However, as most tokens are critical for the security of the applications
they serve, one cannot just load their virtual counterparts on a storage medium
such as a floppy disk. On the one hand, such a medium would not offer any
protection against misuse in case it gets lost or stolen. On the other hand, a
virtual token could be copied at will as it can be read by anyone holding the
medium. One possibility to overcome these difficulties is to use a microchip as
implemented on smart cards to hold the files representing tokens. This way, they
are protected both against misuse by someone else than the legitimate user and
against unauthorized duplication by the holder himself. This paper describes a
new scheme that uses such a chip to realize a secure and practical multifunctional
token.

The remainder of this paper is organized as follows. After a short review
of existing solutions and their most serious shortcomings in the next section,

J. Domingo-Ferrer, J. Posegga, and D. Schreckling (Eds.): CARDIS 2006, LNCS 3928, pp. 16–31, 2006.

the main security requirements of a multifunctional smart card are outlined in section 3. Section 4 contains a description of the new approach. Finally, the last section is devoted to some conclusions summarizing this work.

## 2   State of the Art

The idea of using a single token for multiple purposes is quite an old one. Its simplest and most famous implementation is perhaps that of a master key able to open several locks. Recently, many solutions appeared which aim at grouping many applications on a single smart card, or more generally, on a single microchip. Most of them can be categorized into one of two classes. The first class, denoted by *single ID cards* in this paper, is the simpler one. So called *multi-application smart cards* constitute the second class. They are more comprehensive and consequently more complex than single ID cards. In the following, these two classes are described in more detail sketching their pros and cons.

### 2.1   Single ID Cards

The simplest realization of a single ID card is to have a number (an ID) that uniquely identifies a person across several back-end systems stored on a smart card. Each system keeps its own set of data associated with a given user in its central database. The smart card merely serves as a reference to that account. As all systems share the same number for a given user, a single card suffices to identify him in all of them. Put another way, single ID cards realize an authentication by possession of a person already known to the different systems through a common identification scheme. A more advanced version of this solution uses smart cards capable of producing digital signatures. The idea is to have the user's private key stored on his card, whereas the corresponding public key is shared by all participating back-end systems. The main advantages and drawbacks of this class are presented in the following.

#### Advantages

**Simplicity:** Solutions built on single ID cards are very simple. A single ID card merely identifies a person. Each application maps the ID to a data set associated with the corresponding user. The management of relevant application data is thus differed from the card to the more powerful back-end systems, which facilitates implementation.

**Generic Digital Signature:** In case a digital signature card is used, the card can additionally be used to digitally sign electronic documents. Thus, a large category of applications requiring the authenticity and non-repudiation of electronic documents can be covered. Many countries already have laws that guarantee to certain kinds of digital signatures a legal status equivalent to that of a classical (i.e. manual) signature.

**Drawbacks**

**No Off-Line Functionality:** As the card merely represents a pointer to a data set stored in the back-end system, it can only be used given an online access to the central database. This is especially difficult when the verifier does not belong to the issuer's organization. To verify a student card, an employee sitting at the entrance of a cinema would have to access data from the student office of the corresponding university.

**Privacy Concerns:** As all the back-end systems use the same ID, comprehensive user profiles can be easily constructed by matching the different data sets belonging to a person. This raises privacy concerns because of possible misuse.

**Single Point of Failure:** The different back-end systems all rely on a unique ID per user which is tightly bound to a single card. If this hardware token is lost, stolen, or compromised, all those systems are affected at once. That is, the card holder has no possibility to mitigate the risk resulting from a loss or theft by employing more than one smart card.

**High Demands:** In case a signature card is used, the requirements concerning the card's protection and the key management are very high. This makes sense when the card is used to generate legally recoverable digital signatures. For most use cases, however, such functionality is not needed. A train conductor only has to be convinced that a passenger possesses a valid ticket. He does not need to get the traveller's legally recoverable signature. In such cases, high demands would unnecessarily burden the solution.

## 2.2   Multi-application Smart Cards

This class employs so called *multi-application card operating systems (MACOS)* [14, p. 308] which try, in analogy to computer operating systems, to abstract the underlying hardware in order to make it possible for different applications to run on it. They offer an application programmer interface (API) that can be used to access the card's services. The newer MACOS (e.g. MULTOS [9] or Java Card [19] [8] [5]) do not only provide for the hosting of many applications on the same microprocessor, but also make it possible for the same application to run on different chips by employing a virtual machine. Using the Java Card platform for instance, each system can load its applet (a small application written in Java) on the card where it can be executed together with other applets. In the remainder of this section, the main advantage of multi-application smart cards as well as their drawbacks are discussed.

**Advantage**

**Universality:** The vision of multi-application smart cards is to have a universal chip able to execute arbitrary code. That is to say, the goal consists in the miniaturization of multi-purpose devices such as personal computers or handhelds. This would enable everyone to write applications that do whatever he wants and load them to be executed on card. The employed smart card would bear all the necessary functionality and would not need to rely on any back-end system, thus providing a high level of flexibility and autonomy.

### Drawbacks

**Complexity:** Due to their complexity these systems are far from being mature. This results in the following limitations of current solutions.

- The capabilities of MACOS are restricted due to limitations in processing performance and storage capacities of the underlying hardware. It will take some time before they reach the universality of operating systems running nowadays on personal computers, for instance.
- Many of the current solutions do not offer the possibility of post-issuance loading. The applications are installed on the card before the latter is issued. This is for instance the case when using MULTOS [12]. Java applets can be loaded after the card is issued, but until version 2.2 of the Java Card specification there was no possibility to remove already loaded applets. This shows the kind of difficulties encountered in practice.

**Security:** The main advantage of multi-application smart cards, consisting in their ability to host arbitrary applications and to execute their code, constitutes at the same time a considerable security risk. Some applications running on the card may not be trusted. They could access sensitive data of other applications residing on the same chip. Currently, many efforts are made to secure smart card applets against one another using e.g. so called firewalls [6] [18] or byte code verification [13]. This is a cumbersome task. The cost of evaluating, for instance, an application written for MULTOS according to ITSEC E6 [7] is estimated to be 150% of the overall development cost [4]. Besides, their genericity does not allow to hard-wire once and for ever protection mechanisms needed to ensure the requirements of uniqueness and privacy described in the next section. Instead, each application has to implement its own security framework, possibly leading to new vulnerabilities.

## 3   Security Requirements

A multifunctional smart card as introduced in the first section should satisfy at least the following security requirements.

**Authenticity:** Only a legitimate issuer should be able to produce authentic virtual tokens for a given application. No one besides the student office should be capable of issuing valid student cards.

**Integrity:** A solution has to make sure that, once issued, a virtual token can not be modified, not even by its holder. The student must not be able to change the validity period of his card himself.

**Uniqueness:** Virtual tokens have to be protected against duplication. This is especially important when considering applications where the token is used as a dongle or as a ticket. Imagine a railway ticket that can be duplicated at will.

**Privacy:** This requirement could also be entitled "separability". Physical tokens, although perhaps belonging to the same user, are not a priori linked to each other. Often they are not even associated with their holder. In no way can a car key be linked to any of the other tokens a user has in his pocket, nor is it related to his person. The same should hold when replacing physical tokens by virtual ones. Else, profiles existing in the different systems could be easily matched to get a comprehensive picture of the user. Also, when virtual tokens need to be verified it should be possible to present them separated from each other, though residing on the same chip. All a train conductor has to know is that the traveller paid for his trip. This requires him to look at the passenger's ticket but not to learn his identity.

The requirements of authenticity and integrity are satisfied by letting the issuer digitally sign each virtual token he issues. Verifying this signature ensures that only authentic and untampered virtual tokens are accepted as valid. The scheme described in the next section also guarantees uniqueness and privacy.

## 4   New Approach

The proposed solution is based on the concept of *virtual tokens (VT)* introduced above. These are hosted by a microchip called *digital pocket (DP)* in this paper, in analogy to a pocket that holds physical tokens. VTs can be loaded (e.g. over the Internet) into a DP after the latter is issued (post-issuance loading). They can even be moved by their holder from one DP to another without any intervention by the issuer, which makes the scheme very flexible. In a certain way, VTs resemble attribute certificates as described e.g. in [3]. The main difference is that a VT can only be used in conjunction with a single hardware token (i.e. a DP) at a given time, thus preventing its duplication.

Each DP is embedded into a container that provides it with power supply and a communication interface. The most obvious realization of this idea is to use a smart card in conjunction with a reader providing the required infrastructure. However, it could be implemented as well in a mobile phone, in a wrist watch, or in any other object the user bears with him. For the sake of simplicity a smart card realization is assumed in this paper.

The main actors taking part in the scheme are identified in the next subsection. After sketching DP's architecture and describing the involved key pairs, the scheme is outlined in subsection 4.4. Finally, a short analysis of the trust relationships that have to be assumed among the different roles and a discussion comparing the new scheme to existing solutions are presented.

### 4.1   Roles

The following actors take part in the considered setting. Fig. 1 summarizes their interactions.

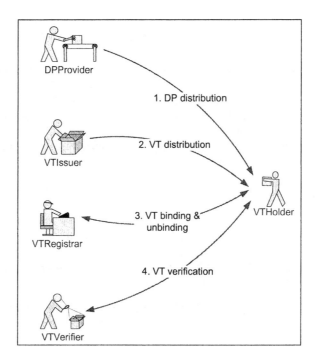

**Fig. 1.** The different roles and their interactions

- *Digital Pocket Provider (DPProvider)*: is the issuer of DPs.
- *Virtual Token Issuer (VTIssuer)*: issues VTs (e.g. the railway company).
- *Virtual Token Holder (VTHolder)*: is a person holding one or more VTs (e.g. a railway passenger).
- *Virtual Token Verifier (VTVerifier)*: verifies VTs (e.g. a train conductor).
- *Virtual Token Registrar (VTRegistrar)*: represents a trusted institution assuring that there is no more than one active copy of a given VT at any time.

These roles may be assumed by distinct persons and/or institutions. However, a single organization may also assume several of them. DPProvider and VTRegistrar could for example be embodied by the same infrastructure operator. Another option is to have VTIssuer ensure the uniqueness of VTs he issues, thereby additionally playing VTRegistrar's role.

### 4.2 Architecture

The proposed solution can be readily implemented using standard hardware components as they can be found on modern smart cards. More precisely, DP's architecture consists of the following elements.

- *Protected Memory (PM)*: represents the area of the chip where VTs and all relevant public keys are stored. This area is accessible to VTHolder after authorization, e.g. using a PIN or some kind of biometrics. The protection is meant to prevent VTVerifier or someone else from randomly reading the content of a DP without VTHolder's consent.[1]

- *Tamper-Resistant Memory (TRM)*[2]: is an area that can not be read from the outside, not even by VTHolder. It serves as a storage for private keys.
- *Tamper-Resistant Processing Unit (TRPU)*: represents a processing unit for the execution of computations involving secrets.
- *Controller*: coordinates the single actions of a DP and provides an interface to the outside world. It handles the communication with VTHolder, VTVerifier and VTRegistrar.

## 4.3 Involved Key Pairs

The presented solution relies on public key cryptography. In the remainder of this paper, a private key used to create a digital signature is always denoted by $S_x$ (for some index $x$), whereas $P_x$ stands for the corresponding public key employed for signature verification. More precisely, the following key pairs are used to generate and verify digital signatures in the different phases of the scheme.

$(S_{\text{VTIssuer}}, P_{\text{VTIssuer}})$: Every VT issued by a VTIssuer is signed with his private key $S_{\text{VTIssuer}}$ and can be checked for validity using the corresponding public key $P_{\text{VTIssuer}}$.

$(S_{\text{VTRegistrar}}, P_{\text{VTRegistrar}})$: VTRegistrar employs his private key $S_{\text{VTRegistrar}}$ to generate binding confirmations that can be verified using $P_{\text{VTRegistrar}}$.

$(S_{\text{VT}}, P_{\text{VT}})$: Each VT is bound to a DP using a dedicated key pair $(S_{\text{VT}}, P_{\text{VT}})$.

$(S_g, P_g)$: Before their distribution, DPs are divided by DPProvider into groups. All the DPs of a given group are assigned the same key pair $(S_g, P_g)$.

DPs are grouped in order to protect the privacy of their holders. That is, all DPs belonging to the same group $g$ share a common key pair $(S_g, P_g)$. Thus, they cannot be distinguished from one another. If each DP had its own key pair, the different identities connected to it could be linked together. This is prevented by letting an individual DP hide in its group much in the same way that a single Internet user hides in a group of surfers when using anonymizer services built on crowds [15]. Although the fact that several chips carry the same private key would appear to increase the security risk, such is not the case. As will become clear from the following description of the scheme, the damage caused by a compromised DP is independent of whether it was assigned a unique key or whether it shares it with a number of other DPs.

---

[1] To make such a protection effective a secure communication channel between VTHolder and DP is needed. This involves an input device (e.g. a keypad) and an output device (e.g. a small display) that are tamper-resistant. However, to keep the system's description simple this point will not be further elaborated in this paper.

[2] As a perfect protection of hardware tokens averting every attack can hardly be achieved [1], the term "tamper-resistant" is used instead of "tamper-proof" to make clear that despite great efforts to protect the microchip, a risk of compromise still exists. The assumption is of course, as with other schemes, that the token's physical protection is sufficient for its purpose.

### 4.4   How It Works

The main phases of the scheme comprise:

**a) Initialization:** Before its delivery to a VTHolder, each DP is initialized by DPProvider. To initialize a group of DPs, DPProvider generates a new key pair $(S_g$ , $P_g)$. The private key $S_g$ is stored in the tamper-resistant memory (TRM) of each card in the group. Further, the corresponding public key $P_g$ is included into *PubList*, which is the list of the public keys of all DPs issued so far.[3]

**b) Distribution:** Once the DPs have been initialized, they can be distributed to VTHolders through any channel. At this stage, all the DPs are identical in the sense that they are neither VTHolder specific nor VTIssuer specific. A VTHolder could just buy an "empty" DP in the supermarket to load his VTs on it.

**c) Virtual Token Generation:** In order to issue a VT, VTIssuer has to write the application dependent data into a file and to sign it with his private key $S_{\text{VTIssuer}}$. The format of this file may be freely chosen by VTIssuer (as long as VTVerifier is able to make sense of it). The signed file constituting a VT can be transferred to VTHolder via e-mail or any other means. If the VT contains confidential data it must, of course, be protected on its way to VTHolder. After receiving a VT, VTHolder has to bind it to a particular DP before it will be accepted by VTVerifier.

**d) Binding:** Binding a VT to a DP ensures that it can not be duplicated (see the requirement of uniqueness in section 3). VTRegistrar knows about every VT he has bound to a DP and is responsible for the prevention of multiple bindings. To do so, he stores the hash value of each VT that he binds in a list called *BoundList*. Storing only a hash value and not the VT itself prevents VTRegistrar from learning the token's content, thus guaranteeing VTHolder's privacy as required in section 3. Moreover, the use of a hash value improves the system's efficiency, especially when a big number of VTs has to be managed. The details of the binding process are depicted in protocol 1 (see also Fig. 2).

*Protocol 1 (Binding of a VT to a DP by VTRegistrar):*

1. TRPU calculates a hash value of VT:

$$h := Hash(\text{VT}).^4$$

2. A new key pair $(S_{\text{VT}}$ , $P_{\text{VT}})$ is generated inside TRPU.
3. $S_{\text{VT}}$ is stored in TRM.

---

[3] An update of PubList is regularly propagated to VTRegistrar (e.g. using a public key infrastructure).

[4] $Hash(\cdot)$ is assumed to be a cryptographically secure hash function, i.e. one that is collision and preimage resistant (see e.g. [11, p. 323]).

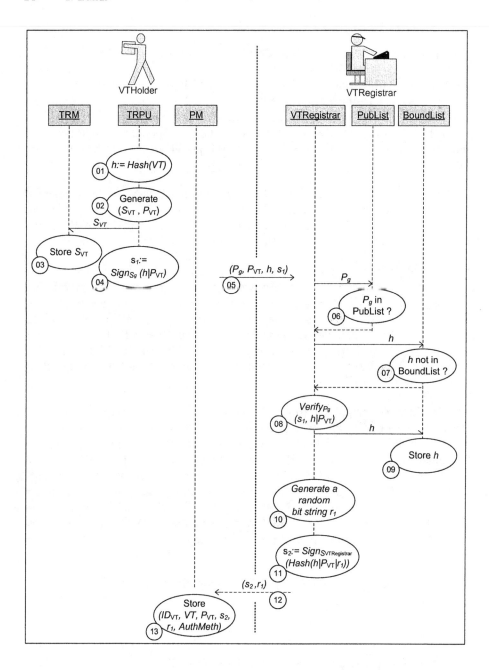

**Fig. 2.** Binding a VT to a DP by VTRegistrar (Protocol 1)

4. TRPU signs the bit string $h|P_{VT}$ using $S_g$:

$$s_1 := Sign_{S_g}(h|P_{VT}).^5$$

5. The tuple $(P_g, P_{VT}, h, s_1)$ is sent to VTRegistrar.
6. VTRegistrar verifies that $P_g$ is contained in PubList.
7. VTRegistrar verifies that $h$ is not yet contained in his list of bound VTs (BoundList).
8. VTRegistrar checks the validity of $s_1$ using $P_g$:

$$Verify_{P_g}(s_1, h|P_{VT}).$$

9. VTRegistrar stores $h$ in BoundList.
10. VTRegistrar generates a random bit string $r_1$.
11. VTRegistrar signs $Hash(h|P_{VT}|r_1)$ with his private key $S_{VTRegistrar}$:

$$s_2 := Sign_{S_{VTRegistrar}}(Hash(h|P_{VT}|r_1)).$$

12. VTRegistrar sends the pair $(s_2, r_1)$ back to VTHolder.
13. The tuple $(ID_{VT}, VT, P_{VT}, s_2, r_1, AuthMeth)$ is stored in PM, where $ID_{VT}$ stands for the ID of the application VT belongs to and $AuthMeth$ for the authentication method to enforce before granting access to this particular VT.[6]

By signing $Hash(h|P_{VT}|r_1)$ in step 11 VTRegistrar confirms that the VT which hashes to $h$ was bound to the DP that holds the corresponding private key $S_{VT}$ in its TRM. Such a confirmation is only issued if three conditions are met:

i. The binding was actually requested using a DP (step 8 of the previous protocol),
ii. that DP is genuine, i.e. its public key $P_g$ is contained in PubList (step 6), and
iii. the VT in case is not yet bound to another DP (step 7).

*Remark 1.* If in step 11 VTRegistrar just signed $h|P_{VT}$ instead of $Hash(h|P_{VT}|r_1)$ then chosen-ciphertext attacks could be feasible. This is why [16, p. 54] points out that "it is foolish to encrypt arbitrary strings".

*Remark 2.* The key pair $(S_{VT}, P_{VT})$ has to be generated securely inside the TRPU so that nobody learns its value. Some smart cards use pseudo random number generators with a seed set by the manufacturer [14]. Such smart cards are unsuitable for this scheme as everyone knowing the seed could deduct the entire pseudo random number sequence. The keys rather have to stem from a physical source of randomness (see e.g. [2] for a true random number generator suitable for integration on smart cards).

---

[5] $b_1|b_2$ stands for the concatenation of the bit strings $b_1$ and $b_2$.
[6] Depending on the use case, $AuthMeth$ is determined either by VTIssuer or by VTHolder.

26    I. Bakdi

**e) Verification:** When a DP is asked to present a given VT to VTVerifier, it first requests an authorization from VTHolder as mentioned in section 4.2. In case VTHolder approves, DP sends VT together with the binding confirmation to VTVerifier who checks their validity. Protocol 2 (depicted by Fig. 3) contains the necessary steps.

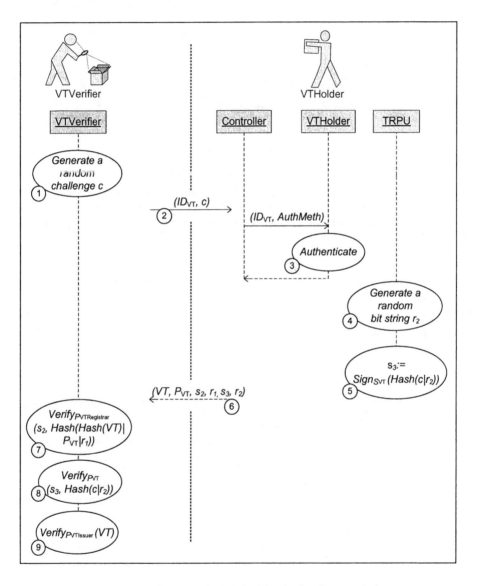

**Fig. 3.** Verification of a VT by VTVerifier (Protocol 2)

*Protocol 2 (Verification of a VT by VTVerifier):*

1. VTVerifier generates a random challenge $c$.
2. VTVerifier requests VT from DP's Controller by sending it the pair $(ID_{VT}, c)$.
3. Controller uses the specified *AuthMeth* to ask VTHolder for permission to show VTVerifier the VT in case.
4. TRPU generates a random bit string $r_2$.
5. TRPU generates the following signature:

$$s_3 := Sign_{S_{VT}}(Hash(c|r_2)).$$

6. Controller sends the tuple $(VT, P_{VT}, s_2, r_1, s_3, r_2)$ to VTVerifier.
7. VTVerifier checks the validity of $s_2$ using $P_{VTRegistrar}$:

$$Verify_{P_{VTRegistrar}}(s_2, Hash(Hash(VT)|P_{VT}|r_1)).$$

8. VTVerifier checks the validity of $s_3$ using $P_{VT}$:

$$Verify_{P_{VT}}(s_3, Hash(c|r_2)).$$

9. VTVerifier checks the authenticity and integrity of VT using $P_{VTIssuer}$.

In step 7 of this protocol, VTVerifier gets convinced that the VT he received is uniquely bound to the DP that holds the private key $S_{VT}$ corresponding to $P_{VT}$. By looking at $s_3$ in step 8, he verifies that he is actually communicating with that DP. Finally, the authenticity and the integrity of the VT itself are verified in the last step.

*Remark 3.* DP could use a suitable zero-knowledge protocol as described e.g. in [11, pp. 405–417] to convince VTVerifier that it holds $S_{VT}$ without divulging it. However, in this paper a digital signature was chosen for this purpose in order to simplify matters.

**f) Unbinding:** VTHolder may want to use more than just one DP and to be able to transfer VTs among them. He could use a DP for his private VTs and a separate one for the VTs he needs at work. When going on a vacation trip he may choose to only take certain VTs with him in order to reduce the damage caused by a possible loss or theft. To satisfy this requirement, a mechanism is needed which enables the unbinding of a VT from the DP it is bound to. Protocol 3 realizes this task.

*Protocol 3 (Unbinding of a VT from a DP by VTRegistrar):*

1. TRPU calculates

$$h := Hash(VT).$$

2. TRPU signs $h$ with $S_{VT}$:

$$s_4 := Sign_{S_{VT}}(h).$$

3. $S_{\mathrm{VT}}$ is removed from TRM.
4. The tuple $(h, P_{\mathrm{VT}}, s_2, r_1, s_4)$ is sent to VTRegistrar.
5. VTRegistrar checks the validity of $s_2$ using his own public key $P_{\mathrm{VTRegistrar}}$:

$$Verify_{P_{\mathrm{VTRegistrar}}}(s_2, h|P_{\mathrm{VT}}|r_1)).$$

6. VTRegistrar checks the validity of $s_4$ using $P_{\mathrm{VT}}$

$$Verify_{P_{\mathrm{VT}}}(s_4, h).$$

7. VTRegistrar removes $h$ from BoundList.

Step 5 of the above protocol ensures that the VT which hashes to $h$ was actually bound to the key pair $(S_{\mathrm{VT}}, P_{\mathrm{VT}})$. In Step 6 VTRegistrar gets convinced that the unbinding request comes from the DP to which VT is currently bound, namely the one holding $S_{\mathrm{VT}}$.

*Remark 4.* So far, a single VTRegistrar was assumed in order to keep the description simple. Nevertheless, the scheme is able to accommodate any number of VTRegistrars. By letting each VTRegistrar manage his own BoundList, a decentralized solution is obtained. The different VTRegistrars do not even need to communicate with each other. In order to designate a VTRegistrar responsible for the uniqueness of a given VT, VTIssuer would include the public key $P_{\mathrm{VTRegistrar}}$ of that VTRegistrar into the VT before signing it. This way, VTVerifier learns which public key he has to employ in order to verify $s_2$ (step 7 of protocol 2). This flexibility is especially important to make a viable business model possible, because it avoids dependency on a single institution. A VTIssuer himself could for instance care about the binding of VTs issued by him. For the sake of completeness, it should be mentioned that the drawback of having many VTRegistrars is the bigger overhead when moving VTs from one DP to another. For each VT being transferred the corresponding VTRegistrar has to be contacted to unbind it from the first DP and to rebind it subsequently to the second one. This could impair the flexibility of the scheme in case VTs are frequently moved.

### 4.5   Who Trusts Whom?

To better understand the dependencies between the single roles their trust relationships are examined in the following.

**VTRegistrar:** The only thing VTRegistrar has to rely on is that the DPs behave correctly, i.e. that they do not divulge private keys and that they execute operations only according to the protocols presented above. In other words, VTRegistrar has to trust DPProvider to only issue DPs that work as specified and to provide him with the correct list of valid public keys (PubList). In all the other actors VTRegistrar does not need to trust.

**VTHolder:** Like VTRegistrar, VTHolder has to trust DPProvider. If his DP functions correctly and keeps its secrets safe, VTHolder does not have to trust VTRegistrar, because the latter does not learn any sensitive information in the course of binding and unbinding VTs. Conversely, assuming the trustworthiness of VTRegistrar, VTHolder cannot be fooled into using a manipulated DP, because he would notice it as soon as he tries to use the chip for the first binding. This renders the distribution channel for DPs uncritical.

**VTIssuer/VTVerifier:** VTIssuer and VTVerifier have to trust VTRegistrar to ensure the uniqueness of VTs, i.e. that binding confirmations are only issued for VTs not already bound. In particular, they have not to rely on the genuineness of a given DP, because VTHolder would not be able to get a binding confirmation from VTRegistrar if his hardware token were not working properly.

*Remark 5.* Someone who learns $S_g$ would be able to request bindings that he may copy. This is because he could generate a key pair $(S_{VT}, P_{VT})$ outside a DP, use $S_g$ to get a binding confirmation from VTRegistrar, and thus know the private key $S_{VT}$ that is necessary for duplication. However, he would not be able to generate a second binding for a given VT using a different pair $(S_{VT}, P_{VT})$, nor could he use any previously bound VT if he lacks the corresponding DP. This is why the consequences of compromising a DP's private key are the same whether it is shared within a group of DPs or not.

*Remark 6.* The scheme described above assumes a running public key infrastructure (PKI). This PKI is, however, only needed in order to manage PubList and the public keys of VTRegistrars and VTIssuers. While PubList has to be accessible to VTRegistrars, the only actor interested in getting authentic public keys of VTRegistrars and VTIssuers is VTVerifier. VTHolders and their DPs have no public keys to be managed by this PKI. This makes the required PKI much simpler than one needed by single ID cards able to generate digital signatures, for instance.

## 4.6   Discussion

The solution proposed in this paper can be seen as a pragmatic compromise between the inflexible single ID cards, on one hand, and the cumbersome multi-application smart cards, on the other hand. While single ID cards represent the simplest solution and have therefore many serious limitations, multi-application smart cards provide the most flexible system, but still need a lot of work to reach their vision. The main difference between the new approach and single ID cards is that the former employs an independent virtual token for each back-end system. The virtual tokens can be used without any online access to a central database and they can be transferred from one hardware token to another without being duplicable. In contrast to multi-application smart cards, a DP merely stores data on the chip, but no application-specific code is executed on it. This makes implementation easier and avoids many security problems. [17] states that "... for many applications, using a smart card securely means understanding it not as a 'trusted' computation platform, but as a data storage device with limited computational abilities".

Nevertheless, there are also applications not covered by the new scheme. These are use cases requiring some application-specific code to be executed on card (e.g. digital signature cards, digital cash cards with a purse-to-purse functionality such as Mondex [10], etc.). Hence, the approach presented above is not meant as a substitute for the other solutions but rather as a complement. Note that it is for example possible to combine a digital signature card with the scheme presented in this paper to cover an even larger set of applications. Summarizing, one could say that the presented approach, although not covering all use cases, is able to avoid undue complexity and still serve a big number of applications adequately.

## 5   Conclusions

A new scheme for a multifunctional hardware token was described in this paper. It is based on the observation that many applications (e.g. driving licenses, student ID cards, credit cards, loyalty cards, pay TV cards, subway tickets, etc.) do not necessarily need the execution of application-specific code on card nor the ability to generate digital signatures. The role of each actor in the scheme, which can be assumed by any person or organization, was clearly defined and the interactions taking place between the different actors were specified. The architecture of a microchip needed to host different virtual tokens was roughly sketched. Unlike attribute certificates, virtual tokens are bound to a single hardware token, which prevents them from being duplicated. Not only does the scheme enable off-line use and post-issuance loading, but virtual tokens can also be transferred among different hardware tokens making the solution very flexible. Moreover, the scheme inherently provides for authenticity, integrity, and privacy. Comparing it to other approaches it was shown that while certainly not providing a universal solution, it may help considerably towards a secure and practical multifunctional smart card.

## References

1. Anderson, Ross and Kuhn, Markus: Tamper Resistance - a Cautionary Note. In: Proceedings of the Second USENIX Workshop on Electronic Commerce, Oakland, CA, USA (1996), 1–11.
2. Bucci, Marco; Germani, Lucia; Luzzi, Raimondo; Trifiletti, Alessandro and Varanonuovo, Mario: A High Speed Oscillator-Based Truly Random Number Source for Cryptographic Applications on a Smart Card IC . In: IEEE Transactions on Computers, No. 4, Vol. 52 (2003), 403–409.
3. Chadwick, David W.: The X.509 Privilege Management Infrastructure. In: Proceedings of the NATO Advanced Networking Workshop on Advanced Security Technologies in Networking, Bled, Slovenia, 2003.
4. Chan, Siu-cheung Charles: Infrastructure of Multi-Application Smart Card (in the concerns of access control). http://home.hkstar.com/~alanchan/papers/multiApplicationSmartCard/, download 2005-02-28 (1997).

5. Chen, Zhiqun: Java Card Technology for Smart Cards: Architecture and Programmer's Guide. Addison-Wesley Professional, Amsterdam (2000).
6. Éluard, Marc; Jensen, Thomas and Denney, Ewen: An Operational Semantics of the Java Card Firewall. In: Proceeding of Smart Card Programming and Security (ESMART), Lecture Notes in Computer Science, 2140, Springer-Verlag, Berlin Heidelberg New York (2001), 95–110.
7. European Union (ed.): Information Technology Security Evaluation Criteria (ITSEC). http://www.bsi.de/zertifiz/itkrit/itsec-en.pdf, download 2005-02-28 (1992).
8. Grimaud, Gilles and Vandewalle, Jean-Jacques: Introducing research issues for next generation Java-based smart card platforms. In: Proceedings of the Smart Objects Conference (SOC), Grenoble, France (2003), 138–141.
9. MAOSCO, Ltd: MULTOS. http://www.multos.com, download 2004-06-07 (2004).
10. MasterCard International: Mondex. http://www.mondex.com, download 2004-06-07 (2004).
11. Menezes, Alfred J.; van Oorschot, Paul C. and Vanstone, Scott A.: Handbook of Applied Cryptography. CRC Press, Boca Raton et al. (1997).
12. Niwano, Eikazu; Hatanaka, Masayuki; Hashimoto, Junko and Yamamoto, Shuichiro: Early Experience of a Dynamic Application Downloading Platform for Multi-Application Smart Cards. In: Proceedings of the Fifth Joint Conference on Knowledge-Based Software Engineering (JCKBSE) Maribor, Slovenia (2002).
13. Posegga, Joachim and Vogt, Harald: Byte Code Verification for Java Smart Cards Based on Model Checking. In: Proceedings of the Fifth European Symposium on Research in Computer Security (ESORICS), Louvain-la-Neuve, Belgium, Lecture Notes in Computer Science, 1485, Springer-Verlag, Berlin Heidelberg New York (1998), 175–190.
14. Rankl, Wolfgang and Effing, Wolfgang: Handbuch der Chipkarten: Aufbau - Funktionsweise - Einsatz von Smart Cards. Hanser Verlag, Munich et al. (2002).
15. Reiter, Michael K. and Rubin, Aviel D.: Crowds: Anonymity for Web Transactions. ACM Transactions on Information and System Security, No. 1, Vol. 1 (1998), 66–92.
16. Schneier, Bruce: Applied cryptography: protocols, algorithms and source code in C. John Wiley & Sons, Inc., New York et al. (1996).
17. Schneier, Bruce and Shostack, Adam: Breaking Up Is Hard To Do: Modeling Security Threats for Smart Cards. In: Proceedings of the USENIX Workshop on Smart Card Technology, USENIX Press (1999), 175–185.
18. Siveroni, Igor; Jensen, Thomas and Éluard, Marc: A Formal Specification of the Java Card Firewall. Nordic Workshop on Secure IT-Systems (2001).
19. Sun Microsystems, Inc.: Java Card Technology. http://java.sun.com/products/javacard/, download 2004-06-07 (2004).

# Implementing Cryptography on TFT Technology for Secure Display Applications

Petros Oikonomakos[1], Jacques Fournier[1,2], and Simon Moore[1]

[1] University of Cambridge, Computer Laboratory, William Gates Building,
15 JJ Thomson Avenue, Cambridge CB3 0FD, UK
po230@cl.cam.ac.uk
[2] GEMPLUS, La Vigie, Avenue des Jujubiers, ZI Athélia IV,
13705 La Ciotat Cedex, France

**Abstract.** Several recent studies have underlined the need for trusted information displays in current and future personal devices. On the other hand, the display market is more and more dominated by low-cost flat-panel structures, driven by Thin-Film Transistor (TFT) circuits. Further, the quality of TFT-based electronics is constantly improving, allowing the fabrication of complicated electronic circuits on TFT technology. We have embarked on a project to implement cryptographic algorithms on polysilicon TFT technology. Our prototype designs will pave the way for secure display realisations combining cryptographic circuits and conventional pixel drivers on the same substrate. An experimental Data Encryption Standard (DES) coprocessor on polysilicon TFT technology is under development, while we are investigating a vector processor architecture to implement Elliptic Curve Cryptography (ECC).

## 1 Introduction

Investigations related to secure and convenient, new or improved financial transaction models are frequently published nowadays. Some of them [1, 2, 3] have identified the improvements in customer security that *trusted* displays have to offer. In this context, a display is trusted (or *secure*) if the content source can be sure that the distributed information will only be presented on the *intended* display. Alternatively, a secure display may be regarded as a means to verify that data is coming from a trusted source. When used in a customer's personal electronic device (PDA, mobile phone, "smart device" etc.), such a display would form part of a secure communication path between a user and a business. An obvious way to develop secure displays is to equip them with decryption electronics, and have the source send encrypted information to them. An unauthorised party not having the adequate key(s) would thus not be able to extract clear display data or display any unauthorised content.

On the display technology front, Organic Light Emitting Diodes (OLEDs) are emerging as a potential market substitute for Liquid Crystal Display (LCD) technology [4]. In the preferred active matrix configuration, both OLED and LCD pixel arrays are driven by Thin-Film Transistors (TFTs), fabricated on

J. Domingo-Ferrer, J. Posegga, and D. Schreckling (Eds.): CARDIS 2006, LNCS 3928, pp. 32–47, 2006.

an insulating substrate (typically glass). The TFT active area is formed either traditionally by hydrogenated amorphous Silicon (a–Si:H) [5], more recently by polycrystalline Silicon (polysilicon, poly–Si) [4], or by continuous grain Silicon (CG–Si), described by Sharp as a next-generation variant of poly–Si [6]. The last two technologies demonstrate higher carrier mobility than a–Si:H, thus producing better quality transistors. It has therefore been possible to fabricate relatively complicated electronic circuits using both poly–Si and CG–Si [7, 8]. Note that the production and material costs of TFT technology are much lower than that of conventional CMOS circuits. This can be understood even from the fact that the former use very cheap materials for the substrate (glass or plastic), while the latter require Silicon. Hence TFTs are economically preferable in large area electronics applications with relatively low performance requirements.

A straightforward way to cryptographically secure an OLED display would be to use a conventional CMOS cryptographic chip for the decryption of the image information sent by the source. The decrypted information could then be suitably directed to the pixel driver array. The non-secure channel between the cryptographic chip and the driver array constitutes the weakest link in most of today's security systems. However, given the recently demonstrated improved capabilities of modern TFT technologies (mentioned in subsection 3.1 of this paper), it would be interesting to investigate whether cryptographic applications can be successfully implemented in such technologies. The motivation behind such an investigation is that consumer portable electronic devices usually occupy relatively large areas. One could therefore use as much of the area as needed for the actual display, while the rest can be occupied by TFT circuits controlling access to the display, by performing cryptographic operations. Figure 1 depicts an over-simplified configuration of a conceptual consumer smart device adhering to the above ideas. The bottom layer of the device in the figure is occupied

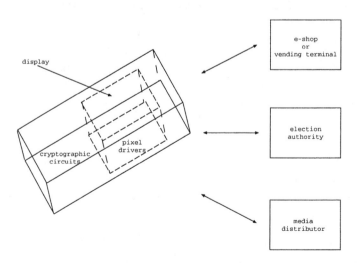

**Fig. 1.** A smart consumer device with a secure TFT display

by TFT electronics, partly driving the pixels of an OLED display, and partly performing cryptographic functions. Of course, several other components (not shown in Fig. 1) would be needed in a consumer smart device, such as a keypad, I/O functionality, a radio antenna etc. The key idea illustrated by the figure, though, is the migration of cryptographic functionality from CMOS to TFT technology, allowing for better area use, promising lower production cost, and completing the end-to-end security chain. The figure also shows three examples of parties that, depending on the application scenario, may communicate with the smart device and would therefore require use of the display; a few such applications will be explained in Section 2.

The rest of this paper is organised as follows. Section 2 establishes the need for secure displays by reviewing a few relevant works. Section 3 provides a brief up-to-date presentation of display technology and TFT drivers, as well as an overview of recent developments in TFT circuits not directly related to displays. In Section 4 we propose our idea for a cryptographic device on poly–Si TFT technology. We report our progress in the direction of a first DES coprocessor prototype, together with our investigations towards a vector processor archi-tecture for Elliptic Curve Cryptography. Section 5 deals with low-level design considerations, particularly by presenting a Programmable Logic Array (PLA) configuration and detailing its operation. Finally, section 6 concludes the paper.

## 2   The Need for Secure Displays

In 1995, Yee and Tygar proposed the use of secure coprocessors in electronic commerce [1]. When used in a point-of-sale terminal scenario, the coprocessor (e.g. a smart-card) communicates with the terminal, the customer reviews the transaction on the terminal display and authorises it using the terminal interface. However, there can be no guarantee about the integrity of the terminal display. It is possible that the customer may be reviewing a transaction of a certain amount, and yet the terminal may be charging the card a different amount. This can be either due to a violation of the terminal security by criminal activity, or even due to merchant fraud. As the authors of [1] mention, the solution to that would be a private visual communication path between the smartcard processor and the end user. An information display on the user side is therefore needed, that would only present data received from the card. Such a trusted display would ensure that the user indeed authorises the same transaction that his or her own card is about to implement.

In a recent patent application [3], a cashless payment method is advocated, using a remote customer terminal (mobile phone, PDA or related apparatus encompassing user interfaces) to communicate with a trader station (e.g. super-market till) and a central station (e.g. bank). The desired amount of money is first read into the trader station, in a conventional way (keyed-in or scanned), and then transmitted to the central station through a data line. The customer reviews the transaction on the trader station display. If the amount is correct, he or she uses the mobile terminal to wirelessly send a unique identifier both to the trader station and to the central station. In response to that, the central station again wirelessly transmits the transaction details to the customer, to be confirmed on the mobile terminal display. Payment proceeds following user authorisation from the mobile terminal to the central station. It can be argued that this model is more secure than that of the previous paragraph, since the user effectively authorises the transaction twice, reviewing payment details submitted from two different sources. Again, however, it is important that the display on the mobile terminal can be trusted to only present information received from the central station. Otherwise the whole model would be vulnerable to "man-in-the-middle" attacks [2], should an attacker interfere between the central station and the customer. Therefore, the mobile terminal will need to be a "smart device" with a secure display.

In 1998 a group of European companies formed the FINancial Transactional IC Card READer (FINREAD) Consortium [9]. Their objective ever since has been to reinforce the level of smartcard security through the specification of a smartcard reader connectable to personal computers, to facilitate home-based e-commerce. Interestingly, the first FINREAD technical specifications mandate, among others, a secure display for the reader. Thus, the consortium of business experts recognise the importance of the integrity of data presented to the user. In a recently accepted paper, Hiltgen et al. [2] describe how such a reader could be used for secure internet banking. In effect, all communication between the card and the bank takes place through the reader and its secure interfaces. The PC plays no active role in manipulating (displaying, encrypting) the card's details. Further, simple knowledge of the card number and details are no longer enough for a malevolent party to access customer accounts, since the bank server only authenticates users by exchanging encrypted card information with the card through the reader.

In another application area, Hortmann published a short tutorial on long distance e-voting [10]. He identifies the problem of potential communication spoofing between a voter's PC monitor and the election authority by online attackers, which is very similar in nature to equivalent scenarios in e-banking. Furthermore, in e-voting it is important not only that the voter sees the correct information on his or her display, but also that nobody else can see the information (for reasons of vote anonymity). Once again, the use of secure displays for end-user voting components is advocated. The author of [10] envisions future PDAs armed with trusted displays functioning as "Personal Security Devices" (PSDs) to realise secure e-voting.

Since 2003, the Open Mobile Alliance (OMA), an industry forum dealing with mobile services, has been working on Digital Rights Management (DRM) schemes to securely distribute and protect data on mobile terminals [11]. Their DRM specification details functional models for the distribution of purchased media applications to mobile consumer devices. In order for such a business model to operate profitably, it is imperative that the distributor be certain that the application can only be enjoyed by the customer, and not widely distributed further. If the application contains images, then encrypting them such that only the buyer's secure display can show them will provide a good solution to this problem.

Through the examples reviewed in the above, this section has demonstrated how secure displays on smart devices can enable trusted communication of private, sensitive data through public networks, in a variety of applications, including e-commerce, e-voting, and wireless distribution of media applications.

## 3   Display Technology and TFTs

Liquid Crystal (LC) based components currently dominate the flat-panel display market. LCDs operate by modulating light generated by a back-light source. In recent years, an alternative emissive technology has been rapidly developing: Organic Light Emitting Diode (OLED) displays. Compared to LCDs, OLEDs demonstrate higher luminous efficiency, brightness, lower production costs and lower operating voltage requirements, in addition to a larger viewing angle. An OLED is a multi-layered electronic structure. One layer is fabricated from an electron transporting material; another from a hole transporting material. In between there exists another layer where the carriers recombine and the excess energy is released as light. The whole structure is often sandwiched between a hole injecting electrode and an electron injecting electrode. Current passing through the OLED causes the emission of light [4].

The pixels of an LC or OLED display can be driven by either a passive or an active matrix (PM or AM respectively), formed by a horizontal address line and a vertical data line. In PM driving, the LCD elements or OLEDs are directly connected to the lines, while AM displays employ actual driving circuits. LCD pixels are voltage-driven; therefore PM driving is a valid low-cost option. In contrast, OLEDs are current-driven. Further, all pixels require a uniform current flow, in order for the OLEDs to provide uniform brightness. It is very difficult to achieve uniform current unless some transistor-based driver circuit is used. It is therefore in practice mandatory to apply active matrix driving of OLED displays. Given the physical dimensions of displays, in most cases it would be economically unwise to use CMOS driving circuits for the active matrix. This is the application area where TFTs on insulating and cheap substrates are useful.

From the above description, it is evident that good quality current sources to be used as AM pixel drivers are the most obviously needed TFT circuits. It is desirable that the drivers not only provide constant current initially, but also continue to do so throughout the expected display lifetime, regardless of any TFT threshold voltage shift over time. A number of designs have been proposed in the literature for this purpose. References [5, 12] deal with a–Si:H TFTs. These TFTs do not demonstrate very good electronic properties. They suffer in particular from low carrier mobility (lower than $1cm^2/V$-s), thus requiring very wide channels to allow sufficient current flow (e.g. Nathan et al. [5] report TFTs with channels as wide as $1000\mu m$). Further, p-channel TFTs are not available in a–Si:H technology [4]. Nevertheless a–Si:H TFT technology is mature and still draws significant research attention. In this context, reference [12] proposes a constant current source composed of 4 TFTs and a storage capacitor. Reference [5] shows an improved version, requiring no storage capacitor.

The driver designs mentioned in the previous paragraph can equally well be used in poly–Si TFT based displays. Poly–Si TFTs demonstrate much greater mobility values than their a–Si:H counterparts (typically by more than an order of magnitude). This allows for much narrower transistors (W/L=2 is achievable). Many poly–Si TFT processes are also able to produce p-channel devices. In [4], Stewart et al. describe a number of refinements to conventional poly–Si TFT fabrication processes that were shown to lead to more uniform TFT characteristics. This way, brightness uniformity can be improved even for driver circuits consisting of only 1 or 2 TFTs.

It is noteworthy that an interesting family of low-temperature poly–Si TFT processes has recently been developed (termed LTPS–TFT) [6]. These processes enable the relatively easy fabrication of TFT circuits on non-conventional substrates, e.g. plastic or various flexible substrates.

## 3.1    Recent TFT Applications

TFT electronics unrelated to information displays are not widespread. However, the availability of p-channel devices, the continuous improvement in electronic properties and the reduced fabrication costs, in addition to unique characteristics such as manufacturability on flexible substrates have recently triggered a certain degree of research activity on other potential uses of poly–Si TFTs, LTPS–TFTs and CG–Si TFTs. Some characteristic examples are presented in this section.

Hashido et al. [13] developed a capacitive fingerprint sensor using LTPS–TFT technology. They initially observe that conventional optical fingerprint authentication systems are very expensive and not portable. Direct-contact fingerprint sensors are a portable alternative; implementing such sensors on TFT technology additionally lowers the production cost. Their sensor is based on the assumption that the capacitance between a given area of the human finger and a sensor plate that the finger touches depends on the morphology of the area (i.e. whether it is a "valley" or a "ridge"). A simple 1-TFT sensor cell is configured that, together with a read-out TFT, converts this capacitance to voltage. The overall sensor chip comprises a matrix of such sensor cells, as well as buffers and shift registers that control the continuous scanning of all rows and columns of the matrix. Their experimental results undoubtedly support their sensing method.

Estrela et al. [14] experiment with poly–Si TFTs for biosensor applications. They observe consistent and repeatable threshold voltage shifts in the current-voltage (I-V) characteristics of TFTs when they come in contact with certain biochemical agents. Based on this, they demonstrate the potential usefulness of poly–Si TFTs as inexpensive disposable pH sensors, penicillin sensors, as well as DNA hybridization sensors.

In a more conventional application, Lee et al. [8] present a full Z80 CPU (8-bit) developed using CG–TFT technology on a glass substrate. CG–TFTs typically demonstrate three times the carrier mobility of LTPS–TFTs [6]. The presented chip comprises 13000 TFTs and runs at 3 MHz when powered at 5

Volts. The authors of [8] report it as the first publicly-announced successful step in the direction of realising full-scale electronic systems on glass substrates ("Systems on Panels").

Finally, Karaki et al. [7] announced the fabrication of an 8-bit LTPS asynchronous microprocessor, named ACT11. Operating asynchronously provides robustness against variations in TFT I-V characteristics as well as power savings. The chip nominally operates at 5 Volts.

## 4   Developing Cryptography on Poly–Si TFTs

The discussion so far established that as TFT technologies mature, they can accommodate more and more complicated digital electronics applications. The integration of substantial functional circuits and display drivers on the same substrate appears to be a matter of time. The state-of-the-art rapidly approaches a stage where high-volume production will demand serious CAD tool support for TFT chip production lines. Motivated by these observations, we have embarked on a research project to implement cryptographic functionality on poly–Si TFT technology. We expect this concept to be particularly useful for the development of secure displays, to be used in financial and other future applications such as these described in Section 2 of this paper. The current capabilities of TFTs cannot cope with clock frequency values above a few MHz (or equivalent asynchronous throughput). However, most of these applications could easily be accommodated by static and slow displays without seriously impairing customer satisfaction. In addition, TFT characteristics are improving rapidly. Therefore it is expected that the commercial relevance of TFT electronics applications will increase continuously in the future. In other words, cryptographic TFT chips may in the future be used even in scenarios requiring fast displays.

To investigate about the implementation of cryptographic functions on poly–Si TFTs, we chose to focus on the simple concept of displaying information

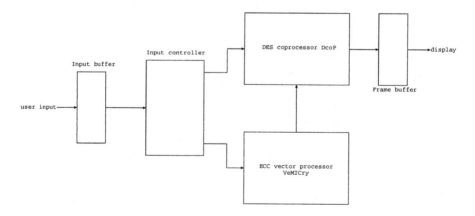

**Fig. 2.** Cryptographic chip architecture

encrypted using DES. In order to securely distribute and refresh the DES keys
we include ECC capabilities in our scheme as illustrated in Fig. 2. Our chip will
work in the following fashion.

- The data received in the input buffer is assumed to be encrypted according
  to the Data Encryption Standard (DES) [15].
- The 56-bit DES keys are transmitted encrypted using an asymmetric
  public-key scheme, in our case Elliptic Curve Cryptography. In the field of
  public-key cryptography, Elliptic Curves (ECs) have performance and key-
  size advantages over the RSA scheme [16]. We therefore choose them for our
  design.
- The environment first provides a number of encrypted DES keys to the input
  buffer.
- The input controller routes these keys to the ECC processor VeMICry shown
  in the figure.
- Processor VeMICry is being designed to include special hardware to implement modular arithmetic needed for ECC. Its overall architecture accords
  to the *vector* processor model [17]. More details are provided in subsection
  4.2 of this paper.
- While VeMICry is decrypting the keys using its private key, the environment
  provides the actual DES-encrypted data to the input buffer.
- The input controller then makes sure the data is routed to the DES coprocessor (DcoP in the figure).
- Coprocessor DcoP is a pure hardware module and makes heavy use of PLAs
  as building blocks. More details on its architecture are given in subsection
  4.1 of this paper.
- When VeMICry finishes decrypting the keys, it sends them to the DES coprocessor, to be used for data decryption.
- Coprocessor DcoP then performs DES decryption and writes the decrypted
  data to the output buffer. In the figure the buffer is termed frame buffer,
  since the chip is intended to feed display drivers.
- While DcoP performs decryption, the environment provides new keys to the
  chip input. The keys are again sent to VeMICry and a new cycle of operation
  begins.

56-bit DES keys are no longer considered to be completely secure [18]. However, one could envisage to refresh the keys frequently enough to discourage any
attack on the DES. In a real application, one could use 3-DES or AES; our chip
is simply a proof-of-concept of cryptography using TFTs. The security of the
overall scheme will also depend on the security of the ECC processor (and its
resistance to side-channel attacks) and how the device's private key is stored.
If implemented and combined with pixel drivers, the architecture will provide
cryptographic protection to the display. With those cryptographic capabilities,
we could for example make sure that only "authenticated" users can access the
display or that distributed images are only visible on that particular display.

Of the blocks shown in Fig. 2, VeMICry and DcoP are currently under development. The input controller is expected to be nothing more complicated than

a state machine, routing a fixed number of input packets to VeMICry, followed by another fixed number of packets to DcoP. The following subsections 4.1 and 4.2 provide architectural details on the design of the two processors.

### 4.1   The DES Coprocessor

The DES coprocessor is being designed purely as a hardware module, comprising three blocks, namely the key schedule, round block, and the controller. It is a straightforward implementation, shown in the block diagram of Fig. 3. The coprocessor receives a 64-bit encrypted data input, directed to the round block, and a 56-bit key, directed to the key schedule block. The environment (ultimately the input controller of Fig. 2) also raises two flags – I and K – as soon as valid data and a valid key have been fed to DcoP. As soon as I and K are raised, the controller state machine orders the key schedule to compute a subkey, again by raising a suitable flag. The key schedule block computes the subkey and feeds it to the round block, while informing the controller about computation completion. The controller further signals to the round block that the subkey is ready. Upon receiving the signal, the round block responds by using the subkey to produce the partial result, and subsequently informs the controller. The same process is repeated sixteen times for all DES rounds [15]. After all rounds, the decrypted output is available at the round block output. The controller informs the environment and waits for new input and key values. Throughout the process, the controller asserts or deasserts suitable signals to make sure the key schedule performs single or double shifts depending on the current round.

It is evident that this simple model can easily be adjusted to perform encryption instead of decryption, by performing left or right shifts in the key schedule block. Further, it can also easily be amended to implement triple DES instead of standard DES.

Behavioural Verilog [19] models for the DcoP blocks have been developed and confirmed by simulation. The actual layout is currently under development. The resulting chip will be the first, to our knowledge, cryptographic application on

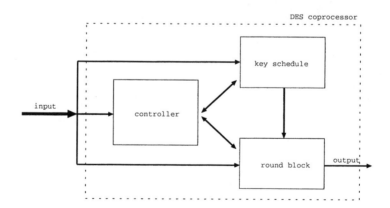

**Fig. 3.** DES coprocessor block diagram

poly–Si TFT technology, and at the same time the first poly–Si TFT chip to feature a 64-bit datapath. It will test the feasibility of cryptography on TFTs and build up our confidence towards full integration of the architecture of Fig. 2. Note that this design can be easily tweaked to execute stronger encryption algorithms like DESX.

## 4.2   A Vector Processor for Elliptic Curve Cryptography

This section provides information about the architecture and functional model of the vector processor with cryptographic support shown in Fig. 2. We have used the acronym VeMICry, for Vectorial MIPS for Cryptography [20]. In essence, VeMICry comprises a simple MIPS-I processor [21] implementing usual, "scalar" instructions, together with a vector coprocessor for the vector instructions. The simplified block diagram of Fig. 4 depicts this idea. The overall processor works very much as a standard MIPS as regards conventional instructions; when *vector* instructions are encountered in the program then the decoder directs them to the vector coprocessor. As the name suggests, vector instructions operate on vectors of registers rather than on individual registers. A total of 17 vector instructions have been defined for VeMICry; a full list is provided in [20]. A few examples – relevant to public key cryptography – are:

- Unsigned Vector Addition: adds the contents of respective elements (registers) of two vectors and writes the result to a third, while propagating carries from the $i$th element to the $i$+1st.
- Vector-Scalar Unsigned Addition: adds a scalar value – stored in a single register – to each vector element and writes the result to a target vector.
- Vector-Scalar Arithmetic Multiplication: multiplies a vector by a scalar value while propagating carries. The result is written to a target vector.
- Vector-Scalar Polynomial Multiplication: multiplies a vector by a scalar value without carry propagation. The result is written to a target vector.

Clearly, the last two instructions can be used to implement modular multiplication, based on Montgomery's reduction algorithm [22], in prime or binary

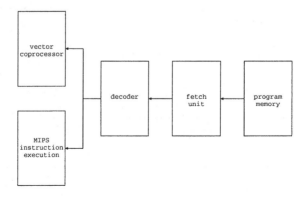

**Fig. 4.** ECC vector processor block diagram

Galois Fields. This multiplication is the most critical opearation of EC point multiplication required for EC decryption.

The reason why we chose a vector architecture is that cryptographic algorithms in general and ECC in particular operate on very wide datapaths and long precision numbers. Decomposing the data into vectors of registers of smaller widths and working on vectors and vector elements *in parallel* is expected to increase performance. Further, a vector processor datapath is modular and scalable, thus can easily be deployed in a variety of applications. Finally, a vector processor has a simpler control path and scheduling logic than other superscalar processors, thus reducing power dissipation [17, 23]. Figure 5 shows the "heart" of the vector coprocessor, that is the vector register file together with vector processing units (VPUs) to implement the instructions. Naturally, the coprocessor also needs peripheral control logic not shown in the figure. In essence, this logic will implement a vector instruction pipeline, separate from and communicating with the scalar MIPS pipeline (Fig. 4). Parameters in the design of the coprocessor include the number of vectors $q$, the number of elements per vector $p$, and the number of processing units $r$ (all three shown in Fig. 5), as well as the register bit-width, currently fixed at 32. The choice of these parameters will influence the processor performance, area, and degree of parallelism. In order to explore the trade-offs between these characteristics, we have built a functional model of the VeMICry using the ArchC simulation tool [24]. Details and simulation results can be found in [20], showing significant performance improvements when the Montgomery algorithm runs on the vector processor model, compared to equivalent realisations on a purely scalar, conventional MIPS.

A Verilog model for the vector processor of Fig. 4 is under development. The architecture will allow us to work on datapaths up to 256 bits wide.

Note that the VeMICry functional model is not restricted to modular multiplication, ECCs or public key cryptography; the AES algorithm [25] has also been simulated on it and again improvements were demonstrated in [20]. While

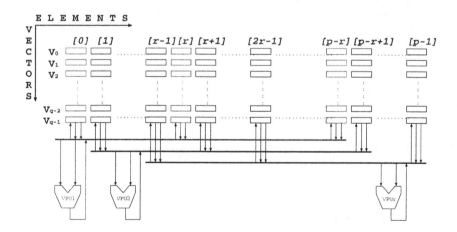

**Fig. 5.** Vector register file and connections to vector processing units

in this particular project it is employed for ECC decryption, it should be regarded as a scalable, high performance processor architecture employable in a variety of cryptographic applications.

## 5   Low-Level Design Considerations

Instead of randomly placed logic gate realisations, in our DES design we are heavily relying on regular structures, in particular PLAs. Due to their geometrically regular layout, PLAs demonstrate timing predictability and controllability. Therefore they are often used in modern CMOS design flows to achieve quick timing closure [26]. In these dynamic-logic structures, power is dissipated only immediately after clock edges [27]. Therefore, the PLA outputs do not experience data-dependent power glitches; this can be regarded as a counter measure against side-channel attacks. In line with the recommendations of [28], we thus provide a degree of security "by design". This may not be very relevant in the case of the architecture in Fig. 2 as in practice an attacker would rather extract the ECC private key than the DES secret keys which are refreshed frequently. However, it is definitely a positive feature for our coprocessor as such, should it be used to implement DES, DESX or triple DES alone.

After reviewing the PLA configurations proposed in the literature and conducting a number of electrical simulations, we decided to use the circuit shown in Fig. 6 as our basic PLA cell. The figure depicts one "AND" and one "OR" plane term, together with an interplane buffer and control logic.

In more detail, the control logic comprises two Muller C-elements and a few inverters constituting a delay line (four inverters are shown for the sake of the illustration – more or less can be used as required). The asynchronous 4-phase single-rail handshaking protocol [29] is thus realised. In the asynchronous

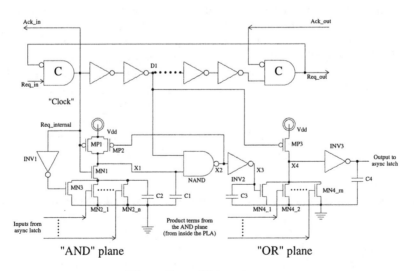

**Fig. 6.** Basic PLA architecture

operation context, the PLA is treated as combinational hardware handling bundled-data coming from an asynchronous latch. The PLA output is also considered to feed the latch of the next logic stage. The PLA is for the most part an asynchronous counterpart of the synchronous design presented by Wang et al. [27]. Indeed, if a clock was applied as shown in the figure ("clock") instead of the asynchronous control signals, then we would have a perfectly working synchronous PLA. For our project, we choose an asynchronous implementation. This is firstly because it is difficult to route a clock distribution network throughout the chip, given that TFT technologies rarely use more than two metal layers [13]. Further, in line with Karaki et al. [7], we acknowledge the importance of I-V characteristic variation tolerance that asynchronous design offers.

The PLA is implemented using n- and p-channel TFTs (nTFTs and pTFTs respectively) in dynamic logic configuration and as such works in two phases, namely "precharge" and "evaluate". When Req_internal=0, the circuit is in the precharge phase, and points X1 and X4 are driven to Vdd (the latter after two inverters' delay). In the subsequent evaluate phase (Req_internal=1), the pulldown network of nTFTs in the AND plane determines the logic value at X1. After two inverter delays, this value is allowed to propagate to the OR plane through the interplane buffer composed of the NAND gate and inverter INV2. The OR plane pull-down network then determines the ultimate PLA output. Capacitors C1 – C3 in the figure model parasitics, corresponding to long lines in the actual layout [27], while C4 signifies the output load.

While the PLA operation described above is typical of dynamic logic, the design of Fig. 6 also includes some non-standard elements. First of all, the first inverting element of the interplane buffer is not a pure inverter but a NAND gate. This ensures that the voltage at point X2 is the logic inverse of X1 only in the evaluation phase. During precharge, the voltage at X2 is kept high, therefore point X3 is kept low and the need for a ground switch in the OR plane is eliminated. This mechanism both speeds up the OR plane, and saves power, since it minimizes the switching activity in the interplane buffer. The second non-standard technique is the charge sharing phenomenon exploited in the AND plane. Notice the nTFT MN1. It is effectively the ground switch of the AND plane, but it has been moved between the precharge pTFT and the nTFTs implementing the function. As soon as Req_internal goes high, capacitor C1 transfers some of its charge to C2 through MN1, regardless of the input pattern. If any of the MN2_i nTFTs are on, then the rest of the charge in C1 will be transfered to ground and X1 will be driven low. The charge sharing effect thus speeds up the discharge process and the overall PLA evaluation phase. If all MN2_i TFTs are off, then C1 loses some charge to C2; this charge is replenished when transistor MP2 is turned on, since X2 is driven low. Thus, the design continues to operate correctly. In the subsequent precharge phase, transistor MN3 turns on and discharges C2. We owe both these ideas to [27].

The addition of two inverter delays between the activation of the AND and the OR planes in the structure of Fig. 6 is our own modification to the original structure of [27]. Indeed, in the design of [27] both planes were activated

```
.i 3      ───────►no of inputs
.o 2      ───────►no of outputs
.p 7      ───────►no of product terms
001 10 |product terms
010 10 |left-hand side:
100 10 |1: variable contributes to the term
111 10 |0: complement of variable contributes to the term
11- 01 |-: don't care
       |right-hand side:
1-1 01 |1: term contributes to the OR-plane sum term
-11 01 |0: term does not contribute to the OR-plane sum term
.e        ───────► end
```

**Fig. 7.** An example of the standard PLA description format

simultaneously by the system clock (equivalent to our Req_internal). Through simulation we found that this created unnecessary and data-dependant glitches on the interplane buffer, consuming power needlessly and potentially creating security hazards.

We have laid out a library of AND- and OR-plane cells and interplane buffers on poly–Si TFT technology using the Electric full-custom VLSI layout tool [30]. We subsequently wrote a relatively simple tool in the Perl language, which uses this library to automatically create full PLA layouts on the paradigm of Fig. 6 when fed by a description of their equations, in the standard PLA format exemplified and explained in the code of Fig. 7. Most logic functions of the DES standard (notably, the S-boxes) will be laid out using this tool. Together with other basic components (latches, multiplexers, barrel shifters, permutation operations – the latter manually designed simply as re-arrangements of wires), they form the building blocks of DcoP, to be connected together manually again using the layout editor of Electric.

## 6   Conclusion

Trusted displays are needed in modern and future applications. In the 'Trusted Computing' model, they will enable content providers to identify the equipment on which protected material is displayed. They may also be used to authenticate any party wishing to present visual information on them. In this paper we have advocated *cryptographically secure displays* and presented their on-going implementation using *polysilicon Thin-Film Transistor* technology. To this end, we have proposed a general cryptographic configuration combining public and secret key cryptography. We have outlined the high-level architectures of its constituent elements, namely a hardware DES coprocessor and a vector processor tailored for cryptographic applications. Finally, we have reported on low-level design considerations, namely by describing a PLA structure and associated automatic layout generator, intended to be used for the production of the main building blocks of our chip layouts.

We are actively working towards a first cryptographic test chip featuring a DES coprocessor on TFTs, and expect to have samples available for measurements within 2006.

## Acknowledgement

Thanks are due to EPSRC for funding this work under grant code GR/S05496/01. The authors would also like to thank Simon Hollis for his useful input during the planning phase of this work, and Ross Anderson for his comments on the paper.

## References

1. Yee, B., Tygar, J.D.: Secure Coprocessors in Electronic Commerce Applications. Proceedings of the 1st USENIX Workshop on Electronic Commerce, July 1995, 155–170
2. Hiltgen, A., Kramp, T., Weigold T.: Secure Internet Banking Authentication. Accepted for publication in IEEE Security & Privacy, available online at http://www.ubs.com/1/ShowMedia/ubs_ch/authentication?contentId=75819& name=IEEE2.pdf
3. Offer, G.: Method and Apparatus for Performing a Cashless Payment Transaction. United States Patent Application #20,020,101,708
4. Stewart, M., Howell, R.S., Pires, L., Hatalis, M.K.: Polysilicon TFT Technology for Active Matrix OLED Displays. IEEE Transactions on Electron Devices, Vol. 48, No. 5, May 2001, 845–851
5. Nathan, A. et al.: Amorphous Silicon Thin Film Transistor Circuit Intergration for Organic LED Displays on Glass and Plastic. IEEE Journal of Solid-State Circuits, Vol. 39, No. 9, September 2004, 1477–1486
6. Sharp Microelectronics of the Americas website: http://www.sharpsma.com/lcd/ lcdguide/Technologies/CG-Silicon.php
7. Karaki, N. et al.: A Flexible 8b Asynchronous Microprocessor based on Low-Temperature Poly-Silicon TFT Technology. Digest of Technical Papers of the 52nd IEEE International Solid-State Circuit Conference (ISSCC) 2005
8. Lee, B. et al.: A CPU on a Glass Substrate Using CG-Silicon TFTs. Digest of Technical Papers of the 50th IEEE International Solid-State Circuit Conference (ISSCC) 2003
9. FINREAD Specification, FINREAD Consortium. http://www.finread.com
10. Hortmann, M.: Tutorial on E-Voting. EURESCOM mess@ge, Issue 3, 2001, page 22, available online at http://www.eurescom.de/~pub/about-eurescom/ message03_2001/message03_2001.pdf
11. Open Mobile Alliance (OMA): DRM Specification V2.0 Candidate Version 2.0-26 April 2005, available online at http://www.openmobilealliance.org/ftp/ Public_documents/BAC/DLDRM/
12. He, Y., Hattori, R., Kanicki, J.: Current-Source a-Si:H Thin-Film Transistor Circuit for Active-Matrix Organic Light-Emitting Displays. IEEE Electron Device Letters, Vol. 21, No. 12, December 2000, 590–592
13. Hashido, R. et al.: A Capacitive Fingerprint Sensor Chip Using Low-Temperature Poly-Si TFTs on Glass Substrate and a Novel and Unique Sensing Method. IEEE Journal of Solid-State Circuits, Vol. 38, No. 2, February 2003, 274–280
14. Estrela, P., Stewart, A.G., Yan, F., Migliorato, P.: Field Effect Detection of Biomolecular Interactions. Electrochimica Acta, Vol. 50, 2005, 4995–5000
15. US Department of Commerce, National Institute of Standards and Technology: Data Encryption Standard (DES). Federal Information Processing Standards Publication 46-3, October 1999

16. Batina, L., Berna Örs, S., Preneel, B., Vandewalle, J.: Hardware Architectures for Public Key Cryptography. Integration, The VLSI Journal, Vol. 34, 2003, 1–64
17. Asanović, K.: Vector Microprocessors. PhD Thesis, University of California Berkeley, 1998
18. Electronic Frontier Foundation: Cracking DES. Secrets of Encryption Research, Wiretap Politics & Chip Design. July 1998
19. Lilja, D.J., Sapatnekar, S.S.: Designing Digital Computer Systems with Verilog. Cambridge University Press, 2004
20. Fournier, J., Moore, S.: A Vectorial Approach to Cryptography Implementation. Proceedings of the 1st International Conference on Digital Rights Management: Technology, Issues, Challenges and Systems, November 2005
21. MIPS Technologies: MIPS Architecture for Programmers Volume II: The MIPS32 Instruction Set. Technical Report MD00086, Revision 0.95, March 2001
22. Montgomery, P.: Modular Multiplication without Trial Division. Mathematics of Computation, Vol. 44, 1985, 519–521.
23. Folegnani, D., González, A.: Energy Effective Issue Logic. Proceedings of the 28th Annual International Symposium on Computer Architecture, June-July 2001, 230–239
24. T.A. team: The ArchC Architecture Description Language – Reference Manual. Technical Report v.1.2, University of Campinas, December 2004
25. US Department of Commerce, National Institute of Standards and Technology: Advanced Encryption Standard (AES). Federal Information Processing Standards Publication 197, November 2001
26. Posluszny, S. et al.: "Timing Closure by Design", A High Frequency Microprocessor Design Methodology. Proceedings of the 37th ACM/IEEE Design Automation Conference, June 2000, 712–717
27. Wang, J.S., Chang, C.R., Yeh, C.: Analysis and Design of High-Speed and Low-Power CMOS PLAs. IEEE Journal of Solid-State Circuits, Vol. 36, No. 8, August 2001, 1250–1262
28. Li, H., Markettos, A.T., Moore, S.: Security Evaluation Against Electromagnetic Analysis at Design Time. Proceedings of the 7th International Workshop on Cryptographic Hardware and Embedded Systems, August-September 2005, 280–292
29. Sparsø, J., Furber, S.: Principles of Asynchronous Circuit Design: A Systems Perspective. Kluwer Academic Publishers, 2001
30. Static Free Software: Using the Electric VLSI Design System, available online at http://www.staticfreesoft.com/manual/

# A Smart Card-Based Mental Poker System

Jordi Castellà-Roca, Josep Domingo-Ferrer, and Francesc Sebé

Rovira i Virgili University of Tarragona,
Dept. of Computer Engineering and Maths,
Av. Països Catalans 26, Tarragona E-43007, Catalonia
{jordi.castella, josep.domingo, francesc.sebe}@urv.net

**Abstract.** On-line casinos have experienced a great expansion since the generalized use of Internet started. There exist in the literature several proposals of systems allowing secure remote gaming. Nevertheless, the security requirements of some game families lead to the use of complex and costly cryptographic protocols. A particularly challenging game family is mental poker. In this paper we present a smart card-based e-gaming system for mental poker with a low computational cost.

**Keywords:** Smart cards and applications in the Internet, Cryptographic protocols for smart cards, E-gambling, Mental poker.

## 1  Introduction

Computer networks, and especially Internet, allow a lot of usual activities to be carried out in a time- and space-independent way. Leisure is a sector that has quickly grasped and exploited the possibilities of the network as a new business outlet. On-line casinos are a particularly visible form of on-line leisure. Increasing sales figures of on-line gambling companies are a clear indicator of the positive evolution in this sector. According to Merryll Lynch the on-line gambling business is expected to grow to $48 billion by 2010 and $177 billion by 2015. This booming turnover must be accompanied by enough security guarantees for on-line players; unfortunately, this is not always the case.

In an on-line casino, players usually go through the following steps:

**Registration:** Prior to accessing the on-line casino, players must register themselves. In the registration step, players give their personal information. This information is used by the on-line casino to create an account for the player. Players will access the on-line casino via their account.

**Authentication:** After registration, players possess the necessary information (typically a username and a password) to authenticate themselves to the casino and log in their accounts.

**Increase credit:** On-line casinos tend to use pre-payment methods. Thus, players must make a payment to the casino before starting to play. The amount of cash that has been paid by a player receives the name of credit, and it is transferred to the account created in the registration step. When a player

J. Domingo-Ferrer, J. Posegga, and D. Schreckling (Eds.): CARDIS 2006, LNCS 3928, pp. 48–61, 2006.

makes a bet, the on-line casino verifies that the player has got enough credit. If the player loses/wins her bet, the on-line casino substracts/adds the bet amount from/to the player's credit.

**Withdraw credit:** The player transfers her game earnings from her casino account to her bank account.

**Bet:** At least one bet is made in every casino game. The game rules specify how many bets are possible and when players can bet.

**Game:** The rules of each game drive its operation. Based on those rules, players obtain one or several random events during the game. The game result, *i.e.* who wins and who loses, is based to some extent on the obtained events.

We can assert that a gaming system is secure if each of the above steps can be done in a secure manner.

### 1.1  Contribution and Plan of This Paper

We present in this paper a gambling system that allows poker to be played remotely, while offering security for the different steps players need to go through.

In the proposed system, each player owns a smart card that runs the security-critical parts of the aforementioned steps. We assume that smart cards are issued by the public authority that regulates on-line gambling. This authority ensures that: i) player registration is made properly; ii) the software inside the smart card is fair.

This paper is organized as follows. A state of the art is given in Section 2. Section 3 justifies the security requirements that will be considered. The architecture of the proposed systems is described in Section 4. The relevant protocols of our system are specified in Section 5. Section 6 is a security analysis. Finally, conclusions are summarized in Section 7.

## 2  State of the Art

Hall *et al.* propose a remote gambling system ([7]). Each player has a key pair of a public-key cryptosystem. Players use their private key to authenticate themselves to the on-line casino, and also to sign each message they send. The paper does not describe how key pairs are generated and distributed; this is a relevant issue, *e.g.* because any minor under the legal age for gambling should be unable to register and get a key pair. The random events used in the game are computed jointly by all players using a cryptographic protocol. The protocol ensures that no player is in a privileged position to influence the outcome of the random event.

In [9] a remote gambling system is described. The system has the same security properties as [7]. Nevertheless, its implementation uses multicast, so the proposed system is more efficient as far as communication is concerned.

Proposals [7] and [9] do not present any protocol to play poker without a trusted third party (TTP). Their authors argue that fulfilling the security properties enumerated in [3] without a TTP is too costly. As an example, they quote the work by Edwards in [6], where an implementation of the protocol [4] on three Sparc workstations is reported to have taken eight hours to shuffle a deck.

Recent proposals, like [2] and [10], improve on [4] from the efficiency point of view. Nonetheless, they use zero-knowledge proofs to satisfy all security requirements enumerated in [3]. Their computational and communication costs preclude their commercial use.

Zhao *et al.* present in [11] a payment method for on-line casinos. The payment protocol uses an optimistic TTP. Each bet includes the payment information in encrypted form. The TTP verifies that payment information is correct. If a player loses a bet and refuses to pay, the TTP reveals the payment information to the winner. Again, zero-knowledge proofs are used, which degrade the performance of the protocol.

Aiello *et al.* propose in [1] a gambling system, where players have an electronic device. The device allows players to play off-line. It is based on a smart card that manages the player's credit and ensures game fairness. Our proposal below is based on the same principle to design an efficient and secure mental poker protocol. The difference is that players are on-line and the smart card does all security-critical operations.

## 3   Security Requirements

In Section 1, we have enumerated the steps done by players in an on-line casino. Now we define the security properties that must be guaranteed at each step:

**Registration:** Registration must collect accurate and truthful information about people wishing to play. This is necessary to detect, *e.g.*, minors under the legal age for gambling, known dishonest players and people with mental diseases related to gambling.

**Authentication:** The authentication method used by players must be a strong one. It must be resistant against common attacks, for instance birthday and replay attacks.

**Credit:** Players increase their credit when they make a payment to the on-line casino and decrese ther credit when they make a withdrawal. Consequently, the action to increase or decrease the player's credit must satisfy the same security requirements as an electronic payment:
 - *Confidentiality.* the payment information is a private business between the payment issuer (player) and the payment receiver (the on-line casino or the bank).
 - *Integrity.* Once the payment has been sent out, no party must be able to modify the payment information.
 - *Authentication.* Each message must include a non-malleable and verifiable proof of who is the message originator.
 - *Non-repudiation.* Once the payer has sent her payment, she must be unable to repudiate it. Moreover, the payer must obtain a receipt of the payment so that the receiver cannot later deny having been paid.

**Bet:** When a player places a bet, the following properties must be satisfied:

- *Integrity.* The bet cannot be modified once it has been sent to the on-line casino, neither the player nor the casino can alter the bet.
- *Authentication.* All messages exchanged in a bet are public to all players and the on-line casino. In this way, any game participant can verify the origin of any message.
- *Non-repudiation.* A player cannot repudiate her bet and the on-line casino cannot repudiate a previously accepted bet.

A bet must have at least the following information:

- Bet amount;
- An identifier of the game;
- The concept of the bet, *e.g.* what condition is being betted on.

**Game:** Poker over a network is one of the most complex games from the security point of view. Crépeau [3] enumerated a list of requirements and properties that must be met by a mental poker protocol:

- *Uniqueness of cards.* Traditional decks of cards can be verified before the game starts, and players can be assured that there are not duplicate cards. In a mental poker protocol players should be able to verify that each card appears once and only once.
- *Uniform random distribution of cards.* In a traditional hand of poker, one player shuffles the deck and the rest of players can see it. Cards are uniform randomly distributed, because the shuffling player cannot influence the result of shuffling. A way to guarantee uniform random distribution in mental poker is for the hand of each player to depend on decisions made by all players.
- *Cheating detection with a very high probability.* A mental poker protocol must detect any attempt to cheat, *e.g* seeing a face-down card, changing a face-up card, etc.
- *Complete confidentiality of cards.* If the deck is face-down then no partial or total information about any card from the deck ought to be disclosed. Also when a player draws a card, the rest of players should not be able to get information on that card.
- *Minimal effect of coalitions.* A secret communication channel between the players of a coalition is possible in mental poker, *e.g.* one player can ring another player to tell her her cards. A mental poker protocol should reduce the effect of coalitions, so that if a player is not cheating then nobody can learn more about her hand, or about the cards in the deck, than what they can infer from the cards in their coalition.
- *Complete confidentiality of strategy.* It is strategically very important in the game of poker that the losing players may keep their cards secret at the end of a hand. The whole concept of bluffing is based on this fact.

## 4   Architecture

TTP-based mental poker proposals share the common feature that the on-line casino performs most of the above steps: the on-line casino registers players, authenticates them, and manages bets, the credit of players and the entire game. Note that it is the casino who generates the game events (card shuffling, etc.) and controls the game rules.

Allowing the casino to act as a TTP places it in a privileged position: the casino controls the game and at the same time takes part in it. Thus, security in the TTP-based paradigm completely depends on the on-line casino. If the casino security is compromised by an external or an internal attacker, then the result of the game can be manipulated against honest players.

Thus, it is desirable to prevent the casino from being critical to security. To that end, we propose a new gambling system where security is distributed among the following parties: regulator, on-line casino and players.

Each player has a smart card. The regulator (public authority, government, etc.) certifies the smart card and the software in it. The certification is a guarantee on the fairness of the gambling system. Thus, trust as far as the smart card is concerned rests on the public regulator. This should give more guarantees than relying on the on-line casino, which is often located off-shore or in some tax paradise. We next describe each party in our architecture:

**Regulator:** In a vast majority of countries, on-line gambling is not regulated. This legal void results in a lack of protection for players, and in some cases for the on-line casinos too [5]. In our proposal the game regulator is the government or a public authority. The regulator watches over the rights of the players and on-line casinos. Moreover, the regulator facilitates to players and on-line casinos the fulfillment of their duties when they must declare their earnings. The game regulator issues the smart cards used by players. Every smart card contains a player's key-pair and a sofware application to play on-line. The software allows the following actions: authenticate to players, increase credit, place a bet and play.

**On-line casino:** The on-line casino authenticates players in a secure way and puts them in touch so that they can start playing with each other. The on-line casino manages the players' accounts (increase credit, decrease credit, place a bet, pay a bet). For each of the above actions, we propose a cryptographic protocol in this paper where the TTP is "distributed" between the regulator and the smart cards. To the extent that they use no centralized TTP, our protocols are TTP-free, albeit in a weak form.

**Players:** We use the term "players" to denote the set of players plus the software and hardware in the smart cards they use to play remotely.

**Protocols:** A protocol is described for each of the steps required in the game.

## 5   The Protocols

The following notation is used in order to describe the protocols and procedures presented.

- $P_{entity}, S_{entity}$: Asymmetric key pair of *entity*, where $P_{entity}$ is the public key and $S_{entity}$ is the private key.

- $S_{entity}[m]$: Digital signature of message $m$ by *entity*, where digital signature means computing the hash value of message $m$ using a collision-free one-way hash function and encrypting this hash value under the private key of *entity*.
- $E_{entity}(m)$: Encryption of message $m$ under the public key of *entity*.
- $H(m)$: Hash value of message $m$ using a collision-free one-way hash function.
- $m_1 \| m_2$: Concatenation of messages $m_1$ and $m_2$.

## 5.1   Player Registration

A player $\mathcal{P}_i$ can play only if she is registered. In the registration process, the player provides her information. This information must be strongly verified, in order to ensure that registered players are legally allowed to gamble.

Carrying out such a verification over the network is a complex problem. However, governments in several countries are promoting the distribution of smart card-based electronic IDs. Basically, such IDs are smart cards containing a key pair certified by the government. The private key never leaves the smart card, so that a high standard of security is achieved. In addition, those smart cards are able to run application software.

We propose to use these electronic IDs in our e-gambling system. The government issuing the IDs (or a governmental authority) is assumed to regulate e-gambling in its territory. This is no extravagant assumption, since most governments have traditionally been involved in gambling or at least gaming (lotteries, etc.). In this way, we can assume that the relevant application software for e-gambling comes already installed in the electronic IDs. Note that including application software in the IDs can be a way to involve the private sector in co-funding electronic ID manufacturing and distribution.

At least, the smart card stores the following data on the player:

$I_{\mathcal{P}_i}$: Player identifier. In our protocols, we will use as identifier the hash value of the player's public key certificate.
$Cert_i$: Digital certificate of $\mathcal{P}_i$'s public key.
$P_{\mathcal{P}_i}, S_{\mathcal{P}_i}$: Public and private keys of player $\mathcal{P}_i$.
$C_{\mathcal{P}_i}$: Credit of $\mathcal{P}_i$, initially set to 0.
$B$: Credit card data for $\mathcal{P}_i$.

## 5.2   Increase/Decrease Credit

Player $\mathcal{P}_i$ wishes to deposit money in her casino account in order to be able to play. Alternatively, she may be interested in withdrawing money. Let $G$ denote the on-line casino and $V$ denote the amount to be deposited or withdrawn (depending on whether it is a positive or negative value). Credit increase/decrease is performed with Protocol 1.

### Protocol 1

*1. $\mathcal{P}_i$ runs Procedure 1 with parameters $Cert_G$ and $V$ in the smart card to increase/decrease her credit and obtain $E_G(A)$ and $S_{\mathcal{P}_i}[E_G(A)]$.*

2. $\mathcal{P}_i$ sends $E_G(A)$ and $S_{\mathcal{P}_i}[E_G(A)]$ to $G$.
3. $G$ does:
   (a) Verify the signature $S_{\mathcal{P}_i}[E_G(A)]$.
   (b) Decrypt $E_G(A)$ using the casino's private key $S_G$ to get $V$ and $B$.
   (c) Verify the deposit/withdrawal data $V$ and $B$.
   (d) Update the credit of player $\mathcal{P}_i$ as $C'_{\mathcal{P}_i} := C_{\mathcal{P}_i} + V$.
   (e) Compute a receipt $R_C$ for the new credit as $R_C = S_G[I_{\mathcal{P}_i} || C'_{\mathcal{P}_i}]$.
   (f) Encrypt $R_C$ and $C'_{\mathcal{P}_i}$ with the public key of $\mathcal{P}_i$ to get $E_{\mathcal{P}_i}(C'_{\mathcal{P}_i}, R_C)$.
   (g) Send $E_{\mathcal{P}_i}(C'_{\mathcal{P}_i}, R_C)$ to $\mathcal{P}_i$.
4. $\mathcal{P}_i$ checks that her credit has been updated by running Procedure 2 in the smart card.

## Procedure 1  $[Cert_G, V]$

1. Randomly obtain a value $r$.
2. Fetch the player's credit card data $B$ (stored in the card).
3. Compute the identifier of the credit update operation $A = r||V||B$.
4. Encrypt $A$ using $G$'s public key (extracted from $Cert_G$) to get $E_G(A)$.
5. Sign $E_G(A)$ with the player's private key $S_{\mathcal{P}_i}$ to get $S_{\mathcal{P}_i}[E_G(A)]$.
6. Return $E_G(A)$ and $S_{\mathcal{P}_i}[E_G(A)]$.

## Procedure 2  $[E_{\mathcal{P}_i}(C'_{\mathcal{P}_i}, R_C)]$

1. Decrypt $E_{\mathcal{P}_i}(C'_{\mathcal{P}_i}, R_C)$ using the player's private key $S_{\mathcal{P}_i}$ to obtain $C'_{\mathcal{P}_i}$ and $R_C$.
2. Verify the digital signature in the receipt $R_C$.
3. Check against the receipt that the credit amount $C'_{\mathcal{P}_i}$ is correct.

### 5.3  Start a Game

Once a player is registered, he can start a game. To start playing, the on-line casino $G$ and players use Protocol 2.

## Protocol 2

1. $G$ computes a game identifier $I_P$ with Procedure 3.
2. $G$ reveals $I_P$ and $S_G[I_P]$ to all players.
3. If a player $\mathcal{P}_i$ wishes to enter game $I_P$, she must go through the following steps:
   (a) Create a request to enter game $I_P$ using Procedure 4, which is run in the smart card and yields as output $\rho_i = S_{\mathcal{P}_i}[S_G[I_P], I_{\mathcal{P}_i}]$ and $Cert_i$.
   (b) Send $S_{\mathcal{P}_i}[S_G[I_P], I_{\mathcal{P}_i}]$ and $Cert_i$ to $G$.
4. Let us assume that $n$ players have requested their participation in the game. $G$ generates a certificate for participants in game $I_P$ by the following steps:
   (a) Sign all requests to participate in the game, that is, $S_G[\rho_1, \ldots, \rho_n]$
   (b) Send $S_G[\rho_1, \ldots, \rho_n]$, $\{\rho_1, \ldots, \rho_n\}$ and $\{Cert_1, \ldots, Cert_n\}$ to players who asked to participate.

5. *Each player who asked to participate verifies $S_G[\rho_1, \ldots, \rho_n]$, $\{\rho_1, \ldots, \rho_n\}$ and $\{Cert_1, \ldots, Cert_n\}$ using Procedure 5 which is run in the smart card.*

## Procedure 3

1. *Generate a random $r$.*
2. *Obtain the current time $T$.*
3. *Obtain the number of past games $N$.*
4. *Compute $I_P = r||T||N + 1$.*
5. *Increase $N$ by one unit.*
6. *Sign $I_P$ using the casino's private key to get $S_G[I_P]$.*
7. *Return $S_G[I_P]$ and $Cert_i$.*

## Procedure 4

1. *Verify the signature $S_G[I_P]$.*
2. *Create a request to participate in the game: $S_{\mathcal{P}_i}[S_G[I_P], I_{\mathcal{P}_i}]$.*
3. *Return $S_{\mathcal{P}_i}[S_G[I_P], I_{\mathcal{P}_i}]$.*

## Procedure 5     $[S_G[\rho_1, \ldots, \rho_n], \{\rho_1, \ldots, \rho_n\}, \{Cert_1, \ldots, Cert_n\}]$

1. *For $i = 1$ to $n$ do:*
   (a) *Verify whether $Cert_i$ has been issued by the regulator's CA.*
   (b) *Verify $\rho_i$ with $Cert_i$.*
2. *Verify $S_G[\rho_1, \ldots, \rho_n]$.*
3. *Store $I_P$ and certificates $\{Cert_1, \ldots, Cert_n\}$ if all verifications are correct.*
4. *Return the verification result (OK or NOT OK).*

### 5.4   Bet Placing

A player $\mathcal{P}_i$ places a bet in a game $I_P$ using the following protocol:

## Protocol 3     $[I_P]$

1. $\mathcal{P}_i$ *requests to place a bet by running Procedure 6 in the smart card and gets $(I_A, I_A^*)$.*
2. $\mathcal{P}_i$ *sends $(I_A, I_A^*)$ to $G$.*
3. *The on-line casino $G$ performs the following steps:*
   (a) *Verify the digital signature $I_A^*$ using the public key of $\mathcal{P}_i$.*
   (b) *Verify the bet data: game identifier $I_P$, bet amount $V$, bet concept $K$ (what is being betted on).*
   (c) *Verify that $\mathcal{P}_i$ has got enough credit, that is, check that $C_{\mathcal{P}_i} - V \geq 0$, where $C_{\mathcal{P}_i}$ is the player credit.*
   (d) *If the player has got enough credit:*
      i. *Update the player's credit as $C'_{\mathcal{P}_i} = C_{\mathcal{P}_i} - V$.*
      ii. *Compute the receipt $R_A$ for the bet $I_A$ as $R_A = S_G[I_A^*]$.*
      iii. *Compute the receipt $R_C$ for the remaining credit as $R_C = S_G[I_{\mathcal{P}_i}||C'_{\mathcal{P}_i}]$.*
      iv. *Send $C'_{\mathcal{P}_i}$, $R_A$ and $R_C$ to $\mathcal{P}_i$.*
      *Otherwise (the player hasn't got enough credit) the bet is not accepted.*

4. $P_i$ runs Procedure 7 in the smart card to verify that the on-line casino has updated her credit.

## Procedure 6 $[I_P, V, K]$

1. Obtain a random value $r$.
2. Compute the bet identifier $I_A = \{I_P||r||V||K\}$, that is the concatenation of the game identifier, $r$, the bet amount and the bet concept.
3. Sign $I_A$ with the player's private key $S_{P_i}$ to get $I_A^* = S_{P_i}[I_A]$
4. Return $(I_A, I_A^*)$.

## Procedure 7 $[R_A, R_C, C_{P_i}]$

1. Verify the digital signature in $R_A$.
2. Verify the digital signature in $R_C$.
3. Check that the credit $C'_{P_i}$ is correct.

At the end of a game, the casino pays her earnings to player $P_i$ using the following protocol:

## Protocol 4 $[I_A, I_A^*, R_A]$

1. G does:
   (a) Verify the signatures on the bet receipt $R_A$ and the bet $I_A^*$.
   (b) Compute the earnings $g$ of $P_i$ in game $I_P$ with bet $I_A$.
   (c) Update the player's credit as $C'_{P_i} = C_{P_i} + g$.
   (d) Compute the receipt of the available credit $R_C$ as $R_C = S_G[I_{P_i}||C'_{P_i}]$.
   (e) Send $R_C$ to $P_i$.
2. $P_i$ verifies that she got paid by running Procedure 8 in the smart card.

## Procedure 8 $[R_C, C_{P_i}]$

1. Verify the signature on $R_C$.
2. Verify that the new credit for $C'_{P_i}$ is correct.

### 5.5   Deck Shuffling

Once the game has started with Protocol 2, the smart card of each player contains the certificates of the rest of players. Based on the key identifier field within the players' certificates, an order between players is established: the first player is the one with the lowest identifier. The first player has a singular role. The smart card of the first player (not the player herself) creates a permutation of 52 values, that is, the smart card shuffles the deck; then, following the prescribed player ordering, the smart card of the first player computes the cards for each player. For each of the remaining players, the first player's smart card computes a digital envelope containing the cards of that player. This digital envelope can only be opened by the corresponding player's smart card (player's cards are managed by the player's smart card).

The method for shuffling the deck is described in Protocol 5.

**Protocol 5**

1. *Let us assume that players $\{\mathcal{P}_1, \ldots, \mathcal{P}_n\}$ and the casino G start a game using Protocol 2.*
2. *Based on her certificate, each $\mathcal{P}_i$ derives her order in the player ordering.*
3. *$\mathcal{P}_1$ does:*
   (a) *Run Procedure 9 in the smart card and obtain a shuffled deck.*
   (b) *For $i = 2$ to $n$ do:*
      i. *Run Procedure 10 in the smart card to obtain the cards for $\mathcal{P}_i$ encrypted under $\mathcal{P}_i$'s public key and signed under $\mathcal{P}_1$'s private key. Denote the output of the smart card by $\xi$ and $S_{\mathcal{P}_1}[\xi_i]$, where $\xi_i$ are the encrypted cards for $\mathcal{P}_i$.*
      ii. *Send $\xi$ and $S_{\mathcal{P}_1}[\xi_i]$ to player $\mathcal{P}_i$;*
4. *Each player $\mathcal{P}_i$ for $i \in \{2, \ldots, n\}$ recovers her cleartext cards by running Procedure 11 inside her smart card.*

Procedure 9 is used by player $\mathcal{P}_1$ to generate a shuffled deck and compute the cards corresponding to each player.

**Procedure 9**

1. *Generate a permutation $\pi$ of 52 elements;*
2. *For $i = 2$ to $n$ do:*
   (a) *Compute the cards for $\mathcal{P}_i$ as $D_i = \{d_{i,1}, \ldots, d_{i,10}\}$, where $d_{i,j} = \pi(5 * (j - 1) + i)$ and $j \in \{1, \ldots, 10\}$;*
3. *Initialize the counter $k$ of requested cards and the counter $l$ of discarded cards to $k = 0$ and $l = 0$, respectively.*

The following procedure encrypts player $\mathcal{P}_i$'s cards under that player's public key and signs the result under player $\mathcal{P}_1$'s private key.

**Procedure 10** *[i]*

1. *Generate a random $R$.*
2. *Encrypt $D_i$, $I_P$ and $R$ under $P_{\mathcal{P}_i}$'s public key to get $\xi = E_{P_{\mathcal{P}_i}}(I_P, D_i, R)$.*
3. *Sign $\xi$ to get $S_{\mathcal{P}_1}[\xi]$.*
4. *Return $\xi$ and $S_{\mathcal{P}_1}[\xi]$.*

Players decrypt their cards by running Procedure 11 in their smart cards.

**Procedure 11** *[$\xi$,$S_{\mathcal{P}_1}[\xi]$]*

1. *Verify the signature $S_{\mathcal{P}_1}[\xi]$ on $\xi$ using the certificate $Cert_1$.*
2. *Decrypt $\xi$ with the player's private key $S_{\mathcal{P}_i}$ and obtain $D_i$, $I_P$ and $R$.*
3. *Check $I_P$ is the current game identifier.*
4. *Store $D_i$ in the smart card.*
5. *Initialize the counter $k$ of requested cards and the counter $l$ of discarded cards to $k = 0$ and $l = 0$, respectively.*

## 5.6   Card Draw

A player's smart card keeps track of how many cards it has given to the player, the set $\tau$ of cards that are in the hand of the player and the set of cards that have been discarded. When the player wants to draw a card, her smart card checks that she is allowed to do so, *i.e.* that she has got less than five cards in her hand. If yes, the next stored card is given to the player and added to the set $\tau$.

**Procedure 12**
*If $k - l < 5$ then*

1. *Retrieve the next card $\tau_{k+1} = d_{k+1}$, where $d_{k+1} \in D_i$.*
2. *Let $k := k + 1$.*
3. *Add $\tau_{k+1}$ to the set $\tau$.*
4. *Return $\tau_{k+1}$.*

*Otherwise return error (player not allowed to draw).*

## 5.7   Card Discarding

In the following Procedure 13, if a user discards a card $\tau_j$, the counter $l$ is incremented and $\tau_j$ is eliminated from $\tau$.

**Procedure 13**   *$[\tau_j]$*

1. *If $\tau_j \in \tau$ then do:*
   (a) *Let $l := l + 1$.*
   (b) *Eliminate $\tau_j$ from $\tau$.*
2. *If $\tau_j \notin \tau$ then return error.*

## 5.8   Card Opening

If a player wants to show the cards in her hand, she runs the following Procedure 14 in her smart card.

**Procedure 14**

1. *Sign $\tau$ to get $S_{\mathcal{P}_i}[I_P\|\tau]$.*
2. *Return $S_{\mathcal{P}_i}[I_P\|\tau]$ and $\tau$.*

# 6   Security Analysis

Security in our mental poker system depends on whether all steps performed by players in the on-line casino are secure. We will examine whether each protocol or procedure described above fulfills the properties enumerated in Section 3.

**Registration:** In Section 5.1, we propose that registration be handled by the public authority issuing electronic IDs. Thus, registration is performed in a controlled environment and offers whatever security is provided to register for an electronic ID.

**Start a game:** In Protocol 2 presented in Section 5.3, the on-line casino acts as a central node that puts players in touch with each other. All actions (game creation, request to participate) done by the parties are signed. Thus message authentication and integrity can be verifies by any player or external party. Also, message non-repudiation is guaranteed.

**Credit increase:** Protocol 1 described in Section 5.2 encrypts and signs all messages between the player's smart card and the on-line casino, so that confidentiality, authentication, integrity and non-repudiation are ensured.

**Bet placing:** In Protocol 3 of Section 5.4 messages between the player and the on-line casino are signed. The digital signature ensures message authentication, integrity and non-repudiation. Non-repudiation is especially important, as it prevents the player from repudiating a lost bet and it also prevents the on-line casino from repudiating an accepted bet.

**Deck shuffling:** The most complex shuffling operations are performed by the smart card. Let us check that Protocol 5 of Section 5.5 meets the security requirements enumerated in Section 3.

– *Uniqueness of cards.* The smart card of $P_1$ follows Procedure 9 to create a permutation of 52 elements that corresponds to the deck. The permutation ensures that there are no duplicated cards. Cards are distributed to each player so that each card belongs only to a player.

– *Uniform random distribution of cards.* The smart card uses its random generator to obtain a shuffling permutation. We assume that the generator is good enough to ensure uniform random distribution of shuffled cards.

– *Cheating detection with a very high probability.* Thanks to its exclusive knowledge of the player's private key (we assume the smart card is tamper-resistant enough for its contents to be safely held), the smart card cannot be bypassed by a cheating player. Thus, any cheater will be unable to sign messages and will be detected.

– *Complete confidentiality of cards.* $P_1$ creates the deck of cards by running Procedure 9 *within the smart card.* Then cards are distributed using Procedure 10: cards exit the smart card encrypted under the public key of the player who requested them. In order to recover a cleartext card, an intruder should be able to decrypt the digital envelope containing the cards; but this cannot be done without the requesting player's private key, which is securely held by that player's smart card.

– *Minimal effect of coalitions.* Cards are initially in the smart card of player $P_1$ and are subsequently sent to the rest of players in encrypted form. There are two possible attacks for a coalition of players to obtain cards which are not theirs: i) extract the cards from player $P_1$'s smart card, which is deemed infeasible because of the tamper-resistance of $P_1$'s smart card; ii) decrypt the cards which are sent in encrypted form, which is deemed infeasible because the private keys needed for decryption are safely held by the smart cards of players having legitimately requested the cards.

  – *Complete confidentiality of the strategy.* Revealing players' strategies is not needed to verify the game fairness at the end of the game. The control exerted by the player's and casino's smart cards is deemed sufficient to ensure game fairness and correctness.

**Card discarding:** Procedure 13 is run inside the smart card. If the discarded card is in the player's hand, the smart card removes it and allows the player to request a new card. The information on the discarded card does not leave the smart card.

**Card opening:** $P_i$ can show her cards using Procedure 14. The digital signature on the game identifier $I_P$ and the player's set of cards $\tau$ can only be computed using the private key that is held by the smart card. This private key never leaves the smart card, so that the latter cannot be bypassed.

## 7   Conclusions

We have presented a system whereby players can play poker over a network with a high degree of security. The different parties (players and casino) must use their tamper-resistant smart cards to take part in the game, which leads to secure and simple protocols. The same approach can be extended to other games over a network.

*Note.* A patent application covering the essentials of the proposed system is in process.

## Acknowledgments

The authors are partly supported by the Catalan government under grant 2002 SGR 00170, and by the Spanish Ministry of Science and Education through project SEG2004-04352-C04-01 "PROPRIETAS".

## References

1. W. A. Aiello, A. D. Rubin, and M. J. Strauss. Using smartcards to secure a personalized gambling device. In *CCS '99: Proceedings of the 6th ACM conference on Computer and communications security*, pages 128–137, New York, NY, USA, 1999. ACM Press.
2. A. Barnett and N. Smart. Mental poker revisited. In *Proc. Cryptography and Coding*, volume 2898 of *Lecture Notes in Computer Science*, pages 370–383. Springer-Verlag, December 2003.
3. C. Crépeau. A secure poker protocol that minimizes the effect of player coalitions. In Hugh C. Williams, editor, *Advances in Cryptology - Crypto '85*, volume 218 of *Lecture Notes in Computer Science*, pages 73–86, Berlin, 1985. Springer-Verlag.

4. C. Crépeau. A zero-knowledge poker protocol that achieves confidentiality of the players' strategy or how to achieve an electronic poker face. In A. M. Odlyzko, editor, *Advances in Cryptology - Crypto '86*, volume 263, pages 239–250, Berlin, 1986. Springer-Verlag. Lecture Notes in Computer Science.

5. Department for Culture Media and Sport of Great Britain. Gambling review body. http://www.culture.gov.uk/role/gambling_review.html, July 17 2001. chapter 13, page 167.

6. J. Edwards. Implementating electronic poker: A practical exercise in zero-knowledge interactive proofs. Masters thesis, Department of Computer Science, University of Kentucky, May 1994.

7. C. Hall and B. Schneier. Remote electronic gambling. In *13th Annual Computer Security Applications Conference*, pages 227–230. ACM, December 1997.

8. R. M. Needham and M. D. Schroeder. Authentication revisited. *ACM Operating Systems Review*, 21(1), 1987.

9. R. Oppliger and J.L. Nottaris. Online casinos. In *Kommunikation in verteilten Systemen*, pages 2–16, 1997.

10. W.H. Soo, A. Samsudin and A. Goh. Efficient mental card shuffling via optimised arbitrary-sized benes permutation network. In *Information Security Conference*, volume 2433 of *Lecture Notes in Computer Science*, pages 446–458. Springer-Verlag, 2002.

11. W. Zhao, V. Varadharajan and Y. Mu. Fair on-line gambling. In *16th Annual Computer Security Applications Conference (ACSAC'00)*, pages 394–400, New Orleans, Louisiana, December 2000. IEEE.

# A Smart Card Solution for Access Control and Trust Management for Nomadic Users*

Daniel Díaz Sánchez, Andrés Marín Lopez, and Florina Almenárez Mendoza

Telematic Engineering Department, Carlos III University of Madrid,
Avda. Universidad, 30, 28911 Leganés (Madrid), Spain
{dds, amarin, florina}@it.uc3m.es

**Abstract.** Increasing efforts are placed on security solutions for no-madic users. Solutions based on smart cards offer physical and logical portability, robustness, low cost, and high security. Nevertheless, such solutions concentrate only on offering the cryptographical capabilities of the smart card, together with key and user certificate storage. Advanced trust management and access control are not addressed. In this article, we propose a scheme to include trust management and attribute certificates for authorization in two widely used cryptographic APIs: Microsoft CryptoAPI and RSA labs PKCS#11.

## 1 Introduction

Increasing efforts are placed on security solutions for nomadic users. VPN clients and https support can be found in mobile devices such as phones and PDAs. The popularity of applications using cryptographic APIs is growing fast, specially in e-business, but also in e-government, e-learning, or e-health. Solutions based on smart cards offer portability (size, weight), robustness (humidity, temperature), wide support (standards, operating systems, readers), low cost, and high security due to their tamper-proof nature.

Smart cards are convenient wallet solutions for average user needs. They are used in a number of applications like e-purse applications, or as the basis of cryptographic APIs to store keys, or user certificates([1], [2,3]). Similar efforts and solutions are needed for trust management, security cornerstone. Nomadic users need solutions offering trust management based on smart cards.

The list of trusted entities (CAs, signers, etc.), the purposes under which this trust is placed, or the level of trust of each entity, are data required to move along with the user, just like secret keys and personal certificates.

Besides, applications also demand access control. ACs, short for Attribute Certificates, are a standard solution [4], though popular applications don't use them yet. ACs lack of support in CryptoAPI and the support that gives PKCS#11 to them is very limited.

---

* This work has been partially supported by UBISEC (IST STREP 506926) and Trust-ES (MEDEA+).

J. Domingo-Ferrer, J. Posegga, and D. Schreckling (Eds.): CARDIS 2006, LNCS 3928, pp. 62–77, 2006.

This work is restricted to applications using Microsoft CryptoAPI [5] (CAPI) and RSA Labs PKCS#11 [1] and PKCS#15 [6]. We are not addressing PGP [7] and GnuPG [8] here, though they are mentioned in the related work section 5. Giving support to CAPI, PKCS#11 and PKCS#15 a huge amount of platforms are covered from desktop computers to mobile phones and PDAs.

## 2   Problem Domain

A brief definition about some topics may help the reader to understand better what is addressed in this paper:

- Nomadicity is the ability of a user to change the network access point as he moves, while the service is completely stopped and started again. Nomadicity implies discrete changes of location.
- User mobility refers to the ability of a user to maintain the same identity irrespective of the terminal used and its network point of attachment. Users on the move may use different types of terminal and applications to access services.
- Ad-hoc interaction. In many cases, a user may desire to interact directly with other peers without being connected to a local network. This situation may be common where there is no available service or just to save battery (roaming and network discovery is expensive in terms of battery life).

Web browsers and mail clients are the most used user applications and those applications typically use CAPI and PKCS#11. We have identified a number of possible scenarios showing the trust management security concerns for a mobile user.

- Alice moves among different terminals always using CAPI applications.
- Bob uses CAPI applications in some computer and PKCS#11 in others and moves among them.
- Yi moves among different terminals using always PKCS#11 applications.

When Alice moves to another computer, she may carry a smart card with her keys and personal certificates. On the other hand, she has to check manually the Certificate Trust List (CTL) in the new computer and the assigned policies and trust levels for that CTL. Everytime she decides to add or remove a new certificate to the CTL or to change the trust level associated with the CTL or the privileges, she must do this in all the computers she uses. She would benefit of carrying the CTL and the trust information in the smart card to avoid this task.

Similarly, Yi may hold a smart card with personal keys and certificates. Since PKCS#11 also allows to store in the token certificates (CKO_CERTIFICATE) with a boolean attribute (CKA_TRUSTED), which is set only by the user OS, or an initialization application. Unfortunately, few applications use this feature and do the CTL management themselves. Yi is also forced to manually control the CTL.

Bob is more flexible and can use more computers and applications. On the other hand, his life is harder: there is no communication among CAPI and

PKCS#11, so he is forced to maintain his security decisions about the CTL and trust levels for both types of applications as he moves to a new machine. He will also benefit of carrying such data in his smart card. Besides, Bob will need some means to ensure that the semantics of PKCS#11 and CAPI are somehow maintained, so that the security information created by PKCS#11 applications is stored in the smart card in some way that it can be accessed by CAPI.

PKCS#15 offers more explicit support for CTL. Any number of Certificate Directory Files (CDFs) can be stored in the smart card, but in the normal case there will only be one or two (one for trusted certificates and one which the cardholder may update). The certificates themselves may reside anywhere on the card (or even outside the card, using a url and a certHash field for verification). Trusted certificates are used in PKCS#15 as trust chain origins (when signalled by the implicitTrust attribute). PKCS#15 also allows certificates to indicate the trustUsage which can be encrypt, decrypt, sign, signRecover, wrap, unwrap, verify, verifyRecover, derive and nonRepudiation.

Unfortunately, these features are not being exploited by applications, though mobile user benefit is clear. Trust management for mobile users implies that the security information regarding the trusted certificates and their level of trust moves along with the user. We claim that smart cards should be used for this purpose, as they are now used for key and certificate storage.

The usage of policies in certificates was the first approach taken in the PKI standard (ITU-T Rec. X.509[9], ISO/IEC 9594-8). Conceptually identity and permissions have different life and life-cycle, and they arise from different sources. This leads to scalability and management problems. A later version of the standard included PMI and attribute certificates (section 2.1), engineered as a more suitable solution for privilege management. Attribute certificates are supported in PKCS#11 and PKCS#15, but not in CAPI.

## 2.1   Attribute Certificates

An Attribute Certificate (AC) [4] is a structure similar to a Public Key Certificate (PKC) but ACs bind identities to privileges and contain no public key (Fig. 1). ACs are issued by Attribute Authorities (AAs). AAs store and manage them independently from Certificate Authorities (CAs). AAs are the source of authorization information, just like CAs are the source of authentication information.

Typically the AAs store the attribute certificates in a Lightweight Directory Access Protocol (LDAP). In this case, both the entity and the service perform authentication. Then the server requests or "pulls" the AC from a repository or an AA. Pull mode allows the use of ACs without changing the clients. This model is more appropriate for inter-domain access where privileges are assigned in the domain of the server, see Fig. 2.

In other environments, as ad-hoc, is more suitable for an entity to "push" ACs to the server. This model simplifies services, because no new connections are needed to obtain authorization information. The push model improves performance since servers have instantly access to the authorization data and fit in ad-hoc environments where services can be located in peers and the access

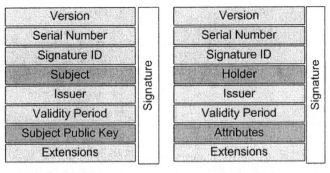

**Fig. 1.** AC structure

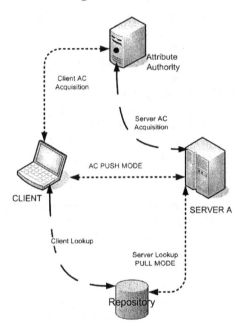

**Fig. 2.** AC exchanges

to Internet is not assured. Details about X509 identity certificate validation (necessary for AC exchange) in ad-hoc environments is covered in section 4.1.

## 3   The Cryptographic APIs

In this section we start by describing briefly the main features of PKCS#11 and Microsoft CryptoAPI. After that, we present why a bridge between them is needed, and the requirements for this bridge.

## 3.1   PKCS#11: Cryptoki

PKCS#11 (Public Key Cryptographic Standard) specifies an API called Cryptoki, short for Cryptographic Token Interface Standard, to devices that hold cryptographic information and performs cryptographic operations. The aim of this standard is to provide a simple object-based approach that allows applications to be independent of the underlying cryptographic hardware. Cryptographic devices are known, in Cryptoki words, as "*Cryptographic tokens* " or "*tokens*". Cryptoki defines a logical model that makes any device logically equal to any other regardless of the devices different technologies. Therefore, outside the library, the hardware details are hidden and the application has only access to the logical view of the *token*.

Cryptographic *tokens* are plugged in the system using "*slots*", which can correspond, for instance, to a smart card reader [10, 11] plugged in the system. *Tokens* can be, as mentioned before, any removable or not removable device plugged in a *slot*.

Cryptoki defines tree classes of objects: *data, certificate* and *keys. Data objects* hold application information, *certificate objects* store certificates and *key objects* store cryptographic keys that may be public, private or secret. Objects can be classified by visibility and lifetime in: *Token Objects*, that are accessible to applications connected to the *token* that are logged in and have sufficient permission. These objects remain on the *token* after all the sessions are closed and the *token* is removed from the *slot*. *Session Objects* remain on the *token* only within a session and are removed when the session finishes. Objects are also classified by accessibility in public and private objects. Public objects can be accessed by an application without login in the *token*, while private objects can only be accessed by authenticated applications (using, for instance, a PIN).

An application should open one or more sessions with a *token* to gain access to the objects contained in the *token*. A *session* is the logical connection between the *token* and the application. *Sessions* can be read-only and read-write ones. The read-only or read-write state refers only to the *token objects* so *session objects* can be written in a *read-only session*.

*Sessions* are referenced outside Cryptoki by the use of handlers. A *session handler* value is different from others. *Object handler* values can be equals for two or more *sessions* regardless of the object that is referenced since any *session* has it own handler space to reference objects.

## 3.2   PKCS#15 and JCCM

Cryptoki alone can not offer interoperability, since it is an API specification aimed at offering applications a uniform interface to cryptographic tokens. Different tokens require different PKCS#11 drivers, and users need to install the different drivers to use different tokens.

There are two workarounds for this problem. PKCS#15 [6] ensures interoperability by establishing a standard which ensures that users, in fact, will be able to use cryptographic tokens to identify themselves to multiple, standards-aware applications; regardless of the application's cryptoki (or other token interface) provider. PKCS#15 does this by establishing a syntax for storing digital credentials (keys, certificates, etc) on the tokens, and how this information are to be accessed. PKCS#15 only requires card compatibility with ISO/IEC 7816-4, ISO/IEC 7816-5, ISO/IEC 7816-6 and ISO/IEC 7816-15 [12]. Extended features, especially advanced PIN management functions and higher level security operations may require support for ISO/IEC 7816-8 or ISO/IEC 7816-9.

Another solution is the one proposed by Java Card Certificate Management [13]. JCCM proposes to move part of Cryptoki semantics to the smart card, so that the host library (cryptoki driver) is the same for all manufacturers. We have used this approach in this work.

## 3.3   CryptoAPI

CryptoAPI [5] is the security API for Microsoft Windows platforms from desktop computers to mobile smartphones and PDAs. It offers an API to: certificate stores, simplified messages, low level messages (PKCS#7), and certificate encode helped by extensible modules that interact each others see Fig. 3.

CAPI manages certificates providing a set of functions that allow searching, retrieving, deleting, and classifying certificates.

The low level cryptographic functions that CAPI export are served by a set of selectable modules or CSPs.

## 3.4   CSPs: Cryptographic Service Providers

A CSP is a software module that implements CryptoSPI API. This API provides to the operating system the ability to manage keys for both symmetrical and asymmetrical algorithms and to perform cryptographic operations as hashing, encrypting and signing. CSPs may interact with hardware, for instance, a card, usb-token or any tamper-proof device providing secure key management.

CryptoSPI is managed by the operating system, who blocks the software module to avoid for instance a man-in-the-middle attack. CryptoSPI is exported outside the operating system to be used by applications as a set of CAPI functions.

The Independent Software Vendor (ISV) model managed by the operating system allows to select among the available CSPs according to user preferences or domain policy enforcements. Using ISV model, developers can interact with more than one CSP to increase security and strength of applications. This structure allows application to have available providers that implements different public key algorithms, symmetric ciphers, and hash algorithms including communication with cryptographic devices (Fig.3).

A CSP maintains a repository of keys organized by *containers*. Containers' names are given by the applications and each *container* has a unique name in the scope of a CSP. A CSP guards *container* structure and maintains the public/private keys stored in those containers from session to session. However, session keys are not preserved from one session to other.

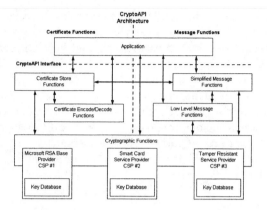

**Fig. 3.** CryptoAPI structure (from MSDN)

CAPI specifies that CSP *containers* should support at least two types of key pair: *"signature key pair"* and *"exchange key pair"*. Moreover, any number of key pairs can be stored besides the default ones, but it depends on the particular CSP implementation. The communication between the application and the CSP is materialized in a *context*. A context should be acquired before performing any operation with a CSP.

### 3.5   Certificate Manager

CAPI exports functions to store, list, retrieve, delete, and verify X.509 certificates. The API offers two main categories of functions for managing certificates: functions that manage **certificate stores**, and functions that work with the certificates, certificate revocation lists (CRLs), and certificate trust lists (CTLs) within those stores.

When a certificate is retrieved from a Store, it is represented by a **Certificate Context** read-only structure. A certificate context can be used for signing, encryption or for authentication processes. CAPI do not attach trust information to a certificate context but allows to develop custom **trust providers** by third parties to manage this type of information, through the *WinTrust* service. Trust providers perform trust verification on a specified object.

Certificate stores can be **System Stores** or **Physical Stores**. System stores are composed by a set of Physical Stores. Physical Stores are organized in store locations served by different **Certificate Store Providers**: system registry, disk file, and memory. These stores classify certificates depending on the intended use. Certificates for trusted certificate issuers are generally kept in the Root store, which is currently stored under a registry subkey.

Besides, each user has a personal "My" store where user's personal certificates are stored; these certificates are used for signing, decrypting user's messages, and mail encryption. "My" store can be at many physical locations including the registry on a local or remote computer, a disk file, a database, directory service, a smart card, or another location. Private keys are generated and stored in key containers in CSPs. Furthermore, CSPs store the keys of the certificates generated by third-party CAs that have been imported to the system.

## 3.6   Bridging Microsoft CryptoAPI to PKCS#11

It is common for nomadic users to use both CAPI applications (like Internet Explorer, Outlook, etc.) and Cryptoki (Mozilla, Firebird, etc.). These users require some means to ensure that the semantics of PKCS#11 and CAPI is somehow maintained, so that the security information created by PKCS#11 applications is stored in the smart card in some way that can be accessed by CAPI.

A solution can be built upon PKCS#15, but this will still require some code to ensure that the information present in Certificate Stores is stored in the smart card.

Another solution is to provide a bridge from CAPI to Cryptoki, so that Cryptoki data objects are used to store such information. Since we work with JCCM, we ensure that the same host library is needed for different smart card providers. The actual version of CAPI does not support attribute certificates, and it needs to be extended for this purpose. Such extension is also considered in the bridge we propose.

## 4   Prototype

User life is not focused on security. Handling different certificates, using different personal devices may be hard unless a common certificate base, trust information and user preferences are shared among applications. This should be done regardless the Cryptographic API used. Our work covers four security cornerstones, by providing a seamless integration of two APIs and sharing credentials and cryptographic capabilities among them. It gives support for nomadic users allowing them to use a card for multiple purposes: authentication, authorization and trust management as well as tamper-proof capabilities.

The middleware developed to achieve this functionality can be divided in four blocks:

- **Trust Manager**: This module handles the trust in PKI and PTM.
- **Public Key Certificate Manager** provides tools to delete, to store, to search and to inspect certificates.
- **Attribute Certificate Manager** allows to handle, to store, to delete and to search Attribute Certificates
- **Key management and ciphersuite** provides cryptographic support to manage keys and to perform cryptographic operations

### 4.1   Trust Manager

Trust information is stored in the card for PKCS#11-aware applications and for CAPI-aware applications through our middleware . Trust is fundamental to validate user's certificates and their certification path. Such validation depends on the list of certificates stored as trustworthy (CTL), therefore, this module calls the CryptoAPI trust chain building functions, `CertGetCertificateChain` and `CertVerifyCertificateChainPolicy`.

After checking the validity of the type of certificate, expiration period, and certificate integrity, is needed to validate the trust chain. CryptoAPI functions perform the traditional validation process, which checks a valid certification path. In this process, the chain is built from the end certificate to a root CA; this latest must be in the Trusted Root Certification Authorities (TRCA) store, or the issuing CA must be in a trusted certification hierarchy or a CTL. During chain building, each certificate in the path will be validated, therefore, communication with each CA is required. When a problem occurs with one of the certificates, for instance, it is revoked, or if it cannot find a certificate, the certification path is discarded as a nontrusted certification path. Finally, the policy constrains are also validated.

Nevertheless, What happens if the root CA is not in the TRCA store or the user is unknown? Would this validation process be suitable for devices with restricted capabilities? or Is remote connectivity always guaranteed? In these cases, we need to use a different trust provider from CryptoAPI functions. Certificates would be validated taking the CTL into account, in this way, each certificate is a trust source. Furthermore, in ad-hoc environments, we could additionally use the cooperation between closed entities to trust in a specific user, instead of verifying long certification chains. In [14], we describe a trust management model (PTM) for open and dynamic spaces, where the presence of ad-hoc networks and peer-to-peer might be frequent. PTM would act as a trust provider according to the context, which is possible due to Windows security architecture allows several trust providers to verity trust in certificates [15].

## 4.2   Public Key Certificate Manager

This module acts as a bridge between CryptoAPI Certificate Manager and PKCS#11. The goal is to provide access to certificates stored in PKCS#11 modules from CryptoAPI Certificate Manager.

We have chosen to access to PKCS#11 modules from CryptoAPI and not the other way around. The reason is that most of the parameters that CryptoAPI attaches to cryptographic information can be extracted from Cryptoki attributes. Besides this "natural"mapping, Cryptoki supports application dependent data management and this can be used to store the information that CAPI needs to handle and the preferences without modifying PKCS#11 API.

It is necessary to describe CAPI internals to find out possible problems when dealing with different repositories: one for certificates and other for private keys. As mention in related work (section 5), other bridges among APIs do not cover certificates but only key management and cryptographic capabilities.

When importing a certificate to a personal store, for instance the System Store "My", the certificate and its public/private key pair are stored separately. Certificates themselves are stored in a Physical Store served by a Certificate Store Provider, that belongs to a System Store, and the private keys in CSPs.

There are some extended properties of a certificate help to solve the problem of having separate repositories, for certificates and private keys, these properties include data that:

− Pertains to the private key to be used with the certificate.
− Indicates the type of hashes to be performed on the certificate.
− Provides user-defined information associated to the certificate.

On Microsoft platforms, values for these properties are attached to a certificate context and move with it, but are not part of the certificate itself. Currently, predefined properties tie a certificate to a particular CSP and, within that CSP, to a particular private key. This properties set also the type of key: signature or key-exchange. This is the way to couple certificates stored in Certificate Stores and private keys guarded by the CSPs at API level. Moreover, these properties describe user preferences so they should be stored in the card in order to support nomadic users as explain the section 4.4.

CAPI Certificate Manager allows to be extended by developing custom certificate store providers, registering the appropriate callback functions in the operating system and registering new Physical Stores within this provider. We have developed a Certificate Store Provider called *PKCS11Store*. This provider is used to register new sibling physical stores under the well known system stores:

− "MY" personal certificates.
− "Root" Trusted root CAs certificates can be loaded into the card from either CryptoAPI or PKCS#11 aware applications and carried by nomadic users
− "TrustedPublisher" maintains a trusted list of software publishers
− "TrustedPeople" certificates from trusted people.

When applications use any of the prior certificate stores, *PKCS11Store* communicates with any PKCS#11 token registered in the system. Then *PKCS11Store* updates the system certificate repository with the information of the card, as can be seen in Fig. 4.

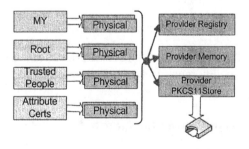

**Fig. 4.** Certificate stores and providers

### 4.3   Attribute Certificate Manager

This module behaves in the same manner as Public Key Certificate Manager does, but it provides another kind of certificates, Attribute Certificates (ACs), to the system.

When an application accesses to certificate stores, it provides, as a parameter, the intended encoding type of the information requested. Currently, CryptoAPI supports the value of the bitwise OR operation of flags X509_ASN_ENCODING or CRYPT_ASN_ENCODING and PKCS_7_ASN_ENCODING.

To distinguish among different types of certificates, a new encoding type flag for ACs has been defined (X509AC_ASN_ENCODING). This enables the use of the same certificate store provider module, in our case *PKCS11Store*, to handle both Public Key Certificates and Attribute Certificates.

*PKCS11Store* in its current state of development is able to extract ACs from PKCS#11 modules and to accept requests from the system through a System Store registered with the convenient encoding type.

At the end of this paragraph, it is shown the "C" declaration of the Public Key Certificate context (defined in CAPI) and the Attribute Certificate context (defined by us) returned by the provider to the O.S. and from the O.S. to the application:

```
typedef struct _CERT_CONTEXT {
    DWORD                   dwCertEncodingType;
    BYTE                    *pbCertEncoded;
    DWORD                   cbCertEncoded;
    PCERT_INFO              pCertInfo;
    HCERTSTORE              hCertStore;
} CERT_CONTEXT, *PCERT_CONTEXT;

typedef struct _ACERT_CONTEXT {
    DWORD dwCertEncodingType;
    BYTE* pbCertEncoded;
    DWORD cbCertEncoded;
    PACERT_INFO pACertInfo;
    HCERTSTORE hCertStore;
} ACERT_CONTEXT, *PACERT_CONTEXT;
```

Where PCERT_INFO and PACERT_INFO contain the most relevant fields of those certificates. The main difference is that attribute certificates do not contain public key.

### 4.4   Key Management and Ciphersuite

As explained, extended properties of certificates are used to "tell" the operating system where to find the private keys of that certificates (in which CSP and container are stored) and to handle user preferences as certificates usages not described in X.509 certificate extensions.

We have built a CSP, *PKCS11CSP*, which is able to interact with PKCS#11 modules. When *PKCS11Store* reads a certificate from a PKCS#11 module and publishes it in "MY" certificate system store, it sets the appropriate extended properties. These properties points to *PKCS11CSP* so the operating system uses *PKCS11CSP* to perform cryptographic operations with the certificate private key.

Bridging CryptoAPI and Cryptoki makes necessary to map both cryptographic APIs at logical level. This is the hardest design constrain, because the logical structure can not be easily mapped from one to other. This section covers the low level mapping from CAPI to PKCS#11: CSPs to PKCS#11.

Some approaches to designing the middleware are described in the following lines. Fist approach may map CSPs to *slots* and *containers* to *tokens*. So *slots* can have plugged more than one *token* as CSPs can manage more than one *container*. The disadvantage is that the creation of a new *container* is associated to the creation of a *token*, but: 1) *tokens* can be physical devices, and 2) Cryptoki does not support *token* creation.

In a second approach, *containers* may be assigned to *certificates* stored in the *token* [16] so container names are derived from the certificates or any of their properties. The problem arises when using a read-write *token* and an application creates a *container*. If no certificate is created according to the name of the container, next time may be infeasible to derive the container name from the certificate, so this approach is only applicable to read-only tokens.

As defined in CryptoAPI a *container* may hold an unlimited number of key pairs but at least two are mandatory: a "signature key pair" and a "key exchange key pair". Thus, assigning a *container* to each *certificate* may not behave properly.

*PKCS11CSP* uses a general purpose object, a Cryptoki *data object*, to store user customization and preferences of CAPI that cannot be derived from the Cryptoki object attributes. Storing this information in a data object enables the user to reproduce his/her preferences everywhere. Data objects are covered by PKCS#11 and Cryptoki does not attach to them any special meaning. The data object (CKO_DATA type) is a persistent object (attribute CKA_TOKEN true), visible without authentication (CKA_PRIVATE false), but it cannot be modified unless the user is authenticated. We store the information in the data object encoded with DER.

The core of the *Key Management and Ciphersuite* module, *PKCS11CSP*, can create a non limited number of *containers* and any *container* can guard "signature key pair", "key exchange key pair" and more. To distinguish among different key types, this information is stored in the data object of the PKCS#11 module and extracted when it is necessary. Furthermore, the container structure is committed to the token data object. Fig. 5 may help the reader to understand the middleware and how blocks interacts each other.

This design doesn't use anything out of the scope of the PKCS#11 standard, so any commercial PKCS#11 [17, 18, 19] module, capable of storing data

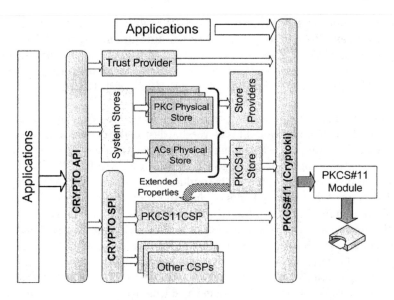

**Fig. 5.** Middleware structure

objects, can be used. Read only tokens can be used, but obviously no changes are committed to the card.

**Context Mapping:** Depending on the type of context requested by the application to the *PKCS11CSP*, the bridge should behave in a different fashion [2]. *PKCS11CSP* provides a GUI to enter PIN when access to private objects of PKCS#11 is requested. The following lines briefly describe most relevant types of CSP *context* and the mapping to PKCS#11 sessions:

- `Normal context (zero value)`: If operations requiring access to private token objects are requested, the context maps to a *R/W user function*. If not, just *R/O access* to public token objects and *R/W access* to session objects will be requested to the PKCS#11 module.
- `CRYPT_VERIFYCONTEXT`: This flag is intended for applications that do not use public/private keys. When this flag is set, the *context* is mapped to a *R/O Public Session*. Attempts to access to private objects should fail.
- `CRYPT_NEWKEYSET`: To create a new *container* with the specified name. R/W access to the token is needed: the data object stored in the *token* needs to be updated with new information. (PIN is needed).
- `CRYPT_DELETEKEYSET`: To delete a *container*. R/W access to token objects is needed to update the data object and to delete the key pairs (PIN is needed).
- `CRYPT_SILENT`: The *PKCS11CSP* should not display any user interface. It is used for unattended applications (*R/O Public Session*).

**Function Mapping:** Key generation and exchange functions exchange, create, configure, and destroy cryptographic keys. In general, functions that require to create a new object should be mapped through calls to Cryptoki function C_CreateObject. If any persistent element is created, the *PKCS11CSP* should update the data object including the name of the involved container and additional data. The additional data will help to find the object faster in following *sessions*, and ensures that the user will access to the same object structure as the last *session*.

Data encryption functions support encryption and decryption. CAPI CPDecrypt and CPEncrypt functions support both single-part operation and multi-part operation (used in hashing and block ciphering). These functions will be mapped with a first call to C_EncryptInit to set up the algorithm. Then, for single-part operations, a unique call to C_Encrypt should be done. In case of multi-part operations, it is necessary to perform a set of calls to C_EncryptUpdate and a last call to C_EncryptFinal.

Hashing and digital signature functions compute hashes and create and verify digital signatures. Cryptoki does not define hash objects. A hash exists as a value during the active Cryptoki hash operation, but not as an object. CSPs define hash objects so they can be destroyed and duplicated. Due to this, no mapping is possible for CSP functions that allow creation, deletion and manipulation of hash objects. These hash objects will be handled by the *PKCS11CSP* library internally, without Cryptoki object manager intervention, and will disappear once the library unloads from memory (session objects). In any case, the hash value will be calculated in the token although the object is managed by the CSP.

Digital signatures generated by CPSignHash (CryptoAPI) will be mapped into calls to C_SignInit, C_Sign, C_SignUpdate and C_SignFinal. Verification process will be handled by calls to C_Verify and C_Verify-Init-Update-Final.

## 5   Related Work

There have been a number of approaches to the interoperation of PKCS#11 and CSPs. The International Cryptography Experiment [20] aimed at a layered cryptographic service architecture, allowing the separation among cryptographic security and applications. ICE provided a bridge from CSP to PKCS#11 similar to CSP11 [20], or ilex's Generic CSP [16]. All them restrict themselves to PKCS#11 basic trust management, and do not take into account CTLs in the smart cards. These approaches lack of mobility support, since users have to set up cryptographic low level details in their personal profiles. GnuPGP [8] deals with CTLs in the smart cards, but the trust model is not compatible with PKI. Our proposal deals with CTLs and builds up a trust model compatible with PKI. We also approach the smart card as attribute certificate holder. Being the smart card an extremely mobile device, it allows a push model more suited for disconnected situations and ad-hoc networks. Besides, the user can require privacy for some of his/her privileges. There are also works for achieving privacy through anonymity. [21] presents an approach to extend X.509 attribute certificates with anonymity, and a protocol based on fair blind signature to obtain certificates preserving user anonymity.

# 6  Conclusions and Future Work

Smart cards offer portability and security at a reasonable price. Nomadic users benefit from existing smart card based solutions, but they require extra management efforts when moving to different platforms. In this article we propose a scheme to include trust management and attribute certificates for authorization in two widely used cryptographic APIs: Microsoft CryptoAPI and RSA labs PKCS#11. Our solution is truly mobile, since platform cryptographic details are stored in the smart card, as a user profile, minimizing thus users' management effort when moving.

We are actually testing the implementation in PCs and Windows CE handhelds (not PDAs). Future work will include usability tests and porting the implementation to Windows Mobile devices (PDAs), which do not support yet PC/SC smart card readers.

Microsoft CAPI will be held in Windows Vista but it will be deprecated in some future version. The brand new API that supersedes CAPI in Windows Vista is known as Cryptographic New Generation (CNG). The information made available by Microsoft about this new API is not detailed enough to review the design at the time this paper was written.

One of the changes that Microsoft provides for new Windows Vista affects our design: the new Smart Card Infrastructure. Currently, a monolithic approach has been used to develop the CSP. A CSP implements the CryptoSPI interface and the communication with the card through PC/SC. CNG provides a Smart Card KSP (Key Store Provider), that seems to be a common middleware, which interacts with other modules that implements the details (i.e. RSA card module). Our next efforts should be directed to implement one of those modules that cover the specific smart card details. This module will be in charge of interacting with PKCS#11. Other parts of our middleware will need to have access to a more detailed documentation from us to be reviewed.

# References

1. RSALabs: Pkcs#11 v2.11: Cryptographic token interface standard (2004)
2. Microsoft:   The smart card cryptographic service provider cookbook (2002) http://msdn.microsoft.com/library/en-us/dnscard/html/smartcardcspcook.asp.
3. Microsoft:   Writing a csp (2004) http://msdn.microsoft.com/library/en-us/ dnscard/html/smartcardcspcook.asp.
4. Farrell, S., Housley, R.: An internet attribute certificate profile for authorization. Technical Report RFC 3281, IETF PKIX Working Group (2002)
5. Microsoft: Cryptography reference (2004) http://msdn.microsoft.com/library/ default.asp?url=/library/en-us/seccrypto/security/cryptography_portal.asp.
6. RSALabs: Pkcs#15 v1.1: Cryptographic token information format standard (2000)

7. Zimmermann, P.R.: The Official PGP User's Guide. MIT Press, Cambridge, MA, USA (95)
8. Team, T.G.: Gnupg (2005)
9. Union, I.T.: The directory: Public-key and attribute certificate frameworks. Technical Report X.509, International Telecommunication Union (2000)
10. ISO/IEC: 7816-4: Integrated circuit(s) cards with contacts. part 4: Interindustry commands for interchange (1995)
11. ISO/IEC: 7816-3: Integrated circuit(s) cards with contacts. part 3: Electronic signals and transmission protocols (1997)
12. ISO/IEC: 7816-15: Integrated circuit(s) cards with contacts. part 15: Cryptographic information application (1997)
13. Campo, C., Marin, A., Garcia, A., Diaz, I., Breuer, P., Delgado, C., Garcia., C.: JCCM: flexible certificates for smartcards with java card. In: Smart Card Programming and Security. Proceedings of the international Conference on Research in Smart Cards, E-Smart 2001, Springer-Verlag (2001)
14. Almenárez, F., Marín, A., Campo, C., García, C.: PTM: A Pervasive Trust Management Model for Dynamic Open Environments. In: First Workshop on Pervasive Security, Privacy and Trust PSPT'04 in conjuntion with Mobiquitous 2004. (2004)
15. Almenarez, F., Diaz, D., Marin, A.: Secure ad-hoc mbusiness: Enhancing windows ce security. In: Trust and Privacy in digital business. First International Conference, (TrustBus 2004, Zaragoza, Spain). Number 3184 in Lecture Notes in Computer Science, Heidelberg, Germany, Springer-Verlag (2004)
16. TEAM, I.S.: Pkcs_csp (2003) http://www.ilex.fr.
17. Gemplus: Gemsafe products: Gemxpresso pkcs#11 documentation (2004) http://www.gemplus.com/products/software/gemsafe_xpresso/.
18. Cucinotta, T.: Smart sign pkcs#11 modules (2005) http://sourceforge.net/projects/smartsign.
19. Axalto: Cyberflex access sdk: Pkcs#11 module for cyberflex (2004) http://www.axalto.com/infosec/cyberflex_access.asp.
20. Libre-entreprise, R.: Cryptographic service provider number 11: How it works (2004) http://csp11.labs.libre-entreprise.org.
21. V.Benjumea, J.Lopez, J.A.Montenegro, J.M.Troya: A first approach to provide anonymity in attribute certificates. In: PKC 2004 International Workshop on Practice and Theory in Public Key Cryptography. LNCS 2947, Springer-Verlag (2004)

# Smart Cards and Residential Gateways: Improving OSGi Services with Java Cards*

Juan Jesús Sánchez Sánchez[1], Daniel Díaz Sánchez[1], José Alberto Vigo Segura[2],
Natividad Martínez Madrid[1], and Ralf Seepold[1]

[1] Universidad Carlos III de Madrid, Departamento de Ingeniería Telemática,
Av. Universidad 30, 28911 Leganés, Madrid, Spain
{jjsanchez, dds, ralf, nati}@it.uc3m.es
[2] Sequel Business Solutions, Peninsular House, 30 Monument Street,
London EC3R 8LJ, United Kingdom
JVigo@sequel.com

**Abstract.** This article proposes an integration of Smart Cards into an environment controlled by a Residential Gateway. In a common scenario, the Residential Gateway offers services with different characteristics. Some services belong to profiles of a user and thus these services have a mobile behavior. As a consequence, these profile-related and thus user-specific services are configured via a Smart Card. The Smart Card serves as a medium easy to transport but it added more features to the scenario like the possibility of cryptographic services, secure payments for example for pay-per-view or environment's customization. The core of this work has been carried out in order to achieve an integration between two existing technologies: OSGi (Open Service Gateway Initiative) and Java Card.

## 1 Introduction

Nowadays, the application fields for residential gateways are increasing as network operators are facing an increasing need for technology that offer customers end-to-end services like triple-play [1]. These new services are ranging from telemedicine [2] to video-on-demand, thus residential gateways will become a key element in the information society.

Currently, a residential gateway is basically an embedded computer with two network cards one that connects to devices on a home network and the other to connect to the Internet. E-services as telemedicine imply that sensitive information is passed via a residential gateway, and this needs specific protection. Since it is not the core of this work to undertake risk studies, more information can be obtained at [3] and [4].

Smart Cards technologies have been proven to be a robust solution for security services based on their cryptographic capabilities and in their almost tamper-proof nature [5]. Furthermore, Smart Cards are suitable for storing users' sensitive personal information as medical records or private keys and furthermore, it is easy to carry them with you.

---

* This work is partly supported by the Spanish Ministry of Industry via the MEDEA+ projects TRUST-eS (A-306) and Planets (A-121).

J. Domingo-Ferrer, J. Posegga, and D. Schreckling (Eds.): CARDIS 2006, LNCS 3928, pp. 78–90, 2006.
© IFIP International Federation for Information Processing 2006

This work proposes an integration of Smart Cards into a platform for residential gateways. As an example for a highly flexible and open environment, the OSGi (Open Service Gateway Initiative) technology has been chosen as the target system. Also the fact that the Smart Card (Java Card) and the residential gateway support JAVA for programming, the integration task can be performed without a huge effort during the implementation of the interfaces. Once both technologies are integrated, several new functionalities as cryptographic services, secure payments for pay-per-view [6] or environment's customization [7] can be offered via the platform and thus it can be used independent from the service.

In the following section 2, an overview of relevant technologies and a brief study of related work is presented. In section 3, the work performed is detailed. The design phase and the different development strategies and test cases are documented. Once the feasibility is proven, in section 4 several practical applications are described. Also the implementation description is given here. Finally, section 5 presents the conclusion and the future work.

## 2  State of the Art

This section reviews the main aspects of Smart Card and Java Card technologies. In each case a brief description of principal features and applications is given. Also the OSGi technology is briefly presented, since it has been chosen as the platform for integration. At the end, relevant related work is referenced and summarized, while the difference to this proposal is stated as well.

### 2.1  Smart Cards

Smart Cards (defined in ISO-7816 standards [8]) are credit card size devices that are able to store and process information using an embedded integrated circuit. It is transmitting information to an external application. These cards do not only store data but they are able to protect them from unauthorized access or tampering. Typical applications are implementing security modules for banking services, mobile telephony or access control.

The smart card's CPU typically has 8 bits and compares to embedded processors its speed typically is slower, i.e. in the range of 10 MHz in case of the ST19XT34 MCU based smart cards [9]. The Smart Card has a ROM (96KB) and a RAM (4KB) memory. The first one is for the operating system and the second for user applications (EEPROM with 32KB or 64KB). Smart Cards have no interface to keyboards, monitors and other peripherals but they provide an I/O interface to communicate with a PC or a set-top box.

The communication between smart cards and external applications is realized via a protocol stack. Here, direct communication between the application within the card and an external application takes place. Control and data exchanges are application specific. At the next (lower) level, the communication is based on the exchange of Application Protocol Data Units (APDUs) [10] these are used to convey commands and data from and to the card based application. In general, the communication model follows a master-slave architecture. The card takes over the *slave* role and waits for APDU commands from an external application. Once the card executes the instruction conveyed in the command, it sends the result of an APDU response.

## 2.2 Java Cards

The development of a smart card application is always tuned to a specific architecture since each card has a different internal behavior depending on the manufacturer, i.e. low-level communication protocols, memory management and hardware specific details may be different. The aim of Java Card [11] technology is to offer an interoperable high-level interface that should be available for Java Card application (written in Java and called applets) in any Java Card compatible smart card.

Java Card specifications include the Java Card Virtual Machine (JCVM) that defines the Java virtual machine and language suitable for Smart Cards, the Java Card Runtime Environment (JCRE) that describes the Java Card execution behavior (for example the memory management and the application management), and finally, the Java Card Application Programming Interface (JCAPI) that describes Java classes and packets available.

In the implementation of the current version 2.2.1 of Java Card and the Java language version several limitations apply, like: there is not dynamic class load neither a garbage collection, threads are not implemented and the packet `java.lang` is reduced and does not include `String`, `char`, `double`, `float` or `long` classes.

For this work, the Cyberflex Access 32K cards from Axalto [12] (former Schlumberger) have been used. All on-card applications (applets or cardlets) are Java Card 2.1.1 complaint.

## 2.3 OSGi

The Open Services Gateway Initiative (OSGi) is an independent, non-profit corporation working to define and promote open specifications for the delivery of managed services to networked environments, such as homes and automobiles. This initiative created an Open Service Platform Specification that defines the OSGi Service Platform, which consists of two parts: the OSGi framework and a set of standard service definitions. The OSGi framework, which is located on top of a Java virtual machine, represents the execution environment for services.

The central component of the OSGi architecture is the Service Platform that works as the execution environment for services. It provides a platform that service providers can use as their own environment using the devices on a local network.

Initially, the targets for the OSGi specifications were digital and analogue set top boxes, Service Platforms and cable/DSL modems. As the standard has developed, it has first applications in consumer electronics, PC's, industrial computers, cars and other areas where the benefits of uniform operating environments, hardware abstraction and service lifecycle management are appreciated.

The OSGi Framework handles the life cycle management of applications and components. It therefore provides the following functions:

- A packaging format for the applications: The OSGi specifications provide the Bundle format. Bundles are applications packaged in a standard Java Archive (JAR) file, which format is fully compatible with the ubiquitous supported ZIP files.
- Install a bundle: The bundle must be prepared and the diverse components installed in the OSGi Framework, ready to be executed.
- Start/Stop a bundle: Installed bundles can be started and stopped in an OSGi Framework. It is important to remark that in a Service Platform, all applications are started in the same JVM, thereby saving memory, resources, and CPU cycles.

Security issues in this framework are addressed only at bundle level by specifying three different security permissions for the bundles, *AdminPermission*, *PackagePermission*, and *ServicePermission*. The purpose of each of these permissions is to grant the authority to the bundle to carry out specific actions. OSGi tries to extend security issues beyond authorization policies and to add new functionalities to the framework.

For a detailed study of the specifications, it is recommended to read the OSGi specifications [13] and the global vision of the whole architecture that is completed in [14].

In this work *Oscar* [15] has been chosen as the implementation platform. Oscar is an open source implementation of the OSGi framework specification. Currently, Oscar is compliant to major components of the OSGi release 3 specifications. As a remark, "Oscar" was also the name of a smart card OS developed by GIS in the UK in 1989 that can be seen as a precursor to Java Card technology.

## 2.4  Related Work

Before starting with a detailed description of the implementation, other initiatives and proposals driven to take advantage of smart card potential in a residential gateway have been evaluated. As a result, two articles had been classified to be relevant: the first one is from the area of telemedicine and the second one focuses on authentication issues in Residential Access Networks.

In [16] an electronic-prescription system for home-based telemedicine is described. This article describes a health-prescription application running on a smart card that communicates with a Personal Digital Assistant (PDA). It uses OSGi as a central coordinating point among the devices. The OSGi environment is aimed to allow intercommunication between the card reader, the patient's PDA application and other devices but there is no detailed description about how the system is implemented neither on the specific security needs required for medical applications with respect to OSGi platforms.

The second approach [4] presents a quite different scenario in which authentication on network access is addressed. In this case, a smart card is used as a mere certificate and key container inserted in the residential gateway. This article is focused on describing an authentication protocol in which smart card encryption and decryption capabilities are used. In this approach, the portability of data and configuration is less important for the application case.

# 3  Integration of OSGi and Smart Card

This section describes in detail the work carried out to create a bundle that adds new capabilities to OSGi gateways. With this new capabilities it is possible to design a Smart Card based application that takes advantage of all the functionalities offered by these devices like secure storage of data or cryptographic operations and thus to port configurations into different residential environments.

## 3.1  First Approach: MUSCLE Applet Loader Integration into an OSGi Gateway

In order to check the feasibility of this proposal, several tests have been made; the more complete was based in the MuscleCard Applet Loader [17] developed by MUSCLE (Movement For The Use of Smart Cards in a Linux Environment) project [18]. The original idea was to develop an OSGi bundle able to load the MuscleCard Applet into a Java Card.

### 3.1.1  MuscleCard
MuscleCard can be conceptually divided into two parts: A cryptographic card edge definition for Java Cards describing the behavior and the protocol of a MuscleCard applet and an API for accessing Smart Card services. Together, they provide a powerful key and object storage solution on smart cards with cryptographic functionality. The range of applications of MuscleCard ranges from logon purposes to document signatures.

The complete specification of the API is defined in [17]. The MuscleCard applet protocol definition is presented in [19]. Additionally, a good overview of MuscleCard technology can be found in [20].

### 3.1.2  MuscleCard Applet Loader
Inside the MUSCLE project, several applications and tools have been created in order to support the application of MuscleCard. The Java based MuscleCard Applet loader developed by Martin Buechler has been chosen to be become the test OSGi bundle. With this loader it is possible to load the MuscleCard applet onto a smartcard. The different components of this application and their functionalities will be described with a higher level of detail in the subsection 3.2.

Since the Java application distribution includes all the necessary components and native libraries to be execute both in Linux and Windows environments, it is a standalone application suitable to be used as a stand-alone OSGi bundle.

### 3.1.3  MuscleCard Applet Loader OSGi Bundle Description
The created bundle's structure is depicted in figure 1. It consists of the Applet Loader components plus a BundleActivator that will execute the applet loader application. These elements are packaged with a manifest file into a bundle file that can be loaded by an OSGi gateway.

An example of the execution of this bundle is shown in figure 2. This figure is based on a screen snapshot showing how an Oscar gateway loads and executes the bundle and how it establishes a communication with the smart card and loads the MuscleCard Applet.

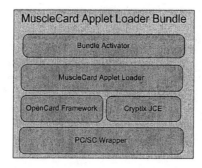

**Fig. 1.** MuscleCard Applet Loader Bundle structure

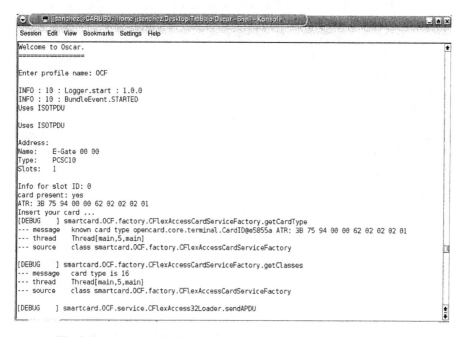

**Fig. 2.** Execution of *MuscleCard Loader OSGi bundle* in an OSGi gateway

This test also shows the feasibility of the planned implementation and thus the following step is introduced: the design of a specific bundle that serves as a library to others bundles.

### 3.2 OCFBundle Description

It is required to provide a bundle that serves as a communication bundle for on-card applications. This bundle will provide a global interface between OSGi applications and their respective Java Card applets.

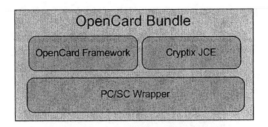

**Fig. 3.** *OpenCard bundle* composition

Therefore, this new bundle allows the communication between applications running on a gateway (as OSGi bundles) and applications running in a Smart Card.

The bundle will be called *OCFBundle* (OpenCard Framework Bundle) and it is based on the basic components of the Applet Loader Bundle. The following components are part of the bundle:

1. OpenCard Framework block: The OpenCard Framework provides a common interface for both the smart card reader and the card s application. It was created as a standardized framework for implementing Smart Card enabled solutions and Smart Card based services. It provides an open architecture and a set of common APIs (Application Program Interfaces). Also CardTerminal and CardService concepts are defined. Both of them are specifically implemented for a particular Smart Card based application. The former is an API to access to the card and reader through standardized protocols such as ISO7816-3 (i.e., T=0 or T=1 protocols) and the latter is an application that uses such an API.

2. Any Client Bundle developed will use these functionalities for communication with applications inside the smart card.

3. Cryptix JCE block: The Java Cryptography Extension (JCE) [21] is a set of packages that provides a framework and implementations for encryption, key generation, key agreement, and Message Authentication Code (MAC) algorithms. Support for encryption includes symmetric, asymmetric, block, and stream ciphers. The software also supports secure streams and sealed objects. For this development, Cryptix JCE [22] has been chosen since it is a complete open-source implementation of the official JCE API published by Sun. Through this API a Client Bundle is able to fulfill the cryptographic operations needed to establish a secure channel between the application and the applet in the card.

4. PC/SC Wrapper block (PC/SC CardTerminal): This wrapper [23] was initially developed by IBM and Gemplus in order to integrate PC/SC in OpenCard Framework [24]. Through this wrapper, an OpenCard based application can be used operating the system's PC/SC capabilities to establish communication with an on-card application.

Finally, the new bundle has been tested on an Oscar 1.0.5 OSGi Gateway running on a Java Runtime Environment 1.5.0_04. The tests were successful, but adjusting and tuning processes are ongoing.

## 4  Applications

In this section, several applications of the proposed architecture are described. In all cases, new functionalities are added to the OSGi Framework, and the majority of these functionalities are related to security issues.

The communication with Smart Card devices is carried out through a further OSGi bundle, the integration of smart based applications can be done seamlessly when designed it as a Java architecture.

An example of how OSGi can improve its functionalities by adding a PC/SC wrapper bundle is depicted in Fig. 4. There are many possible applications fields but only three functionalities are proposed for implementation:

- Environment customization. This has been the first practical application of the proposed architecture; here, smart cards have act as a mean of storing and managing user's preferences in different environments. This application is detailed in the following subsection.
- User's authentication. Smart Cards are able to store users' certificates and private keys and thus they have been widely used as authentication means. With this extension an OSGi bundle is able to check a user's identity.
- Pay-per-view, Micro e-payments and DRM. These three applications fields are currently under investigation by different research centres or companies' alliances. It is foreseen that this technology targets at a growing market.

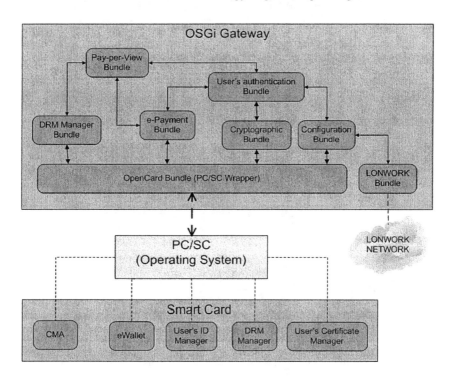

**Fig. 4.** Architecture to integrate Java Card based applications into OSGi Framework

### 4.1 Environment's Customization

This application is based on a previous work [25] in which an architecture for customizing automation was proposed. A possible architecture for a customizable automation environment was described, in such a way that environment's configurations for each user depend on the information stored in a Smart Card device.

Following this scheme, a user will be able to configure and control devices that are connected to the network with the help of a smart card. Many different scenarios are possible; with the help of a Smart Card, a user can control the power of the home lights, the maximum and the minimum temperature of the room's heating, the blinders behavior, preferences in the TV program, etc.

Originally, the proposed solution is based on a specific type of control networks from LonWorks ([26], [27]), which provides a distributed, powerful and open architecture in order to control and manage any kind of sensors and actuators. In this approach, the on-card application, the so-called CMA (Configuration Manager Application) manages the different user's configurations via applets.

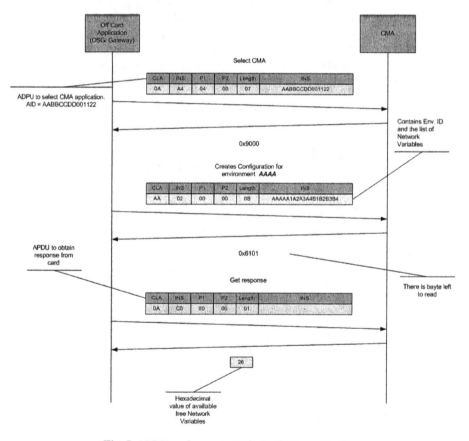

**Fig. 5.** *APDU exchange* example for CMA application

When the card is inserted, the gateway has to select the right application to operate with the card (one card can store different applications). Once the CMA application is successfully selected, it is possible to establish a communication between the program running in the gateway and the on-card application as it is shown Fig 4.

### 4.1.1  CMA Functionalities

In this example, the CMA is a Java Card applet which is responsible element to manage all possible configurations in different environments.

For each given environment, a configuration can be defined as a set of values for different variables: each device can be represented via a group of variables. The values of these variables will define a device's status and the configuration of an environment is made up by the set of all devices' status.

In the implementation, the CMA stores and manages several configurations for the same environment and these configurations may consist of different sets of variables. That implies that when a new configuration is used to set up a specific environment, non-updated variables keep their current values.

The CMA can manage configurations for different environments. This allows users (a cardholder) to have their private configuration for different environments (home, office, car,) stored in the same portable device.

In Figure 6, the different operations available for the current CMA version are shown.

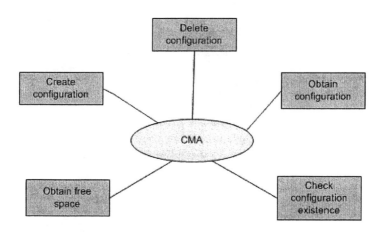

**Fig. 6.** Current *CMA* available *operations*

As shown below, current CMA implementation allows carrying out simple management operations with stored configurations but future efforts will be aimed to add new functionalities.

### 4.1.2  Configuration Bundle

This OSGi bundle will be the one that uses the configurations stored inside the smart card to set up the environment where it has been deployed. That implies of course that any given environment must have an OSGi gateway as one of its core elements since it is the "more intelligent device".

A configuration bundle communicates with the CMA applet through OCFBundle, whose API is used to compound the messages (APDUs) sent to the CMA and to receive its responses. With these messages the bundle is able to obtain configurations stored in the card and to make the required changes in the environment. Besides, it is possible to create a new configuration from the current status of an environment and to store it.

The current version of this bundle is limited and thus it applies first configuration found. It is planned to develop a more complex bundle that includes a Graphic User Interface (GUI). Once the GUI is finished, can a user select among different configurations that apply.

### 4.1.3 LONWORK Bundle

The LONWORK bundle's purpose is to act as an interface between the Configuration Bundle and the LONWORK network, in such a way, that the Configuration Bundle is able to control these devices. Currently, this bundle is in a conceptual status but it is expected to launch the development soon in order to test the whole system connect to an industrial network. Then, other bundles for different automation networks can be created, and this will enable to control more complex environments within different automation networks.

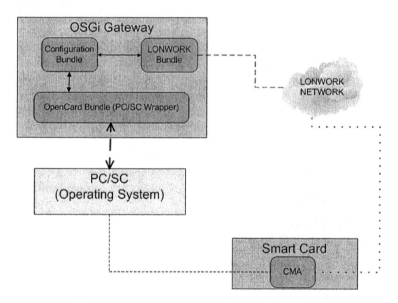

**Fig. 7.** Current *CMA* available *operations*

## 5  Conclusion and Future Work

This article presented a proposal for an integration of smart cards into an OSGi environment. Besides the description of the design and the implementation, several applications have been described. Furthermore, the OCFBundle feasibility has been successfully proven and additional applications have been proposed.

It is planned to offer this bundle to the Oscar Initiative for further discussion and possibly to include it as a regular bundle in the distribution.

Currently, CMA functionalities and Configuration bundle improvements are almost finished. While the implementation of the LONWORK connection is still under development. Since both projects (TRUST-eS and Planets) are running, it is planned to perform the remaining tasks with the help of the regular work flow.

Finally, the convenience of abstracting the CMA application in the OSGi framework as service will be considered. With this service a regular Java interface that hides the implementation details will be provided, in such a way, that any other CMA implementation could be used.

# References

1. D. Ladson: Building a next-generation residential gateway means making tough 0design choices. Texas Instruments, Wireless Net DesignLine July 2005, at www.embedded.com/showArticle.jhtml?articleID=166402757
2. P. O. Bobbie, S. H. Ramisetty, A. Yussiff and S. Pujari: Designing an Embedded Electronic-Prescription Application for Home-Based Telemedicine Using OSGi Framework. Embedded Systems and Applications, Proceedings of the International Conference on Embedded Systems and Applications, ESA '03, June 23 - 26, 2003, Las Vegas, Nevada, USA.
3. A. Herzog and N. Shahmehri: Towards Secure E-Services: Risk Analysis of a Home Automation Service. Proceedings of the 6th Nordic Workshop on Secure IT Systems (NordSec). Copenhagen, Denmark. Pages: 18-26. November, 2001.
4. J. Rossebo, J. Ronan and K. Walsh: Authentication Issues in Multi-Service Residential Access Networks. 2003. Proceedings of 6th International Conference on Management of Multimedia Networks and Services MMNS'2003, LNCS 2839, pages 381-395, Belfast, UK.
5. D. Naccache and D. M'Raihi: Cryptographic Smart Cards. IEEE Micro, pp. 14-24, 1996.
6. J. Domingo-Ferrer, A. Martínez-Ballesté and F. Sebé, Francesc: MICROCAST, Smart Card Based (Micro)Pay-per-View for Multicast Services. CARDIS 2002: 125-134
7. Vigo Segura, J.A., J.J. Sánchez Sánchez, N. Martínez Madrid and R. Seepold: Profile-based configuration of residential networks. ISBN 8-489315-43-4. EUNICE 2005, Networked Applications, 11th Open European Summer School, Colmenarejo, Madrid (Spain).
8. International Organisation for Standardisation (ISO): ISO/IEC 7816. Identification cards - Integrated circuit(s) cards with contacts. Available at www.cardwerk.com/smartcards/smartcard_standard _ISO7816.aspx
9. STMicroelectronics: ST19XT34 Brief Data, Smartcard MCU with MAP, USB/ISO Interface & 34 Kbytes High Density EEPROM. September 2003.
10. International Organisation for Standardisation (ISO): ISO 7816-4: Interindustry Commands for Interchange. Available at www.cardwerk.com/smartcards/smartcard_standard ISO7816-4_7_transmission_interindustry_commands.aspx
11. Sun Microsystems, Inc: Java CardTM Specifications Version 2.2.1. October, 2003. Available at http://java.sun.com/products/javacard/ RELEASENOTES_jcspecs.html
12. Axalto: Cyberflex Access Cards Programmer's Guide. Axalto 2004

13. The Open Services Gateway Initiative Alliance: OSGi Service Platform, Release 3. OSGi 2003. This specification can be downloaded from the OSGi web site: www.osgi.org
14. The Open Services Gateway Initiative Alliance: About the OSGi Service Platform Technical Whitepaper, Revision 3.0. 2004. Available at www.osgi.org/documents/osgi_technology/osgi-sp-overview.pdf
15. Oscar, An OSGi framework implementation. Available at oscar.objectweb.org
16. P.O. Bobbie, A.L. Yussiff, S. Ramisetty and S. Pujari; Designing an Embedded Electronic-Prescription Application for Home-based Telemedicine Using OSGi Framework. Proceedings of the 2003 International Conference on Embedded Systems and Applications (ESA'03), Eds. H. R. Arabnia and L. T. Yang, Las Vegas, June 23-26, 2003, pp. 16-21.
17. D. Corcoran and T. Cucinotta: MUSCLE Cryptographic Card Edge Definition for Java Enable Smartcards. MUSCLE 2001. Available at www.linuxnet.com/musclecard/files/mcardprot-1.2.1.pdf.
18. MUSCLE - Movement for the Use of Smart Cards in a Linux Environment Home-Page: linuxnet.com
19. D. Corcoran and T. Cucinotta: Musclecard Framework Application Programming Interface. version 1.3.0, MUSCLE 2002. Available at www.linuxnet.com/musclecard/files/muscle-api-1.3.0.pdf
20. O. Karsten: MuscleCard. Available at www.inf.tu-dresden.de/ ~ko189283/MuscleCard/MuscleCardArticle.html
21. Sun Microsystems, Inc.: JavaTM Cryptography Extension (JCE) Reference Guide for the JavaTM 2 Platform Standard Edition Development Kit (JDK) 5.0. 2004. Available at java.sun.com/j2se/1.5.0/docs/guide/security/jce/JCERefGuide.html
22. Cryptix JCE Home-Page: www.ntua.gr/cryptix/products/jce
23. PC/SC Wrapper CardTerminal Home-Page. www.gemplus.com/techno/opencard/card terminals/pcsc/doc/README-PCSCWrapper.html
24. OpenCard Home-Page. www.opencard.org
25. J.A. Vigo Segura, J.J. Sánchez Sánchez, N. Martínez Madrid and R. Seepold: Integration of Smart Cards into Automation Networks. IEEE Catalog Number 05EX1101, ISBN 3-902463-03-1. WISES 2005. Hamburg (Germany).
26. Echelon Corporation. Introduction to the LonWorks System, 1999. Available at www.echelon.com/ support/documentation/manuals/078-0183-01A.pdf
27. LonMark Association. LONMARK Application-Layer Interoperability Guidelines version 3.3, 2002. Available at http://www.lonmark.org/products/guides.htm

# Zero Footprint Secure Internet Authentication Using Network Smart Card

Asad M. Ali

Smart Card Research, Axalto,
8311 North FM 620 Road, Austin, TX 78726, USA
amali@axalto.com

**Abstract.** This paper describes the motivation and technological innovation of Network Smart Card, a next generation smart card architecture that supports standard Internet communication and security protocols. It outlines the role of these next generation smart cards in addressing some of the weaknesses inherent in current Internet authentication frameworks. The paper evaluates several common methods of authenticating users as well as servers during online transactions and shows how they can be improved by the use of Network Smart Card. Traditional two-factor authentication techniques require modifications to client machine, remote server, or both. This paper describes a method of achieving the same two-factor authentication for secure Internet access without requiring any modification to host device or remote servers. Finally, the advantages of Network Smart Card are evaluated against other forms of authentication, such as conventional smart cards and OTP tokens.

## 1 Introduction

A fundamental assumption behind online transactions over the Internet is an implicit trust in the identity of the other party, and the confidentiality of the data being transferred. This trust is not gained through personal interactions, but is instead based on a combination of underlying technologies that provide authentication and data encryption. In today's world of ubiquitous network access, where ability to conduct secure online transactions is expected of most, if not all, merchants, there is an ever-increasing need to strengthen these trust enabling authentication technologies without degrading the user's online experience. Since attackers continuously exploit weaknesses in existing modes of authentication, frameworks such as simple password based login systems, which were once considered secure, are no longer adequate [1]. In this perpetually changing landscape of online security threats, next generation smart cards could be extremely useful tools. Conventional smart cards [2] have long been used as secure identity tokens for gaining access to local resources. By supporting standard Internet protocols for communication (TCP/IP) and security (SSL/TLS), the next generation smart cards [3] can bring the same level of security to online transactions. The challenge is to transfer these login credentials from the token to a remote online server without requiring a host application, or modifying the remote server. This paper describes one approach to meet this challenge.

J. Domingo-Ferrer, J. Posegga, and D. Schreckling (Eds.): CARDIS 2006, LNCS 3928, pp. 91–104, 2006.
© IFIP International Federation for Information Processing 2006

## 2   Network Smart Card

To understand the Network Smart Card architecture we first need to look at the current usage of smart cards. Smart card technology has been in use for more than two decades. However, because of the ISO 7816 based standards [4] embraced by the smart card industry, smart cards have evolved in their own niche markets using protocols that are alien to the mainstream computing world. Although there have been key pioneer attempts [5,6,7,8] to break away from smart card specific standards, the use of smart cards as Internet access tokens is still on the fringes of mainstream computing. Smart card advantages such as security, portability, wallet compatible form-factor, and tamper resistance make them increasingly useful in a wide variety of environments such as GSM. However, in other environments such as desktop computing and online access, wide scale adoption of smart cards is hindered by the mismatch between smart card communication standards and the standards of the mainstream computing and networking. When smart cards are connected to host computers, applications cannot communicate with them using standard mainstream network interfaces. Instead, smart card specific hardware and software in the form of reader device drivers and middleware are needed to access smart card services.

### 2.1   Motivation

Applications for conventional smart cards, using ISO 7816 based communication standards, are difficult to develop, and even more cumbersome to deploy and maintain. These deployment hurdles have hindered the acceptance of smart cards as secure devices for Internet commerce more than any other single factor [9].

Smart Cards are extremely useful hardware tokens that provide a secure repository of confidential data. However, a conventional smart card cannot guarantee data security beyond its physical boundary without trusting the host device to which it is connected, or sharing a smart card specific encryption technique with the remote application. These restrictions have limited the appeal of smart cards as secure Internet access devices. Data could be manipulated on the host computer before being forwarded to a remote trusted merchant. While merchants may have very high confidence in data retrieved directly from a smart card, they cannot put the same level of trust in the data forwarded by a host computer. Storing data securely is one thing; using it safely is another. While conventional smart cards provide very strong secure storage, safe use is limited to trusted terminals; there is no mechanism to pass data securely to a standard remote server through an untrusted host or terminal using mainstream communication protocols. The Network Smart Card has been designed to overcome this limitation, so that a remote server can trust data from the smart card.

### 2.2   Architecture

The Network Smart Card solves the communication mismatch by implementing standard Internet protocols on the card. What distinguishes the Network Smart Card technology from some earlier attempts [6,8] at making the smart card network aware, is an architecture based on certain key design choices: implement the TCP/IP network stack and SSL/TLS security layer inside the card; use standard interfaces and drivers that are built into most operating systems, so that no additional middleware deployment is required [3]. This provides seamless connection to host computers and an end-to-end secure data connection with other remote standard Internet nodes.

Figure 1 shows an overview of the Network Smart Card architecture. It contains a USB or ISO 7816 physical layer, a complete network stack consisting of a data link layer, TCP/IP, and SSL/TLS, and various network applications. The data link layer can be either Ethernet/EEM or PPP [10]. If a USB interface is used, then a USB connector is used to connect to the host computer. If an ISO 7816 interface is used, a specialized smart card reader is used to convert this to full duplex serial or USB, and is connected to a serial or USB interface on the host computer. The host computer can be any platform that is configured to permit network access from a serial or USB port. This includes most workstation, desktop, and laptop platforms including Windows, MacOS X, Linux and Unix platforms, as well as some mobile palmtop and handset devices. The host is unaware that the computer being connected is a smart card; it treats the smart card as any other computer requesting a direct connection. No middleware or other smart card specific software is required for any platform. This is an enormous leap in the evolution of smart card design and deployment.

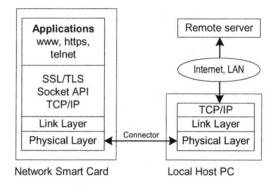

**Fig. 1.** Protocol stack on Network Smart CardLink

The host computer functions simply as a router to connect the smart card to the network. This enables the smart card to access network resources and provide its services through the network without requiring any middleware on the host computer. The remote computers that the smart card communicates with are also unmodified, with no middleware or smart card specific software. As far as the remote computer can tell, the smart card is just another standard computer on the Internet. The ability to establish an end-to-end secure connection with a remote merchant server from any PC can turn the smart card into a portable and secure token for Internet authentication.

## 3   Current Authentication Methods

The HTTP protocol [11] used on the Internet is a stateless, unencrypted and unauthenticated protocol. What makes it secure for online commerce is the SSL [12, 13], or its

IETF flavor TLS [14], protocols. These protocols use public-key cryptography to exchange a secret key and then symmetric cryptography to encrypt the actual data exchanged between a web browser and a web server. However, even with the use of TLS, the security of authenticating users is far from ideal [15,16]. The problem is not with the protocol itself, but with the infrastructure in which it is used.

Figure 2 illustrates various methods of authenticating the identity of users during an online transaction. B1 is a web browser through which a user connects to a merchant server S1. These methods are discussed in the following sections.

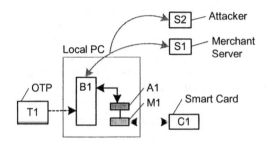

**Fig. 2.** Common Internet authentication frameworks

## 3.1  Password

A username/password pair is perhaps the oldest method of identifying a user at a remote server. This single-factor authentication is now universally considered weak for transactions of high value. Although still widely used by most merchants and financial institutions due to lack of a low cost alternative, authentications based solely on passwords have some inherent shortcomings. Good passwords are difficult to remember, while poor ones are easily compromised using various forms of software attacks. Regardless of the password strength, a password typed manually into a browser is vulnerable to a keystroke logger attack before it is encrypted using TLS. In addition, phishing and spoofing attacks may trick the user into providing the password directly to the attacker.

## 3.2  Automated Password

Automated password entry is achieved using various form-fill applications, A1 (figure 2), that automatically enter the required fields in a web form. This allows use of much stronger passwords that do not have to be remembered by the user. While this approach prevents the typical keystroke logger attack, the data is still kept on the host computer and can potentially be stolen through browser exploits and Trojan horses. It is also vulnerable to spoofing and phishing attacks [17]. Furthermore, this approach is not portable. It can only be used from computers that have application A1 installed and on which the user has previously saved all password data.

### 3.3  Conventional Smart Cards

A safer, and more portable option is to store the password data on a conventional smart card, C1. Smart cards are extremely secure hardware tokens and are excellent repositories for highly confidential information. They provide a two-factor authentication that is missing in simple password based options. However, due to the mismatch between ISO 7816-based smart card communication standards [4] and the communication protocols [10, 18, 19] used by mainstream PC applications, smart cards require special reader drivers as well as middleware application, M1. This overhead is a major impediment to the widespread use of smart card based authentication solutions.

### 3.4  OTP Tokens

OTP tokens are small portable devices that generate a one-time-password code, which can be combined with traditional username/password method to provide a two-factor authentication. This alleviates some of the problems associated with password-only methods. There are two broad categories of OTP generation algorithms: time based algorithms such as the one used with RSA SecureID tokens; and event-based algorithms such as that proposed by the Open Authentication (OATH) consortium. While the latter algorithm is an open standard, the former uses a proprietary technology. Regardless of which option is chosen, the token and the authentication server have to be synchronized. Unit cost of OTP tokens is generally higher than that of smart cards. In addition the cost of token distribution and integration of OTP algorithms in the authentication servers have to be evaluated by merchants when opting for this technology.

### 3.5  Server Authentication

Like user authentication, there are issues with the server authentication as well. For example, the TLS protocol relies on digital certificates to ensure the identity of the two parties. While client authentication is optional, TLS requires the server side to be authenticated before TLS handshake can proceed. This design reflects the general principle of business-to-consumer Internet commerce. It is more important for a user (the client in a TLS handshake) to ensure that the server (typically an online merchant) is who he says he is. After all, securing a connection with the wrong, presumably malicious, merchant can be disastrous. We may like to assume that TLS provides a magic bullet to ensure that we communicate with the correct merchant, but it does not. All it ensures is that we are communicating securely with somebody [20]. To verify that that somebody is actually the correct merchant is left at the discretion of the user. Unfortunately most users do not know how to perform this validation, and of those who know, the vast majority does not make the effort.

Web browsers do assist in this validation process. They compare the intended URL with the corresponding value in the digital certificate received from the merchant. This value is usually the Common Name part of the Subject field in the x.509 certificate that complies with the ITU-T X509 international standard [21]. In case of a mismatch, the browser displays a warning dialog box. The dialog box is also displayed if the certificate has expired, or if the browser does not recognize the Certificate Authority that issued the certificate. These last two warnings are rather rare. Usually, it is the first warning about mismatch of intended URL and actual certificate holder that users overlook. As illustrated in figure 2, a user may think that he is communicating securely with a genuine merchant S1, but in reality could have a secure TLS connection with attacker S2, due to a redirection attack, or simply by mistyping the URL, thereby connecting to a spoofed server.

## 4   Cardholder Verification

Before the Network Smart Card can transfer the user login credentials to remote servers, the user must first be authenticated to the smart card. To achieve this authentication, the user opens a web browser and connects to the web server running on the Network Smart Card. The web server sends a login page into which the user types his PIN. However, a conventional PIN based mechanism where the PIN is typed into a text box opens the possibility of the PIN being compromised. This is particularly true when using public computers that may have malware and keystroke loggers installed on them. The challenge is to enter the PIN on such systems without compromising the PIN.

We use a methodology whereby PIN or password based user authentication can be achieved without compromising the PIN or password as they are entered by the user. There are two mechanisms used, depending upon the balance of ease of use verses security.

The simplest mechanism uses digitally scrambled numeric images at random locations, which are then clicked by the user to show knowledge of the PIN. When more security is required, a second mechanism is added, through which the user applies a mathematical transformation to the PIN, P, using a transformation PIN, T. This transformation is keyed from a random number, R, which is displayed on the login page. The result of this transformation is a virtual PIN, V, which is a one-time password. P and T are secret numeric values known to the user. R is generated by the smart card and is different for each login attempt. The combination of these three values and the transformation logic can produce a virtual PIN, V that is different each time the user logs in.

The transformation logic can vary in complexity depending upon the security requirements or the comfort level of the user. The logic can also be designed in such a way that the selection of a particular transformation PIN, T, can nullify the transformation effect. In this case the virtual PIN, V, is the same as the actual PIN, P.

## 5   Zero Footprint Authentication

Once the user has been authenticated to Network Smart Card, the smart card can act on user's behalf and securely send his login credentials to remote online servers. The technique described in this paper is a zero-footprint technique; requiring no change to either the host computer or the remote servers. It uses JavaScript and a standard web browser on the host computer to transfer login information from Network Smart Card to a remote unmodified server. No additional application software is required on the host. Furthermore, since the Network Smart Card does not require any smart card specific middleware or reader drivers, this approach provides an extremely portable way of carrying the login credentials of multiple existing commercial servers on the smart card and then logging into these servers.

Figure 3 shows a high-level overview of this approach. It is a simple design where a browser B2 connects to the login page of the remote server S1. The user login data is passed from the smart card N1 to the remote server S1 via browser B2. There is no need to have the application A1 or the middleware M1 installed on the host computer.

Figure 4 provides a more detailed view of how the Network Smart Card can be used to achieve this. All arrows indicate data flow over a secure HTTPS connection in response to user clicks or automated script processing.

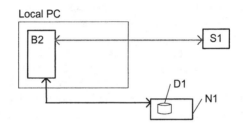

**Fig. 3.** Auto login from smart card without A1 or M1

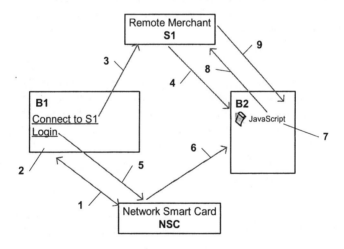

**Fig. 4.** Steps for passing login data from smart card to remote server

The description of each step in Figure 4 is as follows:

1. The user opens a browser B1 and connects to the web server running on the NSC [Network Smart Card]. One way to do this is to type the IP address of the card in the URL bar of the browser. After entering the PIN the user is authenticated to the card.

2. The NSC sends a page to browser B1. This page has the list of remote servers for which the card has login credentials. Each server is represented by a pair of HTML links; one connecting to the login URL of the remote server, and the other back to the NSC.

3. The user clicks on one such server link, e.g. server S1. A connection is made to the login URL of the server.

4. The login page is downloaded from server S1 into a new browser window B2. This allows the server to write any cookies that are necessary during the login process. The cookies are written to the host PC. In case these cookies are session specific they are associated with the browser instance B2.

5. Instead of filling the login information in B2, the user now clicks on the corresponding login link in B1. This link is the second half of the pair of server links picked in step 3. The click sends a request back to the web server on the NSC.

6. The response from the NSC consists of an HTML form template that matches the form used for login at server S1. Along with this form, a small JavaScript code is sent. The form data as well as the JavaScript code are loaded in browser instance B2. This is the same browser that previously contained the login page from server S1. All the form elements are marked as "hidden" so they do not show up in the browser window. Instead a message is displayed indicating that user login information is being sent to server S1.

7. The JavaScript code is automatically launched. It uses data from the NSC to fill the login form, and then calls the submit( ) action on the form.

8. The form containing user login information is sent to the URL on server S1 that authenticates login requests.

9. Once server S1 validates the login credentials sent in step 8, the user is granted access.

This allows the NSC to connect seamlessly to an unmodified remote server. The two-step login procedure that requires the user to click twice (step 3 and 5), though somewhat cumbersome, is designed to work across most common web browser and operating system combinations. It is possible to achieve the same zero-footprint login functionality with a single click if we restrict the browser and OS platform options.

## 6  Authentication Details

The procedure to authenticate a user to remote unmodified web servers uses a combination of HTML form data and JavaScript code to transfer user login credentials from a Network Smart Card to the target server.

### 6.1  Simple Ideal Case

Theoretically, a user login name and password can be sent to a web server using a simple HTML form template. This form template has three elements that are of interest:

- The target URL at the authentication server to which the form data has to be posted, e.g. *https://www.serverS1.com/doLogin*
- The name of the input tag corresponding to the username, e.g. *userID*
- The name of the input tag corresponding to the password, e.g. *userPassword*

Once these three elements are known, a form can be constructed as follows:

```
<form action="https://www.serverS1.com/doLogin">
    <input name="userID" value="myUserID">
    <input name="userPassword" value="myUserPassword">
</form>
```

**Fig. 5.** HTML Form template for sending user login data

The actual values for the *userID* and *userPassword* fields can be stored on a secure hardware token like a Network Smart Card. These values are then read from the smart card and placed in this form template. The form is then submitted to the URL indicated in the action element. In theory this is all that is needed to login to the remote server. In practice this approach seldom works.

### 6.2  The Real World

"In theory, there is no difference between theory and practice. But, in practice, there is" [22]. The reason the simple theoretical case described in section 6.1 does not work in the real world is the use of session cookies by merchant web servers. Servers store cookies on the local client machines for two reasons. The first is to identify users and keep track of their browser session at the server. The second reason is to prevent repeated automated login requests. Servers regard such requests as attempts by a potentially malicious user to break into existing accounts on the server. Therefore, servers reject login requests from browsers that fail to present an adequate set of cookies.

These cookies are written to user's machine when the browser connects to the login page of the server. The server can choose to put one or more cookies for each login session. The cookies can also be time stamped so they cannot be used after their predefined validity period has expired. All this is done to make sure that it is an actual user who is trying to login, and not an automated script with malicious intentions. If the login form is sent directly from the Network Smart Card the corresponding session cookies will be stored on the card itself. The remote server will not recognize the session with a web browser running on the host computer since this browser will not have access to these cookies.

The challenge then is to make the simple ideal case scenario work in the real world environment for transferring data from a smart card to the remote server.

### 6.3  The Solution

One solution is to perform the login process in two steps. This solves the disparity between the simple form submission scenario and the real world authentication environment where commercial web servers use an extensive set of session cookie logic. In the first step the login page from the remote server is downloaded in a browser B2. The remote server is thus given the opportunity to write all authentication related cookies to the local host machine. Once the cookies are written, the same browser instance can be used to load and send the HTML form template of figure 5 to the server. Now the remotes server accepts the login credentials passed by the form and the user is granted access.

JavaScript can be used to automate part of this two-step login process so that the end user can login to unmodified servers with just two clicks; one click to connect to the login page of the server, and second click to pass the user data to the server.

## 6.4  A Complete Example

This section explains the details of HTML and JavaScript code that can be used to pass login data from a smart card to a remote merchant server. Figure 4 is described again, but with actual code examples.

*Step 1:* The user opens a browser B1 and connects to the IP address of the NSC [Network Smart Card]. After entering the PIN the user is authenticated to the card.

*Step 2:* The NSC sends a services page to browser B1. This page has the list of remote servers for which the card has login credentials. Each remote merchant server is represented by a pair of links. The HTML code for one such pair of links is shown in Listing 1.

```
1    <HTML><BODY>
2    <A href="https://www.serverS1.com/login" TARGET=B2> Connect to serverS1 </A>
3     
4    <A href="https://myNetworkSmartCard/serverS1.html" TARGET=B2> Login </A>
5    </BODY></HTML>
```

**Listing 1.** Pair of links to login to a merchant server S1

The key aspects of this code are:

- The link on line 2 connects to the login page of the remote merchant *server S1*.
- The link on line 4 connects to the corresponding page on the smart card that has login data for the merchant server S1. Both the links have browser B2 as their target.

*Step 3:* The user clicks on one such server link, e.g. *server S1*. A connection is made to the login URL of the server, https://www.serverS1.com/login.

*Step 4:* The login page is downloaded from *server S1* into a new browser window B2. This allows the server to write any cookies that are necessary during the login process. The cookies are written to the host PC. In case these cookies are session specific cookies they are associated with the browser instance B2.

*Step 5:* Instead of filling the login information in B2, the user clicks on the login link (line 4, Listing 1) in B1. This is the link corresponding to the server link picked in step 3. This click sends a request ( https://myNetworkSmartCard/serverS1.html ) back to the NSC web server.

*Step 6:* The response from the NSC is displayed in browser B2, over-writing the login page from server *S1*. This response data consists of an HTML form template that matches the form used for login at *server S1*. The HTML code is shown in Listing 2.

```
1   <HTML><BODY>
2   Secured by Axalto Network Smart Card :<br>
3   Your login credentials are being passed to server S1, please wait ...
4   <FORM method="post" name="loginForm" action="https://www.serverS1.com/doLogin">
5   <INPUT type="hidden" name="userID" value="">
6   <INPUT type="hidden" name="userPassword" value="">
7   </FORM>
8   <IFRAME SRC=serverS1Login.html name="autoLogin" ALIGN=bottom FRAMEBORDER=0>
9   </IFRAME>
10  </BODY></HTML>
```

**Listing 2.** serverS1.html file on Smart Card

The key aspects of code in Listing 2 are:

- Line 2 and 3 show a message that is displayed to the user while login data is being sent to *server S1*. This is the only text visible to the user. All other data is hidden.
- Line 4 is the start of a hidden form. The action element of the form is set to the URL at server S1 that processes login requests.
- Line 5 is the input element for userID at server S1. It is hidden.
- Line 6 is the input element for user's password at server S1. It too is hidden.
- Line 8 creates an inline frame on the same page. The source of this page is another HTML file, serverS1Login.html on the smart card. The code for this file is shown in Listing 3. It contains the JavaScript code to fill the username and password data and to automatically submit the form to server S1.

```
1   <SCRIPT LANGUAGE="JavaScript">
2   function setValue() {
3       parent.document.loginForm.userID.value = "myUserID";
4       parent.document.loginForm.userPassword.value = "myUserPassword";
5       parent.document.loginForm.submit();
6   }
7   </SCRIPT>
8   <BODY OnLoad="setValue()">
9   </BODY>
```

**Listing 3.** serverS1Login.html file on Smart Card

The key aspects of code in Listing 3 are:

- Line 3 and 4 set the values of username and password.
- Line 5 submits the form to server S1.
- Line 8 indicates that the function setValue() should be called as soon as this frame is loaded. This allows the login data to be submitted automatically.

*Step 7:* The JavaScript code from serverS1Login.html is automatically launched (see line 8 Listing 3). The confidential user data is kept on the smart card and placed in serverS1Login.html file before it is sent to the browser B2.

*Step 8:* Browser B2 sends the form data containing user login information to the URL (specified in line 4 of Listing 2) at server S1 that processes login requests.

*Step 9:* Once *server S1* authenticates the user, user is granted access.

This example described the use of HTML and JavaScript code to pass user login data to the merchant server. The key is to reuse the same browser instance B2 through which session cookies were initially obtained. This browser reuse is possible through the TARGET element of HREF tag. Another option is to use browser window handle. The first link (that goes to the login page of server S1) creates a window. The handle of this window is saved inside the JavaScript code. The second link (that goes to serverS1.html on smart card) reuses this window handle.

## 7  Comparison

Table 1 compares the security, portability, and deployment cost of various authentication methods. The deployment cost is measured in terms of required changes on both the client machine from which the user logs in, and the remote servers through which the user is authenticated. As shown, the conventional smart cards require no change at the server, but need installation of middleware application and smart card reader device drives on the client machine. Conversely, the OTP based solutions require no change to the client machine, but the OTP algorithm needs to be synchronized with authentication servers. In contrast, the Network Smart Card based solution proposed in this paper requires no change at either the client or the server. It provides a two-factor authentication for passing user identity to existing commercial servers. These servers are not necessarily aware that the identity credentials are coming from a smart card. The only assumption implicit in this approach is that the authentication server does not change its login URL and form template tags. If any one of these things is modified, a corresponding change is required to the login scripts stored on the Network Smart Card. Since the cost of server modification is often an impediment to achieving a stronger authentication framework, this seamless integration with existing servers can be an attractive alternative to conventional smart card or OTP token options.

**Table 1.** Comparison of various authentication methods

| Authentication Methods | Security | Portability | Requires Change at: | |
|---|---|---|---|---|
| | | | Client | Server |
| Manual Password | Low | High | No | No |
| Auto Form-fill | Medium | Low | Yes | No |
| OTP Token | Medium | High | No | Yes |
| Conventional Smart Card | High | Low | Yes | No |
| Network Smart Card | High | High | No | No |

## 8  Progress

This technology was first prototyped and demonstrated as a server at Cartes 2003. Client technology was added in 2004. A second-generation prototype that allows smart card assisted login to unmodified remote online servers, was completed in 2005, and demonstrated at Cartes 2005.

## 9 Conclusion

This paper presented the Network Smart Card architecture and outlined its role in breaking the restrictive mould of conventional smart cards. This new technology recasts smart cards as full-fledged network aware devices that can enhance the trust and security of online authentication frameworks. Network Smart Card can be used for passing user login credentials to remote web servers to gain access to existing site. The user data is kept on the smart card and is sent to the remote server through a secure SSL/TLS connection. This technique has advantages over other existing form-fill software approaches. It provides a more portable way of passing login data from any machine. The user is not restricted to the machine on which form-fill software is installed. The technique is also superior to general OTP-token based methods. It does not require any change on the server side and can, therefore, be used seamlessly with existing commercial servers. In addition, since URLs of legitimate merchant web sites are also stored on the smart card, the user can be protected from potential phishing, spoofing, and DNS poisoning attacks. Since Network Smart Card is a secure computing device supporting standard mainstream communication and security protocol stacks, it is in a much better position to prevent such attacks than conventional smart cards or OTP tokens.

## References

[1] B. Schneier, "Secrets and Lies: Digital Security in a Networked World", pp. 17-39, ISBN 0-471-25311-1, Wiley Computer Publishing, 2000.
[2] Jurgensen, T.M. and Guthery, S.B., "Smart Cards", Pearson Education, Inc., 2002.
[3] Montgomery, M., Ali, A., and Lu, K. "Implementation of a Standard Network Stack in a Smart Card", CARDIS 2004, Toulouse, France, August 2004.
[4] ISO/IEC 7816-3:1997 "Information technology – Identification cards – Integrated circuit(s) cards with contacts – Part 3: Electronic signals and transmission protocols". Available from International Organization for Standards; http://www.iso.org.
[5] Rees, J., and Honeyman, P. "Webcard: a Java Card web server," Proc. IFIP CARDIS 2000, Bristol, UK, September 2000.
[6] Urien, P. "Internet Card, a smart card as a true Internet node," Computer Communication, volume 23, issue 17, October 2000.
[7] Guthery, S., Kehr, R., and Posegga, J. "How to turn a GSM SIM into a web server," Proc. IFIP CARDIS 2000, Bristol, UK, September 2000.
[8] Muller, C. and Deschamps, E. "Smart cards as first-class network citizens," 4th Gemplus Developer Conference, Singapore, November 2002.
[9] J. Vijayan, "Low Draw for Smart Cards: Cost and interoperability problems are slowing companies' adoption of smart card technology". ComputerWorld, February 2004. www.computerworld.com/printthis/2004/0,4814,89924,00.html
[10] Simpson, W. "The Point-to-Point Protocol (PPP)," RFC 1661, July 1994.

[11] Fielding, R., et al. "Hypertext Transfer Protocol -- HTTP/1.1" Network Working Group, RFC 2616, June 1999. The RFC is available at: http://www.w3.org/Protocols/rfc2616/rfc2616.html

[12] Freier, Alan O., et al. "The SSL Protocol, Version 3.0," Internet Draft, November 18, 1996. Also see the following Netscape URL: http://wp.netscape.com/eng/ssl3/.

[13] Elgamal, et al. August 12, 1997, "Secure socket layer application program apparatus and method." United States Patent 5,657,390.

[14] Dierks, T., Allen, C., "The TLS Protocol, Version 1.0," IETF Network Working Group. RFC 2246. The RFC is available at, http://www.ietf.org/rfc/rfc2246.txt.

[15] Jesdanun, A., "Thief captures every keystroke to access accounts," Seattle Post, July, 2003, http://seattlepi.nwsource.com/national/131961_snoop23.html.

[16] Poulsen, K., "Guilty Plea in Kinko's Keystroke Caper," SecurityFocus, July 18, 2003. http://www.securityfocus.com/printable/news/6447.

[17] Poulsen, K. "California reports massive data breach" SecurityFocus, October 19, 2004. http://www.securityfocus.com/news/9758

[18] Postel, J. "Internet Protocol," RFC 791, September 1981.

[19] Postel, J. "Transmission Control Protocol," RFC 793, September 1981.

[20] B. Schneier, "Secrets and Lies: Digital Security in a Networked World", pp. 167-168, ISBN 0-471-25311-1, Wiley Computer Publishing, 2000.

[21] X.509 certificate standard from International Telecommunication Union (ITU-T). See http://www.itu.int/ITU-T/index.html for a copy of the standard.

[22] Jan L. A. van de Snepscheut (1953-1994), Computer scientist and educator.

# An Optimistic NBAC-Based Fair Exchange Method for Arbitrary Items

Masayuki Terada, Kensaku Mori, and Sadayuki Hongo

NTT DoCoMo, Inc., 3–5 Hikari-no-oka,
Yokosuka, Kanagawa, Japan

**Abstract.** Fair exchange protocols are important in realizing safe electronic commerce. In particular, optimistic fair exchange protocols, which involve a trusted third party only when mutual communication between exchanging parties fails, are the most promising development because of their efficiency. Unfortunately, however, existing optimistic protocols place restrictions on the items that can be exchanged, i.e., at least one item must be a "strongly generatable" item such as a digital signature. Without this requirement, only weak fairness that requires (expensive) external dispute resolution processes (e.g. trials in court) after exchange failure can be assured. This paper proposes a novel fair exchange method that enables parties to fairly exchange arbitrary items in an optimistic manner. This is achieved by realizing an optimistic non-blocking atomic commitment (NBAC) protocol between two smartcards and adapting the known result that fair exchange can be reduced to NBAC among trusted processes.

## 1   Introduction

To enable consumers and merchants to securely participate in electronic commerce without fear of fraud, it is essential to guarantee transaction fairness. When buying digital content such as a movie or music, for example, the content data must be exchanged fairly with the payment data; it must be guaranteed that both data transfers are performed or no valuable data is transferred. Such an exchange of data is called a "fair exchange".

Fair exchange is not easy to achieve. To guarantee fairness, several fair exchange protocols apply gradual data release and others involve a trusted third-party (TTP)[1, 2, 3]. In particular, optimistic protocols[4, 5, 6] (often called off-line TTP protocols), which involve a TTP in an exchange only when something goes wrong, appear the most promising approach of their efficiency — they require many fewer messages than gradual protocols while greatly reducing TTP overheads.

All existing optimistic protocols place strong restrictions on the data to be exchanged[3]; optimistic protocols can fairly exchange items only when at least one item is a *strong generatable* item, such as a digital signature (or an item which essentially contains a digital signature, e.g. a payment) or both are electronic vouchers[7, 6]. The other exchanges, e.g. the mutual exchange of digital

J. Domingo-Ferrer, J. Posegga, and D. Schreckling (Eds.): CARDIS 2006, LNCS 3928, pp. 105–118, 2006.
© IFIP International Federation for Information Processing 2006

documents, cannot be performed fairly with existing optimistic protocols, and so another (more inefficient) sort of fair exchange protocols such as online TTP protocols must be used for these exchanges. Even if the restriction is satisfied, an exchange may be unfair if the wrong initiator (who starts the exchange) is selected. These limitations of optimistic protocols force users to carefully use different protocols according to the items and situations, and thus make the practical use of fair exchange difficult and inconvenient.

This paper proposes a novel optimistic fair exchange method that fairly exchanges arbitrary items in an optimistic manner with no restriction on items being exchanged. This is achieved by realizing a smartcard-based optimistic[1] non-blocking atomic commitment (NBAC) protocol that solves the NBAC problem in an optimistic manner, along with the application of the known reduction of fair exchange to NBAC among trusted processes[8]. Since neither the protocol nor the reduction algorithm assumes that the exchanged items have any special property, arbitrary items can be fairly exchanged by this method.

The rest of the paper is organized as follows. Section 2 introduces the definition of fair exchange and discusses the characteristics of existing fair exchange protocols, mainly focusing upon the restrictions placed on items by existing optimistic protocols. Section 3 describes the NBAC definition and the reduction algorithm from fair exchange to NBAC, and discusses the practicality of fair exchange based on previous NBAC protocols. Section 4 details the proposed optimistic NBAC protocol. Section 5 analyzes the NBAC properties of the proposed protocol and the feasibility (and the limitations) of the fair exchange method based on this protocol.

## 2   Fair Exchange

Assume that party A and B have items $i_A$ and $i_B$, respectively, and A wants to obtain $i_B$ from B while B wants $i_A$. Each party has a description of the item to be exchanged; e.g., A knows $d_B = \mathsf{desc}(i_B)$.

An exchange protocol that exchanges items $i_A$ and $i_B$, between exchanging parties A and B, respectively, is called a fair exchange protocol if it satisfies the following properties when party A behaves correctly (and vice versa)[4][2].

**Effectivity.** If B also behaves correctly[3], and both A and B do not want to abandon the exchange, then when the protocol completed, A has $i_B$ such that $d_B = \mathsf{desc}(i_B)$.

---

[1] By *optimistic* we mean that a TTP is involved in an exchange only for exchange resolution. Note that this definition differs from that used in the transaction processing literature, e.g., optimistic transactions, where the resources involved are not locked (to improve concurrency) and any inconsistency is fixed (compensated) later.

[2] In [4], another property called "non-repudiability" is also listed, but we do not discuss this requirement in this paper since it's not a mandatory requirement for fair exchange protocols (as noted in [4]).

[3] From A's point of view. That is, failures in the communication channel between A and B are subsumed in the notion of a misbehaving peer.

**Termination.** A can be sure that the protocol will be completed at a certain point in time. At completion, the state of the exchange as of that point is either final or any changes to the state will not degrade the level of fairness achieved by A so far.

**Fairness.** When the protocol has completed, either A has $i_B$ such that $d_B = \mathsf{desc}(i_B)$, or B has gained no additional information about $i_A$.[4]

Fair exchange protocols can be classified into the following three categories: gradual protocols, online TTP protocols, and optimistic protocols.[1, 2, 3]

In gradual protocols, each exchanging party gradually (i.e. in a "bit by bit" manner) releases the item to be exchanged (or the "privilege" to obtain the expected item). They can exchange items without involving any third-party, however, there are drawbacks to practical use because the fairness achieved by this approach is probabilistic and a lot of interactions are needed to achieve fairness with adequate probability.

Online TTP protocols assure (deterministic) fairness by involving a TTP in every exchange[5]. This approach does not require so many messages (usually less than ten) and can assure fairness deterministically. However, involving a TTP in every exchange incurs message congestion at the TTP when many exchanges are concurrently performed, which degrades scalability and the availability of systems implementing the protocol.

Optimistic protocols also utilize a TTP, but only when the mutual interaction cannot be concluded because of a misbehaving partner or failure of the communication channel. This limited use of the TTP resolves the congestion problem of the online TTP protocols while the number of the messages is comparable to (mostly less than) that required by the online TTP protocols; an optimistic protocol typically requires only four messages in errorless cases.[3, 6]

Existing optimistic protocols do, unfortunately, place restrictions on the items to be exchanged and thus cannot fairly exchange arbitrary items; at least one of the items (the item to be received by the initiator of a protocol, actually) must be *strongly generatable*[6][10, 3]. Strong generatability means that a TTP can always generate the item (or its substitution) when the TTP is invoked to conclude the protocol.

A digital signature is a strongly generatable item since a TTP can generate a substitutive signature that has the same effect as the original signature, provided that the exchanging parties agree upon the substitution in advance (namely "the replacement token" method[4]). Electronic vouchers (or electronic rights)[7, 11] can also be assumed to be strongly generatable, but they require

---

[4] This definition is often called *strong* fairness to distinguish from *weak* fairness which is discussed later.

[5] Protocols wherein the TTP mediates messages are often classified into another category namely "inline TTP protocols"[1, 2].

[6] An optimistic protocol that doesn't require strong generatability but requires a property called "strong revocability" has been proposed[9], but this property is also a strong assumption and only limited items such as closed-loop electronic money are supported.

an exclusive protocol[6] to be fairly exchanged mainly because of the need to prevent duplication of vouchers.

Strong generatability, unfortunately, is not possessed by the many other items, such as digital content and digital documents, exchanged in daily life. Existing optimistic protocols can guarantee fairness when applied to implement *contract signing*, the mutually exchange of two digital signatures, *certified mail*, the exchange of a document and its (signed) receipt, and *voucher trading*, the mutual exchange of two electronic vouchers, however, they guarantee only the weaker notion of fairness called *weak* fairness[7] in other exchanges such as mutual exchange of messages.[3]

Weak fairness requires an external dispute resolution process (e.g. trial in court) if one party wants to recover from some disadvantage. Considering the effort and cost imposed by such a process, weak fairness should be avoided as much as possible.

## 3   Reducing Fair Exchange to NBAC

Apart from developing dedicated protocols to solve the fair exchange problem, several researchers are focusing on the similarity between the notion of fair exchange and the problems in distributed computing, e.g., consensus and (non-blocking) atomic commitment, and have analyzed the relationship among these problems[8, 12]. In particular, [8] showed that fair exchange is reducible to NBAC among trusted processes; i.e., the fair exchange problem can be solved if the NBAC problem among processes on smartcards is solved. Since there is no special assumption (such as item generatability) on the items exchanged, a fair exchange achieved by this approach can exchange arbitrary items.

This section introduces the definition of NBAC and the reduction algorithm from fair exchange to NBAC proposed in [8], as well as discussing the practicality of existing NBAC protocols when applied to fair exchange.

### 3.1   Definition of NBAC

Assume a set of independent processes, each of which has an initial proposed value, yes or no, and try to reach a unanimous decision, commit or abort. A protocol between these processes solves NBAC if it satisfies the following properties[8].

**Termination.** Every correct process eventually reaches a decision.
**Agreement.** No two processes decide differently.
**Commit-Validity (C-Validity).** If all processes propose yes and there is no failure, then the decision value must be commit.
**Abort-Validity (A-Validity).** If at least one process proposes no, then the decision value must be abort.

---

[7] Weak fairness is defined as "if (strong) fairness is not satisfied, then A can prove to an arbiter (a TTP) that B has received (or can still receive) $i_A$ such that $\mathsf{desc}(i_A) = d_A$, without any further intervention from A."[4]

[8] C-Validity and A-Validity are often called "non-triviality" and "uniform-validity", respectively.

## 3.2   Reducing Fair Exchange to NBAC Using Smartcards

The following briefly describes how the fair exchange problem can be solved by NBAC (with help of smartcards).

Assume a system that consists of a set of processes interconnected by a communication network with bidirectional synchronous[9] channels. The processes are divided into two classes, *untrusted* processes and *trusted* processes. The trusted processes are assumed to behave correctly (the untrusted processes are not). Each untrusted process is *associated* with a trusted process, and vice versa. The paired untrusted and trusted processes are adjacent; they are directly connected by a communication channel. Any two untrusted processes are adjacent, while no two trusted processes can be adjacent. This system model can be considered to represent the configuration in which hosts (e.g. PCs and mobile phones) are connected to a network and smartcards are connected to hosts (e.g. a smartcard connected to a PC by a card R/W and a SIM card on a mobile phone).

In this system setting, NBAC among the trusted processes solves fair exchange among the untrusted processes by the algorithm described below:

**FairExchange**(item $i$, description $d$) {
  ⟨send $i$ to exchange partners over secure channel⟩
  **timed wait for** ⟨expected item $i_e$ from exchange partners⟩
    ⟨check $d$ on $i_e$⟩
  **if** (check succeeds and no timeout)
    **then** $vote :=$ yes **else** $vote :=$ no **endif**
  $result :=$ NBAC($vote$)
  **if** ($result =$ commit)
    **then return** $i_e$ **else return** ⟨abort⟩ **endif**
}

The proof that the above algorithm realizes fair exchange is described in [8][10].

## 3.3   Problems in NBAC-Based Approach

Although fair exchange can be (rather easily) resolved by applying NBAC as described above, the NBAC problem itself is known as a *hard* problem[13]. Existing NBAC protocols mostly focus much on multi-party settings, and so fail to match the efficiency of the optimistic protocols introduced in Sect. 2 when used to solve the fair exchange problem.

The well-known two-phase commit (2PC) algorithm that solves the atomic commitment problem (equivalent to NBAC without Termination) cannot solve

---

[9] While synchronity of channels is assumed in this section as to [8], we will relax this assumption in Sect. 4.

[10] To be accurate, [8] uses a different approach to defining the fair exchange problem (mostly same as the definition in [3]) from the definition described in Sect. 2 (follows the definition in [4], which is more rigorous), but they are basically equivalent in the two-party setting.

NBAC, since a crash of the *coordinator* process that gathers votes and distributes a decision may block termination. 2PC can avoid blocking (thus assuring termination) given a resilient coordinator and synchronous channels between the coordinator and other processes; these assumptions might not be infeasible since most TTP-based fair exchange protocols also make similar assumptions (i.e., the TTP are assumed to be eventually reachable from every exchanging party), however, since 2PC requires the coordinator to interact with all processes in every protocol run, the congestion problem is raised as in the online TTP fair exchange protocols.

The three-phase commit (3PC) algorithm, which introduces another phase to elect a coordinator (pre-commit phase), is known to solve NBAC in synchronous systems without assuming a reliable process[14]. However, 3PC is also known as a complicated algorithm that is rarely implemented[15] and introducing an additional phase to 2PC inevitably makes 3PC less efficient than 2PC.

The Monte-Carlo NBAC algorithm[8] solves a weaker variant of NBAC, wherein the Agreement property is satisfied with some probability $p$ $(0 < p < 1)$. This algorithm doesn't involve a coordinator and thus avoids the congestion problem, but probabilistic Agreement implies that achievable fairness is also probabilistic; a large number of interactions are needed to achieve fairness with adequate probability, alike the gradual fair exchange protocols.

## 4   Optimistic NBAC Protocol

As mentioned in Sect. 3, fair exchange based on NBAC among trusted processes doesn't require any special assumptions on the exchanged items. If NBAC can be performed in an optimistic manner, it would be possible to realize optimistic fair exchange that can exchange arbitrary items. This is the key point of our approach.

In this section, we propose an optimistic NBAC protocol between two smartcards. Similar to optimistic fair exchange protocols, this protocol runs in an optimistic manner, i.e., a TTP is involved only when something goes wrong, but solves NBAC rather than fair exchange. This protocol requires only three messages to be passed between the participating smartcards to solve NBAC in errorless cases; this is comparable to existing optimistic protocols, most of which require four messages.

### 4.1   System Model

The system model assumed by this protocol is similar to the system described in Sect. 3.2, except for the following:

- the number of parties (the number of associated pairs) is two,
- a TTP process, which is a reliable trusted process adjacent to each untrusted process is added to the system, and
- untrusted processes are connected by an asynchronous channel instead of a synchronous channel.

The first and second differences are introduced as we consider optimistic exchanges between two parties here. The last difference relaxes the network assumption; because communication channels among hosts pass across a widely-distributed network such as the Internet and mobile phone networks, it is difficult to assume that all communication is synchronous[11].

The channels between each associated pair, i.e., between an untrusted process and a trusted process, stay synchronous as well as those between the TTP and untrusted hosts.

The feasibility of these system assumptions are discussed in Sect. 5.2.

## 4.2   Protocol

Assume trusted processes A and B (on smartcards), which communicate with each other through associated untrusted processes. Both A and B have their own signing key, kept secret from any other party, and the corresponding public key certificate. $vote_A$ is the input $vote$ value of A and $vote_B$ is that of B. $result_A$ and $result_B$ are similar. H() is a collision-resistant one-way hash function (such as SHA1), $\text{Sig}_X(m)$ is $m$ and a digital signature by $X$'s signing key, and $Cert_X$ is $X$'s public key certificate corresponding to $X$'s signing key.

The mutual communication part of this protocol (namely the *main* protocol) is performed as follows. The *abort* subprotocol and the *resolve* subprotocol invoked from this protocol are described later.

1. A generates random number $r$ and calculates $s := H(r)$.
2. A $\rightarrow$ B: $m_1 := \{\text{Sig}_A(s, vote_A), \text{Cert}_A\}$. If $vote_A = $ no, A terminates the protocol with the output $resultA := $ abort after sending $m_1$.
3. B verifies the signature of $m_1$. If this fails, B waits $m_1$ again. If the verification succeeds and $vote_A = $ yes, B proceeds to the next step. If $vote_A = $ no or the reception of (correct) $m_1$ timeouts, B terminates the protocol with the output $result_B := $ abort.
4. B $\rightarrow$ A: $m_2 := \{\text{Sig}_B(s, vote_B), \text{Cert}_B\}$.
5. A verifies the signature of $m_2$. If this fails, A waits $m_2$ again. If the verification succeeds and $vote_B = $ yes, A proceeds to the next step. If $vote_B = $ no, A terminates the protocol with the output $result_A := $ abort. When the reception of $m_2$ timeouts, A abandons this protocol (i.e. ignores $m_2$ even if received later) and invokes the abort subprotocol.
6. A $\rightarrow$ B: $m_3 := r$. After sending $m_3$, A terminates the protocol with the output $result_A := $ commit.
7. Using $s$ in $m_1$ and $r$ in $m_3$, B verifies if $s = H(r)$. If this fails, B waits $m_3$ again. If the verification succeeds, B terminates the protocol with the output $result_B := $ commit. When the reception of $m_3$ timeouts, B invokes the resolve subprotocol.

---

[11] This relaxation does not affect the reducibility from fair exchange to NBAC of the algorithm described in Sect. 3.2, since (besides the NBAC execution) this algorithm use the channels among untrusted processes only to receive item $i_e$ and timing out the reception of $i_e$.

Since the abort subprotocol and the resolve subprotocol are performed in the almost same way, we describe them together. In the following description of the subprotocol(s), $P$ is either A or B that invoked the protocol and $flag$ is a flag that indicates which protocol is being performed; i.e., let $P :=$ A and $flag :=$ abort when performing the abort subprotocol, while $P :=$ B and $flag :=$ commit with the resolve subprotocol.

T is the TTP, which has its own signing key and corresponding certificate $Cert_T$. T manages two sets $S_{abort}$ and $S_{commit}$, whose initial states are $S_{abort} = S_{commit} = \{\phi\}$.

The abort and resolve subprotocols are performed as follows.

1. $P \to$ T: $m_{t1} := \{Sig_P(flag, s), Cert_P\}$.
2. T receives $m_{t1}$ and executes the followings:
   (a) verifies the signature of $m_{t1}$, and waits $m_{t1}$ again if the verification failed, and
   (b) arbitrates whether this protocol should be aborted or committed:
       - if $s \in S_{abort}$, then let $result_T :=$ abort,
       - if $s \in S_{commit}$, then let $result_T :=$ commit, or
       - if neither, then let $S_{flag} := S_{flag} \cup s$ (i.e. add $s$ to $S_{abort}$ when aborting (or $S_{commit}$ when resolving)) and $result_T := flag$.
3. T $\to P$: $m_{t2} := \{Sig_T(result_T, s), Cert_T\}$.
4. $P$ verifies the signature of $m_{t2}$. If this fails, then $P$ waits $m_{t2}$ again. If it succeeds, $P$ terminates the protocol with the output $result_P := result_T$.

## 5    Discussions

### 5.1    Analysis of NBAC Properties

We discuss below how the protocol proposed in Sect. 4.2 satisfies the NBAC properties in Sect. 3.1. In the following analysis, we assume $r$ has enough length and randomness that the possibility of $r$ being predicted before A reveals $m_3$ is negligible.

**Termination Property.** When there is no failure in the communication channels and either party is honest (the associated untrusted process that forward the messages to the other behaves correctly), both A and B can obviously terminate the protocol with a decision in the main protocol[12].

We then discuss the situation in which either process, A or B, can terminate if the execution of the protocol is interupted by failures in the communication channels or a misbehaving partner.

The execution of process A may be interrupted only by the non-arrival of correct $m_2$. In this case, A timeouts and can determine $result_A$ by invoking the abort subprotocol.

---

[12] Since the TTP is not involved in the main protocol, this also confirms that this protocol is an optimistic protocol.

The execution of B may be interrupted by the non-arrival of correct $m_1$ or $m_3$. When $m_1$ doesn't arrive, B can terminate the protocol with $result_B :=$ abort in step 3 of the main protocol. In case $m_3$ doesn't arrive, B timeouts and can determine $result_B$ by invoking the resolve subprotocol.

Hence, either A or B can terminate the protocol and issue result, and the Termination property is satisfied.

**Agreement Property.** First, we show that $(result_A =$ commit$) \Rightarrow (result_B =$ commit$)$.

Process A may terminate the protocol with $result_A =$ commit iff it successfully executes step 6 (and terminates) in the main protocol or the TTP arbitrates that the protocol should conclude by commit (i.e. sends $m_{t2}$ where $result_T =$ commit to A) in the abort subprotocol.

When assuming that A successfully executed step 6 in the main protocol, B must terminate the protocol with $result_B =$ commit by receiving $m_3$, or invoke the resolve subprotocol by timeout of $m_3$, in step 7 of the main protocol. The agreement is obviously reached in the former case. In the latter case, since A is assumed to have successfully executed step 6 in the main protocol, A must not have invoked the abort subprotocol; the resolve subprotocol inevitably concludes with $result_B =$ commit.

If A terminates the protocol by receiving $result_T =$ commit in the abort subprotocol, T must have received $m_{t1}$ from B in the resolve subprotocol before receiving it from A in the abort subprotocol. In this case, the resolve subprotocol must have concluded (or will conclude) with $result_B =$ commit.

Next, we show the converse, $(result_B =$ commit$) \Rightarrow (result_A =$ commit$)$.

Process B may terminate the protocol with $result_B =$ commit iff it successfully received $m_3$ in step 7 of the main protocol, or it received $result_T =$ commit in the resolve subprotocol. In the former case, A must have successfully executed step 6 in the main protocol and terminated with $result_A =$ commit. In the latter case, $m_{t1}$ of the abort subprotocol by A must not have arrived at T yet; A has terminated in step 6 in the main protocol, or $m_{t1}$ from A will arrive at T later. In either case, A terminates with $result_A =$ commit.

As a corollary of the above results,

$$(result_A =$ commit$) \Leftrightarrow (result_B =$ commit$). \tag{1}$$

Since each process decides either commit or abort, $\neg(result_X =$ commit$) \Rightarrow (result_X =$ abort$)$, and therefore,

$$(result_A =$ abort$) \Leftrightarrow (result_B =$ abort$). \tag{2}$$

Hence, A and B do not decide differently, and the Agreement property is satisfied.

**C-Validity Property.** If $(vote_A =$ yes$) \cap (vote_B =$ yes$)$ and there is no failure, then process A terminates with $result_A = commit$ in step 6 in the main protocol and B terminates with $result_B = commit$ in step 7.

The C-Validity property is satisfied therefore.

**A-Validity Property.** If $vote_A =$ no, then process A terminates with $result_A :=$ abort in step 2 in the main protocol. Similarly, B terminates with $result_B :=$ abort in step 3 if $vote_B =$ no. In either case, $result_A = result_B =$ abort according to Eq. (2).

The A-Validity property is satisfied.

## 5.2 Feasibility

In the following, we show that this exchange method based on the optimistic NBAC protocol proposed in Sect. 4.2 and the reduction algorithm introduced in Sect. 3.2 can be feasibly implemented under the system assumptions described in Sect. 4.1.

**Implementation of the Processes.** Besides communication channels, the system consists of associated pairs of an untrusted process and a trusted process, and a trusted third-party (TTP) process. Each exchange party is assumed to be represented by an associated pair.

An untrusted process is easily implemented on a host connected to a network (e.g. a personal computer and a mobile phone). It is not assumed to be reliable and there are no difficulties to implementing it; what it has to do are to input the item to be sent and a description of the item to be received into the associated trusted process, and to forward the messages among trusted processes.

A trusted process (associated with an untrusted process) is required to be implemented on a tamper-resistant user device such as a smartcard connected to a host through a card reader/writer (card R/W) or embedded in a host (like a SIM card in a mobile phone). If not, an exchange becomes completely unfair because a party can obtain the received item regardless of the result of the NBAC run in the reduction algorithm; tamper-resistance is an essential requirement in applying this method. Assuming such a trusted device might be not so impractical nowadays considering the rapid penetration of smartcards; e.g., most GSM phones and 3G mobile phones have (U)SIM cards. However, regarding implementation on a smartcard, the performance bottlenecks associated with smartcards should be carefully considered. Performance estimation of the smartcard implementation is discussed later.

The TTP process will be implemented as a server connected to a network. This server should be managed by a trusted third-party. This server is involved in an exchange when either of the exchanging parties invokes an abort or resolve subprotocol. Since the protocol is optimistic, these invocations are performed only when something goes wrong in mutual interactions between exchanging parties; when many exchanges are conducted concurrently, the TTP server is involved in a part of them. Under the assumption that failures that need arbitration by the TTP are rare, this system will avoid congestion of messages on the TTP and be scalable, like existing optimistic fair exchange protocols.

**Implementation of the Channels.** As described in Sect. 4.1, we assume a system where the channels between untrusted processes are asynchronous and the other channels (the channels between an associated pair and those between the TTP and untrusted processes) are synchronous. When considering to apply the system to exchanges in electronic commerce, the system should be able to be implemented in a widely-distributed and unreliable network such as the Internet and mobile phone networks.

Asynchronous channels between untrusted processes obviously can be implemented in such networks. Since both processes in an associated pair are managed by an exchanging party, the synchronous communication channel between them is mostly local and should be easily implemented; although a user can block interactions between them, e.g., by removing the smartcard from the card R/W, we can treat this as misbehavior of the untrusted process (on the host).

The channels between the TTP process and each untrusted process might not be local; hosts are most likely to communicate with the TTP server through a network. However, different from communicating with another host, which may be unsure where it is and who manages it, the TTP can be expected to be connected to the network continuously. Although the communication channel can be (permanently) lost if the host is disconnected from the network by its user, we can also treat this as misbehavior of an untrusted process. This assumption is, accordingly, also feasible.

**Performance.** The possible bottlenecks of a smartcard implementation are the I/O performance, the processing speed (especially cryptographic calculation) and the number of write operations to non-volatile memory (write operations to EEPROM are much slower than those to RAM). Since no persistent store of data into a smartcard is needed in the proposed exchange, we focus on the I/O interactions and the cryptographic processes.

The proposed NBAC protocol can terminate with unanimous decisions by exchanging three messages between trusted processes in errorless cases (i.e. in the main protocol). In this protocol, the required cryptographic calculations in each trusted process, i.e. each smartcard, are a pair of signature generation and verification (using the corresponding certificate) and a single hash calculation. When something goes wrong in the mutual interaction, an additional round-trip message exchange, which involves another pair of signature generation and verification, with a TTP may be required. This load does not exceed that of existing optimistic protocols, so this protocol can be considered to be practical for implementation on current smartcards.

An optimistic fair exchange protocol for electronic vouchers, which is slightly more complex than the proposed protocol (requires four messages and almost the same cryptographic calculations), performs an exchange in less than two seconds when implemented on mid-range smartcards.[16] This implies that the proposed NBAC protocol can be performed in the same or less time.

On the other hand, the reduction algorithm seems to need some performance improvement for applications that exchange huge data. This algorithm requires trusted processes to send and receive the whole items to be exchanged. However, since the I/O performance of the current smartcards is not so high (approximately 10kbps ~ 400kbps), it might be infeasible to exchange a large amount of data, such as digital content. Some measure, e.g., exchanging encrypted items in advance and exchanging the description keys fairly, could be introduced to exchange large items, but it may make the item verification (i.e. checking the description of the expected item on the received item) difficult. This could be an open problem.

### 5.3  Limitation

Although the proposed NBAC protocol and fair exchange method is more efficient than existing NBAC protocols and fair exchange protocols that can exchange arbitrary items (i.e., gradual and online TTP protocols), respectively, it cannot replace either protocols in general; it lacks applicability to multi-party settings and relies upon trusted devices and a TTP.

Since most exchanges are conducted by two parties, e.g., trades in commerce, the support for two-party setting should be attractive enough to stimulate the frequency of fair exchange. However, distributed transactions often need consistency in three or more (independently managed) resources. This protocol cannot be applied to guarantee atomic commit in such transactions. Secure multi-party computation, which often requires fairness, is another example. These applications will need another protocol to assure consistency or fairness.

Relying upon trusted devices and a TTP should not spoil the feasibility as discussed in Sect. 5.2, however, there may be environments where assuming them is difficult. Our method cannot be adopted in such environments.

### 5.4  Comparison to Existing Smartcard-Based Exchange Protocols

Several protocols have been proposed for fair exchange via smartcards.

One of them is a reduction from fair exchange to a weaker variant of NBAC (Monte-Carlo NBAC)[8], mentioned in Sect. 3. As described before, this has similar characteristic to gradual exchange protocols and shares the same problems (probabilistic fairness and high interaction costs).

A similar approach based on (a variant of) the consensus problem (named Biased Consensus) among trusted processes is introduced in [12]. This achieves deterministic fair exchange if a majority of the untrusted processes are honest (behave correctly), but fairness becomes probabilistic if half or more processes are dishonest; in two-party exchanges, which will be the most common setting, a misbehaved partner is enough to lose the honest majority and thus only probabilistic fairness can be assured.

In [17, 18], several protocols that use a smartcard to achieve optimistic fair exchange between two parties are introduced. These protocols exchange items between a party called *vendor* and another party *customer*, who uses a smartcard (the vendor does not use a smartcard). One of the protocols, called the basic protocol, can exchange arbitrary items[13]; it does not assume generatability or revocability on either item. However, these protocols have a drawback in that

---

[13] The other protocols require one of the items (from the customer to the vendor) to be strongly revocable.

the Termination property (of fair exchange) is not assured to the vendor; the vendor is not assured to be able to know if its item is sold or not.

Another smartcard-based optimistic fair exchange protocol is proposed in [6]. This protocol fairly exchanges electronic vouchers stored in smartcards as well as preventing illegal acts on the vouchers (forgery, alteration, and duplication). This protocol can be applied only to the exchange of particular items, i.e., vouchers stored in smartcards, as it is[14].

# 6 Conclusion

In this paper, we argued that existing optimistic protocols place an excessive restriction on exchanged items, i.e., at least one of the item has to be a strongly generatable item such as a digital signature. To circumvent this restriction, we focused on NBAC-based fair exchange using smartcards, which is based on NBAC between trusted processes, and proposed a novel NBAC protocol that can be performed between smartcards in an optimistic manner. The NBAC properties and feasibility of the protocol were also discussed; the proposed protocol satisfies all of the NBAC requirements and can be efficiently implemented on current smartcards.

NBAC does not only realize fair exchange but is also useful for diverse transactions in electronic commerce. Considering the popularity of mobile phones equipped with smartcards and the rapid improvement of smartcard process technologies, this protocol may broadly contribute to realize safe and secure electronic commerce.

# References

1. Zhou, J., ed.: Non-repudiation in electronic commerce. Artech House, Norwood, MA, USA (2001)
2. Kremer, S., Markowitch, O., Zhou, J.: An intensive survey of fair non-repudiation protocols. Computer Communications **25** (2002) 1606–1621
3. Pagnia, H., Vogt, H., C.Gärtner, F.: Fair exchange. The Computer Journal **46** (2003) 55–75
4. Asokan, N.: Fairness in Electronic Commerce. PhD thesis, University of Waterloo (1998)
5. Schunter, M.: Optimistic Fair Exchange. PhD thesis, Universität des Saarlandes (2000)

---

[14] However, interestingly, its use of a different notion of fairness to prevent duplication of vouchers assures that if one party successfully terminates (i.e. commit) an exchange, then the other party *never* aborts the exchange; this implies the Agreement property of NBAC, while the (original) fairness property doesn't (a misbehaved party can abort if the other party successfully commits). Actually, NBAC is reducible to fair voucher exchange (cf. fair exchange is reducible to NBAC, but not vice versa) and the proposed NBAC protocol can also be considered as a generalization of the voucher exchange protocol.

6. Terada, M., Iguchi, M., Hanadate, M., Fujimura, K.: An optimistic fair exchange protocol for trading electronic rights. In: Proc. 6th Working Conference on Smart Card Research and Advanced Applications (CARDIS'04), IFIP (2004) 255–270
7. Fujimura, K., Eastlake, D.: RFC 3506: Requirements and Design for Voucher Trading System (VTS). (2003)
8. Avoine, G., Gärtner, F., Guerraoui, R., Kursawe, K., Vaudenay, S., Vukolic, M.: Reducing fair exchange to atomic commit. Technical Report 200411, Swiss Federal Institute of Technology (EPFL), School of Computer and Communication Sciences, Lausanne, Switzerland (2004)
9. Vogt, H.: Asynchronous optimistic fair exchange based on revocable items. In: Proc. 7th International Financial Cryptography Conference, IFCA (2003) 208–222
10. Vogt, H., Pagnia, H., Gärtner, F.C.: Modular fair exchange protocols for electronic commerce. In: Proc. 15th Annual Computer Security Applications Conference. (1999) 3–11
11. Terada, M., Kuno, H., Hanadate, M., Fujimura, K.: Copy prevention scheme for rights trading infrastructure. In: Proc. 4th Working Conference on Smart Card Research and Advanced Applications (CARDIS'00), IFIP (2000) 51–70
12. Avoine, G., Gärtner, F., Guerraoui, R., Vukolic, M.: Gracefully degrading fair exchange with security modules. In: Proc. 5th European Dependable Computing Conference (EDCC). (2005) 55–71
13. Guerraoui, R.: Revisiting the relationship between non-blocking atomic commitment and consensus. In: Proc. 9th International Workshop on Distributed Algorithms (WDAG95). (1995) 87–100
14. Skeen, D.: Nonblocking commit protocols. In: Proc. 1981 ACM SIGMOD International Conference on Management of Data. (1981) 133–142
15. Gray, J., Lamport, L.: Consensus on transaction commit. Technical Report MSR-TR-2003-96, Microsoft Research (2004)
16. Terada, M., Mori, K., Ishii, K., Hongo, S., Usaka, T., Koshizuka, N., Sakamura, K.: TENeT: A framework for distributed smartcards. In: Proc. 2nd International Conference on Security in Pervasive computing (SPC2005). Volume 3450 of LNCS., Springer-Verlag (2005) 3–17
17. Vogt, H., Pagnia, H., Gärtner, F.C.: Using smart cards for fair exchange. In: Proc. 2nd International Workshop on Electronic Commerce (WELCOM 2001). (2001) 101–113
18. Vogt, H., Gärtner, F.C., Pagnia, H.: Supporting fair exchange in mobile environments. ACM/Kluwer Journal on Mobile Network and Applications (MONET) 8 (2003) 127–136

# Generic Cryptanalysis of Combined Countermeasures with Randomized BSD Representations

Tae Hyun Kim[1], Dong-Guk Han[2], Katsuyuki Okeya[3], and Jongin Lim[1]

[1] Center for Information and Security Technologies(CIST),
Korea University, Seoul, Korea
{thkim, jilim}@cist.korea.ac.kr
[2] Future University-Hakodate, 116-2 Kamedanakano-cho, Hakodate,
Hokkaido, 041-8655, Japan
christa@fun.ac.jp
[3] Hitachi, Ltd., Systems Development Laboratory,
1099, Ohzenji, Asao-ku, Kawasaki 215-0013, Japan
ka-okeya@sdl.hitachi.co.jp

**Abstract.** In ICICS'04, Sim et al. proposed an attack against the full version of Ha-Moon's countermeasure which is one of enhanced countermeasures. The analysis technique is based on the fact that the probability for the appearance of an intermediate value is $p = 1/2$. By our simulations, however, it is proven to be not true. Thus sometimes the output of their attack might be wrong because there exists the case that the probability $p$ is so small that they can make a wrong decision.

In this paper we repair the above attack, and then propose a generic analytical technique applicable to all BSD type countermeasures combined with some simple power analysis countermeasures. In order to show that the proposed attack is as practical as the usual differential power analysis (DPA), we estimate the number of samples and computational cost. Furthermore, we enhance the proposed attack in two ways such that it works against right-to-left algorithm in a simpler and more efficient way, and also works against one combined with an extra DPA countermeasure.

**Keywords:** Elliptic Curve Cryptosystems, Side Channel Attack, Differential Power Analysis, Refined Power Analysis, Binary Signed Digit (BSD) Representation.

## 1 Introduction

Mobile devices such as smart cards, mobile phones, and handheld computers are penetrating in our daily life in order for us to be convenient. Since mobile devices are equipped with scarce resources only, cryptographic algorithms on them should be optimized. Above all, elliptic curve cryptosystems (ECC) [13, 17] are suitable for implementing on such devices because of the reduced key size

J. Domingo-Ferrer, J. Posegga, and D. Schreckling (Eds.): CARDIS 2006, LNCS 3928, pp. 119–134, 2006.
© IFIP International Federation for Information Processing 2006

required in comparison to other cryptosystems (e.g. a 160-bit ECC has almost the same security as a 1024-bit RSA).

On the other hand, side channel attacks (SCA) have been recognized as menaces to ECC. In SCA, an attacker observes side channel information such as computation timing, power consumption, and electro-magnetic radiation while a cryptographic device performs cryptographic operations, then analyzes the information for revealing the secret stored in the device [12]. Thus constructing an efficient scalar multiplication method which is secure against SCA and analyzing its security are important research topics [3, 10, 26].

For this purpose, many countermeasures against SCA have been proposed. In particular, a popular type of countermeasures is based on inserting random decisions when choosing one representation among several different representations for the same secret scalar. For instance, it includes Oswald-Aigner countermeasure [20], Ha-Moon countermeasure [8], Ebeid-Hasan countermeasure [5], and the countermeasure of Agagliate et al. [1], which are based on randomized Binary Signed Digit (BSD) representations. Moreover, this type of countermeasures on ECC provides us with good performance/efficiency. We call countermeasures using BSD representations *BSD type countermeasure*[1].

Whereas many BSD type countermeasures were proposed, most of them have been broken by many sophisticated simple power analysis (SPA) if we use them as a single countermeasure against SCA [23, 14, 21, 9, 25].

A possible approach to resist the sophisticated SPAs is to combine BSD type countermeasures with an SPA countermeasure using a fixed procedure such as Coron's dummy method [4] or Montgomery ladder methods [19, 22]. An example of BSD type combined with an SPA countermeasure is the full version of Ha-Moon's method [8] composed of a random recoding method and an SPA-immune algorithm using dummy operations. Unfortunately, the full version of Ha-Moon's method has been analyzed by two different methods [6, 24]. The attacks utilize a characteristic of BSD representations generated by a specific random recoding method. Thus, the attacks are ad-hoc in the sense that it is tailored specifically to Ha-Moon's countermeasure. If the target countermeasure is changed from Ha-Moon's countermeasure then the characteristic is also changed. Thus, it is not clear whether the attacks can be applicable to the other BSD type countermeasures or not.

## 1.1   Contributions of This Paper

The proposed attack can break the combined countermeasures without knowledge for the appearance probability of an intermediate point in advance, i.e., it is independent of a random recoding method. Therefore, the proposed attack is applicable to not only Ha-Moon's countermeasure but also *all BSD type countermeasures* under reasonable assumptions. Moreover, to reduce the unwanted

---

[1] The BSD representations use the set of digits $\{-1, 0, 1\}$. Thus, in this paper, we do not deal with countermeasures based on window methods using randomized addition chains.

noise in power signals, we use a model of the signal-to-noise ratio (SNR) for "Zero Exponent Multiple Data" (ZEMD) [15]. In this model, the role of the number of samples used in the ZEMD attack is very important. In this paper, we show how many number of samples are required to obtain the same height of peaks as the ordinary ZEMD attack on unprotected algorithms. From our simulations, we deduce that the proposed attack is as practical as the ordinary ZEMD attack.

In this paper, we propose analysis techniques against the following three targets.

**Target 1.** The BSD type countermeasures combined with an SPA countermeasure using a fixed procedure such as Coron's dummy method [4] or Montgomery ladder methods [19, 22]. An example of SPA countermeasure is the following Addition-Subtraction_Always method.

Addition-Subtraction_Always method

| |
|---|
| INPUT    A point $P$, and $k = \sum_{j=0}^{n-1} k_j 2^j$, $k_j \in \{0, 1\}$ |
|            $d = \sum_{j=0}^{n} d_j 2^j$, $d_j \in \{-1, 0, 1\}$, where $d$ is a recoded number of $k$ |
| OUTPUT $Q = dP$ |

1. $Q[0] \leftarrow \mathcal{O}$, $R[0] \leftarrow P$, $R[1] \leftarrow P$, $R[2] \leftarrow -P$
2. for $j = n$ downto 0
   2.1. $Q[0] \leftarrow$ECDBL$(Q[0])$
   2.2. $Q[1] \leftarrow$ECADD$(Q[0], R[1 - d_j])$
   2.3. $Q[0] \leftarrow Q[|d_j|]$
3. Return $Q[0]$

**Target 2.** The BSD type countermeasures combined with a DPA countermeasure using randomized point representation methods such as Coron's third method called randomized projective coordinates [4] and random isomorphism methods [11].

**Target 3.** The BSD type countermeasures using right-to-left computations.

This paper is organized as follows. In the next section, we introduce some tools for power analysis. In Section 3 we propose a generic attack against Target 1 and show simulation results. In Section 4, we enhance the proposed attack in two ways: against Target 2 and Target 3. In Section 5 we show a comparison of attacks against BSD type countermeasures. Finally, we conclude in Section 6.

## 2 Tools for Power Analysis

To construct an attack against BSD type combined with an SPA countermeasure, we introduce two concepts; discernment point and signal-to-noise ratio.

### 2.1 Discernment Point in ZEMD Attack

In this subsection, we introduce the concept of *discernment point*. A ZEMD attack utilizes a correlation between power consumption and any specific key-dependent bits. In view of ZEMD attack, the three following assumptions support the success of ZEMD attack.

(i) A point that its appearance in the middle of computing provides the attacker with information of (a portion of) the secret key exists. Such a point is referred to as *discernment point*.

(ii) A coordinate of the discernment point is computable or predictable with purposive probability for the attacker.

(iii) The attacker can discern whether the discernment point appears or not using side channel information.

The attacker succeeds in ZEMD attack under the three assumptions.

(1) The attacker classifies input points into two classes depending on the coordinate of the discernment point. ((i) provides the existence of a discernment point, and (ii) provides the attacker's capability of classifying.)

(2) The attacker collects side channel information, and discerns whether the discernment point appears or not. ((iii) provides the attacker's capability of discerning.)

(3) The attacker reveals a portion of the secret key using the (dis)appearance of the discernment point. ((i) provides the attacker's capability of revealing.)

Now, we simply describe a ZEMD attack against SPA-protected Double-Add_Always method by using the above concept of the discernment point.

**Double-Add_Always method**

| | |
|---|---|
| INPUT | A point $P$, and $k = \sum_{j=0}^{n-1} k_j 2^j$, $k_j \in \{0, 1\}$ |
| OUTPUT | $Q = kP$ |

1. $Q[0] \leftarrow P$
2. for $j = n - 2$ downto 0
   2.1. $Q[0] \leftarrow \text{ECDBL}(Q[0])$
   2.2. $Q[1] \leftarrow \text{ECADD}(Q[0], P)$
   2.3. $Q[0] \leftarrow Q[k_i]$
3. Return $Q[0]$

An intermediate point which is actually calculated at the step 2.1 after $j = i$ bit $(k_i)$ calculation in Double-Add_Always method is as follows;

$$- (\sum_{j=i+1}^{n-1} k_j 2^{j-i+1}) \cdot P \text{ if } k_i = 0, \text{ and } (\sum_{j=i+1}^{n-1} k_j 2^{j-i+1} + 2) \cdot P, \text{ if } k_i = 1.$$

Thus the discernment point used in the ZEMD attack on Double-Add_Always method can be one of $(\sum_{j=i+1}^{n-1} k_j 2^{j-i+1}) \cdot P$ and $(\sum_{j=i+1}^{n-1} k_j 2^{j-i+1} + 2) \cdot P$.

## 2.2 Signal-to-Noise Ratio

We introduce the concept of signal-to-noise ratio (SNR) in order to estimate the required number of samples. A successful ZEMD attack requires that an attacker can detect the signal over the noise. To reduce the unwanted noise in the power signal, Messerges et al. used filtering strategies [16]. They proposed a model for the ZEMD signal-to-noise ratio.

**Proposition 1** ([16]). *A ZEMD attack using $R$ samples on an $M$-bit processor in* Double-Add_Always *method, with signal size $\varepsilon$, average nonalgorithmic noise variance $\sigma^2$, and percentage of algorithmic noise $\alpha$, has a voltage intrasignal SNR that can be modeled by*

$$SNR = \frac{\varepsilon\sqrt{R}}{\sqrt{8\sigma^2 + \varepsilon^2(\alpha M + M - 1)}}. \tag{1}$$

## 3   Proposed Attack

In this section, we propose a novel ZEMD attack algorithm against Target 1 and show the results of simulation. (The proofs of several propositions may be found in appendix.)

### 3.1   Notations

Let $k = \sum_{j=0}^{n-1} k_j 2^j$ with $k_j \in \{0,1\}$ be the $n$-bit binary secret key and $d = \sum_{j=0}^{n} d_j 2^j$ with $d_j \in \{-1,0,1\}$ be the $(n+1)$-bit random recoded number generated from $k$ by a random recoding method. Note that $k$ and $d$ are obviously the same number, even though their representations differ. Let $k_{[s_1,t_1]}$ and $d_{[s_1,t_1]}$ denote partial bits from the $s_1$-th bit to the $t_1$-th bit of $k$ and $d$, respectively. Namely $k_{[s_1,t_1]} := \sum_{j=s_1}^{t_1} k_j 2^{j-s_1}$ and $d_{[s_2,t_2]} := \sum_{j=s_2}^{t_2} d_j 2^{j-s_2}$. Here, $0 \leq s_1 \leq t_1 \leq n-1$ and $0 \leq s_2 \leq t_2 \leq n$.

- $R$: The number of executions that an attacker observes, i.e., the number of samples.
- $R^S$: The smallest number of executions to detect the signal over the noise in SNR formula (1) against Double_Add_Always method. If $R$ is chosen as $R \geq R^S$ then an attacker can break Double_Add_Always method.
- $R^M$: The maximum number of execution which an attacker can use in a ZEMD attack. Note that $R^M$ depends on the computational power of an attacker. By the definition, $R^M \geq R$.
- $P_r$: For $1 \leq r \leq R$, the $r$-th input point into Addition-Subtraction_Always method.
- $IP_r^i$: The intermediate point which is actually calculated at the step 2.1 after $j = i$ bit ($k_i$) calculation for the $r$-th input point into Addition-Subtraction _Always method.
- $p$: The appearance probability of a discernment point after the calculation for $k_i$, i.e., $p := Pr[DP_r^i = IP_r^i]^{1 \leq r \leq R}$ during $R$ executions. Note that the probability depends on the secret key and a random recoding method used in BSD type countermeasures.

### 3.2   SNR for Probabilistic Appearance of Discernment Point

As Addition-Subtraction_Always method uses randomized BSD representations, the size of signals may decrease due to probabilistic appearance of discernment points. Thus the SNR model for BSD type countermeasure should be modified as follows:

**Proposition 2.** *Assume that the computational environment is the same as Proposition 1. If the appearance probability of a discernment point is p, then the signal-to-noise ratio is*

$$SNR = \frac{\varepsilon p \sqrt{R}}{\sqrt{8\sigma^2 + \varepsilon^2(\alpha M + M - p)}}. \tag{2}$$

*Thus the SNR is approximately p times larger than the original. In other words, in order to obtain the same SNR as the original, the required samples are $p^{-2}$ times larger than the original.*

*Remark 1.* Since the required number of samples $R$ is determined by the probability $p$, if $p^{-2}R$ is bigger than $R^{\mathcal{M}}$ or less than $R^{\mathcal{S}}$, then he/she may not obtain a useful signal over the noise even if the attacker's guess was right.

### 3.3 Properties of All BSD Type Countermeasures

In all BSD type countermeasures we justify that the following property is satisfied, i.e. the consequence of the following proposition does not depend on the choice of a recoding technique.

**Proposition 3.** $d_{[i,n]}$ *is either* $k_{[i,n-1]}$ *or* $k_{[i,n-1]} + 1$.

From Proposition 3, we can obtain a relation between the $i$-th bit $k_i$ of secret key and intermediate point $(IP_r^i)$.

**Observation 1.**

$$IP_r^i = \left(2^2 \cdot k_{[i+1,n-1]}\right) \cdot P_r \quad \text{or} \quad \left(2^2 \cdot k_{[i+1,n-1]} + 2 \cdot 1\right) \cdot P_r, \quad \text{if } k_i = 0;$$
$$IP_r^i = \left(2^2 \cdot k_{[i+1,n-1]} + 2 \cdot 1\right) \cdot P_r \quad \text{or} \quad \left(2^2 \cdot k_{[i+1,n-1]} + 2 \cdot 2\right) \cdot P_r, \quad \text{if } k_i = 1.$$

Thus we can see that there are three kinds of intermediate points. The intermediate point $IP_r^i = \left(2^2 \cdot k_{[i+1,n-1]}\right) \cdot P_r$ only appears in the case of $k_i = 0$, and $IP_r^i = \left(2^2 \cdot k_{[i+1,n-1]} + 2 \cdot 2\right) \cdot P_r$ only appears in the case of $k_i = 1$. But $IP_r^i = \left(2^2 \cdot k_{[i+1,n-1]} + 2 \cdot 1\right) \cdot P_r$ is related to both $k_i = 0$ and $k_i = 1$.

The above observation helps us to determine a discernment point $DP_r^i$ to recover $k_i$. We concretely describe how to determine discernment points in the next section.

### 3.4 Proposed Attack

Before formally describing our analytical framework, we will make some assumptions more precisely. Our analysis depends on the following assumptions:

**Assumption 1.**

(1) We assume that the scalar multiplication in Target 1 utilizes a *left-to-right computation*, i.e., the secret key is scanned from the most significant bit.

(2) We can repeatedly obtain the measurement of power consumption at the device for the fixed secret key $k$.
(3) Suppose an attacker already knows the highest bits $k_{n-1}, \ldots, k_{i+1}$ of the secret key $k$. The attacker will try to recover the next bit $k_i$ with the ordinary ZEMD attack. Assume the attacker first uses $\left(2^2 \cdot k_{[i+1,n-1]}\right) \cdot P_r$ as the discernment point to check $k_i = 0$.

The second assumption is reasonable. For some elliptic curve schemes, collecting power signals for the fixed secret key may be impossible, like the signature generation of ECDSA. However, some other schemes like ECDH are possible. We can then obtain the following result under Assumption 1.

**Proposition 4.** *If the appearance probability of the discernment point for the target bit $k_i$ is $p$ ($\neq 0$), the use of $p^{-2}R^S$ samples enables the attacker to recover $k_i$; $k_i = 0$ if an appreciable peak occurs, or $k_i = 1$ if not.*

By Proposition 4, if the attacker uses $R$ samples such that $R \geq p^{-2}R^S$ then he/she can recover $k_i$. But, there are two cases that the attacker can not find any appreciable peak over noise in the ordinary ZEMD attack, even though his/her guess is right.

**Problem 1:** The case of the probability $p = 0$. Namely, $IP_r^i = \left(2^2 \cdot k_{[i+1,n-1]} + 2 \cdot 1\right) \cdot P_r$ always occurs during $R$ executions. Thus the attacker may confuse whether $k_i$ is 0 or not.
**Problem 2:** The case that the probability $p$ is so small such that $R = p^{-2}R^S > R^M$. It implies the attacker can't use $R = p^{-2}R^S$ samples to determine $k_i$.

Furthermore, there is one more problem that it is difficult for the attacker to predict the probability $p$ in advance because the probability depends on the secret key and the used recoding method. Thus he/she can not determine the exact number of sample $R$ such that $R \geq p^{-2}R^S$.

*Remark 2.* In [24], Sim et al. assumed that the appearance probability of an intermediate point is always $1/2$ (i.e., $p = 1/2$) because of a random bit. So, they mentioned that the required number of samples should be doubled in order to detect the same height of peaks as that of the ordinary ZEMD attack on unprotected scalar multiplication algorithms. Unfortunately, the assumption is not always true. Actually, the probability depends on both the used random recoding method and the secret scalar. Thus, their attack is not practical in the sense of the number of samples.

We now describe how to solve these problems. Let us assume that we always use the maximum number of samples $R^M$ to recover $k_i$, i.e. $R = R^M$. Then the smallest probability $p$ that we can recognize appreciable peaks is $\sqrt{\frac{R^S}{R^M}}$ by Proposition 2. Let the smallest appearance probability $p = \sqrt{\frac{R^S}{R^M}}$ that an attacker can detect peaks be denoted as $\mathcal{LB}$, i.e., it means a lower bound of the appearance probability. In other words, $p \geq \mathcal{LB}$ is equivalent to $R^M \geq p^{-2}R^S$, that is, the number of used samples $R^{\mathcal{M}}$ is enough to detect some useful peak in the obtained power consumption signal. (Note that $\mathcal{LB}$ depends on the ability of an attacker because the capability to obtain $R^{\mathcal{M}}$ differs each.) From Observation 1, we can construct a new attack strategy as follows.

**The Attack Method by One Bit Guess:**

**Assumption:** We always use $R^{\mathcal{M}}$ samples, i.e., $R = R^{\mathcal{M}}$.

**Step 1:** Use the discernment point $DP_r^i = \left(2^2 \cdot k_{[i+1,n-1]}\right) \cdot P_r$. If some useful peaks appear over noise in SNR, i.e., $p \geq \mathcal{LB}$, then output $k_i = 0$

**Step 2:** Else, use another $DP_r^i = \left(2^2 \cdot k_{[i+1,n-1]} + 2 \cdot 2\right) \cdot P_r$. If some useful peaks appear over noise in SNR, i.e., $p \geq \mathcal{LB}$, then output $k_i = 1$.

**Step 3:** Otherwise, we can not determine whether $k_i$ is 0 or not because $IP_r^i = \left(2^2 \cdot k_{[i+1,n-1]} + 2 \cdot 1\right) \cdot P_r$ is operated with high probability.

We now solve the case that $k_i$ is not determined in Step 3. Assume that we guess more bits instead of one bit in the above attack. For simplicity, we explain the case of two bits guess. For all $(k_i k_{i-1})_2$, the intermediate point $IP_r^{i-1}$ is as follows:

**Observation 2.**

$IP_r^{i-1} = \left(2^3 \cdot k_{[i+1,n-1]}\right) \cdot P_r$      or $\left(2^3 \cdot k_{[i+1,n-1]} + 2 \cdot 1\right) \cdot P_r$,   if $(k_i k_{i-1})_2 = (00)_2$;
$IP_r^{i-1} = \left(2^3 \cdot k_{[i+1,n-1]} + 2 \cdot 1\right) \cdot P_r$   or $\left(2^3 \cdot k_{[i+1,n-1]} + 2 \cdot 2\right) \cdot P_r$,   if $(k_i k_{i-1})_2 = (01)_2$;
$IP_r^{i-1} = \left(2^3 \cdot k_{[i+1,n-1]} + 2 \cdot 2\right) \cdot P_r$   or $\left(2^3 \cdot k_{[i+1,n-1]} + 2 \cdot 3\right) \cdot P_r$,   if $(k_i k_{i-1})_2 = (10)_2$;
$IP_r^{i-1} = \left(2^3 \cdot k_{[i+1,n-1]} + 2 \cdot 3\right) \cdot P_r$   or $\left(2^3 \cdot k_{[i+1,n-1]} + 2 \cdot 4\right) \cdot P_r$,   if $(k_i k_{i-1})_2 = (11)_2$.

From the above observation, we can find some useful relations.

- $IP_r^{i-1} = \left(2^3 \cdot k_{[i+1,n-1]}\right) \cdot P_r$ or $\left(2^3 \cdot k_{[i+1,n-1]} + 2 \cdot 4\right) \cdot P_r$ only appears in the case of $(k_i k_{i-1})_2 = (00)_2$ or $(11)_2$, respectively.
- If $IP_r^{i-1} = \left(2^3 \cdot k_{[i+1,n-1]} + 2 \cdot 1\right) \cdot P_r$ or $\left(2^3 \cdot k_{[i+1,n-1]} + 2 \cdot 3\right) \cdot P_r$ appears, then $k_i = 0$ or 1, respectively.

There is one more good relation; for example, if the appearance probabilities for both $DP_r^{i-1} = \left(2^3 \cdot k_{[i+1,n-1]} + 2 \cdot 1\right) \cdot P_r$ and $\left(2^3 \cdot k_{[i+1,n-1]} + 2 \cdot 2\right) \cdot P_r$ satisfy the condition i.e. $p \geq \mathcal{LB}$, then we can be convinced that $(k_i k_{i-1})_2 = (01)_2$. More exactly, suppose an attacker uses $R^{\mathcal{M}} = 9R^{\mathcal{S}}$, i.e., $\mathcal{LB} = 1/3$, and $p = 0.6$ when $DP_r^{i-1} = \left(2^3 \cdot k_{[i+1,n-1]} + 2 \cdot 1\right) \cdot P_r$ and $p = 0.4$ when $DP_r^{i-1} = \left(2^3 \cdot k_{[i+1,n-1]} + 2 \cdot 2\right) \cdot P_r$. Then he/she can detect $(k_i k_{i-1})_2 = (01)_2$ because these two probabilities $p$, 0.6 and 0.4, are greater than $\mathcal{LB} = 1/3$. By recursively processing the above way, we can recover the remaining bits.

### 3.5  Simulations

In this subsection, we estimate the maximum number of consecutive guess bits and the number of trial guess required in the proposed attack by computing the appearance probability of intermediate points in software written in C-language. We carried out simulations on the proposed attack applied to Ha-Moon's method, Ebeid-Hasan's method, and that of Agagliate et al. as follows.

1. Implement Ha-Moon's method, Ebeid-Hasan's method, and that of Agagliate et al. with Addition-Subtraction Always method on typical microprocessors: Pentium IV/2GHz (32-bit $\mu$P; Windows XP, MSVC).
2. For $i = 1$ to $10,000$ do
   - Choose a 160-bit scalar randomly.
   - Obtain 10,000 random recoded numbers generated from the secret key by random recoding methods.
   - Compute the appearance probability of two intermediate points for all bits using the given 10,000 random recoded numbers, that is, $Pr[d_{[i,n]} = k_{[i,n-1]}]$ and $Pr[d_{[i,n]} = k_{[i,n-1]} + 1]$.
   - For each $\mathcal{LB}$, we recover the secret key by the proposed attack.
   - From the result of the above step, count the maximum number of consecutive guess bits and the number of trial guess.
3. Compute the average of the maximum number of consecutive guess bits and the number of trial guess for each $\mathcal{LB}$. (i.e. sum of the maximum number of consecutive guess bits / 10,000 and sum of the number of trial guess /10,000)

Table 1 shows the number of trial guess in the proposed ZEMD attack against BSD type countermeasures with Addition-Subtraction Always method depending on the ability to obtain $R^{\mathcal{M}}$. The number of trial guess means the number of discernment points used in ZEMD attack. Note that since the original ZEMD attack requires one discernment point to recover one bit, the original ZEMD attack requires $n$ times trial guess for $n$-bit secret key.

Fig. 1 shows the required number of measurements to reveal the secret key depending on the computational power of the attacker (i.e. $\mathcal{LB}$). If an attacker has the capability of guessing consecutive 10 bits then, to obtain the same SNR as Proposition 1, the required samples are about $2R^{\mathcal{S}}$ in Ha-Moon's countermeasure, $1.4R^{\mathcal{S}}$ in Ebeid-Hasan's countermeasures, and $R^{\mathcal{S}}$ in Agagliate et al.'s countermeasure. In the case of Agagliate et al.'s countermeasure, we can recover the secret key with the same number of samples as the ordinary ZEMD attack.

From Fig. 1 and Table 1, we can derive the following conclusion. If we use $10R^{\mathcal{S}}$ samples then $\mathcal{LB} \approx 0.32$. Thus we can determine the whole 160-bits secret key using 1987 trial guess before at most 10-bits consecutive guess in Ha-Moon's method, 596 trial guess before at most 7-bits consecutive guess in Ebeid-Hasan's method, and 2915 trial guess before at most 9-bits consecutive guess in Agagliate

**Table 1.** For a 160-bit secret key, the number of trial guess in the proposed ZEMD attack against BSD type countermeasures with SPA countermeasure depending on the ability to obtain $R^{\mathcal{M}}$

| Countermeasures | $R^{\mathcal{M}}$ | | | | | |
|---|---|---|---|---|---|---|
| | $2R^{\mathcal{S}}$ | $5R^{\mathcal{S}}$ | $10R^{\mathcal{S}}$ | $20R^{\mathcal{S}}$ | $50R^{\mathcal{S}}$ | $100R^{\mathcal{S}}$ |
| Ha-Moon [8] | 16484 | 2716 | 1987 | 1480 | 1019 | 868 |
| Ebeid-Hasan [5] | 1515 | 711 | 596 | 543 | 508 | 478 |
| Agagliate et al. [1] | 4004 | 2917 | 2915 | 2898 | 2896 | 2893 |

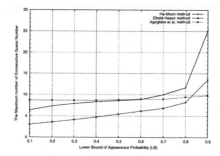

**Fig. 1.** Relationship between the number of samples $R^{\mathcal{M}}$ and the maximum number of consecutive guess bits for a 160-bits secret key

et al.'s method. From these observations, we can see that the proposed ZEMD is as practical as the ordinary ZEMD attack.

## 4    Enhancing the Proposed Attack

The proposed attack can be enhanced in two ways: (1) against *right-to-left* computation. (2) against BSD type countermeasure combined with a *DPA countermeasure*.

### 4.1    Attack for Right-to-Left Algorithm

The proposed attack is also applicable to *right-to-left computation*. In order to construct an attack against a right-to-left algorithm, we use the following property:

**Proposition 5.** $d_{[0,i]}$ *is either* $k_{[0,i]}$ *or* $k_{[0,i]} - 2^{i+1}$.

Proposition 5 is easily derived from Proposition 3. We obtain the relation between $k_i$ and intermediate point $IP_r^i$. Here, $IP_r^i$ denotes the intermediate point which is actually calculated at ECADD after $j = i$ bit $(k_i)$ calculation for the $r$-th execution in a right-to-left version of Addition-Subtraction_Always method.

**Observation 3.**

$$IP_r^i = \left(k_{[0,i-1]} + 2^{i+1}\right) \cdot P_r \quad \text{or} \quad k_{[0,i-1]} \cdot P_r, \qquad \text{if } k_i = 0;$$
$$IP_r^i = \left(k_{[0,i-1]} + 2^i + 2^{i+1}\right) \cdot P_r \quad \text{or} \quad \left(k_{[0,i-1]} + 2^i\right) \cdot P_r, \quad \text{if } k_i = 1.$$

By above observation, the intermediate points for $k_i = 0$ are totally different from those for $k_i = 1$. Thus the proposed attack against right-to-left algorithms can use both cases of intermediate points for $k_i$ as the discernment point, e.g. the discernment point could be $\left(k_{[0,i-1]} + 2^{i+1}\right) \cdot P_r$ or $k_{[0,i-1]} \cdot P_r$ to check $k_i = 0$.

**Proposition 6.** *In Right-to-Left algorithm, the number of try to detect secret key bit $k_i$ is at most two times. As there is no collision between intermediate points for $k_i = 0$ and intermediate points for $k_i = 1$, first we use $IP_r^i = (k_{[0,i-1]} + 2^{i+1}) \cdot P_r$, if we detect useful peaks over noise with SNR then $k_i$ is 0. Otherwise, we try again with $IP_r^i = k_{[0,i-1]} \cdot P_r$. If we find useful peaks over noise with SNR then $k_i$ is 0, otherwise $k_i$ is 1.*

Therefore, the proposed attack against right-to-left algorithms can recover the secret key bit by bit as the similar to the ordinary ZEMD attack. Thus the proposed attack against a right-to-left algorithm is more simple and efficient than that against a left-to-right one.

*Remark 3.* Since Oswald-Aigner's method [20] is a right-to-left algorithm, it is very easily broken using the proposed attack against right-to-left algorithms.

## 4.2   RPA Attack

In this section, we discuss the security of BSD type countermeasures combined with a DPA countermeasure using randomized point representation methods.

In order to strengthen the security of BSD type countermeasures, the BSD type may further be combined with some DPA countermeasures using randomized point representation methods such as randomized projective coordinates [4] or random isomorphisms method [11] before scalar multiplications.

However, Goubin proposed the refined power analysis (RPA) using "special point" $(x, 0)$ and $(0, y)$ that cannot be randomized by randomized point representation techniques [7]. Thus the proposed attack can also break BSD type countermeasures combined with randomized point representation methods by using the "special point" as a discernment point.

Note that other notations and assumptions are the same as those in the previous sections with the exception of combining Addition-Subtraction_Always method with DPA countermeasure. We can then find two differences between DPA and RPA as follows:

**SNR of RPA in the Case Using BSD Type Countermeasures:** Similar to DPA on Addition-Subtraction_Always method described in Proposition 1 and 2, we propose a proposition which deals with SNR of RPA on Addition-Subtraction_Always method with the DPA countermeasure using randomized point representation.

**Proposition 7.** *Assume that the computational environment is the same as Proposition 1. If the appearance probability of the "special" point $P_0$ is $p'$, then the signal-to-noise ratio is*

$$SNR = \frac{\varepsilon p' M \sqrt{R}}{\sqrt{8\sigma^2 + \varepsilon^2 (\alpha M + M - M p')}}. \tag{3}$$

*Thus the SNR is approximately $p'$ times larger than the original RPA. In other words, in order to obtain the same SNR as the original, the required samples are $p'^{-2}$ times larger than the original.*

Note that the proof of it is similar to that of Proposition 2 and refer to the Theorem 3 in [16]. Actually, the appearance probability $p$ of the discernment point in the proposed ZEMD attack is exactly the same as the appearance probability $p'$ of the "special" point $P_0$.

*Remark 4.* Proposition 7 shows that an attacker requires approximately $M^{-2}R$ samples to obtain the same SNR as Proposition 2 (for the proposed ZEMD attack).

**Adaptively Chosen Data Attack:** RPA is an adaptively chosen data attack. Since RPA requires the special point for detecting a specific bit of the scalar, the observed samples cannot be reused. That is, for detecting each bit, the attacker has to observe power consumptions for new data. So, in the proposed RPA attack, the maximum number of samples that the attacker can use for each trial guess is $R^M$/*the number of trial guess* on average. Thus, the symbol $\mathcal{LB} = \sqrt{R^S/R^M}$ used in the new attack strategy in section 3.4 is replaced with $\sqrt{(R^S \times \textit{the number of trial guess})/R^M}$ For a more successful attack we can use more smaller samples if $R^M$/*the number of trial guess* $> R^M/M^2$ and more larger samples if not, but the total number of samples should be less than $R^M$.

*Remark 5.* We can easily convert the RPA attack into the attack on a right-to-left computation using Proposition 5.

## 5    Comparison

As described in the previous sections, the basic BSD type countermeasures are vulnerable to various attacks. So, the BSD type countermeasures should be combined with additional countermeasures to resist SPA and DPA. In the section, when some countermeasures are added to BSD type countermeasures we compare the proposed attack with previously known attacks introduced by Fouque et al. and Sim et al. and the hidden Markov model (HMM) attack [2] [14] for the left-to-right computation and the right-to-left computation, respectively.

Table 2 shows the possibilities of attacks against several combined countermeasures and the direction of computation. We first consider BSD type countermeasures combined with the SPA countermeasure. Fouque et al. and Sim et al. analyzed the full version of Ha-Moon's method. So, the possibility of their attacks against the other BSD type countermeasures may be determined according to the given random recoding method. However, the attack of Fouque et al. is based on detection of internal data collisions, so their attack may be able to apply without regard to the direction of computation algorithms at a glance. On the other hand, the HMM attack is available under the assumption of distinguishability between ECADD and ECDBL. Thus, the HMM attack seems unable to break the BSD type combined with SPA countermeasures.

---

[2] The attack introduced by Karlof and Wagner utilizes the hidden Markov model (HMM) to break BSD type countermeasure, which is a cryptanalytic framework for countermeasures that utilizes a probabilistic finite state machine.

**Table 2.** Comparison of possibility for several combined BSD type countermeasures

| Attacks | Left-to-Right computation | | Right-to-Left computation | | Attack Model |
|---|---|---|---|---|---|
| | with SPA C. | with DPA C. | with SPA C. | with DPA C. | |
| Fouque et al. | Dependent | Infeasible | Dependent | Infeasible | MESD |
| Sim et al. | Dependent | Infeasible | Infeasible | Infeasible | ZEMD |
| HMM | Infeasible | Infeasible | Infeasible | Infeasible | HMM |
| Ours | Feasible | Feasible | Feasible | Feasible | ZEMD |

*Note.* SPA C. and DPA C. denote SPA countermeasure and DPA countermeasure, respectively.
*Note.* We consider the fixed procedure type such as Coron's dummy method or Montgomery ladder method as an SPA countermeasure, and the randomized point representation type such as randomized projective coordinates or random isomorphisms as a DPA countermeasure.
*Note.* "Feasible" means that the attack can break all combined countermeasures, "Infeasible" means that the attack can not break any combined countermeasure, and "Dependent" means that the possibility of the attack depends on random recoding methods.

In the case of BSD type countermeasures combined with the DPA countermeasure, the attack of Fouque et al., the attack of Sim et al., and the HMM attack can not break the combined BSD type countermeasures. However, we have shown that BSD type countermeasures combined with DPA countermeasures using randomized point representations such as randomized projective coordinates [4] or random isomorphisms [11] are vulnerable to the proposed RPA attack.

*Remark 6.* In order to strengthen the security of BSD type countermeasures there are other possible approaches, that is, if BSD type countermeasures are combined with the indistinguishable operations type using the same addition formulae [2] or random point blinding type such as Coron's second method and random initial point method [18], then BSD type countermeasures may be secure against not only the proposed attacks but also the other attacks.

In addition, another difference between the proposed attack and the attack of Fouque et al. is the analysis model. The model of Fouque et al. is based on the collision detection, which is rather different from the usual SCA model. To find collisions their attack utilizes "Multiple Exponent Single Data" (MESD) technique. The MESD requires that an attacker has two identical devices with the same algorithm: one with an unknown secret scalar and the other with a chosen scalar by oneself. In order to recover the unknown secret scalar, we compare the power consumptions of two devices. If the power consumptions are similar then the scalars equal each other, otherwise, the scalars differ. However, such a situation may be less practical than ZEMD technique, which only requires a device with an unknown secret scalar.

## 6   Concluding Remarks

In this paper, we have enhanced the existing attacks against the full version of Ha-Moon's method, and then we have proposed a practical attack applicable to all BSD type countermeasures combined with an SPA countermeasure. We showed that the proposed attack is as practical as the original ZEMD attack by the simulations on the target countermeasures.

We have further enhanced the proposed attack in two ways. The proposed attack is extended to a right-to-left computation and BSD type combined with a DPA countermeasure. That is, in order to repair the security, if BSD type countermeasures are combined with a right-to-left computation or DPA countermeasures such as randomized projective coordinates or random isomorphisms, then it may be vulnerable to the proposed attack.

## Acknowledgments

Tae Hyun Kim and Jongin Lim were supported by the MIC(Ministry of Information and Communication), Korea, under the ITRC(Information Technology Research Center) support program supervised by the IITA(Institute of Information Technology Assessment). Dong-Guk Han was supported by the Korea Research Foundation Grant. (KRF-2005-214-C00016).

## References

1. Agagliate, S., Guillot, P., Orcière, O., *A Randomized Efficient Algorithm for DPA Secure Implementation of elliptic curve Cryptosystems*, in the proceedings of Workshop on Coding and Cryptography 2003 (WCC 2003), (2003), 11-19.
2. Brier, É., Joye, M., *Weierstrass Elliptic Curves and Side-Channel Attacks*, Public Key Cryptography (PKC2002), LNCS2274, (2002), 335-345.
3. Chevallier-Mames, B., Ciet, M., Joye, M., *Low-cost solutions for preventing simple side-channel analysis: side-channel atomicity*, IEEE Trans. Computers, Vol.53, No.6, (2004), 760-768.
4. Coron, J.S., *Resistance against Differential Power Analysis for Elliptic Curve Cryptosystems*, Cryptographic Hardware and Embedded Systems (CHES'99), LNCS1717, (1999), 292-302.
5. Ebeid, N., Hasan, A., *Analysis of DPA Countermeasures Based on Randomizing the Binary Algorithm*, Technical Report of the University of Waterloo, No. CORR 2003-14. http://www.cacr.math.uwaterloo.ca/techreports/2003/corr2003-14.ps
6. Fouque, P.A., Muller, F., Poupard, G., and Valette, F., *Defeating Countermeasures Based on Randomized BSD Representations*, Cryptographic Hardware and Embedded Systems 2004 (CHES 2004), LNCS3156, (2004), 312-327.
7. Goubin, L., *A Refined Power-Analysis Attack on Elliptic Curve Cryptosystems*, Public Key Cryptography, (PKC 2003), LNCS2567, (2003), 199-211.
8. Ha, J., and Moon, S., *Randomized Signed-Scalar Multiplication of ECC to Resist Power Attacks*, Cryptographic Hardware and Embedded Systems 2002 (CHES 2002), LNCS2523, (2002), 551-563.
9. Han, D.-G., Okeya, K., Kim, T.H., Hwang, Y.S., Park, Y.-H., Jung, S., *Cryptanalysis of the Countermeasures Using Randomized Binary Signed Digits*, Applied Cryptography and Network Security (ACNS'04), LNCS3089, (2004), 398-413.
10. Joye, M., Paillier, P., Schoenmakers, B., *On Second-Order Differential Power Analysis*, Cryptographic Hardware and Embedded Systems (CHES'05), LNCS3659, (2005), 293-308.

11. Joye, M., Tymen, C., *Protections against differential analysis for elliptic curve cryptography: An algebraic approach*, Cryptographic Hardware and Embedded Systems (CHES'01), LNCS2162, (2001), 377-390.

12. Kocher, C., Jaffe, J., Jun, B., *Differential Power Analysis*, Advances in Cryptology - CRYPTO '99, LNCS1666, (1999), 388-397.

13. Koblitz, N., *Elliptic curve cryptosystems*, Math. Comp. 48, (1987), 203-209.

14. Karlof, C., Wagner, D., *Hidden Markov Model Cryptanalysis*, Cryptographic Hardware and Embedded Systems (CHES 2003), LNCS2779, (2003), 17-34.

15. Messerges, T.S., Dabbish, E.A., Sloan, R.H., *Power Analysis Attacks of Modular Exponentiation in Smartcards*, Cryptographic Hardware and Embedded System (CHES 1999), LNCS1717, (1999), 144-157.

16. Messerges, T.S., Dabbish, E.A., Sloan, R.H., *Examining Smart-Card Security under the Threat of Power Analysis Attacks*, IEEE Trans. Computers, Vol.51, No.5, (2002), 541-552.

17. Miller, V.S., *Use of elliptic curves in cryptography*, Advances in Cryptology - CRYPTO '85, LNCS218, (1986), 417-426.

18. Mamiya, H., Miyaji, A., and Morimoto, H., *Efficient Countermeasures Against RPA, DPA, and SPA*, Hardware and Embedded System (CHES 2004), LNCS3156, (2004), 343-356.

19. Montgomery, P. L., *Speeding the Pollard and elliptic curve methods of factorization*, Mathematics of Computation, Vol.48, No.177, (1987), 243-264.

20. Oswald, E., Aigner, M., *Randomized Addition-Subtraction Chains as a Countermeasure against Power Attacks*, Cryptographic Hardware and Embedded Systems (CHES 2001), LNCS2162, (2001), 39-50.

21. Okeya, K., Han, D.-G., *Side Channel Attack on Ha-Moon's Countermeasure of Randomized Signed Scalar Multiplication*, INDOCRYPT 2003, LNCS2904, (2003), 334-348.

22. Okeya, K., Sakurai, K., *Power Analysis Breaks Elliptic Curve Cryptosystems even Secure against the Timing Attack*, INDOCRYPT 2000, LNCS1977, (2000), 178-190.

23. Okeya, K., Sakurai, K., *On Insecurity of the Side Channel Attack Countermeasure using Addition-Subtraction Chains under Distinguishability between Addition and Doubling*, The 7th Australasian Conference in Information Security and Privacy, (ACISP 2002), LNCS2384, (2002), 420-435.

24. Sim, S.G., Park, D.J., Lee, P.J., *New power analyses on the Ha-Moon algorithm and the MIST algorithm*, Sixth International Conference on Information and Communication Security (ICICS 2004), LNCS3269, (2004), 291-304.

25. Walter, C.D., *Issues of Security with the Oswald-Aigner Exponentiation Algorithm*, The Cryptographers' Track at the RSA Conference 2004 (CT-RSA'04), LNCS2964, (2004), 208-221.

26. Walter, C.D., *Simple Power Analysis of Unified Code for ECC Double and Add*, Cryptographic Hardware and Embedded Systems (CHES'04), LNCS3156 , (2004), 191-204.

# A    Several Proofs

**Proposition 2.** *Assume that the computational environment is the same as Proposition 1. If the appearance probability of a discernment point is $p$, then the signal-to-noise ratio is*

$$SNR = \frac{\varepsilon p \sqrt{R}}{\sqrt{8\sigma^2 + \varepsilon^2(\alpha M + M - p)}}. \tag{4}$$

*Thus the SNR is approximately p times larger than the original. In other words, in order to obtain the same SNR, the required samples are $p^{-2}$ times larger than the original.*

*Proof.* Recall that SNR is defined as the ratio of the average signal divided by its standard deviation.

Since the discernment point appears with the probability $p$, the signal is $p$ times larger than the original; $E[signal] = \varepsilon p$. If the discernment point does not appear, we can consider such a case as noise; $E[noise] = 0$.

On the one hand, non-algorithmic noise does not depend on the input data. On the other hand, algorithmic noise can be seen as $(M - signal/\varepsilon)$ random bits; $(M - p)$ random bits. Thus, it is easy to see that the variance of the signal is $V[signal] = 4(\sigma^2 + \varepsilon^2(M - p)/4)/R$. If the discernment point does not appear, the variance of the noise is $v[noise] = 4(\sigma^2 + \varepsilon^2 \alpha M/4)/R$.

Hence, in the current case, the average is $p\varepsilon$ and the standard deviation is

$$\sqrt{8\sigma^2 + \varepsilon^2(\alpha M + M - p)}/\sqrt{R}.$$

In other words, SNR satisfies the equation (2).    □

**Proposition 3.** $d_{[i,n]}$ *is either* $k_{[i,n-1]}$ *or* $k_{[i,n-1]} + 1$.

*Proof.* $d = d_{[i,n]} \cdot 2^i + d_{[0,i-1]}$ and $k = k_{[i,n-1]} \cdot 2^i + k_{[0,i-1]}$. As $d = k$, $(d_{[i,n]} - k_{[i,n-1]}) \cdot 2^i = k_{[0,i-1]} - d_{[0,i-1]}$. As $-2^i < k_{[0,i-1]} - d_{[0,i-1]} < 2^{i+1}$, $-1 < (k_{[0,i-1]} - d_{[0,i-1]})/2^i < 2$. Here, $(k_{[0,i-1]} - d_{[0,i-1]})/2^i$ must be an integer since it is equal to $d_{[i,n]} - k_{[i,n-1]}$. Hence, $d_{[i,n]}$ is either $k_{[i,n-1]}$ or $k_{[i,n-1]} + 1$.    □

**Proposition 4.** *Assume that an attacker can recognize whether the peak occurs or not using $R^S$ samples in the case of* Double_Add_Always *method. If the appearance probability of the discernment point for the target bit $k_i$ is $p$, the use of $p^{-2}R^S$ samples enables the attacker to recover $k_i$; $k_i = 0$ if an appreciable peak occurs, or $k_i = 1$ if not.*

*Proof.* First we discuss the case of $k_i = 0$. When Addition-Subtraction_Always _method manipulates the $i$-th bit $d_i^{(r)}$, $d_{[i,n]}^{(r)}$ is computed, which is equal to $2 \cdot k_{[i+1,n-1]}$ or $2 \cdot k_{[i+1,n-1]} + 1$ because of Proposition 3, The next iteration of the flow computes $\left(4 \cdot k_{[i+1,n-1]}\right) \cdot P$ or $\left(4 \cdot k_{[i+1,n-1]} + 2\right) \cdot P$. Note that the former is the discernment point. From the assumption, the appearance probability of the discernment point is $p$. Proposition 2 shows that the use of $p^{-2}R^S$ samples enables the attacker to recognize the peak because of the assumption for his/her capability. Since the peak shows that the attacker's guess is correct, he/she reveals $k_i = 0$. The discussion on the case for $k_i = 1$ is similar.    □

# Amplifying Side-Channel Attacks with Techniques from Block Cipher Cryptanalysis

Raphael C.-W. Phan[1] and Sung-Ming Yen[2,*]

[1] Information Security Research (iSECURES) Lab,
Swinburne University of Technology (Sarawak Campus), 93576 Kuching, Malaysia
rphan@swinburne.edu.my
[2] Laboratory of Cryptography and Information Security (LCIS),
Dept of Computer Science and Information Engineering,
National Central University, Chung-Li, Taiwan 320, R.O.C.
yensm@csie.ncu.edu.tw
http://www.csie.ncu.edu.tw/~yensm/

**Abstract.** We introduce the notion of *amplified side-channel attacks*, i.e. the application of block cipher cryptanalysis techniques to amplify effects exploitable by side-channel attacks. Such an approach is advantageous since it fully exploits the special characteristics of each technique in situations where each thrives the most. As an example, we consider the integration of block cipher cryptanalysis techniques into a particular type of side-channel attack, the differential fault attack (DFA). In more detail, we apply the DFA on the AES key schedule or on intermediate states within the AES and then exploit distinguishers based on Square attacks and impossible differential cryptanalysis to cover the remaining rounds. The use of techniques from conventional differential cryptanalysis in DFAs is not new; however, to the best of our knowledge, more advanced differential-like attack techniques have so far not been applied in collaboration with DFA. Further, while previous DFA attacks can only be mounted if faults are induced in the last or first (but with more restrictions) few rounds, our attacks alternatively show that even when faults are induced into some middle rounds, the DFA attacks still work, complementing existing results in literature; and thus showing that DFA attacks work regardless of where faults are induced. This is of importance because redundancy is a costly countermeasure against DFA and thus it is vital to study which rounds have to be protected. We hope that this completes the picture on the applicability of DFAs to block ciphers, and motivates thoughts into applying other advanced block cipher cryptanalysis techniques into other types of side-channel attacks.

**Keywords:** Attacks and countermeasures in hardware and software, side-channel attacks, cryptanalysis, fault attacks, Advanced Encryption Standard.

* S.-M. Yen's research in this work was supported in part by the National Science Council of the Republic of China under contract NSC 94-2213-E-008-009 and also the University IT Research Center Project.

J. Domingo-Ferrer, J. Posegga, and D. Schreckling (Eds.): CARDIS 2006, LNCS 3928, pp. 135–150, 2006.

# 1    Introduction

Since the introduction of side-channel attacks [11, 27, 28], the importance of designing block ciphers resistant to these attacks has been in the limelight, and this resistance is now part of a cipher's design criteria. Security against side-channel attacks is especially significant in situations where ciphers are implemented in hardware like smart cards or tamper-resistant devices, where secrets are meant to be closely guarded and thus no room for compromise via leakage of secrets.

The study of block cipher cryptanalysis has developed tremendously in recent years. Attacks on block ciphers can typically be grouped into two major types, namely block cipher cryptanalysis which attacks the block cipher's design, and the side-channel attacks (also known as physical cryptanalysis [39]) which attack the block cipher's implementation. Each of these two categories of cryptanalysis has its own cryptanalytic assumption and theoretical foundation. Block-cipher cryptanalysis has been considered extensively in literature, while the physical cryptanalysis is still a somewhat new branch of research in applied cryptography.

Block cipher cryptanalysis refers to attacks that exploit the intrinsic weaknesses of block cipher components, e.g. differential cryptanalysis (DC) [7], linear cryptanalysis [30], slide attacks [9] and rectangle attacks [5]. Meanwhile, side-channel attacks are those that exploit potential physical properties or signal leakages, or bugs that occur when these block ciphers are implemented in particular situations and devices. Such attacks include timing analysis [27], power analysis [28], electromagnetic (EM) analysis [1], and fault analysis [8, 11].

Different though they be, both block cipher cryptanalysis and side-channel attacks have their own individual advantages over each other. More recently, block cipher cryptanalysis has considered more realistic attack models by fully exploiting advances of every kind of computing machine, e.g., developing specific cryptanalysis hardware based on reconfigurable devices e.g. field programmable gate arrays (FPGAs). Block cipher cryptanalysis has hence gone beyond pure theoretical work and now also considers practical issues. On the other hand, side-channel attacks in recent years have gone much further than merely exploiting implementation bugs. They sometimes fully exploit fundamental characteristics of the underlying cipher or related algorithms used to implement the cipher, and at times these attacks might reveal a possible vulnerability of the cipher. Side-channel attacks have hence moved towards theoretical design aspects. As both types of attacks gradually progress towards each other, it seems feasible therefore to consider bridging the gap by directly integrating attacks of both types so that we could exploit and use either type to suit the situation in which they thrive the most. This is the intent of this paper.

We discuss attempts to integrate side-channel attacks, including those in [2, 33, 38]. We then proceed with the first main contribution of this paper, i.e. to introduce the notion of *amplified side-channel attacks* which refers to the integration of one or more block cipher cryptanalysis techniques into side-channel attacks. In particular, we show that in situations where the effects due to conventional side-channel attacks on their own may be lost after some rounds of the cipher, we can apply techniques from block cipher cryptanalysis to amplify these effects so that they cover more rounds and become more distinguishable.

To illustrate this, we consider the particular integration of the Square attack and the impossible differential attack into the differential fault analysis (DFA) [8], a type of side-channel attack. We apply this to the AES [13].

The second main contribution of this paper is that our approach of integrating block cipher cryptanalysis techniques into the DFA makes a much *weaker* assumption on the fault location in that it does not restrict the fault location to be within the last (or sometimes first[1]) few rounds only, as is the case with previous DFAs [10, 12, 15, 19, 32]. This leads to a more reasonable attack from the view point of fault attacks, and a less restricted attack model.

We therefore see that the advantages of our amplified approach is twofold. One, it allows the individual power of block cipher cryptanalysis techniques to be fully exploited by side-channel attacks. Side-channel attacks on their own would not be able to cover as many rounds of a cipher. Two, it allows DFA attacks to be mounted with a more flexible attack model, that faults could be induced even in rounds where previous DFAs are inapplicable. This study is important because redundancy is a costly countermeasure against DFA, thus one should ascertain exactly which rounds need to be protected.

Our attacks do not improve on previous work in situations where previous attacks are applicable, but our contribution is in showing that situations previously not susceptible to DFAs can now be attacked. Our work here therefore complement previous work; and together they show the universality of DFAs and how important it is to guard against them.

In the process, our discussions also provide an insight into the link between side-channel attacks and techniques from block cipher cryptanalysis.

## 1.1   Attack Models: Block Cipher Cryptanalysis vs Side Channels

Block cipher cryptanalysis assumes an attacker has access to or control over input plaintexts and corresponding output ciphertexts – and even secret key relationships in the case of related-key (RK) attacks. He has no access to or control over what happens within the cipher's encryption process but knows the internal structure of the block cipher and exploits this to his advantage.

In contrast, side-channel attacks assume an attacker has much more access or control, not only over the inputs and outputs but also able to induce differences into intermediate rounds (via DFA) and/or predicting behaviour in these intermediate rounds (via timing, power or EM traces). Similarly, he also exploits his knowledge of the internal block cipher structure.

Therefore, the attack model used in side-channel attacks is much more powerful compared to that used in block cipher cryptanalysis. In fact, the former can be considered a superset of the latter.

---

[1] But with a higher text complexity or stricter text requirements.

## 1.2 Outline of This Paper

We describe the AES in Section 2. We recall in Section 3 previous attempts to integrate different side-channel attacks, and propose the notion of amplified side-channel attacks. In Section 4, we review past work on the DFA of the AES. We also comment on limitations of three DFA countermeasures proposed in [12] and argue that they would still allow for DFA to work. This observation recalls the importance of the DFA and its applicability to the proposed attacks considered in this paper. We then show in Section 5 how we could exploit techniques from the Square attack and impossible differential cryptanalysis to cause DFAs to work in situations where they were previously inapplicable. We conclude in Section 6.

## 2   The AES

The AES is a 128-bit block cipher which uses a 128-, 192- or 256-bit secret key, where the number of rounds are then 10, 12 and 14, respectively. For the rest of this paper, we will use AES to refer to the much-analysed 128-bit secret key version, unless otherwise stated. The 128-bit data block of the AES can be represented as a matrix of $4 \times 4$ bytes.

The input 128-bit block is passed through a round function, $\rho$ iterated $R$ times, hence $R$ is the number of rounds. Simultaneously, the secret key, $K$ is input to a key schedule to produce round keys $RK_i$ ($i \in \{0 \ldots R\}$) for use in each round. Each round function consists of four components applied in sequence:

- SubBytes,SB: a non-linear byte substitution.
- ShiftRows,SR: a cyclic shift of each row by different byte amounts.
- MixColumns,MC: a linear combination of all 4 bytes in the same column.
- AddRoundKey,AR$_i$: an exclusive-OR of data block with round key, $RK_i$.

Each round is identical except that an additional AddRoundKey is added before the first round and MixColumn is excluded from the last round.

## 3   Amplified Side-Channel Attacks

In this section, we first discuss previous attempts to integrate side-channel attacks, and then introduce the notion of *amplified side-channel attacks*.

In side-channel attacks, the attacker derives the embedded secret key by collecting and analyzing the obtained side-channel signals, or abnormal behavior and response in the case of fault-based attacks. Integrating several side-channel attacks means that the attacker collects multiple side-channel signals simultaneously and tries to obtain more information than what would be achieved from each attack if only applied individually. This enables the attacker to deduce possible secrets from each side-channel, then either intersect the results from individual side-channels to obtain the secret key, or deduce the secret key from the union of all collected side-channel signals. Furthermore, the secret key can sometimes be deduced from some useful relationship between different side-channel signals. To summarize, the purpose of integrating side-channel attacks is to optimize the information retrieved from the limited amount of individual side-channel information.

Agrawal et al. [2] proposed a formal *multi-channel attack* framework for integrating multiple side-channel attacks, in particular by simultaneously collecting the power and electromagnetic signals. They demonstrated that integrating such multiple side-channel signals in the scenario considered in their work will lead to a two- to three-fold reduction in the requirement of samples needed for a traditional *differential power analysis* (DPA) attack [28]. In [38], another combined side-channel attack was developed by Walter and Thompson which employs previous techniques for timing attacks in order to exploit useful timing information from power signals. Note that this combined side-channel attack is applicable to a pure timing-attack-resistant and pure power-attack-resistant device. Later on, the efficiency of this integrated attack was enhanced by a factor of five and generalized considerably by Schindler [33].

### 3.1  Integrating Block Cipher Cryptanalysis with Side Channels

Though most side-channel attacks apply to full rounds of the cipher, they also have restrictions. For example, the differential fault analysis (DFA) requires that the attacker induce faults into some final rounds of a cipher. Faults induced earlier cannot be exploited by conventional DFA attacks. It is therefore reasonable to consider integrating block cipher cryptanalysis techniques into side-channel attacks to cover more rounds of the attacked cipher.

Referring to our example of the DFA, its limitation of requiring faults to be induced in the final rounds of the cipher can be overcome by allowing faults to be induced much earlier, and then applying block cipher cryptanalysis techniques to the rounds after where the fault was induced. Later in Section 5, we will show two examples of such *amplified side-channel attacks* on the AES, namely the Square-DFA and Impossible-DFA attacks.

Also in [34, 35], Schramm et al. proposed to overcome limitations of collision attacks on cipher implementations by using techniques from either the power analysis [28] or electromagnetic (EM) analysis [1], both of which are side-channel attacks. In more detail, collision attacks had so far been applied successfully to hash functions [14] and are essentially variants of the differential cryptanalysis in that they study the propagation of a collision − which is a non-difference − between a pair through some internal rounds. Nevertheless, collisions eventually disappear as the rounds increase, due to the diffusing nature of round functions, and hence cannot be directly observed at the output. Schramm et al. overcame this limitation by measuring the power or EM traces of the cipher implementation in the second round in order to predict whether collisions had occurred in the first round. To trigger such collisions, they collected sufficiently many chosen plaintext pairs with certain differences for input to the cipher.

Therefore, the collision side-channel attack proposed by Schramm et al. can in fact be viewed as the combination of differential cryptanalysis techniques with the power or EM attack. We remark that this attack also falls into our amplified side-channel attack framework, though in direct complement to our Square/Impossible-DFA in Section 5. Whereas our Square/Impossible-DFA uses block cipher cryptanalysis techniques to enhance the effects of side-channel attacks, Schramm et al.'s collision side-channel uses side-channel techniques to enhance the effects of block cipher cryptanalysis.

We consider the unique advantages of each of the relevant block cipher cryptanalysis techniques or side-channel attacks:

- KP attack: allows attacker to obtain random plaintexts.
- CP attack: allows attacker to choose plaintexts with specific differences.
- RK attack: allows attacker to know or choose relationships (differences) between two or more unknown secret keys.
- DC attack: studies the propagation of differences between pairs through rounds of a cipher, and checks for corresponding differences at cipher output.
- DFA: allows attacker to induce differences into an intermediate round of a cipher.
- Timing/Power/EM attack: allows attacker to predict the behaviour (eg. difference or non-difference/collision) in some intermediate round of a cipher.

With this, we formalize the notion of the amplified side-channel attack:

**Definition 1.** *The amplified side-channel attack integrates block cipher cryptanalysis techniques with side-channel attacks, and consists of the following steps:*

1. (a) Use KP attack to collect some random plaintexts and/or RK attack to control relationship between two or more secret keys, OR
   (b) Use CP attack to control input plaintexts and/or RK attack to control relationship between two or more secret keys, OR
   (c) Use FA (fault attack) to induce differences into intermediate rounds of the cipher.
2. (a) Use DC attack to study propagation of differences through rounds and further use observed output to guess secret key bits, OR
   (b) Use timing, power or EM attack to predict difference or non-difference behaviour in intermediate rounds to guess secret key bits.

We can now express block cipher cryptanalysis, side-channel attacks or their combination under this amplified side-channel framework. e.g. differential cryptanalysis is simply the sequence of steps <1(b),2(a)>, timing/power/EM attack is <1(a),2(b)> or at times simply <2(b)>, DFA is <1(c),2(a)>, collision side-channel is <1(b),2(b)> and Square/Impossible-DFA (Section 5) is <1(c),2(a)>.

## 4    Previous DFAs on the AES and Countermeasures

In this section, we review past work on the DFA of AES. We also comment on the limitations of three DFA countermeasures proposed in [12] and argue that they would still allow for the DFA to work. All this recalls the importance of the DFA and the difficulty of guarding against it. This will motivate the choice of integrating the block cipher cryptanalysis techniques into the DFA in Section 5.

## 4.1    Previous DFAs on the AES

Blömer and Seifert [10] first considered the DFA on AES but worked with a restricted fault model. Their first attack required that a certain chosen bit of the intermediate state just after $AR_0$ be forced to 0, and required 128 faulty ciphertexts in order to determine the full key. Their second attack is implementation-dependent, and requires 256 faulty ciphertexts to obtain the full key.

This was followed by two attacks on the AES by Giraud [19]. The first attack also required to induce a bit fault at the beginning of the last round, $R$, and required 50 faulty ciphertexts. The second attack required 250 faulty ciphertexts and the faults had to be induced on a byte of the round keys, $RK_{R-2}$, and $RK_{R-1}$, and on the intermediate state before the second to last round, $R - 1$.

Later, Dusart, Letourneux and Vivolo [15] presented another attack that required a fault to be induced on a byte before MC in the second to last round, $R - 1$ and required about 50 faulty ciphertexts.

Chen and Yen [12] improved on Giraud's second attack to require about 30 faulty ciphertexts. Their attack similarly needed several byte faults to be induced in the last few rounds, but all on the round keys and none on intermediate states. In particular, faults had to be induced one at a time on one of four bytes of $RK_{R-1}$, followed by faults one at a time on each of 7 bytes of $RK_{R-2}$. Their attack model is efficient on AES key schedules that are generated on the fly.

Piret and Quisquater [32] presented two attacks on the AES. Their first attack required 8 faulty ciphertexts and that a byte fault be induced on the intermediate state between MC in round $R - 2$ and MC in round $R - 1$. Their second attack requires 2 faulty ciphertexts and that a byte fault be induced on the intermediate state between MC in round $R - 3$ and MC in round $R - 2$.

## 4.2    Comments on Countermeasures Against DFA

In [12], Chen and Yen presented a DFA on the AES key schedule based on three stages. The first stage involves inducing a fault in a byte of the 9th round key, $RK_9$. The next stage involves inducing a fault in a byte of the 8th round key, $RK_8$. Finally, the last stage involves inducing another fault in a different byte of the 8th round key, $RK_8$. All in all, the attack requires less than 30 faulty ciphertexts. Their attack depended on a fault being induced in the middle of the key schedule, as the round keys are generated on the fly, and hence relies on an induced fault in a round key inducing further faults on subsequent round keys and propagating the faults all the way to the ciphertext output.

Therefore, such an attack would have to occur during key accesses, during which faults are induced as the round keys are generated. Besides this limitation of their fault model, Chen and Yen also suggested some countermeasures [12].

Their first countermeasure suggests that in order to prevent DFA on the AES key schedule, round keys should not be generated on the fly, but should be pre-generated and then stored in memory. This eliminates the need for a key schedule, and also prevents the DFA attack described in [12].

We agree that such a countermeasure prevents the DFA attack on the AES key schedule described in [12]. However, even though round keys have been pre-generated and stored in memory, it is still possible to induce faults into them. In fact, it is at times even more desirable since faults induced in a round key would not cause any further faults in other subsequent round keys. This allows the attacker to have more control over the position of the faults that will be induced. Also, this removes the limitation that the attacker *must* induce the faults *during* key accesses when the round keys are generated. Since now the round keys are residing in memory all the time, the attacker could induce the faults at any time convenient to him, and hence is able to attack under a less restricted time duration. Therefore, it appears that this first countermeasure does not entirely prevent DFA attacks on the key schedule. On the contrary, it gives the attacker more control of the location and propagation of the faults induced, and less restrictions on when to induce the faults. This suggests that permanently storing the round key may not be sufficient to prevent DFA attacks. In Section 5, we will describe DFA attacks that work *especially* with this countermeasure.

The second countermeasure suggests to generate the round keys once whenever there is a need for an update. But again, for the round keys to be used, they would need to be stored somewhere in memory. Therefore, though this prevents the DFA attacks in [12], it falls to the same problem as the first countermeasure.

The third countermeasure suggests to apply a two-dimensional parity check on the round keys that are generated. Nevertheless, we point out that such an error check would inherit the limitations of conventional two-dimensional parity checks, that 4-bit errors or in this case faults would be undetectable. Therefore, this countermeasure will not prevent DFA attacks on the AES key schedule that involve inducing faults into 4 specific bits of the round keys. Though it may be argued that it is hard to induce 4 bits into exactly specified positions, this is not at all impossible with the optical fault induction attack that requires just US$30 worth of equipment bought at a second-hand camera shop [36].

## 5   Amplified Differential Fault Attacks on the AES

We describe two special cases of amplified side-channel attacks by exploiting techniques of block cipher cryptanalysis to enhance the DFA. These serve solely to illustrate the idea behind the notion of amplified side-channel attacks. Sections 5.1 and 5.2 respectively discuss how to integrate the Square attack and impossible differential cryptanalysis into the DFA.

### 5.1   Square-DFA on the AES

To mount a Square attack [13] on the AES requires us to use a Square distinguisher that works for three rounds of the AES. Suppose we have a group of 256 plaintexts that are totally identical to each other except for one byte in which they would have entirely different values. Then the Square distinguisher specifies that after encryption by 3 rounds of the AES, the 256 texts would have the property that the XOR of all the 256 ciphertexts would result in a zero for all byte positions. This is a very interesting property and has been previously exploited to attack the AES up to 7 rounds [16, 18, 29].

Consider if we use equipment similar to that described in [36] but replaced with a suitable laser to increase precision, to induce a bit of fault in a byte of the 6th round key, $RK_6$, and repeating for 255 times, each time inducing one or more bits of fault into that same byte of $RK_6$ such that it would have all 256 (one correct and 255 faulty) values. These faults will not affect any of the other round keys. However, they will affect the AES encryption starting from the 6th round onwards. Therefore at the end of round 6, the 1 correct encryption and 255 faulty encryptions under these $RK_6$ values would be identical except for that one byte in which they would all have different values. By the Square distinguisher, this would propagate through the next three rounds until the end of round 9 when the XOR of all these 256 texts would result in a zero in all byte positions. What we have basically done is using the DFA to induce faults into $RK_6$ so that we can apply a 3-round Square distinguisher from rounds 7 to 9.

We can now guess all possible values of any byte of $RK_{10}$ and partially decrypt these 256 (one correct and 255 faulty) ciphertexts by one round up to the output of round 9, and then check if their XOR gives a zero. The correct byte value of $RK_{10}$ will always satisfy this, while a wrong value would only satisfy this with a very low probability, so it is almost guaranteed that only the right byte value remains. In the same way, move on to guess all possible values of another byte of $RK_{10}$. Repeat this for all 16 bytes of $RK_{10}$.

In summary, we need 1 correct ciphertext and 255 faulty ciphertexts, which can be reused for guessing all 16 bytes of $RK_{10}$. To guess each byte of $RK_{10}$, we make 256 guesses of the key byte and do 256 single-round AES encryptions, so in total $256 \times 256 \times 16 = 2^{20}$ single-round AES encryptions or $2^{20}/10 \approx 2^{16.5}$ AES encryptions for this DFA-induced Square attack.

**Generalizations.** Our attack considered inducing faults on one byte of $RK_6$. It equally applies when faults are induced on the *intermediate state* between MCs in rounds 6 and 7, or more generally between the MCs in rounds $R - 4$ and $R - 3$. In order to generalize this further, we recall that our attack outlined above induces the byte faults between the MCs in rounds $R - 4$ and $R - 3$, and applies a 3-round Square distinguisher in the rounds $R - 3$ to $R - 1$. In fact, we could also induce the byte faults a bit deeper into the middle of the AES, in particular between the MCs in rounds $R - 5$ and $R - 4$, in either the intermediate state or the corresponding round key, and again apply the 3-round Square distinguisher to the rounds $R - 4$ and $R - 2$. Then, to attack the last two rounds, we guess any column of $RK_9$ and the corresponding 4 bytes of $RK_{10}$, partially decrypt our ciphertexts by those last two rounds up to just before round 9 and check if the XOR is zero in any byte of the column corresponding to that column of $RK_9$. Repeating this four times, we obtain the entire $RK_9$ and $RK_{10}$ with the same number of faulty ciphertexts.

Alternatively, we could also induce the byte faults between the MCs in rounds $R - 3$ and $R - 2$, in either the intermediate state or the corresponding round key, and hence apply the first 2 rounds of the 3-round Square distinguisher to the rounds $R-2$ and $R-1$. In this case, we are guaranteed that after round $R-1$ we would always have all 256 unique values in each byte of the correct and the faulty encryptions. This allows one to consider each byte of the last round key, $RK_{10}$ at a time and performing an attack similar to the above with the same number of faulty ciphertexts, except that instead of computing the resultant XOR value, one would further have to check that all 256 unique values exist.

Finally, we can induce the faults between the MCs in rounds $R-2$ and $R-1$ and apply the first round of our 3-round Square distinguisher to the round $R-1$. This states that after round $R-1$ we would always have all 256 unique values in the column in which the fault was induced. We guess at a time each of the 4 bytes of $RK_{10}$ that correspond to that column, each time reusing the same faulty ciphertexts. We repeat this four times to obtain all 4 columns of the key, and hence requiring a total of $2^{10}$ faulty ciphertexts.

**Discussion.** Our attacks are the *only* DFA-style attacks that can be applied to the AES if faults can only be injected between the rounds $R-4$ and $R-3$, and between the rounds $R-5$ and $R-4$, which would be the case for AES implementations that incorporate countermeasures against standard previous DFAs. Previous DFAs do not work for these rounds at all, even with the entire code book! Our results therefore stress that one should guard against DFAs in any round of the AES, and not just the outer (first or last) few rounds.

## 5.2   Impossible-DFA on the AES

Before we proceed with a description of the attack, we briefly introduce a 3-round impossible differential of the AES, which is a variant of the 4-round impossible differential discussed in [6]. Specifically, our 3-round impossible differential states that given a pair of plaintexts equal in all bytes (called *passive bytes*) except one (*active*) byte in which the pair differs, then the ciphertexts after 3 rounds cannot be equal in any of the 16 bytes at the state just before MC in round 3. Note that only the ShiftRows and MixColumns operations affect the number and positions of the active bytes, and that MC and AR are invariant of each other [13].

We use this distinguisher for our attack. Consider that a fault is induced on any byte of the 6th round key, $RK_6$ that is stored in memory. This fault will not affect any of the other round keys. However, it will affect the AES encryption starting from the 6th round onwards. A correct and a faulty encryption would then differ in a byte prior to the 7th round. This difference will propagate to 4 bytes after round 7, and if we consider our 3-round impossible differential distinguisher previously discussed, this will suggest that after round 9 we would never have any equal byte between the correct and the faulty encryptions at the state just before MC in round 9. We will henceforth denote this state as $X$.

We have in essence used concepts from the DFA to induce a fault into any byte of $RK_6$, in order to cause a byte of difference between a correct and a faulty encryption prior to the 7th round. We then apply the 3-round impossible differential from rounds 7 to 9 up to $X$, and with this in place, we guess all $2^{32}$ possible values of the four bytes of the last round key, $RK_{10}$ that correspond to any column at $X$, say the first column, partially decrypt the correct and the faulty ciphertexts by one round up to $X$ and check if we get any equal bytes in that column of $X$. If this is the case, then the guessed values of $RK_{10}$ are wrong since they caused the impossible differential to occur. These values are removed from the list of $2^{32}$ possible values of $RK_{10}$. Doing this with one faulty encryption causes about $(1 - 2^{-6}) \times 2^{32}$ possible key values to remain[2] [6]. Repeating this with a sufficient number of faulty encryptions, in this case about $2^{11}$, will leave $2^{32}(1 - 2^{-6})^{2^{11}} \approx 0$ wrong key values, so only the correct key value remains [6]. With this, we obtain 4 bytes of $RK_{10}$ that correspond to that column of $X$. We can repeat the same steps for the bytes of $RK_{10}$ that correspond to the other 3 columns of $X$, and hence obtain the entire $RK_{10}$.

To obtain each column of $RK_{10}$, the attack needs 1 correct ciphertext and $2^{11}$ faulty ciphertexts which can be reused. Also, to obtain each column of $RK_{10}$, we do $2^{32}$ single-round AES encryptions, so this makes it $2^{34}$ single-round AES encryptions or $2^{32}/10 \approx 2^{28.5}$ AES encryptions.

**Generalizations.** This can be generalized similarly to Section 5.1, hence the flexibility of inducing the byte fault in the round key or in the intermediate state between the MCs in rounds $R - 4$ and $R - 3$. However, in contrast to the case of the DFA and Square attacks, it is not possible to further generalize and make this attack work when the fault is induced at other locations simply because the first few rounds of the 3-round impossible differential are in fact probability-one differentials, so the propagation of the active and passive would always occur irrespective of the guessed key values, hence cannot be used for filtering wrong keys. For AES-192 (respectively AES-256), one could consider applying the 4-round (respectively 5-round) impossible differentials reported by Kim et al. [24].

**Discussion.** As was the case with our attacks in Section 5.1, our attacks in this section are the *only* DFA-style attacks that can be applied to the AES if faults can only be injected between the rounds $R - 4$ and $R - 3$.

# 6   Concluding Remarks

We have introduced the notion of amplified side-channel attack, and illustrated specifically with Square-DFA and impossible-DFA attacks on the AES. In Table 1, we compare between previous DFAs and our amplified DFA attacks on the AES. We have indicated in Table 1 the best DFAs based on the fault location. Clearly, Dusart, Letourneux and Vivolo's [15] attack is the best for faults induced in round $R - 1$ while Piret and Quisquater's [32] attacks are the best for faults induced between the rounds $R - 3$ and $R - 1$. Our amplified DFA attacks are the best and only attacks that are applicable for faults induced between the rounds $R - 5$ through to $R - 3$. Therefore, we can think of all these attacks as complementing each other. Depending on where the faults can be induced, the

---

[2] The probability of getting a passive byte is $2^{-8}$ so the probability of getting any passive byte in a column is $2^{-6}$.

**Table 1.** Comparison of DFAs on AES

| Attack type | Fault model | Fault location (Which round) | Faulty texts | Source | Best attack |
|---|---|---|---|---|---|
| DFA | Bit faults | 1 (after $AR_0$) | 128 | [10] | |
| DFA | Impl-depend. | - | 256 | [10] | |
| DFA | Bit faults | $R - 1$ (after $AR_{R-1}$) | 50 | [19] | |
| DFA | Byte faults | $R - 1$ (after SR) | 50 | [15] | ✓ |
| DFA | Byte faults | $R - 2$ and $R - 1$ ($RK_{R-2}$, and $RK_{R-1}$) | 250 | [19] | |
| DFA | Byte faults | $R - 2$ and $R - 1$ ($RK_{R-2}$, and $RK_{R-1}$) | 30 | [12] | |
| DFA | Byte faults | Between MCs in $R - 2$ and $R - 1$ | 8 | [32] | ✓ |
| Square-DFA | Byte faults | Between MCs in $R - 2$ and $R - 1$ | $2^{10}$ | This paper | |
| DFA | Byte faults | Between MCs in $R - 3$ and $R - 2$ | 2 | [32] | ✓ |
| Square-DFA | Byte faults | Between MCs in $R - 3$ and $R - 2$ | 256 | This paper | |
| Impossible-DFA | Byte faults | Between MCs in $R - 4$ and $R - 3$ | $2^{11}$ | This paper | |
| Square-DFA | Byte faults | Between MCs in $R - 4$ and $R - 3$ | 256 | This paper | ✓ |
| Square-DFA | Byte faults | Between MCs in $R - 5$ and $R - 4$ | 256 | This paper | ✓ |

Note: Best attack is indicated based on various different fault locations.

cryptanalyst has the option to choose the best that is currently available. Our results also complete the picture of applying DFAs to the AES, and demonstrate that it is sometimes useful to apply techniques from block cipher cryptanalysis to amplify effects caused by side-channel attacks. The integration of two or more cryptanalysis techniques often results in a more powerful attack. This is due to the fact that since we are using more than one attack, we could selectively exploit the special features of each attack in situations or parts of the cipher where it thrives the most. Thus, we ensure the most suitable attack is applied to block cipher components most susceptible to it in order to get an optimum result.

# References

1. D. Agrawal, B. Archambeault, J.R. Rao, P. Rohatgi, "The EM Side-Channel(s)," *CHES '02*, LNCS 2523, pp. 29–45, Springer-Verlag, 2002.
2. D. Agrawal, J.R. Rao, P. Rohatgi, "Multi-Channel Attacks," *CHES '03*, LNCS 2779, pp. 2–16, Springer-Verlag, 2003.
3. E. Biham, "New Types of Cryptanalytic Attacks using Related Keys," *Advances in Cryptology – EUROCRYPT '93*, LNCS 765, pp. 398–409, Springer-Verlag, 1994.

4. E. Biham, A. Biryukov, A. Shamir, "Miss in the Middle Attacks on IDEA, Khufu and Khafre," *Advances in Cryptology - EUROCRYPT '99*, LNCS 1636, pp. 124–138, Springer-Verlag, 1999.

5. E. Biham, O. Dunkelman, N. Keller, "The Rectangle Attack – Rectangling the Serpent," *Advances in Cryptology - EUROCRYPT '01*, LNCS 2045, pp. 340–357, Springer-Verlag, 2001.

6. E. Biham, N. Keller, "Cryptanalysis of Reduced Variants of Rijndael," Submitted to 3rd AES Conference, U.S., 2000.

7. E. Biham, A. Shamir, "Differential Cryptanalysis of the Data Encryption Standard," Springer-Verlag, 1993.

8. E. Biham, A. Shamir, "Differential Fault Analysis of Secret Key Cryptosystems," *Advances in Cryptology - CRYPTO '97*, LNCS 1294, pp. 513–525, Springer-Verlag, 1997.

9. A. Biryukov, D. Wagner, "Slide Attacks," *FSE '99*, LNCS 1636, pp. 245-259, Springer-Verlag, 1999.

10. J. Blömer, J.-P. Seifert, "Fault Based Cryptanalysis of the Advanced Encryption Standard," *Financial Cryptography '03*, LNCS 2742, pp. 162–181, Springer-Verlag, 2003.

11. D. Boneh, R.A. Demillo, R.J. Lipton, "On the Importance of Checking Cryptographic Protocols for Faults," *Advances in Cryptology - EUROCRYPT '97*, LNCS 1233, pp. 37–51, Springer-Verlag, 1997.

12. C.-N. Chen, S.-M. Yen, "Differential Fault Analysis on AES Key Schedule," *ACISP '03*, LNCS 2727, pp. 118–129, Springer-Verlag, 2003.

13. J. Daemen, V. Rijmen, "AES proposal: Rijndael (version 2)," Updated Documentation and Complete Specification, 1999.

14. H. Dobbertin, "Cryptanalysis of MD4," *Journal of Cryptology*, vol. 11, pp. 235–271, Springer-Verlag, 1998.

15. P. Dusart, G. Letourneux, O. Vivolo, "Differential Fault Analysis on A.E.S.," IACR Cryptology ePrint Archive, No. 010, 2003.

16. N. Ferguson, J. Kelsey, S. Lucks, B. Schneier, M. Stay, D. Wagner, D. Whiting, "Improved Cryptanalysis of Rijndael," *3rd AES Conference*, 2000.

17. S. Furuya, "Slide Attacks with a Known-Plaintext Cryptanalysis," *ICISC '01*, LNCS 2288, pp. 214–225, Springer-Verlag, 2002.

18. H. Gilbert, M. Minier, "A Collision Attack on 7 Rounds of Rijndael," *3rd AES Conference*, 2000.

19. C. Giraud, "DFA on AES," IACR Cryptology ePrint Archive, No. 008, 2003.

20. M. Hellman, S. Langford, "Differential-linear Cryptanalysis," *Advances in Cryptology - CRYPTO '94*, LNCS 839, pp. 17–26, Springer-Verlag, 1994.

21. T. Jakobsen, L.R. Knudsen, "The Interpolation Attack on Block Ciphers," *FSE '97*, LNCS 1267, pp. 28–40, Springer-Verlag, 1997.

22. G. Jakimoski, Y. Desmedt, "Related-Key Differential Cryptanalysis of 192-bit Key AES Variants," *SAC '03*, LNCS 3006, pp. 208–221, Springer-Verlag, 2004.

23. J. Kelsey, T. Kohno, B. Schneier, "Amplified Boomerang Attacks against Reduced-round MARS and Serpent," *FSE '00*, LNCS 1978, pp. 75–93, Springer-Verlag, 2001.

24. J. Kim, S. Hong, J. Sung, S. Lee, J. Lim, S. Sung, "Impossible Differential Cryptanalysis for Block Cipher Structures," *Progress in Cryptology - INDOCRYPT '03*, LNCS 2904, pp. 82–96, Springer-Verlag, 2003.

25. J. Kim, G. Kim, S. Hong, S. Lee, D. Hong, "The Related-Key Rectangle Attack – An Application to SHACAL-1," *ACISP '04*, LNCS 3108, pp. 123–136, Springer-Verlag, 2004.

26. L.R. Knudsen, D. Wagner, "Integral Cryptanalysis," *FSE '02*, LNCS 2365, pp. 112–127, Springer-Verlag, 2002.
27. P. Kocher, "Timing Attacks on Implementations of Diffie-Hellman, RSA, DSS, and Other Systems," *Advances in Cryptology – CRYPTO '96*, LNCS 1109, pp. 104–113, Springer-Verlag, 1997.
28. P. Kocher, J. Jaffe, B. Jun, "Differential Power Analysis," *Advances in Cryptology – CRYPTO '99*, LNCS 1666, pp. 388–397, Springer-Verlag, 1999.
29. S. Lucks, "Attacking Seven Rounds of Rijndael under 192-bit and 256-bit Keys," *3rd AES Conference*, 2000.
30. M. Matsui, "Linear Cryptanalysis Method for DES Cipher," *Advances in Cryptology – EUROCRYPT '93*, LNCS 765, pp. 386–397, Springer-Verlag, 1994.
31. R.C.-W. Phan, S. Furuya, "Sliding Properties of the DES Key Schedule and Potential Extensions to the Slide Attacks," *ICISC '02*, LNCS 2587, pp. 138–148, Springer-Verlag, 2003.
32. G. Piret, J.-J. Quisquater, "A Differential Fault Attack Technique against SPN Structures, with Application to the AES and KHAZAD," *CHES '03*, LNCS 2779, pp. 77–88, Springer-Verlag, 2003.
33. W. Schindler, "A Combined Timing and Power Attack," *PKC '02*, LNCS 2274, pp. 263–279, Springer-Verlag, 2002.
34. K. Schramm, G. Leander, P. Felke, C. Paar, "A Collision-Attack on AES: Combining Side Channel- and Differential-Attack," *CHES '04*, LNCS 3156, pp. 163–175, Springer-Verlag, 2004.
35. K. Schramm, T. Wollinger, C. Paar, "A New Class of Collision Attacks and its Application to DES," *FSE '03*, LNCS 2887, pp. 206–222, Springer-Verlag, 2003.
36. S.P. Skorobogatov, R.J. Anderson, "Optical Fault Induction Attacks," *CHES '02*, LNCS 2523, pp. 2–12, Springer-Verlag, 2003.
37. D. Wagner, "The Boomerang Attack," *FSE '99*, LNCS 1636, pp. 156–170, Springer-Verlag, 1999.
38. C.D. Walter, S. Thompson, "Distinguishing Exponent Digits by Observing Modular Subtractions," *Topics in Cryptology – CT-RSA '01*, LNCS 2020, pp. 192–207, Springer-Verlag, 2001.
39. S.-M. Yen, S. Kim, S. Lim, S.-J. Moon, "A Countermeasure Against One Physical Cryptanalysis May Benefit Another Attack," *ICISC '01*, LNCS 2288, pp. 414–427, Springer-Verlag, 2001.

# A     Integrated Block Cipher Cryptanalysis

In this appendix, we summarize previous attempts to integrate block cipher cryptanalysis techniques. This is hoped to motivate more work in this direction. The first was notably the *differential-linear cryptanalysis* [20] in 1994, which combined differential cryptanalysis (DC) [7] with linear cryptanalysis [30]. Denote the block cipher, $E(P) = E_2(E_1(P))$ as the composition of two halves[3], where $E_1$ (respectively $E_2$) denotes the earlier (respectively later) half of the cipher. Then the differential-linear cryptanalysis applies differential cryptanalysis to $E_1$ to enable linear cryptanalysis to be applied to $E_2$. Differential cryptanalysis is a *chosen-plaintext* (CP) attack where the attacker needs to obtain encryptions

---

[3] Not necessarily consisting of the same number of rounds.

of plaintexts with a certain chosen difference between them. Meanwhile, linear cryptanalysis is a *known-plaintext* (KP) attack in that the attacker simply needs to be able to obtain some known plaintext values and their corresponding ciphertexts. CP attacks that are of the differential cryptanalysis naturally can be converted to KP attacks but with a considerably high increase in text complexity. In particular, suppose that we need $m$ pairs of CPs with a certain difference between them. Then with $2^{n/2}\sqrt{2m}$ random KPs, we can form $2^n \times m$ pairs of KPs, of which the probability of getting a pair with a certain difference is $2^{-n}$, and therefore we get $m$ pairs of CPs with the desired difference [7].

In 2001, Furuya [17] considered combining the slide attacks [9] with KP attacks such as linear cryptanalysis. We consider that such attacks should rightly be called the *slide-KP attacks*. These apply the slide attacks to the entire cipher $E$ to enable KP attacks to be applicable to some outer rounds of $E$. Slide attacks are generally KP attacks, but if chosen-plaintext queries are possible, the attacker could mount the slide attacks with a much reduced text complexity.

In 2002, the *integral-interpolation attacks* [26] where presented, which applies integral cryptanalysis [26] to $E_1$ to enable the interpolation attacks [21] on $E_2$. Integral cryptanalysis is a CP attack while interpolation attacks are KP attacks.

Finally, in cases where it is possible for the attacker to obtain the encryptions of plaintexts under two related keys, $K$ and $K'$, he could then mount related-key versions of any of these block cipher cryptanalysis attacks. Examples of such considerations include the related-key differential attacks [3], related-key slide attacks [3], related-key square attacks [16], related-key impossible differential cryptanalysis [22], and the related-key rectangle attack [25].

As an aside, we note that some attacks have been proposed that apply the same kind of attacks to both $E_1$ and $E_2$. In this respect, we consider such attacks as a special case of integrated block cipher cryptanalysis. For instance, the *boomerang attack* [37] uses chosen plaintexts to mount differential cryptanalysis to $E_1$ and then enables differential cryptanalysis on $E_2$ by making adaptively-chosen ciphertext queries from the other end of the cipher. Note that adaptively-chosen plaintext-ciphertext attacks are much harder to mount than CP or KP attacks. The *amplified boomerang attack* [23] and *rectangle attack* [5] are enhancements of the boomerang attack. They similarly apply differential cryptanalysis to $E_1$ but the number of chosen plaintext queries used is increased considerably such that enough texts with the desired chosen difference appear probabilistically after $E_1$ to allow differential cryptanalysis to be further mounted on $E_2$. The *inside-out attack* [37] obtains a high number of known plaintexts such that enough texts with the desired chosen difference appear probabilistically in the middle of the cipher so that the difference will propagate outwards in both directions through $E_1$ and $E_2$. The *miss-in-the-middle attack* [4] applies differential cryptanalysis to both $E_1$ and $E_2$ in such a way that the differences between the texts in the middle of the cipher contradict each other.

Our main observation is that one starts by first applying a CP attack or a KP attack on $E_1$, to enable a KP attack to be mountable on $E_2$. In some cases where it is possible to considerably increase the number of texts obtained, then one could also apply CP attacks to $E_2$.

**Definition 2.** *Integrated block cipher cryptanalysis applies different types of cryptanalysis attacks to the first and second halves of a cipher, E. In particular, CP or KP attacks are applied to $E_1$ to enable KP attacks on $E_2$.*

**Fact 1.** *CP attacks can be converted to KP by increasing the text complexity.*

**Corollary 1.** *In some cases one could also mount CP attacks on $E_2$ when it is possible to considerably increase the number of texts obtained.*

**Corollary 2.** *In cases where it is only possible to apply CP or KP attacks on one sequence of rounds (one half instead of two) within E, then this can be viewed as a special case of integrated block cipher cryptanalysis where the attack is applied to either $E_1$ or $E_2$.*

The notion of integrated block cipher cryptanalysis opens doors to numerous possible attacks where previous attacks on their own failed. In general, any integration of CP and KP attacks could be mounted on ciphers. Further, related-key versions of the aforementioned integrated attacks are also possible.

In Table 2, we consider previous integration of CP and KP attacks, where the rows and columns indicate attacks applied to $E_1$ and $E_2$, respectively: differential-differential attacks e.g. the boomerang [37], inside-out [37], amplified boomerang [23], rectangle [5], and miss-in-the-middle [4]; we also have differential-linear attacks [20] and integral-interpolation attacks [26]. The slide-linear attack [17] is just one of the ways one could mount his proposed slide-KP attacks, another variant he suggested being the slide-partitioning attacks [17]. On this note, we also remark that it would be possible to have slide-interpolation attacks. The slide-slide (double slide) attack [31] has also been considered.

**Table 2.** Previous integration of block cipher cryptanalysis attacks

|  | Differential | Integral | Linear | Interpolation | Partitioning | Slide |
|---|---|---|---|---|---|---|
| Differential | [37, 23, 5, 4] |  | [20] |  |  |  |
| Integral |  |  |  | [26] |  |  |
| Linear |  |  |  |  |  |  |
| Interpolation |  |  |  |  |  |  |
| Partitioning |  |  |  |  |  |  |
| Slide |  |  | [17] | New | [17] | [31] |

# Power Analysis to ECC Using Differential Power Between Multiplication and Squaring

Toru Akishita[1] and Tsuyoshi Takagi[2]

[1] Sony Corporation, Information Technologies Laboratories, Tokyo, Japan
akishita@pal.arch.sony.co.jp
[2] Future University - Hakodate, Japan
takagi@fun.ac.jp

**Abstract.** Power analysis is a serious attack to implementation of elliptic curve cryptosystems (ECC) on smart cards. For ECC, many power analysis attacks and countermeasures have been proposed. In this paper, we propose a novel power analysis attack using differential power between modular *multiplication* and modular *squaring*. We show how this difference occurs in CMOS circuits by counting the expectation of signal transition frequency, and present a simulation result on our ECC co-processor. The proposed attack is applicable to two efficient power analysis countermeasures based on unified addition formulae and elliptic curves with Montgomery form.

**Keywords:** Smart cards, elliptic curve cryptosystems, power analysis, DPA, modular multiplication.

## 1 Introduction

Elliptic Curve Cryptosystems (ECC) offer the same level security with much shorter key length than RSA cryptosystems, so that they are suitable for implementing on resource-constraint devices such as smart cards. In recent years, a new class of attacks has been proposed to extract some secret information from a cryptographic device using side channel information (execution time, power consumption, etc.), that are called side channel attacks. Power analysis attacks, the most typical side channel attacks, are real threats to smart cards since the power consumption during cryptographic protocols is relatively dominant in such devices. These attacks include Simple Power Analysis (SPA) and Differential Power Analysis (DPA) [11]. SPA utilizes a power consumption trace during a single execution, whereas DPA requires many power consumption traces and analyzes them with statistical tools.

For ECC, many SPA/DPA attacks and countermeasures have been investigated since Coron generalized power analysis attacks to a scalar multiplication $dP$ [5], where $d$ is a secret scalar and $P$ is a point on an elliptic curve. In 2002, Brier and Joye proposed unified addition formulae that make a point addition and a point doubling indistinguishable on an elliptic curve with Weierstrass form [4]. This indistinguishability guarantees SPA-resistance and enables the

J. Domingo-Ferrer, J. Posegga, and D. Schreckling (Eds.): CARDIS 2006, LNCS 3928, pp. 151–164, 2006.

use of efficient addition chains such as Non-Adjacent Form (NAF) and so-called window methods. In the meantime, Montgomery ladder always repeats a point addition and doubling, thus an SPA attacker cannot know any bit information of a secret scalar [16]. Montgomery ladder on an elliptic curve with Montgomery form requires much less costs than that on an elliptic curve with Weierstrass form [15, 16]. One can easily enhance these two SPA countermeasures to be DPA-resistant by combining them to randomized projective representation [5, 17] or randomized curve isomorphism [9].

In this paper, we propose a novel attack to these DPA countermeasures. We firstly describe the difference of power consumption between modular *multiplication* and modular *squaring*. Messerges et al. experimented DPA attacks to modular exponentiation using distinguishability between *multiplication* and *squaring* [13], but there is no investigation about this bias in CMOS circuits. We give detailed descriptions of the bias by estimating the transition probability for each gate in carry-save adder tree, which is a main component of a multiplier, during Montgomery modular multiplication algorithm. We performed a net-list timing simulation of our ECC co-processor and confirmed sharp peaks in the difference between Montgomery modular *multiplication* and Montgomery modular *squaring*.

Secondly, we apply this bias to the above mentioned two SPA/DPA countermeasures. For unified addition formulae, an attacker can distinguish whether the formulae work as a point addition or doubling, and detect a secret scalar. For Montgomery ladder on a Montgomery-form curve, we utilize a "special" point that equalizes both inputs of a certain modular multiplication in a point doubling. The point satisfies $x^2 + (A - 4)x + 1 = 0$, and the proposed attack is effective to ECC on any curve that has this point.

The rest of this paper is organized as follows: in section 2 we briefly review power analysis attacks and countermeasures to ECC. Section 3 provides detailed description of the bias between Montgomery modular *multiplication* and Montgomery modular *squaring* together with a simulation result. In section 4, we apply the bias to two power analysis countermeasures. Finally, we conclude in section 5.

## 2    Elliptic Curve Cryptosystems and Power Analysis

In this section, we introduce power analysis attacks and countermeasures against elliptic curve cryptosystems, including unified addition formulae and elliptic curves with Montgomery form. More details are described in [3, Chapter IV and V].

### 2.1    Elliptic Curve Cryptosystems

The Weierstrass form of an elliptic curve $E_W$ over a prime field $\mathbb{F}_p$ ($p > 3$) is represented by

$$E_W : y^2 = x^3 + ax + b \quad (a, b \in \mathbb{F}_p, \ 4a^3 + 27b^2 \neq 0).$$

**Table 1.** Binary method

| **Input:** an $n$-bit scalar $d$, a point $P$ |
| :--- |
| **Output:** scalar multiplication $dP$ |
| 1. $Q \leftarrow P$ |
| 2. For $i = n - 2$ downto 0 do: |
|    2.1. $Q \leftarrow \text{ECDBL}(Q)$ |
|    2.2. if $d_i = 1$ then |
|          $Q \leftarrow \text{ECADD}(Q, P)$ |
| 3. Return($Q$) |

**Table 2.** Double-and-add-always method

| **Input:** an $n$-bit scalar $d$, a point $P$ |
| :--- |
| **Output:** scalar multiplication $dP$ |
| 1. $Q[0] \leftarrow P$ |
| 2. For $i = n - 2$ downto 0 do: |
|    2.1. $Q[0] \leftarrow \text{ECDBL}(Q[0])$ |
|    2.2. $Q[1] \leftarrow \text{ECADD}(Q[0], P)$ |
|    2.3. $Q[0] \leftarrow Q[d_i]$ |
| 3. Return($Q[0]$) |

The set of all points on $E_W$ and a point of infinity $\mathcal{O}$ forms an additive group, where $\mathcal{O}$ is a neutral element. Let $P_0 = (x_0, y_0)$, $P_1 = (x_1, y_1)$ be points on $E_W$. The addition $P_2 = (x_2, y_2) = P_0 + P_1$ is defined in different formulae depending on whether $P_0 = P_1$ or not as following: $x_2 = \lambda^2 - x_0 - x_1$, $y_2 = \lambda(x_0 - x_2) - y_0$, where $\lambda = (y_1 - y_0)/(x_1 - x_0)$ for $P_0 \neq \pm P_1$, and $\lambda = (3x_0^2 + a)/(2y_0)$ for $P_0 = P_1$. We call $P_0 + P_1$ ($P_0 \neq \pm P_1$) an elliptic curve addition (ECADD) and $P_0 + P_1$ ($P_0 = P_1$), namely $2P_0$, an elliptic curve doubling (ECDBL). In practice, both ECADD and ECDBL are implemented in Jacobian coordinates by $x = X/Z^2, y = Y/Z^3$ because an inversion is much more expensive than any other arithmetic (addition, subtraction, multiplication) over $\mathbb{F}_p$. In this case, both are also implemented with different formulae.

In order to construct Elliptic Curve Cryptosystems (ECC) we need to compute a scalar multiplication: computing a point $dP = \underbrace{P + \cdots + P}_{d}$ given a scalar $d$ and a point $P$. On the other hand, the security of ECC is based on the hardness of Elliptic Curve Discrete Logarithm Problem (ECDLP): computing $d$ given $P$ and $dP$. Therefore, in most ECC protocols, $d$ is used as a secret key; $P$ and $dP$ are made to be public. The basic method to compute a scalar multiplication is called as the binary method. Let $d = (d_{n-1} \cdots d_1 d_0)_2$ be a binary representation of $d$. The binary method is shown in Table 1.

### 2.2 Power Analysis Attacks and Countermeasures

Power analysis attacks are serious on resource-constraint devices such as smart cards. An attacker can successfully reveal some secret information by observing the power consumption on a device during cryptographic protocols. Simple Power Analysis (SPA) and Differential Power Analysis (DPA) are typical ones; SPA requires a power consumption trace during only a single execution, whereas DPA utilizes many power consumption traces with statistical analysis [11]. These attacks utilize a correlation between secret information and power consumption, and are also applicable to ECC.

The binary method shown in Table 1 is vulnerable to SPA. It computes ECADD only when $d_i = 1$, although ECDBL is always computed regardless of $d_i$. ECADD and ECDBL are different operations as described above, and thus an attacker can easily distinguish ECDBL and ECADD by observing a power consumption trace and detect secret bit $d_i$. Many SPA countermeasures against ECC have been proposed, and they are principally divided into two types as follows.

(S1) repeating regular pattern

(S2) unifying ECADD and ECDBL

(S1) includes the double-and-add-always method in Table 2 [5], which repeats ECDBL and ECADD by appending dummy ECADD to the binary method, and Montgomery ladder [15], which is discussed in section 2.4. (S2) includes Hessian curves [10], Jacobi curves [12], and unified addition formulae [4], which is shown in section 2.3.

The resistance against SPA doesn't always guarantee the resistance against DPA because a power consumption trace depends on not only a type of operations, namely ECADD or ECDBL, but also intermediate values. A DPA attacker collects many power consumption traces during the scalar multiplication and guesses a bit of the secret scalar by analyzing correlation between these traces and intermediate values [5]. In order to resist DPA, intermediate values must be randomized. There are three standard randomization methods as follows.

(D1) blinding scalar [11, 5]

(D2) randomized projective representation [5, 17]

(D3) randomized curve isomorphism [9]

These three DPA countermeasures together with the SPA countermeasure (S1) or (S2) enables SPA/DPA resistance. (D1), however, requires more additional costs than (D2) and (D3), so that the combination of either (S1) or (S2) and either (D2) or (D3) is thought to be an optimal SPA/DPA countermeasure.

In 2003, Goubin presented a new power analysis attack called Refined Power Analysis (RPA) [6]. This attack utilizes a "special" point $(x, 0)$ or $(0, y)$ that can be fully randomized by neither (D2) nor (D3). In the addition, an attacker can pick up the point only in a few power consumption traces because a power trace in processing this point is distinctive [2]. RPA with a point $(x, 0)$ can be easily discarded by multiplying co-factor on the underlying curve to an input point $P$ since the order of $(x, 0)$ is 2 [18]. On the other side, RPA with a point $(0, y)$ cannot be discarded because $(0, y)$ has large order. Therefore, RPA is effective on a curve that has a point $(0, y)$.

We extended RPA to Zero-value Point Attack (ZPA) using other "special" points [2]. We pointed out that, even if a point has no zero coordinate, intermediate values in addition or doubling formulae might become zero. ZPA using a point addition is actually difficult for a large scalar $d$, but ZPA using a point doubling is as effective as RPA if the point that causes zero-value in a point doubling exists on the underlying curve. Therefore, RPA and ZPA using a point doubling may oblige not only (D2) or (D3) but also (D1), or another countermeasure such as randomized initial point countermeasure [7, 14], which leads to extra costs or memories.

## 2.3    Unified Addition Formulae

Brier and Joye proposed "unified addition formulae" for an elliptic curve addition (ECADD) and an elliptic curve doubling (ECDBL) on a Weierstrass-form elliptic curve as an SPA countermeasure [4]. In their formulae for affine coordinates, a denominator becomes no longer zero in ECDBL as follows.

**Unified Addition Formulae.** $P_2 = P_0 + P_1$

$$x_2 = \left( \frac{x_1^2 + x_1 x_0 + x_0^2 + a}{y_1 + y_0} \right)^2 - x_0 - x_1$$

$$y_2 = \left( \frac{x_1^2 + x_1 x_0 + x_0^2 + a}{y_1 + y_0} \right) (x_0 - x_2) - y_0$$

Izu and Takagi proposed the exceptional procedure attack that forces a denominator to become zero for ECADD by inputting two points $(x_0, y_0)$ and $(x_1, y_1)$, which satisfy $y_0 + y_1 = 0$, but it seems difficult to find a couple of such points for a large scalar [8].

An SPA attacker cannot distinguish whether the unified formulae work as ECADD or ECDBL, thus she knows only a hamming weight of a secret scalar $d$ even if the binary method is used. Moreover, an efficient addition chain such as Non-Adjacent Form (NAF) or window-based methods leads great efficiency. The unified addition formulae for projective coordinates were also proposed. The combination with a DPA countermeasure (D2) or (D3) enables the compatibility of efficiency and SPA/DPA resistance.

*Remark 1.* In [21], Walter proposed an SPA attack to unified addition formulae based on the existence of a final subtraction in Montgomery modular multiplication. This attack, however, is easily eliminated by computing a final subtraction in any case.

## 2.4    Elliptic Curve with Montgomery-Form

The Montgomery form of an elliptic curve $E_M$ over $\mathbb{F}_p$, $(p > 3)$ was proposed by Montgomery to speed up integer factorization [15], and represented by

$$E_M : By^2 = x^3 + Ax^2 + x \quad (A, B \in \mathbb{F}_p, \ (A^2 - 4)B \neq 0).$$

About 40% of elliptic curves with Weierstrass form are transformed into Montgomery form, and the order of a Montgomery-form elliptic curve is always divisible by 4 [16]. On a Montgomery-form elliptic curve $E_M$, $x$-coordinate of the addition of two points can be computed without $y$-coordinate if $x$-coordinate of the difference of these points is known. Affine coordinate $x$ is transformed into projective coordinates $(X : Z)$ by $x = X/Z$. Let $P_0 = (X_0 : Z_0)$ and $P_1 = (X_1 : Z_1)$ be points on $E_M$. In the following we describe Montgomery addition formulae $P_2 = (X_2 : Z_2) = P_0 + P_1$, where $P_0 \neq \pm P_1$ and $P' = (X' : Z') = P_0 - P_1$, and Montgomery doubling formulae $P_2 = (X_2 : Z_2) = 2P_0$.

**Table 3.** Montgomery ladder

| |
|---|
| **Input:** an $n$-bit scalar $d$, a base point $P$ |
| **Output:** scalar multiplication $dP$ |
| 1. $Q[0] \leftarrow P$, $Q[1] \leftarrow 2P$ |
| 2. For $i = n - 2$ downto 0 do: |
|   2.1. $Q[1 - d_i] \leftarrow \text{mECADD}([Q[0], Q[1])$ |
|   2.2. $Q[d_i] \leftarrow \text{mECDBL}([Q[d_i])$ |
| 3. Return($Q[0]$) |

**Montgomery Addition Formulae (mECADD).** $P_2 = P_0 + P_1$ $(P_1 \neq \pm P_0)$

$$X_2 = Z'((X_0 - Z_0)(X_1 + Z_1) + (X_0 + Z_0)(X_1 - Z_1))^2$$
$$Z_2 = X'((X_0 - Z_0)(X_1 + Z_1) - (X_0 + Z_0)(X_1 - Z_1))^2$$

**Montgomery Doubling Formulae (mECDBL).** $P_2 = 2P_0$

$$4X_0Z_0 = (X_0 + Z_0)^2 - (X_0 - Z_0)^2$$
$$X_2 = (X_0 + Z_0)^2(X_0 - Z_0)^2$$
$$Z_2 = (4X_0Z_0)((X_0 - Z_0)^2 + ((A + 2)/4)(4X_0Z_0))$$

A scalar multiplication $dP$ can be computed by so-called Montgomery ladder in Table 3. Montgomery ladder always repeats mECADD and mECDBL whether $d_i = 0$ or 1. Therefore, an SPA attacker cannot guess any bit information of a secret scalar $d$ [16]. Montgomery ladder on an elliptic curve with Weierstrass form was also proposed, but the costs of a point addition and a point doubling on a Weierstrass-form curve are much larger than mECADD and mECDBL. One can enhance Montgomery ladder to be DPA-resistant by applying randomized projective representation [17]. In the addition, RPA and ZPA are easily eliminated by checking whether $4P$ is a point at infinity or not for a input point $P$ because the order of a point $(0, y)$ for RPA, $(-1, y)$ and $(1, y)$ for ZPA are 2, 4 and 4, respectively.

# 3    Differential Power Between Multiplication and Squaring

Here we show that there exists the difference of power consumption between modular *multiplication* and modular *squaring* in CMOS circuits. We estimate the transition probability of each signal in some full adders, and present a result of net-list timing simulation in order to confirm this difference.

## 3.1    Montgomery Modular Multiplication

We assume the following standard smart card environment. The embedded CPU on a smart card, typically an 8 or 16 bit CPU, has only so poor computing

**Table 4.** 160-bit Montgomery modular multiplication using a 32-bit multiplier

| |
|---|
| **Input:** $M = (M_4 \cdots M_0)_b$, $X = (X_4 \cdots X_0)_b$, $Y = (Y_4 \cdots Y_0)_b$, |
| $\quad b = 2^{32}$, $R = b^5$, $\gcd(m, b) = 1$, $m' = M_0^{-1} \bmod b$ |
| **Output:** $XYR^{-1} \bmod M$ |
| 1. $A \leftarrow 0$ $((A = (A_5 \cdots A_0)_b)$ |
| 2. For $i$ from 0 to 4 do: |
| $\quad$ 2.1. $temp \leftarrow 0$ |
| $\quad$ 2.2. For $j$ from 0 to 4 do: |
| $\qquad \{temp, A_j\} \leftarrow X_j Y_i + A_j + temp$ |
| $\quad$ 2.3. $A_5 \leftarrow temp$, $temp \leftarrow 0$, $u_i \leftarrow A_0 m' \bmod b$ |
| $\quad$ 2.4. For $j$ from 0 to 5 do: |
| $\qquad \{temp, A_j\} \leftarrow M_j u_i + A_j + temp$ |
| $\quad$ 2.5. $A \leftarrow A/b$ |
| 3. If $A \geq M$ then $A \leftarrow A - M$ |
| 4. Return($A$) |

power that we usually equip a co-processor for implementing ECC. An addition, subtraction, multiplication and inversion over a base field $\mathbb{F}_p$ are implemented in an ECC co-processor to compute elliptic curve operations such as a point addition, point doubling and scalar multiplication. The modular multiplication is the most frequently used among those modular operations.

Recall that Montgomery modular multiplication algorithm is a standard algorithm for computing modular multiplication over general prime fields. In this paper we analyze a 160-bit Montgomery modular multiplication with 32-bit word size is shown in Table 4, which is a standard size in current implementation of ECC. In this algorithm there are three 32-bit multiplications computed by a 32-bit multiplier, namely $X_j Y_i$ in step 2.2, $A_0 m'$ in step 2.3, and $M_j u_i$ in step 2.4.

We will later show that signal transition probability in a 32-bit multiplier during computing $X_j Y_i$ is biased if the inputs of Montgomery modular multiplication, $X$ and $Y$, satisfy $X = Y$.

### 3.2 Structure of a Multiplier

In this section we deal with a 6-bit multiplier instead of a 32-bit multiplier because of space limitation. All observations, however, are applicable to a 32-bit multiplier.

In general, a multiplier consists of three stages: Partial Product Generator (PPG), Partial Product Accumulator (PPA) and Final Stage Adder (FSA). The PPG stage generates partial products from multiplicand and multiplier in parallel. The PPA stage then performs multi-operand addition for all partial products and produces their sum in carry-save form. Finally, the carry-save form is converted to the binary output at the FSA stage.

In Fig.1, we show the detailed structure of a 6-bit multiplier $x * y$ using simple XORs as PPG and Wallace tree as PPA, where $x = (x_5 x_4 x_3 x_2 x_1 x_0)_2$ and $y = (y_5 y_4 y_3 y_2 y_1 y_0)_2$ are binary representations of $x$ and $y$, respectively. All

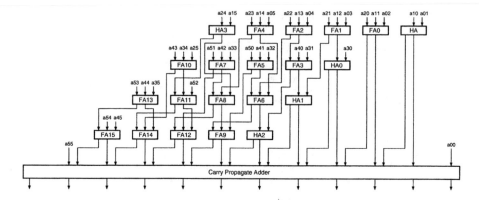

**Fig. 1.** 6-bit multiplier with Wallace tree

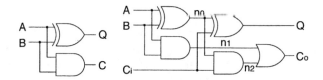

**Fig. 2.** Half Adder (HA) and Full Adder (FA)

partial products $a_{ij} = x_i \& y_j$ for $0 \leq i, j \leq 5$ are summed in carry-save form at Wallace tree that is composed of Half Adders (HA) and Full Adders (FA) shown in Fig.2. In the final stage, a carry propagate adder generates a product from 11-bit sum and 9-bit carry.

### 3.3   Biased Signal Transition Probability in a Multiplier

Power consumption in CMOS circuits depends on the transition probability of signals without power consumption caused by the leakage current, which is determined by the characteristics of the CMOS process. Therefore, regarding to power analysis, we have only to consider transition probability of signals [19, 20]. When the transition probability in two cases is biased, the difference of power consumption occurs.

Here we estimate the signal transition probability of FA0, FA1, FA2, FA4, FA5, FA7, FA10 and FA13, depth-1 full adders of Wallace tree, in Fig.1. The all three inputs $A, B, C_i$ of these full adders consist of partial products $a_{ij}$. We consider the following two cases about the inputs $(x, y)$ of the 6-bit multiplier:

(i) transition from $(s, t)$ to $(s', t)$,
(ii) transition from $(s, t)$ to $(t, t)$,

where $s, s'$ and $t$ are 6-bit random values, respectively. $a_{ij} = 1$ generally occurs with probability $1/4$ by $a_{ij} = x_i \& y_j$.

**Table 5.** Signal transition probability of Full Adders (FAs)

| signal | transition | TypeN | TypeA1 | TypeA2 | TypeA3 | TypeA4 |
|--------|-----------|-------|--------|--------|--------|--------|
| $A$ | $0 \to 1$ | 1/8 | 1/8 | 1/8 | 1/4 | 1/8 |
|  | $1 \to 0$ | 1/8 | 1/8 | 1/8 | 0 | 1/8 |
| $B$ | $0 \to 1$ | 1/8 | 1/8 | 1/8 | 1/8 | 1/4 |
|  | $1 \to 0$ | 1/8 | 1/8 | 1/8 | 1/8 | 0 |
| $C_i$ | $0 \to 1$ | 1/8 | 1/8 | 1/4 | 1/8 | 1/8 |
|  | $1 \to 0$ | 1/8 | 1/8 | 0 | 1/8 | 1/8 |
| $n_0$ | $0 \to 1$ | 3/16 | 3/16 | 3/16 | 1/4 | 1/4 |
|  | $1 \to 0$ | 3/16 | 3/16 | 3/16 | 1/8 | 1/8 |
| $n_1$ | $0 \to 1$ | 9/128 | 9/64 | 9/64 | 3/32 | 3/32 |
|  | $1 \to 0$ | 9/128 | 3/64 | 3/64 | 1/32 | 1/16 |
| $n_2$ | $0 \to 1$ | 3/64 | 3/54 | 3/64 | 3/32 | 3/32 |
|  | $1 \to 0$ | 3/64 | 3/64 | 3/64 | 1/32 | 1/32 |
| $Q$ | $0 \to 1$ | 7/32 | 1/8 | 1/4 | 1/4 | 1/4 |
|  | $1 \to 0$ | 7/32 | 5/16 | 3/16 | 3/16 | 3/16 |
| $C_o$ | $0 \to 1$ | 13/128 | 5/32 | 21/128 | 21/128 | 5/32 |
|  | $1 \to 0$ | 13/128 | 1/16 | 9/128 | 9/128 | 1/16 |
| Total | | 2 | 33/16 | 133/64 | 133/64 | 33/16 |

In case (i), all the eight FAs have the same transition probability of inputs, internal nodes and outputs as TypeN shown in Table 5. Meanwhile, in case (ii) FA4 and FA5 also have the same probability as TypeN, but the other FAs are divided into four types, which have different probability from TypeN in Table 5, as follows.

**TypeA1** $A = C_i$ and $B = a_{ii}$  (FA0, FA13)
**TypeA2** $B = C_i$  (FA1, FA10)
**TypeA3** $C_i = a_{ii}$  (FA2)
**TypeA4** $A = a_{ii}$  (FA7)

This biased transition probability results from the following biased state: $a_{ij} = a_{ji}$ and $a_{ii} = 1$ with probability $1/2$ when $(x, y) = (t, t)$. The expectation of the total transition frequency for these FAs in case (ii) is larger by $13/32$ than that in case (i). Moreover, the biased transition probability of outputs $Q, C_o$ in these FAs influences transition probability of depth-2/3 adders in Wallace tree and the carry propagate adder. Therefore, the power consumption traces of the 6-bit multiplier in case (i) and (ii) differ, which will not depend on the bit-width and structure of a multiplier — the difference will occur, for example, when using a 32-bit multiplier with booth encoder as PPG and 4:2 compressor tree as PPA.

We denote Montgomery modular multiplication with inputs $X$ and $Y$ satisfying $X = Y$, namely Montgomery modular squaring, by $SQR$ and Montgomery modular multiplication with general $X$ and $Y$ by $MUL$. Let $C_S$ and $C_M$ be power consumption traces during $SQR$ and $MUL$, respectively. During $SQR$, the inputs of multiplier transit from $(X_{i-1}, X_i)$ to $(X_i, X_i)$ at $j = i$ in step 2.2, which corresponds to case (ii). On the other hand, during $MUL$, the inputs of multiplier then transit to from $(X_{i-1}, Y_i)$ to $(X_i, Y_i)$, which corresponds to case (i). Therefore, the difference $\Delta C = C_S - C_M$ will present a peak at $j = i$

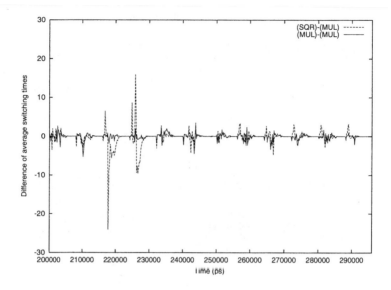

**Fig. 3.** Simulation result of the differential power between $SQR$ and $MUL$

in step 2.2. Similarly, $\Delta C$ also will show a peak at $j = i + 1$ because the biased transition from biased state to random state occurs in a multiplier during $SQR$.

### 3.4   Simulation Result

We performed a net-list timing simulation of Montgomery modular multiplication circuits in our ECC co-processor, reported in [1]. We used a 90-nm CMOS standard cell library and then made estimated power consumption traces by counting the number of gate switching times in every 200ps. In Fig.3, the dotted line shows the difference of average switching times between $SQR$ and $MUL$ for random 10000 inputs at $i = 2$ in step 2.2; the solid line shows the difference between both $MUL$ for random 10000 inputs. The dotted line shows sharp peaks at the 3rd and 4th cycles, namely at $j = 2$ and 3.

*Remark 2.* The power consumption is biased between modular *multiplication* and modular *squaring* for any modular multiplication algorithm because the multiplication of inputs $X$ and $Y$ is required.

## 4   Application to Elliptic Curve Cryptosystems

We apply the difference of power consumption between *multiplication* and *squaring* to the above-mentioned two DPA countermeasures, namely unified addition formulae and Montgomery ladder on a Montgomery-form curve.

## 4.1   Attack to Unified Addition Formulae

The distinguishability between modular *multiplication* and modular *squaring* is applicable to an attack to a scalar multiplication $dP$ for a secret scalar $d$ and a point $P$ using unified addition formulae. We notice the modular multiplication $x_1 x_0$, denoted by **MUL1**, in the affine coordinate version of unified addition formulae in section 2.3. The formulae work as ECADD when $x_1 \neq x_0$ and as ECDBL when $x_1 = x_0$. Hence, if an attacker can distinguish whether **MUL1** is a modular *multiplication* or a modular *squaring*, she knows whether the corresponding operation is ECADD or ECDBL and detects bit information of the secret scalar $d$.

Assume that randomized curve isomorphism is used as a DPA countermeasure. $P_0 = (x_0, y_0)$ and $P_1 = (x_1, y_1)$ is transformed to its isomorphic class like $P_0' = (\lambda^2 x_0, \lambda^3 y_0)$ and $P_1' = (\lambda^2 x_1, \lambda^3 y_1)$ for a random value $\lambda \in \mathbb{F}_p^*$. In the case, the modular multiplication $(\lambda^2 x_1)(\lambda^2 x_0)$ is computed as **MUL1**. Thus **MUL1** remains a modular *multiplication* when $P_0' \neq P_1'$ and a modular *squaring* when $P_0' = P_1'$.

In the following, we present the precise algorithm to search the bit of $d$ for a scalar multiplication $dP$ using unified addition formulae. We assume that the scalar multiplication is computed by the binary method. The unified addition formulae is computed $m = l(d) + h(d) - 1$ times during a single scalar multiplication, where $l(d)$ is the bit length of $d$ and $h(d)$ is the hamming weight of $d$; precisely $h(d) - 1$ times as "A" (ECADD) and $l(d)$ times as "D" (ECDBL).

**[Bit search algorithm for unified addition formulae]**
1. Measure power consumption traces of $dP$ $L$ times and average them.
2. Extract the average traces $C_i$ $(1 \leq i \leq m)$ when computing **MUL1** during the $i$-th execution of the formulae.
3. Assume "A" if $\Delta C_i = C_i - C_1$ $(2 \leq i \leq m)$ shows a peak and "D" if not.
4. Regard "DA" as a bit "1" and the remaining "D" as a bit "0".

The first execution of **MUL1** corresponds to a modular *squaring* because the scalar multiplication always computes ECDBL in the beginning. Therefore, if $\Delta C_i$ shows a peak, $x_1 x_0$ is a modular *multiplication* and the execution corresponds to ECADD.

*Remark 3.* The proposed attack is also applicable to the projective coordinate version of unified addition formulae [4].

## 4.2   Attack to Elliptic Curve with Montgomery-Form

As described in section 2.4, there is no "special" point of small order for RPA and ZPA in Montgomery doubling formulae (mECDBL). Therefore, Montgomery ladder on a Montgomery-form curve together with randomized projective representation is secure against SPA/DPA/RPA/ZPA. $P_0 = (X_0 : Z_0)$ is transformed to its random projective representation like $P_0 = (\lambda X_0 : \lambda Z_0)$ for a random value $\lambda \in \mathbb{F}_p^*$. Here we propose another "special" point that equalizes both inputs of a certain modular multiplication in mECDBL. We notice the modular multiplication $(4X_0Z_0)((X_0 - Z_0)^2 + ((A+2)/4)(4X_0Z_0))$, denoted by **MUL2**, in mECDBL.

Let $E = 4X_0Z_0$ and $F = (X_0 - Z_0)^2 + ((A+2)/4)(4X_0Z_0)$. **MUL2**, of course, becomes a modular *squaring* when $E = F$. The condition satisfying $E = F$ is that x-coordinate $x_0 = X_0/Z_0$ of $P_0$ satisfies $x_0^2 + (A - 4)x_0 + 1 = 0$ by

$$E - F = -(X_0^2 + (A - 4)X_0Z_0 + Z_0^2)$$
$$= -Z_0^2(x_0^2 + (A - 4)x_0 + 1).$$

Even if projective representation of $P_0$ is randomized as $P_0 = (\lambda X_0 : \lambda Z_0)$, the condition of $E = F$ still implies $x_0^2 + (A - 4)x_0 + 1 = 0$ by $-\lambda^2 Z_0^2(x_0^2 + (A - 4)x_0 + 1) = 0$.

Let $R = (x_R, y_R)$ of order $\#R$ be the point satisfying $x_R^2 + (A - 4)x_R + 1 = 0$ and exist on the underlying Montgomery-form curve. If the input point of mECDBL is $R$, **MUL2** becomes a modular *squaring* despite randomized projective representation. Suppose that a scalar multiplication $dP$ for a secret scalar $d$ and a point $P$ is computed by Montgomery ladder (Table 2) and randomized projective representation, where $P$ can be adaptively chosen by an attacker. Here we assume that she knows $(n - i - 1)$ most significant bits $(d_{n-1} \cdots d_{i+1})$ of $d$. In Table 2, for any given input point $P$, the points $Q[0]$ and $Q[1]$ obtained at the beginning of the $i$-th step of the loop are $Q[0] = (\sum_{j=i+1}^{n-1} d_j 2^{j-i-1}) \cdot P$ and $Q[1] = (\sum_{j=i+1}^{n-1} d_j 2^{j-i-1} + 1) \cdot P$. We then have two cases:

- If $d_i = 0$, the input point of mECDBL is $(\sum_{j=i+1}^{n-1} d_j 2^{j-i-1}) \cdot P$.
- If $d_i = 1$, the input point of mECDBL is $(\sum_{j=i+1}^{n-1} d_j 2^{j-i-1} + 1) \cdot P$.

Thus, **MUL2** becomes a modular *squaring* at the $i$-the step of the loop in the following two cases:

- $d_i = 0$ and $P = [(\sum_{j=i+1}^{n-1} d_j 2^{j-i-1})^{-1} \bmod \#R] \cdot R$,
- $d_i = 1$ and $P = [(\sum_{j=i+1}^{n-1} d_j 2^{j-i-1} + 1)^{-1} \bmod \#R] \cdot R$.

In these cases biased power consumption occurs in **MUL2** compared to a modular *multiplication*.

We present the algorithm to search the bit of a secret scalar $d$ from the most significant bit.

**[Bit search algorithm for Montgomery-form curve]**
1. Measure power consumption traces for $L$ random input points $P$ and average them by $C_t$.
2. $i \leftarrow n - 2$.
3. Compute $P_0 = [k^{-1} \bmod \#R] \cdot R$ and $P_1 = [(k + 1)^{-1} \bmod \#R] \cdot R$ for $k = \sum_{j=i+1}^{n-1} d_j 2^{j-i-1}$.
4. Measure power consumption traces $L$ times for the input point $P_0$ and average them by $C_0$.

5. Measure power consumption traces $L$ times for the input point $P_1$ and average them by $C_1$.
6. Compute $\Delta C_0 = C_0 - C_t$ and $\Delta C_1 = C_1 - C_t$.
7. Assume that $d_i = 0$ if $\Delta C_0$ during **MUL2** at the $i$-th step of the loop has larger peaks than $\Delta C_1$ and $d_i = 1$ otherwise.
8. If $i = 0$, terminate; else $i \leftarrow i - 1$ and go to 3.

The average power trace $C_t$ is used as a standard one where **MUL2** is a modular *multiplication* at every step of the loop.

# 5   Conclusion

We presented detailed descriptions of the biased power consumption between Montgomery modular *multiplication* and Montgomery modular *squaring*. However, it must be emphasized that the bias occurs in any modular multiplication algorithm. We applied this bias to unified addition formulae and Montgomery ladder on a Montgomery-form elliptic curve. We should randomize not only a base point but also a secret scalar for these power analysis countermeasures.

# References

1. T. Akishita, K. Iizuka, and H. Sato, "Hardware Implementation of Elliptic Curve Cryptosystems for Contactless IC Card", Proceedings of SCIS 2002, 15B-1, pp.1107-1112, 2002 (in Japanese).
2. T. Akishita and T. Takagi, "Zero-Value Point Attack on Elliptic Curve Cryptosystems", *Information Security - ISC 2003*, LNCS 2851, pp.218-233, Springer-Verlag, 2003.
3. I.F. Blake, G. Seroussi, and N.P. Smart, *Advances in Elliptic Curve Cryptography*, Cambridge University Press, 2005.
4. E. Brier and M. Joye, "Weierstrass Elliptic Curve and Side-Channel Attacks", *Public Key Cryptography - PKC 2002*, LNCS 2274, pp.335-345, Springer-Verlag, 2002.
5. J.-S. Coron, "Resistance against Differential Power Analysis for Elliptic Curve Cryptosystems", *Cryptographic Hardware and Embedded Systems - CHES '99*, LNCS 1717, pp.292-302, Springer-Verlag, 1999.
6. L. Goubin, "A Refined Power-Analysis Attack on Elliptic Curve Cryptosystems", *Public Key Cryptography - PKC 2003*, LNCS 2567, pp.199-211, Springer-Verlag, 2003.
7. K. Itoh, T. Izu, and T. Takenaka, "Efficient Countermeasures against Power Analysis for Elliptic Curve Cryptosystems", *Sixth Smart Card Research an Advanced Application IFIP Conference - CARDIS 2004*, pp.99-114, Kluwer, 2004.
8. T. Izu and T. Takagi, "Exceptional Procedure Attack on Elliptic Curve Cryptosystems", *Public Key Cryptography - PKC 2003*, LNCS 2567, pp.224-239, Springer-Verlag, 2003.
9. M. Joye and C. Tymen, "Protection against Differential Analysis for Elliptic Curve Cryptography", *Cryptographic Hardware and Embedded Systems - CHES 2001*, LNCS 2162, pp.377-390, Springer-Verlag, 2001.

10. M. Joye and J.-J. Quisquater, "Hessian Elliptic Curves and Side-Channel Attacks", *Cryptographic Hardware and Embedded Systems - CHES 2001*, LNCS 2162, pp.402-410, Springer-Verlag, 2001.
11. P. Kocher, J. Jaffe, and B. Jun, "Differential Power Analysis", *Advances in Cryptology - CRYPTO '99*, LNCS 1666, pp.388-397, Springer-Verlag, 1999.
12. P.-Y. Liardet and N.P. Smart, "Preventing SPA/DPA in ECC Systems Using the Jacobi Form", *Cryptographic Hardware and Embedded Systems - CHES 2001*, LNCS 2162, pp.391-401, Springer-Verlag, 2001.
13. T.S. Messerges, E.A. Dabbish, and R.H. Sloan, "Power Analysis Attacks of Modular Exponentiation in Smartcards", *Cryptographic Hardware and Embedded Systems - CHES '99*, LNCS 1717, pp.144-157, Springer-Verlag, 1999.
14. H. Mamiya, A. Miyaji, and H. Morimoto, "Efficient Countermeasure against RPA, DPA, and SPA", *Cryptographic Hardware and Embedded Systems - CHES 2004*, LNCS 3156, pp.343-356, Springer-Verlag, 2004.
15. P.L. Montgomery, "Speeding the Pollard and Elliptic Curve Methods of Factorization", *Mathematics of Computation*, vol.48, pp.243-264, 1987.
16. K. Okeya, H. Kurumatani, and K. Sakurai, "Elliptic Curves with the Montgomery-Form and Their Cryptographic Applications", *Public Key Cryptography - PKC 2000*, LNCS 1751, pp.238-257, Springer-Verlag, 2000.
17. K. Okeya, K. Miyazaki, and K. Sakurai, "A Fast Scalar Multiplication Method with Randomized Projective Coordinate on a Montgomery-Form Elliptic Curve Secure against Side Channel Attacks", *Information Security and Cryptology - ICISC 2001*, LNCS 2288, pp.428-439, Springer-Verlag, 2002.
18. N.P. Smart, "An Analysis of Goubin's Refined Power Analysis Attack", *Cryptographic Hardware and Embedded Systems - CHES 2003*, LNCS 2779, pp.281-290, Springer-Verlag, 2003.
19. D. Suzuki, M. Saeki, and T. Ichikawa, "Random Switching Logic: A Countermeasure against DPA based on Transition Probability", IACR Cryptology ePrint Archive 2004/346, 2004. http://eprint.iacr.org/2004/346/
20. D. Suzuki, M. Saeki, and T. Ichikawa, "DPA Leakage Model for CMOS Logic Circuits", *Cryptographic Hardware and Embedded Systems - CHES 2005*, LNCS 3659, pp.366-382, Springer-Verlag, 2005.
21. C.D. Walter, "Simple Power Analysis of Unified Code for ECC Double and Add", *Cryptographic Hardware and Embedded Systems - CHES 2004*, LNCS 3156, pp.191-204, Springer-Verlag, 2004.

# Designing Smartcards for Emerging Wireless Networks

Pascal Urien[1] and Mesmin Dandjinou[2]

[1] ENST 37/39 rue Dareau, Paris 75014, France
[2] Université Polytechnique de Bobo-Dioulasso, Burkina Faso
Pascal.Urien@enst.fr
Mesmin.Dandjinou@voila.fr

**Abstract.** This paper presents our work relating to introduction of EAP smartcards in emerging wireless LAN like Wi-Fi or WiMax. We analyse basic characteristics involved in authentication protocols from feasibility and performances points of view. We shortly introduce our open Java architecture, and underline some observed interoperability issues. We present and analyze results obtained with five different smartcards, for two authentication scenarios: the first one works with an asymmetric algorithm (EAP-TLS, a transparent transport of the well known SSL standard), and the second method uses the EAP-AKA protocol, which is an adaptation of the symmetric Milenage algorithm. We introduce a new class of smartcard which acts as EAP server, and that has been successfully tested in operational networks. Finally we suggest a new way to manage and use smartcards, remotely and securely, by using Trusted EAP Modules.

## 1 Introduction

In 1999, the IEEE 802 committee ratified the 802.11 standard [3] which introduced the first wireless Ethernet network, later enhanced with 802.11i standard [9]. Wi-Fi technology became the foundation stone of cheap IP radio LAN. Two years after, an *"Air Interface for Fixed Broadband Wireless Access Systems"* was proposed in [6] that extends wireless IP connectivity at a campus scale. The emerging IEEE 802.16e [14] standard, *"Air Interface for Fixed and Mobile Broadband Wireless Access Systems"*, provides enhancements to [6] in order to support subscriber stations moving at vehicular speeds.

But unlike the GSM network, no security module was specified in the so called *Wi-Technologies*. There is however a common denominator between [5] and [6], both of them supports the *Extensible Authentication Protocol* [10]. EAP is a light protocol, used prior to IP address allocation, that may transport multiple authentication scenari like EAP-TLS [2] or EAP-AKA [13].

An EAP dialog occurs between an EAP client, that wants to gain access to network resources, and an EAP authenticator which is the heart of an AAA (Authentication, Authorization and Accounting) system. An EAP session is a set of (server) requests and (client) responses; at the end of this exchange the server delivers either a success or a failure message. Upon success both EAP entities compute a shared secret referred as the AAA key. EAP messages are transported either by non IP protocols like EAPoL [5] or PKM-EAP [14] on the wireless media (between the access point / base station and the client), or by routable protocols such as RADIUS [8] or DIAMETER [17] over the Internet network (between the access point / base station and the AAA server).

J. Domingo-Ferrer, J. Posegga, and D. Schreckling (Eds.): CARDIS 2006, LNCS 3928, pp. 165–178, 2006.

In this paper we introduce smartcards associated to EAP clients and EAP servers. Section 2 shortly reviews basic services that must be supported by EAP cards. Section 3 describes the software architecture of an open implementation for Java cards. Section 4 presents experimental results with five kinds of Java cards. Section 5 defines EAP servers for Java cards and gives early results. In the last section we introduce the Trusted EAP Module (TEAPM), an innovative architecture that will improve usage and remote management of smartcards.

## 2  EAP Java Cards Issues

They are two main issues concerning the use of smartcards for computing the EAP protocol: the protocol complexity and the computing speed.

Protocol complexity must be compatible with Java cards computing resources. As an illustration, byte code size is about 20 kB for EAP-TLS implementation, and 16 kB for EAP-AKA implementation; that is well-suited with today Java cards characteristics.

The need for Java cards performance estimation is not new, for example *a performance comparison of Java cards for micro payment implementation* was discussed in [4]. More recently, an initiative for *open benchmark for Java card technology* has been launched by [12], in order to setup a missing and useful tool for the smartcards industry. A study of Java cards performances has been recently presented in [18].

In our approach we classify processing operations in three categories: data transfer, cryptographic operations, and software overhead. So, the processing time of an application can be written like:

$$T_{Application} = T_{Transfer} + T_{Crypto} + T_{SoftwareOverhead} \cdot \tag{1}$$

Our applications embed test functions that are used to identify critical parameters.

### 2.1  Data Transfer

In protocols dealing with X.509 certificates like EAP-TLS, several kilobytes of data are sent/received to/from the smartcard. Due to the lack of RAM memory, these information are written or read in the non-volatile memory ($E^2PROM$, flash memory,...). Therefore we call data transfer, the time required for transporting EAP packets between a terminal that controls the smartcard and the application running in this device. From a practical point of view it is easy to measure this time, but we shall not try to estimate the different elements that make up this value, like transfer delays between terminal and reader, transfer duration between reader and smartcard, internal software delays (introduced for example by java operations) and time consumed by memories accesses (writing and reading). Named $T_{Transfer}$, it is expressed like:

$$T_{Transfer} = T_{TransferReader} + T_{TransferSmartcard} + T_{SoftwareOverhead} + T_{MemoriesAccesses} \cdot \tag{2}$$

Figure 1 presents transfer characteristics measured with four smartcards labeled A, B, C and D; the reader is the same excepted for device A which integrates an USB interface. Reading and writing operations (respectively from and to a smartcard) require similar times. The transfer law is quite linear ($T_{Transfer} = a + b \times Length$) with $a$ corresponding to a factor around 50 ms and $b$ to a factor around 0.6 ms/byte for A and D devices, and 1.7 ms/byte for B and C devices.

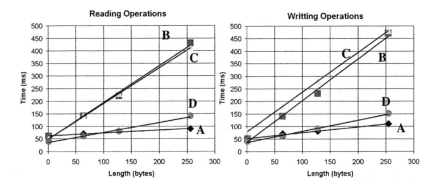

**Fig. 1.** Measured times for reading and writing operations

## 2.2 Cryptographic Operations

In a Java card context, cryptographic functions are invoked via specific APIs. For the authentication methods studied in this paper, the main cryptographic procedures are MD5, SHA1, RSA and AES.

Figure 2 shows MD5 and SHA1 speed; the time required by a digest operation is proportional to the number of computed blocs whose size is 512 bits. The time required by bloc is respectively (by alphabetical device name order ) 15.3 ms, 8.5 ms, 10.2 ms, 3.0 ms for MD5, and 33.2 ms, 14.8 ms, 17.3 ms, 4.4 ms for SHA1. Because smartcards are usually optimized for RSA functions, these operations are rather "fast". During the TLS protocol, three RSA calculations are performed: firstly during server certificate checking (public key decryption), secondly for pre-master key encryption (public key encryption), and thirdly for client's authentication (private key encryption). As demonstrated by Table 1, these procedures consumed less than 500 ms.

In our experiments we only get one smartcard (device E) that supports the AES algorithm. We observe for this device a computing time of about 11.3 ms per bloc of 128 bits.

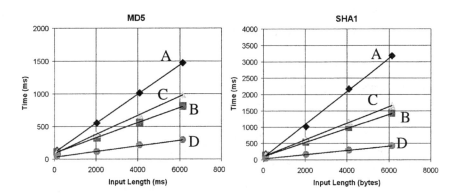

**Fig. 2.** Computing times for MD5 and SHA1 digests

**Table 1.** Estimation of RSA computing times

|   | RSA (1)+(2)+(3) ms | Private Key Encryption (1) | Public Key Decryption (2) | Public Key Encryption (3) | Private Key Decryption (4) |
|---|---|---|---|---|---|
| A | 320 | 230 | 50 | 40 | 220 |
| B | 320 | 160 | 110 | 50 | 230 |
| C | 322 | 191 | 61 | 70 | 200 |
| D | 150 | 110 | 20 | 20 | 120 |

### 2.3 Software Overhead

All resources that are not available through APIs are supplied by the embedded (Java) application. This includes extra software needed for packets analysis, messages construction, additional cryptographic services like keyed MAC (HMAC), pseudo random functions (PRF), or some specific services like X.509 certificates parsing.

### 2.4 Performances Issues

The timing constraints induced by smartcards usage in wireless environments are linked to EAP and DHCP [21] protocols requirements.

On the authenticator side, the EAP server sends requests and waits for responses before a timeout; and this waiting time called *txPeriod* lasts [5] 30 s by default (with 3 retries). If the smartcard computing time exceeds this value a retransmission occurs. On Windows platforms, DHCP is a parallel event, independent of EAP authentication, that starts once network interface comes up. If the IP client doesn't receive a DHCP acknowledgement within a reasonable period of time, usually 60 s, the terminal OS resets the network interface, and therefore restarts both DHCP and EAP processes.

In summary the two main timing requirements are:

- computing an EAP request in less than 30 s, *and*
- processing an authentication scenario in less than 60 s.

This last value also includes the time consumed by the user to enter, if necessary, its PIN code.

## 3   OpenEapSmartcard

The basic idea behind an open platform [16] [20] is to define a simple Java framework (whose APDUs interface is described in [15]) working with most of commercial Java cards, and supporting as many EAP methods as possible.

The software architecture comprises four Java components:

1. The EapEngine that manages several methods and/or multiple instances of the same one. It implements the EAP core, and acts as a router that sends and receives packets to/from authentication methods. At the end of authentication

process, each method computes a master cryptographic key (*AAA Key*) which is read by the terminal operating system.

2. The Authentication interface that defines all mandatory services in EAP methods, in order to collaborate with the EapEngine. The two main functions are *Init()* and *Process-Eap()*. First initializes method and returns an Authentication interface; second processes incoming EAP packets. Methods may provide additional facilities dedicated to performances evaluations.

3. The Credential objects that, each one associated to a method, encapsulate all the information required for processing the given authentication scenari.

4. The Methods that correspond to the specific authentication scenarios to process. Once initialized, the selected method analyses each incoming EAP request and delivers corresponding response.

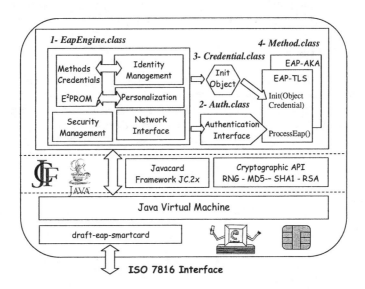

**Fig. 3.** OpenEapSmartcard software architecture

Due to the Java language universality, we could hope that the same code works with all smartcards; the reality is a little bit different because almost all devices present minor differences or even bugs. Here is a brief description of some observed interoperability issues:

- in TLS, the RSA algorithm is issued in conjunction with the PKCS#1 padding rules. Sometimes this functionality is not available (only NO_PAD option is working), and therefore an additional Java code is required;
- digests functions use *Update()* function for digest updating and *DoFinal()* procedure for digest closing. Sometimes *Update()* is not supported, and therefore it is necessary to concatenate all data in the non-volatile memory, in order to compute the output value;
- in some cases we observed erroneous values produced by the *Update()* method invoked with a "long" (a few thousand bytes) input value;

– with some components it is only possible to deal with one instance of MD5 or SHA1 object. As a result an interoperable application can only use one instance which implies multiple writings in non-volatile memory, so that the performances decrease (TLS produces three MD5 and SHA1 calculations).

Our EAP-TLS method takes into account these constraints. It works with RSA algorithm with no padding byte; it is compatible with single digest instance, and manages bugged or missing *Update()* methods.

# 4  Experimental Results

The same EAP-TLS application, including minor adaptations dealing with devices particularities (detailed in section 3), was downloaded in our four different Java cards A, B, C and D. EAP-AKA was tested with device E only.

## 4.1  With EAP-TLS

EAP-TLS [2] is a transparent transport of the TLS protocol [1] which has two working modes (see figure 4). The first one, referred as *full mode*, is asymmetric and uses a mutual authentication based on RSA, and that requires certificates exchange for both server and client. The second mode qualified *session resume* works according to a symmetric scheme and deals with a shared secret, the *master secret* computed during a previous full session identified by a *session-id* parameter. A detailed analysis of the EAP-TLS application was described in [11].

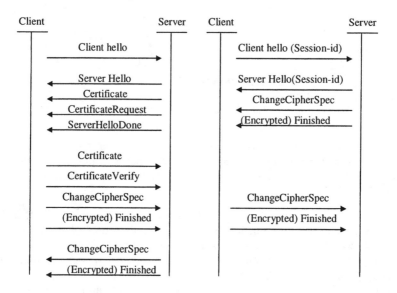

**Fig. 4.** TLS message exchange, *full* mode (left part) and *session resume* mode (right part)

With 1024 bits RSA keys, a *full* mode typically has the following characteristics:

- 2500 bytes of information are exchanged between the TLS client and the TLS server, for the duration of $T_{Transfer}$;
- three RSA calculations are performed (public key decryption, public key encryption and private key encryption) and need a total time $T_{RSA}$;
- approximately 266 blocs of 512 bits are processed by MD5 and SHA1 functions. If we call $T_{Digest}$ the average time for computing a bloc ($T_{MD5}/2+ T_{SHA1}/2$), these calculations cost 532 times $T_{Digest}$;
- other operations, like X.509 certificate parsing, EAP and TLS messages processing are handled by Java procedures and consume a time $T_{SoftwareOverhead}$.

Because all cryptographic resources are seen from a practical point of view as APIs, we called $T_{Crypto}$ the time consumed by these facilities and expressed it as:

$$T_{Crypto} = T_{RSA} + 532 \times T_{Digest}. \tag{3}$$

As a consequence, the time spent in EAP-TLS computing named $T_{EAP-TLS}$ can be split in three categories according to the following formula:

$$T_{EAP-TLS} = T_{Transfer} + T_{Crypto} + T_{SoftwareOverhead}. \tag{4}$$

Total computing time ($T_{EAP-TLS}$) and data transfer duration ($T_{Transfer}$) are obtained by direct measurements. $T_{Crypto}$ is deduced from basic parameters presented in section 2.2. So, $T_{SoftwareOverhead}$ value can be deduced as:

$$T_{SoftwareOverhead} = T_{EAP-TLS} - T_{Transfer} - T_{Crypto}. \tag{5}$$

Table 2 presents experimental results, and a detailed comparison of Java cards performances is presented in *Appendix 1*; the reading of [11] may be useful for understanding these exhaustive comparisons.

The *session resume* mode typically presents the following characteristics:

- no RSA calculation is performed;
- 230 bytes of information are exchanged between TLS client and TLS server, which require a time called $T_{Transfer}$;
- approximately 158 blocs of 512 bits are processed by MD5 and SHA1 functions. If we call $T_{Digest}$ the average time for computing a bloc ($T_{MD5}/2+ T_{SHA1}/2$), these calculations cost 316 times $T_{Digest}$;
- other operations, like EAP and TLS messages processing, are handled by Java procedures and consume a time $T_{SoftwareOverhead}$.

Because all cryptographic resources are seen from an applicative point of view as APIs, we called $T_{Crypto}$ all the time consumed by these facilities and we expressed it as:

$$T_{Crypto} = T_{RSA} + 532 \times T_{Digest}. \tag{6}$$

**Table 2.** EAP-TLS *full* mode performances

|  | A | B | C | D |
|---|---|---|---|---|
| $T_{Transfer}$ (ms) | 2492 | 5326 | 5219 | 1433 |
| $T_{Crypto}$ (ms) | 13221 | 6507 | 7648 | 2117 |
| $T_{SoftwareOverhead}$ (ms) | 62618 | 21914 | 14784 | 6827 |
| $T_{EAP-TLS}$ (ms) | 78331 | 33747 | 27651 | 10377 |

As a result, the time spent in EAP-TLS computing named $T_{EAP\text{-}TLS}$ is shared in three categories:

$$T_{EAP\text{-}TLS} = T_{Transfer} + T_{Crypto} + T_{SoftwareOverhead}. \tag{7}$$

Table 3 shows experimental results, where $T_{SoftwareOverhead}$ is deduced as previously.

**Table 3.** EAP-TLS *session resume* mode performances

|  | A | B | C | D |
|---|---|---|---|---|
| $T_{Transfer}$ (ms) | 140 | 450 | 460 | 110 |
| $T_{Crypto}$ (ms) | 7663 | 3675 | 4352 | 1169 |
| $T_{SoftwareOverhead}$ (ms) | 41697 | 19675 | 8688 | 4221 |
| $T_{EAP\text{-}TLS}$ (ms) | 49500 | 23800 | 13500 | 5500 |

## 4.2  With EAP-AKA

EAP-AKA [13] is a quite transparent transport of the Milenage algorithm [7]. A full authentication session is made of one request and one response. The request message which is 68 bytes long includes three attributes: a random number RAND (16 bytes)

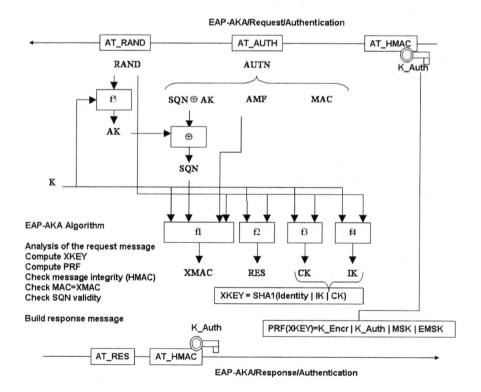

**Fig. 5.** EAP-AKA, Full authentication summary

an authentication value AUTH (16 bytes) and a HMAC-SHA1 trailer (20 bytes). Upon success, the response message whose length is 40 bytes returns two attributes: a signature RES (8 bytes) and a HMAC-SHA1 trailer (20 bytes). This exchange is summarized in figure 5.

The $f_i$ functions ($f_1$, $f_2$, $f_3$, $f_4$, $f_5$) are invoked by the EAP-AKA application, and imply 5 AES calculations. HMAC-SHA1 requires processing of 9 blocs of 512 bits, while the XKEY estimation costs 4 blocs. The pseudo random function (PRF) works with a modified version of SHA1 using a null padding bytes algorithm; the production of 100 bytes requires the calculation of 5 blocs of 512 bits each. Because current versions of Java cards do not support this modified version of SHA1, the procedure is fully written in Java and generates an important software overhead.

In summary the EAP-AKA cost is given by the following expressions:

$$T_{EAP-AKA} = T_{Transfer} + T_{Crypto} + T_{SoftwareOverhead} \cdot \qquad (8)$$

$$\text{with } T_{Crypto} = 5 \times T_{AES} + 18 \times T_{Digest} \cdot \qquad (9)$$

But according to our full software implementation of the PRF function (which computes five modified SHA1 values), we get the formula:

$$T'_{Crypto} = 5 \times T_{AES} + 13 \times T_{Digest} + T_{PRF} \cdot \qquad (10)$$

**Table 4.** Experimental EAP-AKA performances for device E, $T_{Digest} = 4.8$ ms, $T_{AES} = 11.3$ ms

| $T_{EAP-AKA}$ (ms) | $T_{Transfer}$ 108 bytes (ms) | $5 \times T_{AES}$ $f1...f5$ (ms) | $13 \times T_{Digest}$ HMACs and XKEY (ms) | $T_{PRF}$ (ms) | $T_{SoftwareOverhead}$ (ms) |
|---|---|---|---|---|---|
| 5950 | <190 | 56 | 64 | 5650 | >0 |

As shown in table 4, most of computing time is consumed by the PRF function. EAP-AKA should be very efficient, if this function was available via a cryptographic API. Under this hypothesis, the authentication time should be less than 350 ms.

## 5 EAP Server

According to the EAP protocol, clients process requests which are issued by servers. From a software point of view, the EAP server application is very close to the client one. The cryptographic load is quite the same, but messages processing is significantly different. As illustrated by figure 6, we designed [19] a first EAP-TLS server. This server works with real network, but needs a specific RADIUS implementation, that dispatches EAP messages encapsulated in RADIUS packets, to one or more EAP-Server smartcards. In this architecture EAP data are transported by various layers (802.11 frames, RADIUS), but the authentication dialog directly occurs between two EAP smartcards, acting as SAM (Secure Authentication Modules) components.

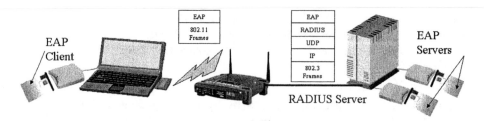

**Fig. 6.** EAP-Server deployment in real networks

**Table 5.** Comparison between EAP client and server performances

|  | B | D |
|---|---|---|
| $T_{EAP\text{-}TLS}$ Client (s) | 33.8 | 10.4 |
| $T_{EAP\text{-}TLS}$ Server (s) | 45.2 | 13.0 |

Table 5 presents measured performances for B and D devices which are used alternatively as clients and servers. We observe that EAP-TLS servers require an additional time of about 30%. We attribute this difference to extra information transfers from $E^2PROM$ to $E^2PROM$, needed for messages construction or data concatenation, induced by digest operations.

## 6   The Trusted EAP Module - TEAPM

Following the results obtained firstly about smartcards performances and secondly concerning OpenEapSmartcard environment for security improvement, and according the perspective of the future advances in smartcard technologies relatively to Moore's law, we suggest a new protocol stack which transforms the usage of smartcards by changing them to a kind of secure electronic pocket deposit box remotely manageable: the Trusted EAP Module.

As it appears in figure 7, EAP protocol and EAP-TLS or other EAP methods represent the heart of this protocol stack. Their presence make possible the mutual authentication establishment which can be followed by a secure exchange and storage of credentials like keys, certificates, account numbers, passwords, profiles, … in the OpenEapSmartcard-based smartcard. In this way, we offer to the users an pocket electronic component which functionally looks like the immutable TPM developed by TCG for trusted computing platforms [22].

With the ISO 7816-4 presence on the one hand of the application layer, we maintain the opening platform aspect by keeping compatibility with existing smartcard applications that use APDUs.

Finally, the choice of HTTP 1.1 and XML protocols on the other hand of the application layer welcomes the development of Web services, on either client side or/and server side.

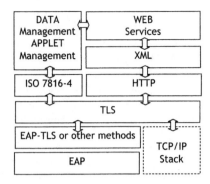

**Fig. 7.** The protocol stack of TEAPM

The implementation and test of this new platform on Java cards are going on. Our wish is to try later the same implementation on a SIM card, and right now nothing prevents from doing it. Surely, this will extend the capacities for secure remote management of services using smartcards, the "air" interface like in GSM network [23] [24], and Web services.

## 7  Conclusion

In this paper we have described a software architecture for EAP smartcards and experimental performances obtained with five devices. These results clearly demonstrate that today smartcards may be successfully introduced for enhancing security in emerging wireless networks. However authentication delays are yet very important in comparison with classical software solutions, probably because firstly some Java cards APIs are missing, and secondly more powerful components are needed, specially for EAP server. The lack of RAM memory leads to a slowdown of data storage in E$^2$PROM, for protocols that exchange several kilobytes of information, like TLS. But this architecture is working with standard Java cards, and it seems likely that performances will follow the Moore's law, and therefore that EAP smartcards will be more and more a credible alternative to traditional software. It is the reason why we propose the Trusted EAP Module, which will facilitate remote management and usage of network security services.

## References

1. RFC 2246, "The TLS Protocol Version 1.0", January 1999.
2. RFC 2716, "PPP EAP TLS Authentication Protocol", B. Aboba, D. Simon. October 1999.
3. Institute of Electrical and Electronics Engineers, "Wireless LAN Medium Access Control (MAC) and Physical Layer (PHY) Specifications", IEEE Standard 802.11, 1999.
4. J. Castellà, J. Domingo-Ferrer, J. Herrera-Joancomartí, J. Planes, "A Performance Comparison of Java Cards for Micro payment Implementation", Proceedings of the Fourth Working Conference on Smart Card Research and Advanced Applications, CARDIS 2000, September 20-22, 2000, Bristol, UK.

5. Institute of Electrical and Electronics Engineers, "Local and Metropolitan Area Networks: Port-Based Network Access Control", IEEE Standard 802.1X, September 2001.
6. Institute of Electrical and Electronics Engineers, "IEEE Standard for Local and Metropolitan Area Networks, part 16, Air Interface for Fixed Broadband Wireless Access Systems,", IEEE Standard 802.16, 2001.
7. 3GPP TS 35.206 V5.0.0, "3rd Generation Partnership Project; Technical Specification Group Services and System Aspects; 3G Security; Specification of the MILENAGE Algorithm Set: An example algorithm set for the 3GPP authentication and key generation functions f1, f1*, f2, f3, f4, f5 and f5*; Document 2: Algorithm Specification", 3GPP, June 2002.
8. RFC 3559, "RADIUS (Remote Authentication Dial In User Service) Support For Extensible Authentication Protocol (EAP)", B. Aboba, P. Calhoun, September 2003.
9. Institute of Electrical and Electronics Engineers, "Supplement to Standard for Telecommunications and Information Exchange Between Systems - LAN/MAN Specific Requirements - Part 11: Wireless LAN Medium Access Control (MAC) and Physical Layer (PHY) Specification for Enhanced Security", IEEE standard 802.11i, 2004.
10. RFC 3748, "Extensible Authentication Protocol, (EAP)", B. Aboba, L. Blunk, J. Vollbrecht, J. Carlson, H. Levkowetz, Ed. June 2004.
11. P. Urien, M. Badra, M. Dandjinou, "EAP-TLS Smartcards, from Dream to Reality", 4th Workshop on Applications and Services in Wireless Networks, ASWN'2004, Boston University, Boston, Massachusetts, USA, August 8-11, 2004.
12. J.-M. Douin, P. Paradinas, C. Pradel, "Open Benchmark for Java Card Technology", e-Smart'2004, Sophia Antipolis, France, September 22-24, 2004.
13. Internet Draft, ."Extensible Authentication Protocol Method for 3rd Generation Authentication and Key Agreement (EAP-AKA)", draft-arkko-pppext-eap-aka-15.txt, December 2004.
14. Institute of Electrical and Electronics Engineers, "Approved Draft IEEE Standard for Local and metropolitan area networks part 16: Air Interface for Fixed and Mobile Broadband Wireless Access Systems Amendment for Physical and Medium Access Control Layers for Combined Fixed and Mobile Operation in Licensed Bands", IEEE 802.16e, December 2005.
15. Internet Draft, "EAP-Support in Smartcard", draft-eap-smartcard-09.txt, October 2005.
16. P. Urien, M. Dandjinou, "The OpenEapSmartcard project", short paper, Applied Cryptography and Network Security 2005, ANCS 2005, Columbia University, June 7-10, New York, USA, 2005.
17. RFC 4072, "Diameter Extensible Authentication Protocol (EAP) Application", P. Eronen, T. Hiller, G. Zorn, August 2005.
18. V. Guyot, "Smartcard, a mobility vector", Phd defense, September 30th 2005, University of Paris 6, Paris, France.
19. P. Urien, M. Dandjinou, M. Badra, "Introducing micro-authentication servers in emerging pervasive environments", IADIS International Conference WWW/Internet 2005, Lisbon, Portugal, October 19-22, 2005.
20. OpenEapSmartcard WEB site, http://www.enst.fr/~urien/openeapsmartcard
21. RFC 2131, "Dynamic Host Configuration Protocol, DHCP", March 1997.
22. TCG, "TPM Main Part 1: Design Principles, Specification Version 1.2 Revision 85", February 2005.
23. 3GPP TS 11.14, "Digital cellular telecommunications system (Phase 2+); Specification of the SIM Application Toolkit (SAT) for the Subscriber Identity Module - Mobile Equipment (SIM-ME) interface", 2003.
24. 3GPP TS 03.48, "Digital cellular telecommunications system (Phase 2+); Security mechanisms for the SIM Application Toolkit; Stage 2", 2001.

## Appendix 1 – Details of EAP-TLS Operations

| EAP-TLS Message | Operation Class | Smartcard | | | |
|---|---|---|---|---|---|
| | | A | B | C | D |
| **First Message** | | | | | |
| Request/Start | Transfer | 510 | 601 | 321 | 151 |
| | | | | | |
| Response/ClientHello | Transfer | 30 | | 120 | 20 |
| **Second Message** | | | | | |
| Request/ServerHello, 1st fragment | Transfer | 210 | 491 | 491 | 130 |
| | Transfer | 140 | 451 | 470 | 110 |
| | Transfer | 131 | 450 | 471 | 120 |
| | Transfer | 140 | 450 | 461 | 110 |
| | Transfer | 130 | 461 | 480 | 130 |
| | | | | | |
| Response/ACK | Transfer | 220 | 410 | 411 | 100 |
| **Third Message** | | | | | |
| Request/ServerHello, 2nd fragment | Transfer | 20 | | 50 | 10 |
| | | | | | |
| Response/ClientFinished | | | | | |
| Certificate Checking | RSA.pub.decrypt+ Other | 2524 | 1312 | 931 | 390 |
| VERIFY | RSA.pub.encrypt+ Other | 8192 | 6400 | 1012 | 541 |
| SHA1+MD5 (VERIFY) | DualHash(Verify) | 1863 | 1121 | 1212 | 381 |
| RSA(VERIFY) | RSA.priv.encrypt+ Other | 530 | 361 | 460 | 261 |
| PRF(MasterSecret) | PRF(MasterSecret) | 9825 | 3294 | 3005 | 1162 |
| PRF(KeyBlock) | PRF(KeyBloc) | 12628 | 4166 | 3825 | 1472 |
| MD5+SHA1+PRF(ClientFinished) | DualHash+PRF(Finished) | 6099 | 2503 | 2524 | 901 |
| MD5+SHA (ServerFinished) | DualHash(ServerFinished) | 2002 | 1222 | 1322 | 410 |
| HMAC-MD5 | HMAC-MD5.compute | 1011 | 451 | 450 | 251 |
| RC4-INIT | RC4.init | 5818 | 691 | 802 | 371 |
| RC4-ENCRYPT | RC4.encrypt | 1813 | 821 | 450 | 310 |
| | | | | | |
| | Transfer | 140 | 480 | 431 | 161 |
| | Transfer | 141 | 470 | 421 | 90 |
| | Transfer | 140 | 471 | 420 | 90 |
| | Transfer | 130 | 310 | 321 | 61 |
| **Fourth Message** | | | | | |
| Request/ServerFinished | | | | | |
| RC4-INIT +RC4-DECRYPT | RC4.init + RC4.decrypt | 7110 | 1292 | 1031 | 441 |
| CHECK HMAC-MD5 | HMAC-MD5.check | 741 | 311 | 381 | 160 |
| PRF(ServerFinished) | PRF(Finished) | 4267 | 1332 | 1342 | 521 |
| PRF(PMK) | PRF(PMK) | 11416 | 3144 | 3685 | 1372 |
| | | | | | |

**Fig. 8.** Detailed EAP-TLS application performances for various smartcards

| Response/ACK | Transfer | 290 | 140 | 160 | 80 |
|---|---|---|---|---|---|
|  |  | 60 |  | 50 | 40 |
| Fifth Message |  |  |  |  |  |
| GET PMK KEY | Transfer | 60 | 141 | 141 | 30 |
|  |  |  |  |  |  |
| Total Time |  | 78331 | 33747 | 27651 | 10377 |

**Fig. 8.** (*continued*)

# Smartcard Firewalls Revisited

Henrich C. Pöhls and Joachim Posegga

Universität Hamburg, FB Informatik,
Sicherheit in Verteilten Systemen (SVS),
Vogt-Kölln-Str. 30, D-22527 Hamburg
svs-office@informatik.uni-hamburg.de

**Abstract.** Smartcards are being used as secure endpoints in computer transactions. Recently, the connectivity of smartcards has increased and future smartcards will be able to communicate over the TCP/IP protocol. In this work, we explore options for using a smartcard as an active node in a communication network rather than as an endpoint.

We envision in particular a proxy firewall running on a smartcard and combining the best of both worlds: the smartcard as a secure environment, and the proxy firewall for securing the network. Facilitating the various security options smartcards offer, we show how to design a secure network firewall on a smartcard. We illustrate the usefulness of such a device in several scenarios.

*Life was simple before World War II.*
*After that, we had systems.*

Rear Admiral Grace Murray Hopper

## 1 Introduction

Smartcards of the latest generation are becoming "network citizens" [13], they are able to participate natively in TCP/IP based networks and possess their own implementation of a TCP/IP stack [12, 6, 5]. We will refer to these as *networked smartcards* throughout the paper.

The core idea of this paper is to design a network firewall within a networked smartcard and route TCP/IP traffic between a single host system and the Internet through this card. Note that this differs from what is known as "applet firewalls" in Javacard[1]: this is a software feature of the Java Card platform to isolate Java objects within the card. Our approach instead suggests that the whole card works as a network firewall for a single network host – a personalized firewall on a smartcard.

We will illustrate the concept of a firewall on a smartcard and provide design ideas on how the concept can be implemented on networked smartcards that will emerge in the near future. An implementation of a firewall on a networked smartcard itself is not documented at this stage, as the cards themselves are still prototypes and hardly available outside the labs of card manufacturers.

J. Domingo-Ferrer, J. Posegga, and D. Schreckling (Eds.): CARDIS 2006, LNCS 3928, pp. 179–191, 2006.
© IFIP International Federation for Information Processing 2006

A firewall on a smartcard would be a small device that has a smartcard with two Ethernet connectors; each one provides its own TCP/IP stack, natively implemented on the smartcard. Today's networked smartcard prototypes are offering just one TCP/IP connection, usually connected over Universal Serial Bus (USB); having two separate connections, however, is technically feasible. We use an additional layer of routing on an intermediate system, to overcome the current restriction of a single network interface.

Our usage model of a smartcard as a network firewall differs from the predominant usage model of smart cards: Instead of the card being an end-point of a communication, we envision the networked smartcard as a transparent network node that acts as a traffic filtering node. Let us consider this more closely.

Cheswick, Bellovin and Rubin define a firewall as "a collection of components placed between two networks, that collectively have the following properties:

- All traffic from inside to outside, and vice-versa, must pass through the firewall.

  Only authorized traffic, as defined by the local security policy, will be allowed to pass.
- The firewall itself is immune to penetration." [17, page 13]

Implementing such firewall functionality on a smart card allows us to take advantage of the secure environment a card provides, thus firewall functions executed in a smartcard environment are better protected than those running on conventional platforms built upon complex operating systems.

The security environment offered by smartcards therefore allows us to come closer to the third property in the above list.

Furthermore, Smartcards provide additional security features that can be facilitated by a firewall running on a smartcard:

- Secure storage for firewall rule sets,
- storage for cryptographic credentials (e.g. certificates) used for network login,
- cryptographic functions to validate credentials or to cryptographically protect network communication (e.g. VPN connections).

We also physically separate the firewall from the host system: This has, among others, the following advantages:

- It eliminates the need to handle security critical firewall functionality in a potentially untrusted host system.
- The "mobility" of the smartcard allows to easily move a user's "personalized" firewall from one host PC to another.
- The "physical" form factor of a firewall in a smart card can make the use of a firewall more comprehensible for the average user[1].

---

[1] It will show its presence/absence more clearly.

## 1.1  Paper Outline

Our paper is organized as follows:

We first consider the network architecture needed for a network firewall (Section 2) and show how this can be implemented on future smartcards even though they will only feature a single network connection. Further, we suggest a design for a simple firewall that would actually run on a smartcard (Section 3). In Section 4, we condense all the security assumptions made and discuss the level of security reached by a firewall on a smartcard. We sketch a few application scenarios to illustrate scenarios for using a firewall on a smartcard in Section 5. After reviewing related work (Section 6) we draw conclusions of our research in Section 7.

## 2  Network Architecture

Our goal is to move all (or at least security-relevant) firewall operations from an untrusted host system to a smartcard. To offer network firewall functionality, all incoming (and outgoing) Internet packets need to pass through the card. The firewall on the smartcard will then decide upon routing or discarding packets according to the rule set stored locally in card.

### 2.1  Emerging "Networked" Smartcard

A networked smartcard natively supports TCP/IP connections by implementing a card-internal TCP/IP stack and it provides a Universal Serial Bus (USB) connector for outward connections [12, 6].

This means no additional hardware or software needs to be installed on the PC: A Plug-and-Play (PnP) aware operating system (OS) will detect the card once it is inserted into the systems USB port. The OS will then automatically install the card as a network device. Depending on the implementation the OS may also route TCP/IP messages from and to the Internet via the system's regular network connection.

According to smartcard vendors, networked smartcards provide a single network connection to the host via USB (at least) through one of the following options [12]:

1. USB → encapsulated Serial → PPP → RAS
2. USB → Remote NDIS[2]
3. USB → CDC[3] Ethernet Emulation Model (EEM)[4] → Ethernet drivers

There might be other options to connect a host to the networked smartcard, but these seem to be most common [12, 6].

---

[2] Remote NDIS (RNDIS) is a Microsoft specification for network devices on dynamic Plug and Play I/O buses such as USB [11].

[3] Also known as Communications Device Class (short CDC), the USB standard also defines an Ethernet Control Model (short CDC Ethernet)[3], but CDC EEM is newer and seems to be favoured.

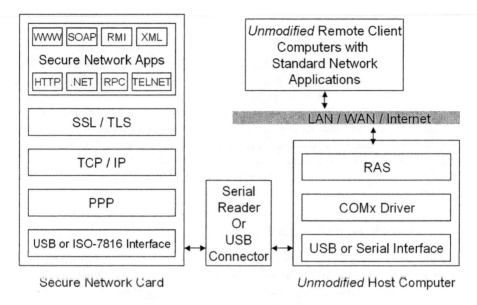

**Fig. 1.** Secure Network Card Architecture [12]

Figure 1 depicts the general architecture of Schlumberger/Axalto's version of such a networked card: Their smartcard offers TCP/IP functionality and can be connected via USB to a host computer, which can then be used to gain access to a network.

A clear benefit of a network connection over USB is that it requires little or no modifications to the host system as it relies on standards that are (or should be) supported by most operating systems. This provides interoperability and mobility.

Since networked smartcard are extensions of today's non-networked smartcards, an off-the-shelf networked smartcard will likely provide:

- a "Java-based operating system" [6]
- a 32-bit chip [6]
- a minimum of 24k RAM [6]
- a 64 kByte EEPROM
- a USB 2.0 connection [6]

The throughput of the smartcard's network connection is limited by the speed of the underlying USB 2.0 connection: Theoretical performance of USB 2.0 in HiSpeed mode is 480 Mbit/s, but measuring TCP/IP connections over a USB 2.0 port shows actual speeds between 7 Mbit/s and 80 Mbit/s[4]. This provides an estimate of the maximum load the firewall, connected over the USB link, can cope with.

---

[4] Measured with NETIO[15] using a packet size of 32 kBytes and 4 kBytes on two Windows XP computers connected by a USB ethernet adapter (D-LINK DUB-E100[2]).

## 2.2   Towards a Firewall on a Networked Smartcard

In order to securely act as a network firewall, all TCP/IP packets must be securely routed through the smartcard and subsequently through the firewall application running on it.

To avoid circumvention the smartcard has to support two network communications: One connection to the untrusted network ("outside") and one to the host ("inside"), often called a "dual homed" system. Rigorously, this can only be achieved if the smartcard provided two physical connections and two separate TCP/IP stacks; off-the-shelf networked smartcards will likely not offer two separate physical connections in the first instance.

To assess firewalls inside a smartcard, we can reduce the restrictions of having two physically separate connections: In order to test a prototype implementation we only need two logically separate network connections to the smartcard.

## 2.3   Routing Packets Through a Smartcard

To establish two at least logically separated connections to the firewall we use an intermediate system; such a system has three physical interfaces:

  – Two physical interfaces, one to the untrusted network (outside), one to the computer that will be protected (inside), and
  – one internal interface over the USB connection to the smartcard, which runs the firewall application.

The intermediate system needs to take care that all packets will travel through the smartcard. The networked smartcard uses its single physical connection (TCP/IP-over-USB) and the resulting network adapter on the intermediate system will be assigned two IP addresses to it. Logical separation will then be based on two distinct IP addresses (either source or destination). Figure 2 shows the concept.

This setting hides a "single homed" smartcard with a firewall from the client and the untrusted network: they only have connections to the intermediate system, and this appears "dual homed".

For security reasons we must of course assume reliable and secure routing of packets within the intermediate system. The security-relevant routing (filtering) is, however, not done on the host. The security impact of this decision is analysed in Section 4. For a prototype implementation, this is not the most relevant aspect, since the goal is only to demonstrate that a network firewall on a smartcard is possible and to assess implications thereof. Once an "ideal" smartcard hardware with two physical network interfaces becomes available, the routing can be moved back to the realm of the card with little impact on the software design.

The intermediate system would also allow us to use a non-networked smartcard as well, but we focus on networked smartcards (see Section 4).

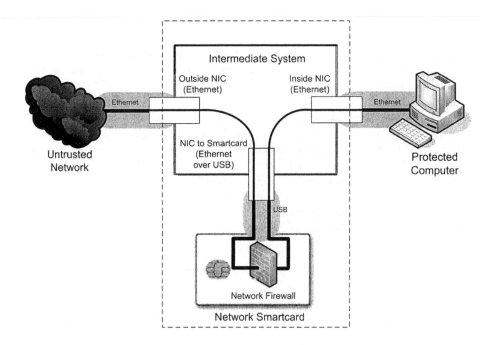

**Fig. 2.** Single connection over USB to smartcard is hidden by intermediate system

## 3    Firewall Design

In the previous section we discussed how to overcome the missing two physical network interfaces. We will now present the design of the firewall software.

In order to provide firewall functionality on a per-packet basis (or packet-filter mode) all IP packets arriving at the smartcard need to be inspected by the firewall implementation: it will decide whether to discard or accept a packet according to a local rule set. The firewall must be invoked for each and every packet that is handled by the TCP/IP network stack to enforce this, which is normally achieved by using hooks. Hooks allow for example the Linux firewall "netfilter" (also known as "iptables") to be invoked whenever a packet is received: "Netfilter is a set of hooks inside the Linux kernel that allows kernel modules to register callback functions with the network stack. A registered call-back function is then called back for every packet that traverses the respective hook within the network stack"[14].

Firewall code then depends on the possibility to register callback functions. These need to be provided by the network stack's code. In the case of off-the-shelf networked smartcards we do not expect to have such hooks available, and it will not be possible (for non-technical reasons) to modify the TCP/IP stack implementation for the card holder/user. So there is no way to build firewall functionality on a per packet basis.

Without modification of the smartcard's TCP/IP stack code, a firewall must run as an application on the networked smartcard. This has the disadvantage of not being able to catch malformed or unwanted packets on the lower levels (i.e. TTL or IP-Flags). The firewall serves as a proxy (proxy-mode), so decisions can be based on both IP addresses (source and destination), both ports and potentially the contents of the network protocol data.

This functionality can be programmed using sockets, and we assume that socket functionality is available on a networked smartcard. Assuming further a Java-based OS, there will be functions like Socket, ServerSocket or Datagram-Socket as in the Java package java.net [16]. Using sockets we are able to design a firewall on a TCP/UDP proxy level.

The procedure for proxying HTTP is straightforward:

1. Opening a listening proxy on the service's port that is to be controlled (e.g. port 80 for HTTP)
2. Listening for an incoming connection and waiting for a HTTP request (HTTP version 1.1)
3. On request: Analysing the request to find the server the client wishes to connect to
4. Filtering of the request according to the firewall rule set
5. If the request is allowed: Opening of a new socket connecting to the server and forwarding the HTTP request
6. Receiving the server's answer
7. Filtering the answer according to the firewall rule set
8. If the answer is allowed: Forwarding the server's answer to the client using the existing connection to the client

The firewall will close/abort the connection to the client or to the server if the request or the answer is denied.

For a fully operational HTTP proxy the above code outline needs to be extended with the following additional features (which can be omitted in a concept prototyping[5]):

1. Resolving host names (found in requests) to IP addresses (used to send the request to the server) by DNS lookups.
2. Handling of multiple concurrent connections.
3. Handling server responses (ICMP destination unreachable) elegantly for the requesting client.

### 3.1  Smartcard Security Features

Following the "best of both worlds"-approach we want to build upon the security functions offered by smartcards as often as possible (see also Section 4); for example:

---

[5] The first two features will be limited by the number of concurrent connections offered by the smartcard's TCP/IP stack. The additional features will also increase the amount of memory needed.

The rule set is stored in a file protected by the smartcard. Using command-oriented access conditions "write" or "update" commands are only executed if the administrative credential (or: PIN) is presented to the card. This enforces authorization for rule set changes.

In the case of an HTTP proxy, SSL-secured connections provide an easy starting ground for the use of the smartcard's functionality. For example the validation of the server credential (SSL certificate) can be left to the smartcard's cryptographic functions. As a next step, the secure storage of the smartcard could hold the user's key and certificate for mutual authentication. The smartcard will only use the user's key to authorise to the server after the user has been authenticated/authorized.

### 3.2   Towards Running Proxy Code on a Networked Smartcard

The proxy code can be implemented for HTTP connections and extended to HTTPS to make use of the aforementioned smartcard security functions. In a first simple implementation the proxy can be written as a single thread, opening a maximum of two concurrent connections. The actual code is lean and our assumed technical specifications (see Section 2.1) make it feasible to implement this design on a networked smartcard.

To provide security for the user's network connections the firewall in a smartcard needed to provide proxy functionality for all protocols used by the user's client. This ranges from simple variants like HTTP to more complex protocols as FTP. The more complex protocols will require more connections, more logic, and thus consume more memory (both for the code and during runtime). As a next step we plan to implement a simple proxy firewall (for IP address-based HTTP requests) on a networked smartcard prototype.

## 4   Security - Assumptions and Gains

In this section we will shortly summarize security decisions and assumptions we made throughout the previous sections, to highlight the overall security reached by a network firewall on a smartcard.

### 4.1   Security Assumptions

We showed that the lack of a second interface can be mitigated by an intermediate system. The following security properties of this intermediate system were assumed:

- The OS of the intermediate system reliably routes all network packets through the smartcard. No packets can travel directly from the inside to the outside interface or vice versa.
- The intermediate system provides at least tamper evidence, so that an educated user can detect that the intermediate device has been manipulated.

- The intermediate system is small, so it is easy to carry the firewall system (smartcard together with intermediate system). Small firewall appliances are already available – not based on smartcards though (more details in Section 5). This physical aspect also means that intermediate systems are not shared: Instead smartcard and intermediate system are given to the user from the same trusted authority.

Smartcards are secure and tamper-resistant computing environments. Additionally to the security properties usually credited to smartcards, we make some assumptions on the smartcard's network connection:

- An attacker is not able to attack the smartcard's OS or a running application in the card by sending maliciously formed packets to the network interface. The TCP/IP stack is robust and secure.
- The firewall is the only application running on the card.
- The smartcard's TCP/IP implementation allows the smartcard to receive arbitrary, but standard-conform, network packets and will transfer them to the firewall code.
- For a firewall in proxy-mode: The smartcard's OS handles packets not addressed to a listening port on the smartcard in a secure fashion (i.e. drop/reject the packet). This makes attacks or connections at lower IP levels impossible.
- For a firewall in packetfilter-mode: The smartcard's OS provides "hooks"[6] that allow the firewall to intercept network packets at IP level. Once an application registered with such a hook all packets are handed over to the application and further processing is delayed.

## 4.2   Security of Firewall on Smartcard

Under the above assumptions the firewall running on the networked smartcard can offer increased security compared to firewalls embedded in traditional computers and operating systems. The secure computing environment provided by the smartcard increases the security of the firewall. It physically separates it from the host system, and provides additional security functionality. Furthermore, a networked smartcard with an embedded TCP/IP stack means increased security of the firewall's TCP/IP handling, as it runs in a secure environment. In the ideal case, all routing of packets through the firewall would be carried out by the trusted smartcard itself using two physical interfaces. But the intermediate system needs only very limited functionality, as it barely acts as a router. This can be implemented more securely than on the general purpose computer that is behind the firewall. However, the role of the intermediate system is solely for prototyping, to show that an implementation of a network firewall on a smartcard is feasible.

As assumed, malformed network traffic is correctly handled by the underlying network stack. So, the firewall only needs to handle packets conforming to

---

[6] A hook allows registering callback functions.

standards. Especially the proxy firewall code will only receive TCP/UDP connections on the ports it is listening to. The proxy firewall will check whether the rule set allows or forbids such a connection from the TCP/IP information available. It will then additionally be able to inspect the data part if it is a correctly formed request. All packets that are not addressed to the service's port that the proxy firewall listens to, are automatically and securely discarded. This allows to restrict the services that are allowed, and it makes the code leaner and more clearly, thus reducing software or configuration errors.

The rule set is needed to make the firewall's decision. Storing this rule set in a file protected by the smartcard using command-oriented access conditions limits the access to this rule set. Only if the administrative credential (PIN) is presented to the smartcard "write" or "update" commands are allowed. Thus, authorization for rule set changes can be enforced. The smartcard's access control can also be used to restrict certain connections: Either restricting the service as such, by providing access control on the opening of a socket for listening. Or restricting connections to certain servers by controlling the access to less restrictive rule sets.

We can also envision the use of the smartcard firewall for securing connections: As a secure network node, the smartcard can ensure that the traffic that traverses it is additionally secured or validated. This involves the validation and use of credentials (SSL certificates, encryption Keys), which can again be stored in protected files in the smartcard. Finally, the smartcard's cryptographic functions can care for encryption, decryption, certificate verification, signing, etc.. In the simplest case, the user's connection is "proxied" via SSL to the server.

## 5   Possible Applications

This section sketches a few possible applications of a firewall on a smartcard. They are discussed separately, to highlight certain aspects, but could be combined into one firewall on smartcard. The focus of this section is to motivate the application of networked smartcards as a secure network node, it does not present market-ready applications. Some of the presented scenarios likely require more processing or memory power than today's smartcards offer, but advances in hardware will make them implementable in the future.

### 5.1   Portable Firewall Box

To overcome the problem of the lacking separate hardware connections, and to further increase the security and portability of a firewall on a smartcard, an embedded system can perform the operations of the intermediate system. Such an embedded system would come with two Ethernet ports (RJ45 connectors) for the network connections and a smartcard reader. It would care for routing network packets and would provide a "dual homed" system, hiding the smartcard from the host. This would prevent a malicious (manipulated) host from modifying the routing of packets and circumventing the firewall. The device could be powered by batteries, an external power-supply (perhaps from a free USB-port), or it would rely upon power-over-ethernet.

There are small, portable security devices on the market: Examples are the mGuard smart from Innominate [10] and ZyXEL's ZyWALL P1 [18]. The approach of using a smartcard as a platform for the firewall enhances the security and could reduce the device's size further.

### 5.2  Managed Firewall for Mobile Access or Personal Use

The firewall's rule set can be stored on the smartcard and the smartcard's access control allows us to restrict access in such a way, that the rule set can be altered solely by authorized principals. In this application scenario the firewall rule set is centrally managed.

One option is central management using a policy server to deploy secure mobile access to certain servers, e.g. for managing access of a mobile workforce in a company. The network connection between the smartcard and the central policy server can be protected with SSL and mutual authentication. Every time the firewall is connected to the network, it first tries to connect to the policy server to download, verify, and install the latest firewall rule set. In such a way a company can enforce its security policy even for mobile clients.

For personal use, the customization of the firewall's rule could be provided as a service to "end"-users. This meant secure firewall configuration without the need of local configuration. The need for customised configurations could be indicated on a Web page presented by the smartcard. The smartcard would then forward the request to the service provider, who exclusively maintains the card-internal firewall's rule set.

### 5.3  Secure Remote Network Access

The mobile client might already use Virtual Private Networks (VPN) and certificates to authenticate to the servers.

The smartcard's firewall application could establish a secure tunnel for remotely accessing e.g. a corporate network. The user's credentials can be securely stored on the smartcard. The user would need to connect to the smartcard with a Web browser and enter the password to unlock her credentials. The smartcard's firewall application would then mutually authenticate to the server and establish session keys for an encrypted tunnel. All signing, encrypting, and certificate-checking during this process can done by the firewall in the smartcard. Thus, the networked smartcard acts as a secure VPN gateway. All this is carried out outside the user's computer, and the use of a VPN is transparent to the user, the user's operating system, and the user's applications.

## 6   Related Work

Related work on network connected smartcards either concentrates on the implementation of network capabilities in the smartcard, or on the implementation of servers running inside smartcard.

Honeyman and Rees showed in [9] that smartcards can indeed become part of the network: "The Webcard is a TCP/IP stack and web server written in Java that runs on a Schlumberger Cyberlfex card; the card is connected to the Internet via an ISO 7816 T=0 serial link at 55.8 Kbps. The card terminal is connected to an OpenBSD server running a simple daemon that forwards packets between the card and the Internet via a tunnel device. All ip, tcp, and http processing is handled by the card, and all web content is stored on the card." [9]

Guthery, Kehr, and Posegga [7, 8] have presented a related approach where a Web server in a GSM SIM smartcard provided services to he Internet.

Muller and Deschamps [13] showed that smartcards can be networked and act as connection endpoint as either clients or servers.

Our usage of a network-capable smartcard is different in that we go beyond the point of being a connection endpoint: we also consider cards as part of a network infrastructure. Our firewall on a smartcard provides network functionality as a network node, rather than being an endpoint.

## 7   Conclusion and Outlook

TCP/IP stacks will be an integral part of tomorrows smatcards, turning the cards into network nodes; the consequences of this, both in terms of applications using smartcards, as well as in terms of security implications for the usage of cards are still to be explored[7].

Whilst most approaches we have encountered so far consider networked smartcards as communication end points, we took the concept further and considered smartcards as part of a network infrastructure. Consequently, we suggest to implement security-critical applications on such cards, for instance a network firewall, which is what we explored in this paper.

Our approach combines the security of a smartcard environment and the network security offered by firewalls: The smartcard provides a high security platform for the firewall to run on, and the firewall protects a network "behind" the smartcard.

TCP/IP stacks are part of future smartcards and so the smartcard is facilitated to provide security for network connections. Furthermore, we envision that the secure storage of credentials and the cryptographic functions of a smartcard provide a strong basis for network security devices.

Our paper introduced the the design of a proxy firewall that run as an application on a network smartcard without modification of the smartcard's network stack. Lower levels of a firewall would require modifications to the networked smartcard's TCP/IP stack implementation; still a proxy allows restricting network traffic: As it is located at the highest layer in the protocol stack it even allows filtering unwanted content and access control based on user authentication. Under the assumption that the underlying network stack is not vulnerable, a highly secure implementation of a proxy firewall is possible.

---

[7] As an example: The concept of proximity between a card and the card holder will be gone, since traditional routing of TCP/IP packets does not care about it.

There are obvious limitations of our approach, one is bandwidth to the (USB-) smartcard, another is the lack of a second network interface in the upcoming generation of networked smartcards. Both restrictions are likely to vanish over time with advances in technology, but we believe that even the current restrictions allow for reasonable applications.

## References

1. Zhiqun Chen. *Java Card Technology for Smart Cards: Architecture and Programmer's Guide*. Addison-Wesley, 2000.
2. D-Link. Usb 2.0 fast ethernet adapter dub-e100. `www.dlink.com/products/?model=DUB-E100`.
3. USB Implementers Forum. Universal serial bus class definitions for communication devices. `www.usb.org/developers/devclass_docs/usbcdc11.pdf`, January 1999.
4. USB Implementers Forum. Universal serial bus communications class subclass specification for ethernet emulation model devices rev. 1.0, February 2005.
5. Gemplus. Press release: Gemplus paves the way for future java card platform. `www.gemplus.com/press/archives/2005/rd/27-06-2005-javaone.html`, June 2005.
6. Giesecke & Devrient GmbH. Internet smart card. `www.gi-de.com/portal/page?_pageid=36,53930&_dad=portal&_schema=PORTAL`.
7. Scott Guthery, Roger Kehr, and Joachim Posegga. How to turn a GSM SIM into a web server. In Josep Domingo-Ferrer, David Chan, and Anthony Watson, editors, *Proc. IFIP Fourth Working Conference on Smart Card Research and Applications (CARDIS 2000)*. Kluwer Academic Publishers, 2000.
8. Scott Guthery, Roger Kehr, Joachim Posegga, and Harald Vogt. GSM SIMs as Web servers. In *Seventh Intern. Conf. on Intelligence in Services and Networks*, Athens, Greece, Februar 2000. Short Paper.
9. Peter Honeyman and Jim Rees. Webcard: a java card web server. In Josep Domingo-Ferrer, David Chan, and Anthony Watson, editors, *Proc. IFIP Fourth Working Conference on Smart Card Research and Applications (CARDIS 2000)*. Kluwer Academic Publishers, 2000.
10. Innominate. Datasheet: mguard smart. `www.innominate.com/images/stories/documents/datasheets/db_smart_en.pdf`, 2005.
11. Microsoft. Ndis - network driver interface specification. `www.microsoft.com/whdc/device/network/ndis/default.mspx`.
12. Michael Montgomery, Asad Ali, and Karen Lu. Secure network card - implementation of a standard network stack in a smart card. In *Proc. IFIP Fourth Working Conference on Smart Card Research and Applications (CARDIS 2000)*. Kluwer Academic Publishers, 2000.
13. Christophe Muller and Eric Deschamps. Smart cards as first-class network citizens. 4th Gemplus Developer Conference, Singapore, November 2002.
14. netfilter. website. `www.netfilter.org`.
15. Kai Uwe Rommel. Netio - network throughput benchmark, version 1.14, 1997.
16. SUN. Package java.net description. `java.sun.com/j2se/1.4.2/docs/api/java/net/package-summary.html`.
17. Aviel D. Rubin William R. Cheswick, Steven M. Bellovin. *Firewalls and Internet Security 2nd ed.* Addison Wesley, 2003.
18. ZyXEL. Datasheet: Zywall p1. `ftp://ftp.zyxel.com/ZyWALLP1/document/ZyWALLP1_v2.0_Datasheet.pdf`, March 2005.

# Multi-stage Packet Filtering in Network Smart Cards

HongQian Karen Lu

Smart Cards Research, Axalto, Inc., 8311 North FM 620 Road, Austin, TX 78726, USA
karenlu@axalto.com

**Abstract.** *Network smart cards* are smart cards with networking capabilities. They have opened new opportunities for the use of smart cards in Internet applications. At the same time, network smart cards are exposed to network security threats just as other computers on the Internet. Unfortunately, existing designs of network security mechanisms, such as packet filtering, may not be best suited for smart cards because the computing resources of the cards are too limited. This paper presents a new packet filtering approach that overcomes this difficulty. The packet filtering is performed in multiple stages. It drops unwanted packets as early as possible, starting at the I/O interrupt level. This builds a network firewall inside smart cards and reduces resource usage for packet processing. It can be used with different hardware and software configurations and with various filter rules. Advantages of this approach include better security, reduced memory usage, and enhanced performance.

## 1  Introduction

An exciting new phenomenon in the smart card industry is the emergence of *network smart cards*, which are smart cards with networking capabilities [1]. The network smart cards can provide services and access resources on the Internet, opening new opportunities for the smart card industry. On one hand, because of their security, portability and tamper-resistance, network smart cards provide security and convenience over the Internet, which is better than other secure tokens [2]. However, on the other hand, network smart cards are exposed to network security threats just as other computers on the Internet. Therefore, they require security protections as well. Unfortunately, existing designs and implementations of network security mechanisms, such as packet filtering, may not be best suited to network smart cards because of the cards' computing resource limitations.

Packet filtering is a key component of the network firewall technique. In the Internet world, a firewall is a network security mechanism. It is typically used to prevent unauthorized Internet users from accessing private networks connected to the Internet. Firewalls can be implemented in hardware, software, or a combination of both. Packet filtering is typically done at protocol layers. However, allocating memory for a packet, processing the packet through layers, and then filtering out the packet waste CPU time and memory resources.

Smart cards have very limited memory resources compared to other network devices or computers. For example, a network smart card may have only 6K bytes of RAM, which seems to be plenty for a smart card. However, this memory is very little

J. Domingo-Ferrer, J. Posegga, and D. Schreckling (Eds.): CARDIS 2006, LNCS 3928, pp. 192–205, 2006.
© IFIP International Federation for Information Processing 2006

for a network device because it must deal with a large amount of data in real-time. The resource need is even higher when communicating over a secure channel. In addition, once connected to the network, the network smart card may face a large number of unwanted messages. If not managed properly, the card's memory buffers may be used up very quickly. Furthermore, network smart cards must protect themselves from network attacks. Therefore, new methods of packet filtering that are practical and efficient for network smart cards must be developed. This paper presents one such method called the *multi-stage packet filtering*. It is a software method that is adaptable to hardware configurations.

The new packet filtering method has two goals: security and resource management. The goals are approached by performing packet filtering as early as possible before more resources are consumed. The filtering has multiple stages starting from the I/O interrupt service routine. The amount of filtering at each stage is configured according to multiple factors, including filtering rules, the hardware configuration, hardware capability, the nature of the data link layer, memory buffering scheme, and the network stack process model.

The multi-stage packet filtering drops unwanted packets early to build a network firewall inside the network smart card, to save memory resources, and to reduce CPU usage for packet processing. It is a general framework of efficient packet filtering, which can be used with a variety of hardware and software configurations and with various filter rules. The method has several advantages over existing packet filtering designs, including better security, reduced memory usage, and enhanced performance. The approach is applicable to a variety of small resource-constrained embedded network devices.

The rest of the paper is organized as follows. Section 2 discusses the related work. Section 3 provides an overview of the multi-stage packet filtering method. Sections 4 through 6 present the details of the packet filtering at each of the multiple stages. The implementation is discussed in Section 7. Section 8 concludes the paper.

## 2  Related Work

A great deal of literature is available on network firewalls and packet filtering [3][4][5] . Many commercial products are also available. The packet filtering is typically done at Ethernet, IP, and TCP/UDP layers, that is, at the protocol processing stage. Extensive research on packet filtering in the past twenty years has produced excellent results and made many applications possible, such as network monitoring, traffic collection, performance measurement, packet classification in routers, firewall filtering and intrusion detection. The references [6][7] offer examples of the packet filtering research, which focus on flexible, extensible, and generalized filter abstractions and show how to compile the high-level abstractions to efficient implementations. These research were mostly based on modern operating systems and computing systems, such as workstations (in the past) and personal computers (at present). The packet filter is normally one module of the operating system, which executes at the protocol processing stage or is parallel to the protocol-processing module [6].

In contrast, the work described herein focuses on the design and implementation of packet filtering for small resource-constrained embedded network devices, such as network smart cards. The main purposes of the filtering here are security and efficient resource management. The packet filtering executes at more than one stage in order to drop unwanted packets as early as possible and to best use limited computing resources.

In a previous paper, we have proposed a front-end packet filtering at the AHDLC layer for resource-constrained network devices [8]. This AHDLC packet filtering method is applicable for devices using PPP as network connections. The multi-stage packet filtering presented in this paper is a further elaboration of the front-end packet filtering concept. This elaboration includes three main aspects: (1) the front is pushed further to the I/O interrupt service routine; (2) the filtering is partitioned into stages; and (3) the main focus is moved to USB/Ethernet smart cards. The following sections describe the new method in details.

## 3  Method Overview

The multi-stage packet filtering method has two main purposes: network security and resource management. Both are extremely important and necessary for network smart cards. The key concept of the method is the front-end filtering, that is, to perform packet filtering as early as possible before more resources, such as memory and CPU time, are consumed. The filtering is done at multiple stages starting from the hardware I/O interrupt service routine. This front-end filtering also makes the device more secure because it blocks malicious packets upfront.

The amount and type of filtering at each of the multi-stages depend on multiple factors, including filtering rules, the hardware configuration (e.g. USB, UART), data link layers (e.g. CDC, EEM, Ethernet), hardware I/O interrupt mechanisms (e.g. byte, frame, DMA), memory buffering schemes (e.g. straight buffer, chained buffer), hardware capability, and the network stack process model. The implementation of this method also depends on these factors.

### 3.1  Network Smart Cards

A network smart card is a smart card that is also an Internet node. The network smart card implements standard Internet protocols and security protocols inside the card. Figure 1 illustrates a network smart card that connects to the Internet through a host computer. The smart card can provide services or access resources over the Internet. The protocol stack on the network smart card is the same as those on other Internet nodes.

A traditional smart card communicates with a host using the smart card standard ISO 7816. The host has smart card specific middleware installed in order to communicate with the card. Through the host, the smart card provides security services to the host or over the network that the host is connected to. In contrast, the network smart card communicates with the host computer or a remote computer using Internet protocols. The host does not have to be trusted [2][9]. No middleware is required on the host computer or on the remote computer in order to talk with the network smart card.

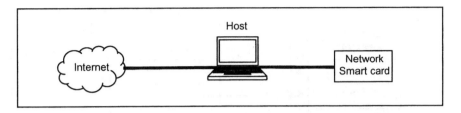

**Fig. 1.** A network smart card connects to the network via a host computer

Moving from proprietary computing environment to the mainstream networking environment opens many opportunities for smart cards. For example, network smart cards can establish direct secure connections with remote servers over the Internet [9]. This capability enables the cards to secure online transactions for Internet applications, such as online banking, online shopping, e-business, e-government, and e-health care.

Network smart cards present numerous engineering challenges mainly due to their computing resource limitations. For example, our first network smart card had only 6K bytes of RAM. The bandwidth was limited by the ISO 7816-3 interface and a bridging protocol [10]. The card resource is scarce considering that it must deal with real-time network traffic. The computation and communication demands for the card are even higher for secure communications because of cryptographic computations and increased network traffic. Many efforts have been made to provide network smart card functionalities in such resource-constrained environment [1][8][10]. This paper presents a continued effort to provide security and to manage limited resources for the card.

Network smart cards connect to the Internet through a host computer using USB or standard smart card interface ISO 7816. Smart cards with full speed USB interface use standard USB networking interface [11]. For smart cards that have only ISO 7816 interface, a bridging protocol, called Peer I/O, is required, which sits above the ISO 7816 layer and below the network protocols layer [10]. A device driver or a reader implements the Peer I/O on the host side to provide a full-duplex serial interface for the ISO 7816 device. Even this case does not require additional middleware because host computers know how to network through a serial interface.

The multi-stage packet filtering approach does not require a particular hardware interface. It is applicable to a variety of hardware and software configurations. For the convenience of discussion, we use USB smart cards as an example. In Section 7 we discuss the case of network smart cards with standard ISO 7816 interface.

Figure 2 illustrates an example of the protocol stacks for a USB network smart card and a host computer. The hardware connection between the smart card and the host computer is the USB. On top of the USB driver is a USB EEM (Ethernet Emulation Model) driver, which carries Ethernet frames using USB packages [11].

The network layer is the Internet Protocol (IP). Ethernet frames carry IP datagrams. The transport layer is TCP or UDP. IP datagrams carry TCP or UDP segments. Figure 3 illustrates the protocol encapsulations.

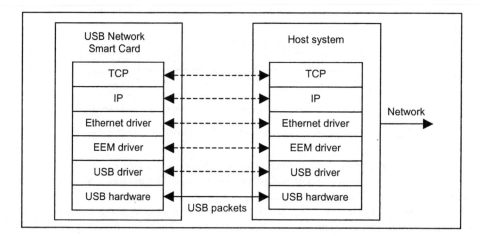

**Fig. 2.** Network stacks in a USB network smart card and the host computer[1]

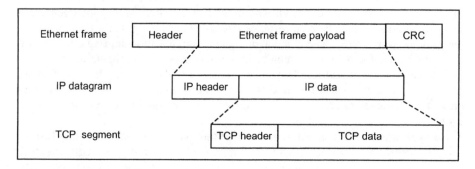

**Fig. 3.** Protocol Encapsulations

The TCP/IP network is a packet-switched network. Messages are divided into *packets* before they are transmitted. Each packet contains a source address and a destination address. Packets can follow different routes to their destinations. Once all packets forming a message arrive at the destination, they are recompiled into the message. In short, the TCP/IP network transmits messages via packets. Packet filtering filters packets to decide whether or not to let the packets pass, or to classify the packets. Packet filtering can be performed on in-bound packets as well as out-bound packets. This paper focuses on filtering of in-bound packets for security purposes.

## 3.2   Filter Rules

Packet filtering has been studied and used for over twenty years for network monitoring, firewall, and other purposes. Filter rules specify how packet filtering should be

---

[1] The full speed USB interface and network stack for smart cards are being proposed as an ETSI smart card standard.

performed. For security purposes, the basic idea is to block all packets, except those that the filter rules allow to pass [4].

In general, filter rules specify packet pass or drop conditions based on information in protocol headers. Packet filters look at protocol headers of a packet and check against filter rules to decide whether or not to let the packet pass. A network stack normally does not look into the payload (or user data) of a packet.

Some of the filter rules are static; others are dynamic. For example, the network device's MAC address is normally fixed, and thus the filter rule associated with the address is a static rule. In contrast, the permissible target IP address list is dynamic and, hence, its corresponding filter rules are also dynamic.

Some of the filter rules are stateless while others are stateful. For example, the TCP layer maintains a state machine for each connection. Rules for checking addresses or protocol types are stateless, because they do not require any state information. Rules that depend on the state of a connection are stateful rules. Figure 4 illustrates a classification of filter rules. The stateful rules may also be classified into static and dynamic rules. For the purpose of the multi-state filtering, this further classification is unnecessary.

There are different ways to model the packet filtering, including a Boolean expression tree and a directed acyclic control flow graph (CFG) [6][7]. The two models are computationally equivalent. Figure 5 illustrates a filter example with these two representations. Research has shown that CFG leads to more efficient implementations [7].

Packet filter rules are hierarchical, as shown in their representations. Once one filter rule decides to drop the packet, the remaining rules need not be checked; the packet is dropped. After a packet passes one filter rule, it still needs to pass other rules down the hierarchy in order to get to its destination.

The multi-stage packet filtering method is a general packet filtering framework. It does not depend on a particular filter rule set. It can be used for various filter rule configurations. The filter rules specification is out of the scope of this paper.

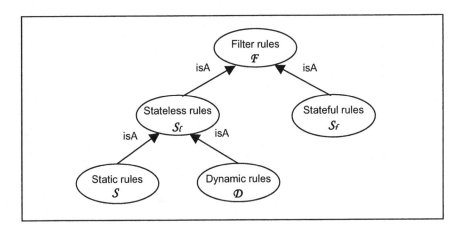

**Fig. 4.** A classification of filter rules

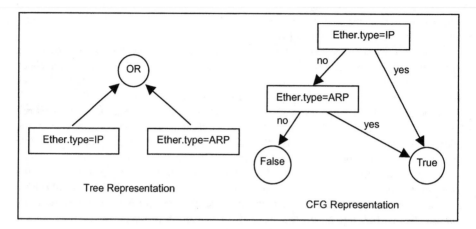

**Fig. 5.** Filter Function Representations

## 3.3   Software Models

This section examines several stages of an embedded system in which the multi-stage packet filtering may be performed. When a packet comes into a network smart card, the I/O hardware of the chip generates an interrupt. The corresponding interrupt service

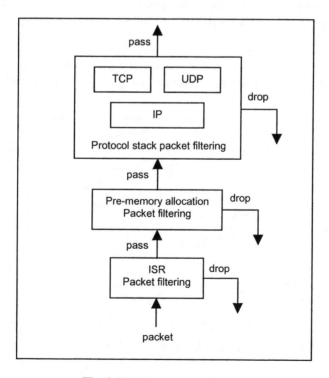

**Fig. 6.** Multi-stage packet filtering

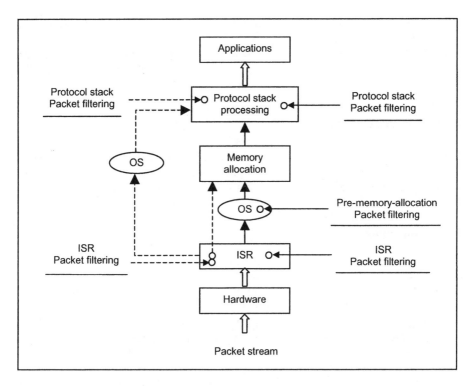

**Fig. 7.** Stages of the packet filtering depend on the software configuration

routine (ISR) handles the interrupt to get the incoming data. This is the first stage of packet handling. We may start filtering inside the ISR. This is called the *ISR packet filtering*. Then, a memory buffer, e.g. a byte array or a buffer chain, is allocated to store the packet for processing. This is a second stage. The filtering may be done just before the memory allocation, which is called the *pre-memory allocation packet filtering*. The protocol stack processes the packet, making a third stage. We call the filtering at this stage the *protocol stack packet filtering*. Depending on the interrupt handling, memory buffer scheme, and protocol stack, these three stages may not be completely separated. Figure 6 illustrates these three general stages. It should be noted that the protocol stack packet filtering might be further distributed among protocol layers.

Figure 7 illustrates two examples of the multi-stage packet filtering. The solid arrow path shows one example of a software configuration in which the memory allocation for the in-coming packet is outside of the ISR. This example uses a three-stage packet filtering. The dashed arrow path shows another example of a software configuration, with which the memory allocation is inside the ISR. This example uses a two-stage packet filtering method in which the ISR filtering is executed before the memory allocation.

Due to time limitation and other constraints of an interrupt service routine, a limited filtering is done at the interrupt service stage. If the memory allocation is outside of the interrupt service routine, much of the stateless filtering is performed before the memory buffer allocation so that unwanted packets do not use additional memory buffers. The protocol stack filtering applies remaining filter rules, especially stateful rules, to the packets. Other software models may have additional stages, which may perform packet filtering. The key of this method is to drop unwanted packets as early as possible. This blocks malicious packets up front, avoids allocating memory buffers for these packets, and avoids or reduces processing time for the packets. The next few sections describe each of the filtering stages in more detail.

# 4   ISR Packet Filtering

This section describes the packet filter in the input event interrupt service routine (ISR). This is also called the front-end packet filtering. We first discuss the constraints of the ISR. We then describe what an ISR packet filter must do to live with these constraints.

## 4.1   Constraints

An I/O interrupt service routine is a software routine that handles I/O events. How an I/O event triggers an interrupt and how the microprocessor invokes the interrupt service routine depend on the chip architecture, the I/O hardware, and the software/hardware interface that the chip manufacture provides. Some chips let a software programmer write hardware interrupt service routines. Other chips provide a hardware/software interface layer to deal with hardware interrupts in which case a software programmer writes interrupt service routines triggered by the interface layer. The interrupt service routine may be called when a byte arrives, when a packet arrives, or when a larger amount of data arrives. For example, with USB devices, the interrupt service routine is typically invoked when a USB packet arrives. With full speed USB bulk data transfer, this may mean that 64 bytes of data have just arrived.

An interrupt service routine normally does some quick and simple things to handle the interrupt. The program goes back to the routine that was interrupted as soon as possible. Typically, the ISR has timing constraints. For example, the ISR must finish before the next input event happens. For USB full speed bulk data transfer on an otherwise idle bus, the maximum possible speed per pipe is nineteen 64-byte transactions per frame, where one frame is 1 millisecond. This takes about 82% of the bus bandwidth. Hence, the minimum time interval between the arrivals of two consecutive USB data packets is 43 microseconds. The ISR must finish within this time.

Another constraint for an ISR is the availability of other resources. For example, the input interrupt may happen when the CPU is doing a non-volatile memory write. In this case, typically the ISR cannot do a non-volatile memory write. In general, the ISR should avoid any non-volatile memory write.

A third constraint for an ISR is variable access. An I/O interrupt may happen when the program is changing a variable. If the ISR tries to access this variable or, worse, to change the variable, the result is unpredictable. This is known as the data-sharing problem. Therefore, either the ISR should try to avoid accessing or changing a variable or the variable must be protected, for example, using critical sections. To avoid the data-sharing problem and to reduce the interrupt latency, the ISR packet filtering must not access any variables, which means only checking static filter rules.

## 4.2    Packet Filtering

The input event ISR extracts Ethernet frames (called packets) from the underlying link layer protocols. Performing packet filtering inside the ISR is feasible because protocol headers, such as headers of EEM, Ethernet, and IP, are at fixed positions within their outer protocol packets. For example, an EEM packet has a two-byte header; the Ethernet packet header has fourteen bytes; and the IP header starts immediately after the Ethernet header. With such fixed positions, the ISR can access header elements directly.

The basic packet filtering rules are very simple and involve only constants. The following is an example of a set of basic filter rules. These are static rules to be applied first and can be done in the ISR.

Rule 1:      If (Ethernet destination address == my Ethernet address)
             Pass the packet.

Rule 2:      If the packet passed Rule 1, and if
             Type == IP
             Pass the packet.

Rule 3:      If (Ethernet destination address == ff:ff:ff:ff:ff:ff)  and  (Type == ARP)
             Pass the packet.

Rule 4:      If the packet passed Rule 3, and if
             Target IP address == my IP address
             Pass the packet.

Rule 5:      If the packet passed Rule 2, and if
             Destination IP address == my IP address
             Pass the packet.

Rule 6:      If the packet passed Rule 5, and if
             (Protocol type == TCP) or (Protocol type == UDP)
             or (Protocol type == ICMP)
             Pass the packet.

The amount of packet filtering in an ISR depends on the CPU speed, the timing constraints for the ISR, and the amount of necessary work that the ISR must do. For the example mentioned earlier, the ISR has as little as 43 microseconds to do its job. One of our implementations can check the above filter rules in 1.67 microseconds in the worst-case scenario. That is a sufficiently short execution time to fit into the ISR. Section 7 provides more details about our implementations.

During software development, one could measure the time needed for the normal ISR work without the packet filtering. The difference between the allowable time for the ISR and the time needed for the ISR function is the time interval that the packet filter can use. Some chips may only have time for checking one filtering rule for an Ethernet packet header; while other chips may have enough time for checking all static filter rules inside the ISR.

The packet filtering at ISR is especially useful if the input event ISR allocates memory buffers for incoming packets. The filtering should be done before the memory allocation. Regardless whether the allocated memory is a single contiguous memory or a chained memory buffer, once the ISR decides to drop the packet according to filtering rules, it will require no memory allocation and no further processing to this packet. This leads to a reduced memory usage and enhanced performance. For zero-copy protocol stack implementations, being able to drop packets at ISR still prevents further processing of the unwanted packets. This again enhances the performance of the system.

In addition to reduced memory usage and enhanced performance, the unwanted packet does not go further into the system. This makes the system less susceptible to network attacks and, hence, results in a more secure system.

## 5   Pre-Memory-Allocation Packet Filtering

For some hardware and software configurations, the interrupt service routine or the Direct Memory Access (DMA) puts the incoming packets into a fixed contiguous memory location. Outside of the ISR, the network protocol stack processes and queues the packet. Before or during this process, the packet is taken out from the fixed memory location and put into a dynamically allocated memory buffer or a buffer chain. The contiguous memory is ready for the ISR or DMA to put in the next packet. This provides another opportunity for early packet filtering, which filters the packets before the memory allocation.

This pre-memory-allocation packet filtering, if performed outside the ISR, can check against all the remaining stateless filter rules, including static rules that were not checked by the ISR packet filter and dynamic rules. Once one rule decides to drop the packet, the remaining rules need not be checked; the packet is dropped. The packet filtering at this stage, again, prevents allocation of memory buffer for un-wanted packets.

One example of dynamic filter rules that can be performed at the pre-memory-allocation stage checks the destination port number of an incoming packet. Each TCP or UDP packet contains a destination port number $P_d$. For example, an http server has a well-known port number 80; a secure http server has a well-known port number 443. The network smart card maintains a permissible destination port number list, $L_d$, which contains port numbers that the card allows the incoming packets to target at a given time. Then, we have the following rule:

Permissible destination port number rule:

If $P_d \in L_d$, then pass the packet.

If an incoming packet's destination port number $P_d$ is not in the list $L_d$, the packet is dropped. This list is static if the network smart card is a network server only. The list is dynamic if the card can be a client as well as a server.

For example, a network smart card provides a secure web server. The permissible destination port number list $L_d$ initially has only one entry 443. The card is also an Internet client or an agent. When the card initiates a connection to a remote server using an ephemeral port number $x$, then $x$ is added to $L_d$. When this connection fin-ishes, the $x$ is removed from $L_d$. Therefore, the list $L_d$ changes; the associate filter rule is dynamic.

If a smart card chip has DMA (Direct Memory Access), the incoming data stream is transferred directly to a pre-specified contiguous memory location without passing through the CPU. The packet filtering may be performed from the DMA memory directly to decide whether or not to drop a packet. Note that the packet filtering in this case may or may not be inside the ISR. If the filtering is inside the ISR, it should leave the check of the dynamic filtering rules to the next filtering stage.

## 6  Protocol Stack Packet Filtering

The protocol stack includes a data link layer (e.g. Ethernet), a network layer (IP), and a transport layer (e.g. TCP, UDP). Conventional packet filters work on the protocol stack or side-by-side to the protocol stack [6]. With the multi-stage method, the packet filtering at the protocol processing stage is reduced because of the filtering already done at previous stages. The filtering at this stage checks remaining filter rules. The stateful filtering is always done here because it requires state information. The amount of filtering at this stage depends on how much has been performed in previous stages. The following are three examples.

1. The protocol stack packet filter does the entire packet filtering work. (There has been neither ISR nor pre-memory-allocation packet filtering.) This is the conventional packet filtering.
2. The protocol stack packet filter does a part of the stateless static filtering, stateless dynamic filtering, and stateful filtering. (There is an ISR packet filter, but no pre-memory-allocation packet filter.)
3. The protocol stack packet filter does stateful filtering only. (There is an ISR and a pre-memory-allocation packet filtering.)

## 7  Implementations

Several smart card companies, such as Axalto, Giesecke & Devrient, and Gemplus, have demonstrated network smart cards, which have been called Internet smart cards or web cards, at various conferences in the past few years. We have implemented a network smart card on a smart card chip from Samsung, which was demonstrated at Cartes in 2003 and other smart card conferences.

We are currently using a faster USB smart card chip that has a 33 MHz microprocessor, 16K of RAM, 128K of ROM and 64K of EEPROM. The network smart card uses the new USB networking standard, EEM, for the lower link layer to carry Ethernet frames [11]. For the multi-stage packet filtering, from the software implementation perspective, the most critical part is the filtering in the interrupt service routine. For USB bulk data transfer with full speed USB, the ISR has a little less than 43 microseconds. Our implementation of an ISR packet filter using the sample rules, listed in Section 0, executes in 55 machine cycles in worst-case scenarios. The ISR packet filter was programmed using the C language. With the chip's 33 MHz microprocessor, this takes 1.67 microseconds. Even assuming a 20 MHz practical processor speed, the ISR filtering, in the worst- case scenario, takes 2.75 microseconds. It could take less time if coded in an assembly language. Therefore, the proposed packet filtering approach is practical and effective.

In a previous work, we have proposed packet filtering at the AHDLC layer [8]. This is especially useful for smart cards that have ISO 7816 interface and do not have USB. For example, our first network smart card prototype used Samsung's S3FC9BJ smart card chip, which had only ISO 7816 interface. In this case, the network smart card uses PPP [12], instead of Ethernet, as the data link layer to carry TCP/IP Internet protocol packets. The AHDLC layer does framing for the PPP layer [13]. The multi-stage packet filtering method is also applicable in this situation. If the AHDLC processing is performed during the interrupt service routine, the filtering that can be performed in the AHDLC layer is under the constraints of the ISR filtering, which is described in Section 4. Otherwise, if the AHDLC processing is outside of the interrupt service routine, stateless packet filtering can be done during the AHDLC processing as described in the reference [8]; stateful packet filtering is done at the upper layer protocol processing stage. In both cases, there can be at least two stages of packet filtering.

# 8   Conclusions

The multi-stage packet filtering method presented in this paper builds a network firewall inside network smart cards. It drops unwanted packets as soon as possible to save memory resources and to reduce CPU usage for packet processing. This is a general framework of efficient packet filtering for network smart cards. It can be used with a variety of hardware and software configurations and with various filter rules. The method has several advantages over existing packet filtering designs, including better security, reduced memory usage, and enhanced performance. The approach is applicable to a variety of small resource-constrained embedded network devices to enhance their security and success on the Internet.

# References

[1] Montgomery, M., Ali, A., and Lu, H.K., "SECURE NETWORK CARD - Implementation of a Standard Network Stack in a Smart Card," Sixth Smart Card Research and Advanced Application IFIP Conference (Cardis), Toulouse, France, August 23-26, 2004.

[2] Ali, A. and Montgomery, M., "Secure Internet Access and the Role of Network Smart Card," Proc. of the 4th IASTED Int. Conf. on Communications, Internet and Information Technology. Cambridge, MA, USA. Oct 31 - Nov 02, 2005, page 259-265.

[3] Cheswick, W.R., Bellovin, S.M. and Rubin, A.D., Firewalls and Internet Security, Addison-Wesley, 2003.

[4] Lockhart, A., Network Security Hacks, O'Reilly, 2004.

[5] Zwicky, E.D., Cooper, S. and Chapman D.B., Building Internet Firewalls, O'Reilly, 2000.

[6] McCanne, S. and Jacobson V., The BSD Packet Filter: A New Architecture for User-level Packet Capture. In Proceedings of the Winter 1993 USENIX Conference, pages 259-290, January 1993.

[7] Mogul, J., Rashid, R. and Accetta. M., The Packet Filter: An Efficient Mechanism for User-level Network Code. In Proceedings of the Eleventh ACM Symposium on Operating Systems Principles, pages 39-51, November 1987.

[8]  Lu, H.K., "Firewall at AHDLC Layer," The 2005 International Conference on Embedded Systems and Applications, June 27-30, 2005, Las Vegas, USA.

[9]  Lu, H.K. and Ali, A., "Prevent Online Identity Theft - Using Network Smart Cards for Secure Online Transactions," 7th Information Security Conference (ISC), Palo Alto, CA, USA, September 27-29, 2004.

[10] Lu, H.K., "New Advances in Smart Card Communication," International Conference on Computing, Communications and Control Technologies (CCCT), Austin, TX, USA, August 14-17, 2004.

[11] Universal Serial Bus Communications Class Subclass Specification for Ethernet Emulation Model Devices, http://www.usb.org/developers/devclass_docs/CDC_EEM10.pdf.

[12] PPP – RFC 1662.

[13] Calson, J., PPP Design, Implementation, and Debugging, Addison-Wesley, 2000.

# Anonymous Authentication with Optional Shared Anonymity Revocation and Linkability

Martin Schaffer and Peter Schartner

Computer Science, System Security,
University of Klagenfurt, Austria
{m.schaffer, p.schartner}@syssec.at

**Abstract.** In this paper we propose three smartcard-based variants of anonymous authentication using unique one-time pseudonyms. The first variant can be used to authenticate a user. However, his identity cannot be revealed and linked to other pseudonyms unless solving the computational Diffie-Hellman problem. In the second variant a set $R$ of revocation centers is able to revoke the anonymity in collaboration with a trust center $T$ but they are not able to link the revealed identity to other pseudonyms of the same user. Using the third variant additionally provides linkability if $R$ and $T$ cooperate. Some selected applications for the proposed protocols include physical access control, secure auctions, eCoins and online gambling.

## 1   Introduction

Nowadays smartcards appear to be a building block in several applications. Once mainly used for physical access control, their usage has been extended to more general applications related to different areas like eCommerce in the recent years. When using a smartcard, a user normally authenticates to the smartcard by entering a personal identification number. Then the smartcard itself authenticates to an instance (e.g. device (un)locking a door or service provider). Several standard methods exist, how to perform a unilateral authentication process, most of which do not really provide the anonymity of the user. So a lot of research has taken place to provide anonymous authentication based on zero-knowledge proofs. Such protocols have two advantages. First, the anonymity can be provided and second, collected communication data of several protocol runs of the same smartcard – depending on the particular solution – are not linkable by an eavesdropper. However, several standard proofs of identity require the same public input on the verifier's side during every authentication process (e.g. proof of knowledge of a private key, where the verifier must have access to the public key). Thus, the usage of the smartcard is traceable.

Providing authentication processes with anonymity and unlinkability protects the user's privacy. However, the verifier of the authentication process has to be protected as well, namely against malicious behaviour of the smartcard-holder in the protocols run thereafter. So we also need a mechanism to revoke

J. Domingo-Ferrer, J. Posegga, and D. Schreckling (Eds.): CARDIS 2006, LNCS 3928, pp. 206–221, 2006.
© IFIP International Federation for Information Processing 2006

the user's anonymity and – if required – the ability to make user's activities traceable by disclosing linking information.

Over the last years several solutions have been proposed in this area. Many of them are based on group signatures, which allow users to prove the membership of a group without revealing their identity [1, 2, 5, 7]. Others are based on threshold privacy where a user remains anonymous when accessing a service up to a limited number of times [18, 26]. Revocation of anonymity and (un)linkability are a main requirement in anonymous credential systems [4, 19] or electronic money [13, 15, 17]. A solution optimized for power-limited devices has been proposed in [14]. Our scheme is neither based on group signatures nor on threshold privacy (as described in [23]). Compared to more general solutions such as traceable signatures [16] our approach is more specific – namely – optimized for smartcards. We designed the protocols in a simple way based on already known techniques providing anonymous authentication and mechanisms to revoke the anonymity and linkability of a user. A second reason for using smartcards is the fact that we use a particular technique to generate globally unique pseudorandom numbers which requires the use of smartcards [21, 22].

When considering authentication schemes based on – but not limited to – smartcards, we come to the following requirements:

- *Unforgeability.* The user must not be able to forge the authentication process.
- *Anonymity.* The anonymity of the user (identifier) has to be provided during every protocol run.
- *Unlinkability.* Any two authentication processes (protocol transcripts) must not be linkable.
- *Optional Anonymity Revocation and Linkability.* Given the protocol transcript, the anonymity of the user should be revocable by some additional information (trapdoor). Moreover, disclosure of linking information should lead to the identification of all corresponding authentication processes.

In the upcoming sections we present several variants of a smartcard-based anonymous authentication, based on unique one-time pseudonyms (OTPs). Depending on the used variant of the protocol, the anonymity is revocable by a set $R$ of revocation centers so that its owner can be identified by the trust center $T$. If required, the protocol can be extended, so that the revealed identity can be linked to all its corresponding OTPs. The paper provides three variants of the anonymous authentication protocol ANONAUTH:

1. ANONAUTH$_1$: No Anonymity Revocation / No Linkability.
2. ANONAUTH$_2$: Optional Anonymity Revocation / No Linkability.
3. ANONAUTH$_3$: Optional Anonymity Revocation / Optional Linkability.

The proposed authentication protocols are based on OTPs containing a user-generated globally unique identifier *id*, blinded by a pseudorandomly chosen value $b$. These one-time pseudonyms are generated and signed by $T$ in a tamper resistant device (TRD) so that there exists no linking information to the user data accessible by $T$. The output of the TRD is an encrypted batch of authentication data containing the used blinding values and the signatures proving that the OTPs have been generated by $T$. The batch can only be decrypted by the owner of the corresponding unique identifier.[1]

Knowing only a OTP and the corresponding signature, does not reveal any information about the holder of the pseudonym. Additionally, OTPs of the same holder are mutually unlinkable. Hence, only the owner of a pseudonym is able to prove its ownership using a zero-knowledge proof which does not reveal private information.

## 1.1  Three Authentication Protocols

The proposed protocols are generally done in three steps:

1. The user imports authentication data to his smartcard and decrypts it.
2. Then he sends the one-time pseudonym and the corresponding signature to the verifier, who verifies the validity.
3. The user proves in zero-knowledge that he knows the pre-image(s) of the one-time pseudonym: the unique identifier $id$ and/or the blinding value $b$.

We provide the following three authentication protocols:

ANONAUTH$_1$ – *No Anonymity Revocation / No Linkability.* Here the user proves in zero-knowledge that he knows $id$ and $b$ without revealing information. However, no one is able to revoke the anonymity or link OTPs to the user except himself by publishing private information.

ANONAUTH$_2$ – *Optional Anonymity Revocation / No Linkability.* Here the user attaches the blinding value $b$ encrypted by the public key of $R$ to the second step of the authentication protocol. In the third step he proves in zero-knowledge that the correct $b$ is contained in the ciphertext. Thus, the user's anonymity can only be revoked by a set of revocation centers by using threshold decryption which acts as a partial trapdoor to the OTP-generation process. However, the revoked information can only be used to identify the owner of a specific pseudonym but cannot be used to find other pseudonyms of this user.

ANONAUTH$_3$ – *Optional Anonymity Revocation / Optional Linkability.* Here the user additionally attaches encrypted linking information. In the third step he proves in zero-knowledge that the correct linking information is contained in the ciphertext. Shared decryption of $b$ and the linking information acts as full trapdoor to the OTP-generation process. The disclosure of the pre-images of the used one-time pseudonym enables the trust center to identify all one-time pseudonyms that belong to the revealed unique identifier.

## 1.2  Core Components

*User $U_i$.* The user owns a smartcard containing the unique Integrated Chip-Card Serial Number ($ICCSN_i$). During the setup and registration phase his

---

[1] The TRD might be replaced by a solution based on multi-party computation [12].

smartcard is provided with a unique user identifier and several keys. Encrypted authentication data is stored on $U_i$'s local machine and can only be decrypted by $U_i$'s smartcard. The user's part of the authentication process is done exclusively on his smartcard.

*Trust Center T.* The trust center owns the commitment of the user's identifier linked to the user's passport data, user's public key and signature. Moreover, the trust center owns a TRD which has two tasks:

1. Signing the user's data during the registration process.
2. Generating user's encrypted authentication data.

*Bulletin Board BB.* Encrypted authentication data is posted here, so that the user is able to download it if required.

*Revocation Centers $R_1, \ldots, R_n$.* In the second variant of the authentication protocol, a set of revocation centers is able to decrypt the blinding information, which leads to the anonymity revocation at $T$. In the third variant, they are able to decrypt linking information as well so that all OTPs of the revealed unique identifier can be found.

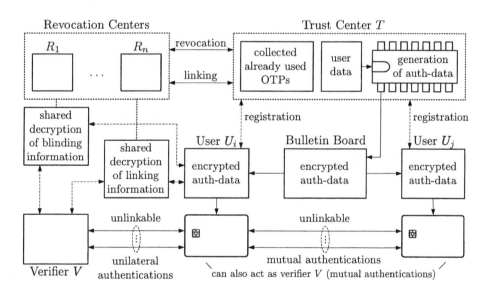

**Fig. 1.** System Architecture

### 1.3   Selected Applications

*eCoins.* The proposed system can be used for "double spending detection" of eCoins. Therefore, the authentication data may contain information about the value of the eCoin and the user would have to pay for each authentication data according to its value. If he uses an eCoin he simply runs the proposed authentication process. Later on, the receiver of the eCoin sends the corresponding pseudonym to a double spending detection server which logs the used eCoins. If an eCoin has been sent twice, it is obvious that it has been used twice. In this case $R$ and $T$ can identify the cheating party.

*Secure Auctions.* Here, the participants can remain anonymous until one wins the auction. In this case the winner may have an interest to reveal his identity. If he refuses to pay, the auction chair can reveal his identity with the help of $R$ and $T$.

*Patent Search.* The proposed scheme can be used for research activities in patent databases. Thus, a business rival is not able to link e.g. queries and hence is not able to associate them to a common identifier.

*Physical Access Control.* The standard application according to smartcards is physical access control. Using our scheme, the holder of a smartcard is not traceable anymore within buildings. If he (physically) misbehaves, his anonymity can be revoked. Moreover, his path through a building can be traced then as well.

*Authenticity of Casino-Chips.* Assume that every chip is provided with a contact-less smart device. For instance, when a player places a chip in a roulette session, it automatically authenticates to the gambling-table. This makes the usage of forged chips detectable. Depending on the used authentication mechanism, the chip can be made traceable or not.[2]

*Traceability of Gamblers.* Assume that every gambler is provided with a Personal Digital Assistant that is used for online gambling in a casino. When playing (e.g. roulette), a person authenticates himself using the proposed protocols. If he loses a game he has to pay or his identity will be revealed for this particular game. Additionally all the games in which he participated can be linked to him if required. The advantage is that the behaviour of the player is untraceable as long as the linking information has not been decrypted by $R$.

## 2   Preliminaries and Notation

### 2.1   The Discrete Logarithm Problem Family

The unlinkability and security of our system relies on the security of the discrete logarithm problem (DLP), the computational Diffie-Hellman problem (CDP) as well as the decisional Diffie-Hellman problem (DDP). Let $g$ be the generator of a cyclic group $\mathbb{Z}_q^*$, then it is hard to compute $x$ by only knowing $g^x$ (DLP). Moreover, it is hard to compute $g^{x \cdot y}$ by only knowing $g^x$ and $g^y$ (CDP). Given

---

[2] Note: Unlike the system proposed in [6] our scheme aims at *physical* casino-chips containing cryptographic hardware.

the values $g^x$, $g^y$ and $Z$ it his hard to decide whether $Z = g^{x \cdot y}$ or $Z$ has been chosen at random (DDP). A triple $(g^x, g^y, g^{x \cdot y})$ is called Diffie-Hellman triple. Several variations of the Diffie-Hellman problem can be found in [3].

## 2.2 ElGamal's Cryptosystem and Signature Scheme

Let $h$ be the generator of a cyclic group $\mathbb{Z}_q^*$. Then the ElGamal key generation outputs the encryption key $e = h^d$ and the decryption key $d$. The encryption/decryption is done as follows [10]:

$$E(m, a, e) = (C_1, C_2), \quad C_1 = h^a, \quad C_2 = m \cdot e^a, \quad a \in_R \mathbb{Z}_q^*$$
$$D((C_1, C_2), d) = m, \quad m = C_2 \cdot (C_1^d)^{-1}$$

We abstract the encryption of larger plaintext by $E'(m, e) = C$. The signature generation/verification is performed over sign key $s$/verification key $v$:

$$S(m, s) = \sigma, \quad V(m, \sigma, v) \in \{\text{true, false}\}$$

Note, that we defined $S$ and $V$ as blackbox-functions because they can be replaced by any other signature scheme.

## 2.3 ElGamal Threshold Decryption

If we consider a single party not to be trustworthy enough to perform a decryption only on request, then there is a need to share the decryption function over a set of instances. In [9] Desmedt and Frankel proposed a shared variation of ElGamal's decryption function. Therefore, the private key $d$ has to be generated in a distributed way by using e.g. the protocol in [11] providing each decryptor $P_i$ with a share $d_i$. In the following we consider the shared decryption protocol as a blackbox-function:

$$\widetilde{D}((C_1, C_2), (d_1, \ldots, d_n)) = m$$

## 2.4 Locally Generated Globally Unique Pseudorandom Numbers

In [22] a method to locally generate globally unique pseudorandom numbers has been proposed. Therefore, a smartcard, a unique identifier and a symmetric cryptosystem are needed. In the current paper we use this method to generate the unique user identifier and the blinding values. A globally unique pseudorandom number $UN$ can be generated in the user's smartcard as follows [22]:

$$UN = E_{DES}(ICCSN||Pad, \tau_k)||\tau_k$$

where $Pad$ is a random padding up to the input-size. Here, $\tau_k$ is a randomly chosen DES-key and $E_{DES}$ is the DES encryption function. Due to the fact that $UN$ is never accessible by unauthorized instances (we only use its discrete logarithm (DL) commitment $g^{UN}$), it is computationally hard to reveal it. Thus, the security of DES does not play a role, because the ciphertext is never available to an attacker. A similar approach which is based on the RSA cryptosystem [20] can be found in [21]. There $UN$ can be uniquely generated as follows:

$$UN = E_{RSA}(ICCSN||Pad, \tau_e)||\tau_e||\tau_n$$

where $(\tau_e, \tau_n)$ is a randomly chosen RSA public key. We use the RSA-version for the generation of unique ElGamal keys (UKG). For a proof of uniqueness we refer to [21] and [22] respectively.

## 2.5   Unique One-Time Pseudonyms

In this paper we use OTPs of the form $\eta_j = (g^{b_j}, g^{b_j \cdot id_i})$. We require each pseudorandom value $b_j$ to be uniquely generated in the TRD. Moreover, we require the unique user identifier to be locally generated by the user himself (in his smartcard). For both values we use the unique pseudorandom number generation (URNG) based on symmetric encryption as described in section 2.4. To avoid local doublets when generating $b_j$, the TRD has to include a counter to the generation process. Due to the fact, that $b_j$ is unique $g^{b_j}$ is unique as well. The second part of $\eta_j$ commits $id_i$ to the pseudonym, so that all pseudonyms of the same holder can be linked to his unique identifier if required.

## 2.6   Used Zero-Knowledge Proofs

We use a very efficient abstract notation for proofs of knowledge (PK) introduced in [5]. For detailed information on the following proofs we refer to [24] and [25].

**Schnorr's Proof of Knowledge.** This proof is required by the first authentication protocol, where a one-time pseudonym can neither be opened nor linked without the cooperation of the user. Let $X = g^x$ be a public value in $\mathbb{Z}_q^*$ with secret pre-image $x$. Then the prover can convince the verifier in zero-knowledge that he knows $x$ using Schnorr's proof of knowledge [24]. Using the abstract notation Schnorr's PK looks as follows:

$$PK\{(\alpha) : X = g^\alpha\}$$

Mapping:   $\alpha = x$

**Stadler's Proof of Knowledge.** Let $X = g^x$ and $(C_1, C_2) = (h^a, x^{-1} \cdot e^a)$ an ElGamal ciphertext. In [25] Stadler proposed a PK where one can prove, that $(C_1, C_2)$ is a correct ElGamal ciphertext and contains the inverse of $x$. This can only be done by the prover iff he knows $a$ and $x$. In our scheme this proof can be used to prove that the pre-images of a OTP are contained in an attached ElGamal ciphertext. Using the abstract notation Stadler's PK looks as follows:

$$PK\{(\alpha, \beta, \gamma) : X = g^\alpha \wedge (C_1, C_2) = E(\gamma, \beta, e)\}.$$

Mapping:   $\alpha = x$   $\beta = a$   $\gamma = x^{-1}$

**Concurrent Executions.** By using the techniques described by Damgard in [8] the above protocols can be made concurrent zero-knowledge. This means, that even if they are executed in parallel, they remain zero-knowledge. Such a modification is of extreme importance for our scheme, because we use smartcards on the user's side. Hence, we have to keep the number of sent messages as minimal as possible.

## 3    On the Linkability of the Used One-Time Pseudonyms

In the following we consider several variations of how to identify the holder of a pseudonym. Moreover, we discuss the ability of $T$ to link pseudonyms to a user $U_i$. For our consideration we assume that all generated pseudonyms are available to $T$ without linkage to the corresponding unique identifier.

Table 1 shows the possible unique identifier with its linking-property based on the amount of open information resulting in the following 6 variations:

1. For every $\eta_j = (\eta_{j1}, \eta_{j2})$ $T$ verifies if $\eta_{j1}^{id_i} = \eta_{j2}$ holds. Each successful verification links the pseudonym to $U_i$.
2. Opening $\eta_j = (g^{b_j}, g^{b_j \cdot id_i})$ results in $g^{id_i}$. For each $id_i'$ $T$ has to verify if $g^{id_i'} = g^{id_i}$ holds. If one holds the owner of the pseudonym has been found. The linkability does not depend on the anonymity revocation.
3. Opening $\eta_j = (g^{b_j}, g^{b_j \cdot id_i})$ results in $id_i$ which speeds up the identification of a user because $T$ does not have to perform the verifications described in 2. Again, the linkability does not depend on the revocation.
4. For each $\eta_j = (\eta_{j1}, \eta_{j2})$ $T$ would have to verify if $\eta_{j1}^{id_i} = \eta_{j2}$ holds. To perform such verifications $T$ has to solve the CDP because he only knows $g^{id_i}$.
5. Opening $\eta_j = (g^{b_j}, g^{b_j \cdot id_i})$ results in $g^{id_i}$. Thus, the owner $U_i$ can be identified by $T$ but no open information of his other pseudonyms is revealed.
6. Opening $\eta_j = (g^{b_j}, g^{b_j \cdot id_i})$ results in $id_i$. For each $g^{id_i'}$ $T$ has to verify if $g^{id_i'} = g^{id_i}$ holds. If one holds the owner of the pseudonym has been found. Moreover, all pseudonyms of $U_i$ can be revealed as described in 1.

**Table 1.** Linkability of User $U_i$ to his OTPs

| unique identifier | amount of open information | | |
|---|---|---|---|
| | nothing | $b_j$ | $b_j$ and $id_i$ |
| $id_i$ | 1. linkable by $T$ | 2. linkable by $T$ | 3. linkable by $T$ |
| $g^{id_i}$ | 4. unlinkable (CDP) | 5. unlinkable (CDP) | 6. linkable by $T$ |
| | anonymity not revocable | anonymity revocable | |

## 4    The Authentication Scheme

### 4.1    Setup

First the system parameters have to be generated in a secure environment. A suitable cyclic group $\mathbb{Z}_q^*$, $q \in \mathbb{P}$ and the according generators $h$ (for ElGamal) and $g$ (for OTPs) have to be chosen. The value $n$ denotes the number of revocation centers and $t$ the threshold of tolerated dishonest revocation centers. The parameter $l$ specifies the number of OTPs included in a batch of authentication data generated in the TRD. The security parameter $k$ specifies the number of necessary rounds of the used zero-knowledge proof. We now assume that each instance of the system is provided with all necessary system parameters.

The user $U_i$ generates a globally unique identifier $id_i$ and an ElGamal keypair $(e_i, d_i)$ where $d_i$ is the private key:

$$id_i = E_{DES}(ICCSN_i||Pad, \tau_{k_i})||\tau_{k_i}$$
$$d_i = E_{RSA}(id_i||Pad, \tau_{e_i})||\tau_{e_i}||\tau_{n_i}, \quad e_i = h^{d_i}$$

such that $id_i, d_i \in \mathbb{Z}_q^*$. The TRD generates a globally unique sign key $s_t$:

$$s_t = E_{RSA}(TRDID||Pad, \tau_{e_t})||\tau_{e_t}||\tau_{n_t}, \quad v_t = h^{s_t}$$

such that $s_t \in \mathbb{Z}_q^*$. The verification key $v_t$ is exported to $T$. The set of revocation centers generate a decryption key $d_r$ in a shared way (e.g. with the solutions in [11]) without reconstructing it, resulting in the private-key-shares $d_{r_1}, \ldots, d_{r_n}$ and the corresponding (reconstructed) public key $e_r$.

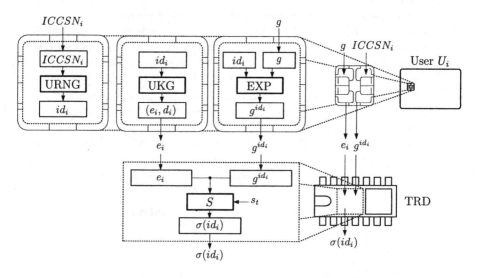

**Fig. 2.** User Registration – Computations on the Smartcard and the TRD respectively

## 4.2    User Registration

First of all $U_i$ computes $g^{id_i}$ and sends the pair $(g^{id_i}, e_i)$ to $T$ – more precise to the TRD – during a face-to-face authentication. The TRD signs $(g^{id_i}, e_i)$ with the sign key $s_t$ resulting in the signature $\sigma(id_i)$. Then $T$ stores the data of unique identification $UI_i = ($passport data$, g^{id_i}, e_i, \sigma(id_i))$ of $U_i$ to the database and returns $(v_t, e_r)$ to $U_i$'s smartcard.

### 4.3   Establishing a Batch of Authentication Data

Prior to generating authentication data, the TRD has to verify if $(g^{id_i}, e_i)$ has been signed with $s_t$ during the registration process. Therefore, it verifies if $\sigma(id_i)$ is the corresponding signature. Iff the verification succeeds, TRD's task is to perform the function $GAD$ (Generate Authentication Data) for $g^{id_i}$ without revealing information about the internally chosen pseudorandom blinding values $b_1, \ldots, b_l$ and the corresponding signatures $\sigma_1, \ldots, \sigma_l$:

$$GAD(g^{id_i}, e_i, s_t, g, l) = (\lambda_1, \ldots, \lambda_l) := \Lambda(id_i)$$
$$\forall_{1 \le j \le l}: \quad b_j = E_{DES}(TRDID\|Cnt, \tau_{k_t})\|\tau_{k_t}, \quad \eta_j = (g^{b_j}, (g^{id_i})^{b_j}),$$
$$\sigma_j = S(\eta_j, s_t), \quad \lambda_j = E'(b_j\|\sigma_j, e_i)$$

where $TRDID$ is the unique identifier of the TRD and $Cnt$ a counter to gain uniqueness. The batch $\Lambda(id_i)$ is posted on $BB$ indexed by $g^{id_i}$ or $e_i$. Now user $U_i$ is able to access $\Lambda(id_i)$ and store it to his local machine. Depending on the capacity of the smartcard, $U_i$ can import the whole batch or only a subset.

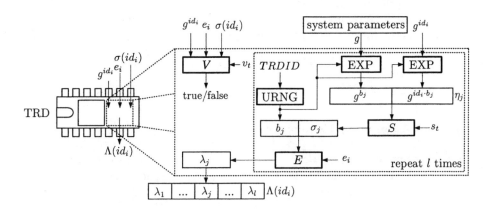

**Fig. 3.** Establishment of Authentication Data – Computations in the TRD

### 4.4   Unilateral Anonymous Authentication

Assume that the user $U_i$ wants to authenticate himself to a verifier $V$ using $\lambda_j$ which corresponds to $\eta_j = (g^{b_j}, g^{b_j \cdot id_i})$.

#### No Anonymity Revocation / No Linkability

*Protocol 1* (ANONAUTH$_1$). User $U_i$ holds $id_i$ and $v_t$ in his smartcard and $\lambda_j$ on his local machine. The verifier $V$ holds $v_t$.

1. $U_i$ imports $\lambda_j$ to his smartcard and decrypts it resulting in $b_j\|\sigma_j$.
2. (a) $U_i$ computes $\eta_j = (g^{b_j}, g^{b_j \cdot id_i})$ and verifies its correspondence to $\sigma_j$.

(b) The tuple $(\eta_j, \sigma_j)$ is sent to $V$.

(c) $V$ verifies if $\sigma_j$ is the signature to $\eta_j$.

3. $U_i$ proves in zero-knowledge (concurrent executions of Schnorr's PK) that he knows the pre-images of $\eta_j$:

$$PK\{(\alpha, \beta) : \eta_{j1} = g^{\alpha} \wedge \eta_{j2} = g^{\beta}\}.$$

Mapping:     $\alpha = b_j \quad \beta = b_j \cdot id_i$

## Optional Anonymity Revocation / No Linkability

*Protocol 2* (ANONAUTH₂). User $U_i$ holds $id_i$, $e_r$ and $v_t$ in his smartcard and $\lambda_j$ on his local machine. The verifier $V$ holds $e_r$ and $v_t$ respectively.

1. $U_i$ imports $\lambda_j$ to his smartcard and decrypts it resulting in $b_j \| \sigma_j$.

2. (a) $U_i$ computes $\eta_j = (g^{b_j}, g^{b_j \cdot id_i})$ and verifies its correspondence to $\sigma_j$.

  (b) $U_i$ computes $r_j = E(b_j^{-1}, a, e_r)$.

  (c) The triple $(\eta_j, \sigma_j, r_j)$ is sent to $V$.

  (d) $V$ verifies if $\sigma_j$ is the signature to $\eta_j$.

3. $U_i$ proves in zero-knowledge (concurrent executions of Stadler's PK) that $r_j$ contains the inverse of the pre-image of $\eta_{j1}$:

$$PK\{(\alpha, \beta, \gamma) : \eta_{j1} = g^{\alpha} \wedge r_j = E(\gamma, \beta, e_r)\}.$$

Mapping:     $\alpha = b_j \quad \beta = a \quad \gamma = b_j^{-1}$

## Optional Anonymity Revocation / Optional Linkability

*Protocol 3* (ANONAUTH₃). User $U_i$ holds $id_i$, $e_r$ and $v_t$ in his smartcard and $\lambda_j$ on his local machine. The verifier $V$ holds $e_r$ and $v_t$ respectively.

1. $U_i$ imports $\lambda_j$ to his smartcard and decrypts it resulting in $b_j \| \sigma_j$.

2. (a) $U_i$ computes $\eta_j = (g^{b_j}, g^{b_j \cdot id_i})$ and verifies its correspondence to $\sigma_j$.

  (b) $U_i$ computes $r_j = E(b_j^{-1}, a, e_r)$ and $l_j = E((b_j \cdot id_i)^{-1}, a', e_r)$.

  (c) The tuple $(\eta_j, \sigma_j, r_j, l_j)$ is sent to $S$.

  (d) $V$ verifies if $\sigma_j$ is the signature to $\eta_j$.

3. $U_i$ proves in zero-knowledge (concurrent executions of Stadler's PK) that $r_j$ contains the inverse of the pre-image of $\eta_{j1}$ and $l_j$ contains the inverse of the pre-image of $\eta_{j2}$:

$$PK\{(\alpha, \beta, \gamma, \delta, \varepsilon, \zeta) : \eta_{j1} = g^{\alpha} \wedge r_j = E(\gamma, \beta, e_r) \wedge$$
$$\eta_{j2} = g^{\delta} \wedge l_j = E(\zeta, \varepsilon, e_r)\}.$$

Mapping:     $\alpha = b_j \qquad \beta = a \qquad \gamma = b_j^{-1}$
$\delta = b_j \cdot id_i \quad \varepsilon = a' \quad \zeta = (b_j \cdot id_i)^{-1}$

The proposed protocols can also be used for mutual authentication as well. Therefore, the steps of the interactive proofs have to be teethed.

## 4.5   Shared Revocation

If the anonymity of an authentication process has to be revoked the verifier has to convince at least $t + 1$ revocation centers and $T$ to agree with the revocation process. If only the user identifier $g^{id_i}$ has to be revealed the revocation centers need the used OTP $\eta_j$ and the encrypted open information $r_j$. $U_i$'s anonymity can be revoked as follows:

$$\eta_{j2}^{\widetilde{D}(r_j, (d_{r_1}, \ldots, d_{r_n}))} = \eta_{j2}^{b_j^{-1}} = g^{b_j \cdot id_i \cdot b_j^{-1}} = g^{id_i}$$

If it is additionally required that all pseudonyms belonging to $U_i$ need to be found, the revocation centers need $l_j$ as well. Then they are able to compute $id_i$ as follows:

$$\widetilde{D}(l_j, (d_{r_1}, \ldots, d_{r_n}))^{-1} \cdot \widetilde{D}(r_j, (d_{r_1}, \ldots, d_{r_n})) = b_j \cdot id_i \cdot b_j^{-1} = id_i$$

Once the anonymity has been revoked including linkability information, each used pseudonym of the user can be linked to $g^{id_i}$. If we do not require the user's future-used OTPs to be linkable, he has to locally generate a new user-id and re-register at $T$.

## 5   Efficiency and Pre-computation

For efficiency reasons the used zero-knowledge proofs have to be run with the modifications described in [8]. Thus, we achieve concurrent executions without loosing the zero-knowledge property. Protocol ANONAUTH$_1$ uses Schnorr's PK which can be run in one round only computing one first-message. This is possible because the challenge space is $\mathbb{Z}_q^*$ in the concurrent model. However, the other two protocols use Stadler's PK whose challenge space is $\{0,1\}$. Thus, concurrent executions require the computation of $k$ first messages. This means in our case, that a smartcard has to perform $O(k)$ exponentiations in $\mathbb{Z}_q^*$ which – depending on the bit-length – can be time-consuming. If this appears to be a problem (which depends on the used type of smartcard) the proposed scheme can be extended so that the TRD pre-computes the $k$ first-messages for each OTP which will then be contained in the encrypted authentication data.[3] Hence, the smartcard only has to compute $k$ third-messages which can be done by negligible $O(k)$ multiplications in $\mathbb{Z}_q^*$. In any case we suggest using ElGamal based on the elliptic curve discrete logarithm problem to speed up all protocols.

## 6   Security Analysis

In this section we analyze the security of the proposed scheme. Therefore, we consider the security according to the requirements stated in section 1. First

---

[3] Note: For efficiency reasons the authentication data should be encrypted using hybrid encryption (e.g. AES + ElGamal).

of all, we analyse the possible dishonest behaviour of the verifier and external adversaries to gain any information about the user's identity or the linking (prover's point of view). Then, we analyse how an external attacker would try to impersonate a registered user (verifier's point of view).

## 6.1    Prover's Point of View

### Anonymity

*User Registration.* The user $U_i$ generates his unique identifier $id_i$ locally without interaction. He only sends $g^{id_i}$ to $T$. So $T$ is not able to extract $id_i$ due to the discrete logarithm problem. The uniqueness of $id_i$ has been proven in [22].

*Establishment of Authentication Data.* The batches of authentication data are generated by the TRD. The input of $GAD$ has to be authentic – otherwise the TRD could be faked. Therefore, the user data $(g^{id_i}, e_i)$ must have been signed by the TRD during the user registration. The output of the TRD is encrypted with $c_i$. An adversary would have to break the ElGamal cryptosystem to get information about the blinding values which would reveal $g^{id_i}$. The security mainly relies on the tamper resistant property of the used device and the CDP.

*Protocol 1* (ANONAUTH₁). In every protocol run a OTP and the corresponding signature is sent to the verifier. The verifier neither gains information about $id_i$ out of the OTP (due to the CDP) nor out of Schnorr's PK (which is proven to be zero-knowledge if used correctly).

*Protocol 2* (ANONAUTH₂). Here the verifier additionally receives an ElGamal ciphertext containing the blinding value of the used OTP. To extract $id_i$, the verifier would have to break Stadler's PK (which is proven to be zero-knowledge). To receive $g^{id_i}$, he would have to break the ElGamal cryptosystem or compromise at least $t + 1$ revocation centers.

*Protocol 3* (ANONAUTH₃). Here the verifier additionally receives an ElGamal ciphertext containing the linking information of the used OTP. To extract $id_i$ the verifier would either have to break the ElGamal cryptosystem or Stadler's PK or compromise $t + 1$ revocation centers.

*External Adversary.* An external adversary would have to compromise $U_i$'s smartcard, compromise trust center $T$ and solve the DLP, break the ElGamal cryptosystem to retrieve $g^{id_i}$ (or $id_i$) or compromise at least $t + 1$ revocation centers.

### Unlinkability

*Adversary knows $g^{id_i}$.* If the adversary knows $g^{id_i}$ and has access to all OTPs of the system, he would have to solve the DDP that is for any OTP $\eta_j = (\eta_{j1}, \eta_{j2})$ to decide whether $(g^{id_i}, \eta_{j1}, \eta_{j2})$ forms a Diffie-Hellman triple or not. Due to the fact that the used proofs of knowledge are zero-knowledge, the adversary does not gain any information about $id_i$.

*Adversary knows $id_i$.* If the adversary knows $id_i$ and has access to all OTPs, then he is able to find all pseudonyms linked to $U_i$ (see section 3).

## Optional Anonymity Revocation and Linkability

*Protocol 1* (ANONAUTH₁). In this protocol the user does not give encrypted open information to the verifier. Even if he behaves dishonest after a successful authentication process the verifier is never able to reveal the user's identity except he compromises him or solves the CDP.

*Protocol 2* (ANONAUTH₂). Here the user additionally sends encrypted open information to the verifier. In case of malicious behaviour the verifier has to convince at least $t + 1$ revocation centers to decrypt the blinding value and reveal $g^{id_i}$. Knowing $g^{id_i}$, the trust center is able to identify the user via the linked passport data.

*Protocol 3* (ANONAUTH₃). Here the user sends the encrypted open- and linking information to the verifier. If required at least $t + 1$ revocation centers are able to decrypt both. Knowing the resulting plaintext the revocation centers can compute $id_i$. So $T$ can identify the user via the linked passport data. If all used OTPs of the system are available, $U_i$'s pseudonyms can be found as well.

### 6.2    Verifier's Point of View

*Forging OTPs.* If an adversary knows $g^{id_i}$ he would be easily able to forge OTPs of $U_i$, but then he would have to be able to forge the corresponding signature as well. Therefore, he would have to compromise the TRD or the used signature scheme.

*Replay Attacks.* If the communication process is not encrypted, an eavesdropper can make a copy of the used OTP and the corresponding signature. If he tries to use the stolen OTP in a different authentication process he would have to fake the used zero-knowledge proof.

For security considerations of the used PK we refer to [24] and [25].

## 7    Conclusion and Future Research

In this paper we proposed three protocols providing anonymous authentication. The first protocol allows a user to prove that he is registered. However, there is no chance to revoke the user's anonymity. Moreover, the authentication processes are mutually unlinkable. This protocol is very useful if the user himself has a strong interest in revealing his identity himself if required (e.g. secure auctions). The second protocol gives the verifier the possibility to revoke the user's identity together with a set of revocation centers and the trust center. Such a protocol can be used if the verifier has a strong interest in the user behaving honest in the protocols performed *after* the authentication process. The third protocol enables the verifier in collaboration with the revocation centers and the trust center to make a user traceable if he behaves dishonest.

We are currently optimizing the protocols with the following goals:

- Multi-party solution to replace the TRD by a set of standard PCs.
- A simple way to establish OTPs where the user only receives one root-OTP and a root-signature based on which he is able to derive several globally unique OTPs and the corresponding signatures.
- An improved version of Stadler's PK, that is more efficient concerning the number of messages for concurrent executions (larger challenge space).
- Some variations of the protocols optimized for selected applications.

## Acknowledgements

The authors would like to thank Dieter Sommer for his useful comments.

## References

1. G. Ateniese, et al. A practical and provably secure coalition-resistant group signature scheme. Adv. in Crypt.: CRYPTO 2000, LNCS 1880, pp. 255–270, Springer-Verlag, 2000.
2. M. Bellare, H. Shi, C. Zhang. Foundations of Group Signatures: The Case of Dynamic Groups. Cryptology ePrint Archive: Report 2004/077.
3. F. Bao, R.H. Deng, H. Zhu. Variations of Diffie-Hellman Problem. Proc. of ICICS'03, LNCS 2836, Springer Verlag, 2003.
4. J. Camenisch, A. Lysyanskaya. An Efficient System for Non-transferable Anonymous Credentials with Optional Anonymity Revocation. Adv. in Crypt.: EURO-CRYPT'01, LNCS 2045, pages 93+, Springer Verlag, 2001.
5. J. Camenisch, A. Stadler. Efficient group signature schemes for large groups. Adv. in Crypt.: CRYPTO'97, LNCS 1296, pp. 410–424, Springer Verlag, 1997.
6. J. Castella-Roca et al. Digital chips for an on-line casino. Proc. of ITCC'05, IEEE Computer Society, vol. I, pp. 494–499, 2005.
7. D. Chaum, E. van Heyst. Group signatures. Adv. in Crypt.: EUROCRYPT'91, LNCS 547, pp.257–265, Springer-Verlag, 1991.
8. I. Damgard. Efficient Concurrent Zero-Knowledge in the Auxiliary String Model. Adv. in Crypt.: EUROCRYPT'00, LNCS 1807, pp. 418–430, Springer Verlag, 2000.
9. Y. Desmedt, Y. Frankel. Threshold Cryptosystems. Adv. in Crypt.: CRYPTO'89, LNCS 435, pp. 307–315, Springer-Verlag, 1990.
10. T. ElGamal. A Public-Key Cryptosystem and a Signature Scheme Based on Discrete Logarithms. Adv. in Crypt.: CRYPTO'84, LNCS 196, pp. 10–18, Springer-Verlag, 1985.
11. R. Gennaro et al. Secure Distributed Key Generation for Discrete-Log Based Cryptosystems. Adv. in Crypt.: EUROCRYPT'99, LNCS 1592, pp. 295–310, Springer-Verlag, 1999.
12. O. Goldreich et al. How to play any mental game – a completeness theorem for protocols with honest majority. Proc. 19th ACM STOC, pp. 218–229, 1987.

13. M. Jakobsson, M. Yung. Revokable and Versatile Electronic Money. In Proc. of the 3rd CCCS, pages 76–87, ACM press, 1996.
14. J. Kim, et al. Anonymous Authentication Protocol for Dynamic Groups with Power-Limited Devices. Proc. of SCIS2003, vol 1/2, pp 405–410, 2003.
15. H. Kim, et al. Design and Implementation of Revocable Electronic Cash System based on Elliptic Curve Discrete Logarithm Problem. Proc. of WISA'02, pp. 85–102, Korea, 2000.
16. A. Kiayias, Y. Tsiounis, M. Yung. Traceable signatures. Adv. in Crypt.: EURO-CRYPT'04, LNCS 3027, pp. 571–589, Springer-Verlag, 2004.
17. T. Nakanishi, M. Shiota, Y. Sugiyama. An Unlinkable Divisible Electronic Cash with User's Less Computations Using Active Trustees. In Proc. ISITA2002, pp. 547–550, Xi'an, 2002.
18. L. Nguyen, R. Safavi-Naini. Dynamic $k$-Times Anonymous Authentication. Proc. of ACNS'05, LNCS 3531, pp. 318–333, Springer-Verlag, 2005.
19. A. Pashalidis, C.J. Mitchell. A Security Model for Anonymous Credential Systems. IFIP Conf. Proc. 148, pp. 183–189, Kluwer Academic Publishers, Boston, 2004.
20. R. Rivest, A. Shamir, L. Adelman. A Method for Obtaining Digital Signatures and Public-Key Cryptosystems. Communications of the ACM, 21 (1978), pp. 120–126.
21. P. Scharnter, M. Schaffer. Unique User-generated Digital Pseudonyms. Proc. of MMM-ACNS'05, LNCS 3685, pp. 194–206, Springer-Verlag, 2005.
22. P. Schartner. Security Tokens – Basics, Applications, Management, and Infrastructures. IT-Verlag (2001).
23. K. Sako, S. Yonezawa, I. Teranishi. Anonymous Authentication: For Privacy and Security. NEC Journal of Advanced Technology, Vol. 2, No. 1, p. 79–83, 2005.
24. C.P. Schnorr. Efficient Signature Generation for Smart Cards. Adv. in Crpyt.: EUROCRYPT'88, LNCS 330, pp. 239–252, Springer Verlag, 1990.
25. A. Stadler. Publicly Verifiable Secret Sharing. Adv. in Crypt.: Eurocrypt'96, LNCS 1070, pp. 190–199, Springer-Verlag, 1996.
26. L. Teranisi, J. Furukawa, K. Sako. $k$-Times Anonymous Authentication. Adv. in Crypt.: ASIACRYPT'04, LNCS 3329, pp. 308–322, Springer-Verlag, 2004.

# SEA: A Scalable Encryption Algorithm for Small Embedded Applications

François-Xavier Standaert[1,3], Gilles Piret[2],
Neil Gershenfeld[3], and Jean-Jacques Quisquater[1]

[1] UCL Crypto Group,
Laboratoire de Microélectronique, Université Catholique de Louvain,
Place du Levant, 3, B-1348 Louvain-La-Neuve, Belgium
[2] Ecole Normale Supérieure, Département d'Informatique,
45, Rue d'Ulm, 75230 Paris cedex 05, France
[3] Center for Bits and Atoms, Massachusetts Institute of Technology,
20 Ames Street, Cambridge, MA 02139, USA
{standaert, quisquater}@dice.ucl.ac.be
Gilles.Piret@ens.fr, neilg@cba.mit.edu

**Abstract.** Most present symmetric encryption algorithms result from a
tradeoff between implementation cost and resulting performances. In addition, they generally aim to be implemented efficiently on a large variety
of platforms. In this paper, we take an opposite approach and consider a
context where we have very limited processing resources and throughput
requirements. For this purpose, we propose low-cost encryption routines
(*i.e.* with small code size and memory) targeted for processors with a
limited instruction set (*i.e.* AND, OR, XOR gates, word rotation and modular addition). The proposed design is parametric in the text, key and
processor size, allows efficient combination of encryption/decryption,
"on-the-fly" key derivation and its security against a number of recent
cryptanalytic techniques is discussed. Target applications for such routines include any context requiring low-cost encryption and/or
authentication.

## 1 Introduction

Resource constrained encryption does not have a long history in symmetric cryptography. Noticeable examples of such ciphers are the Tiny Encryption Algorithm TEA [32] or Yuval's proposal [33]. Both of them are relatively old and
their security against attacks such as linear and differential cryptanalysis was
hardly evaluated. Present block ciphers, like the Advanced Encryption Standard
Rijndael [17, 18] rather focus on finding a good tradeoff between cost, security
and performances. While this approach is generally the most convenient, there
exist contexts where more specialized ciphers are useful. As a motivating example, ICEBERG [30] is targeted for hardware implementations and shows significant
efficiency improvements on these platforms compared to other algorithms.

In this paper, we consequently consider a general context where we have very
limited processing resources (*e.g.* a small processor) and throughput

J. Domingo-Ferrer, J. Posegga, and D. Schreckling (Eds.): CARDIS 2006, LNCS 3928, pp. 222–236, 2006.

requirements. It yields design criteria such as: low memory requirements, small code size, limited instruction set. In addition, we propose the flexibility as another unusual design principle. $SEA_{n,b}$ is parametric in the text, key and processor size. Such an approach was motivated by the fact that many algorithms behave differently on different platforms (*e.g.* 8-bit or 32-bit processors). In opposition, $SEA_{n,b}$ allows to obtain a small encryption routine targeted to any given processor, the security of the cipher being adapted in function of its key size. Beyond these general guidelines, alternative features were wanted, including the efficient combination of encryption and decryption or the ability to derive keys "on the fly". Those goals are particularly relevant in contexts where the same constrained device has to perform encryption and decryption operations (*e.g.* authentication). Finally, the simplicity of $SEA_{n,b}$ makes its implementation straightforward.

Embedded applications such as building infrastructures present a significant opportunity and challenge for such new cryptosystems. For example, introducing programmability into the configuration of lights and switches, thermostats and air handlers, promises to improve the cost of construction, flexibility in occupancy, and energy efficiency of buildings. But meeting this demand on a scale compatible with the economics of the construction industry is going to require secure lightweight implementations of peer-to-peer networks in resource-constrained systems. The Internet-0 approach to end-to-end modulation for interdevice internetworking is typically appropriate in this limit [20]. $SEA_{n,b}$ constitutes a suitable solution for low-cost encryption/authentication within such networks. RFID's or any power/space-limited applications are similarly targeted.

The rest of the paper is structured as follows. Section 2 presents the algorithm specifications. Section 3 discusses security concerns. Performances are evaluated in Section 4 and Conclusions are in Section 5.

## 2   Specifications

### 2.1   Parameters and Definitions

$SEA_{n,b}$ operates on various text, key and word sizes. It is based on a Feistel structure with a variable number of rounds, and is defined with respect to the following parameters:

- $n$: plaintext size, key size.
- $b$: processor (or word) size.
- $n_b = \frac{n}{2b}$: number of words per Feistel branch.
- $n_r$: number of block cipher rounds.

As only constraint, it is required that $n$ is a multiple of $6b$. For example, using an 8-bit processor, we can derive 48, 96, 144, ...-bit block ciphers, respectively denoted as $SEA_{48,8}$, $SEA_{96,8}$, $SEA_{144,8}$, ...

Let $x$ be a $\frac{n}{2}$-bit vector. In the following, we will consider two representations:

- Bit representation: $x_b = x(\frac{n}{2} - 1)\ x(\frac{n}{2} - 2)\ \ldots,\ x(2)\ x(1)\ x(0)$.
- Word representation: $x_W = x_{n_b-1}\ x_{n_b-2}\ \ldots\ x_2\ x_1\ x_0$.

## 2.2  Basic Operations

Due to its simplicity constraints, $\text{SEA}_{n,b}$ is based on a limited number of elementary operations (selected for their availability in any processing device) denoted as follows: (1) bitwise XOR $\oplus$, (2) substitution box $S$, (3) word (left) rotation $R$ and inverse word rotation $R^{-1}$, (4) bit rotation $r$, (5) addition mod $2^b$ $\boxplus$. These operations are formally defined as follows:

**1. Bitwise XOR $\oplus$:** The bitwise XOR is defined on $\frac{n}{2}$-bit vectors:

$$\oplus : \mathbb{Z}_2^{\frac{n}{2}} \times \mathbb{Z}_2^{\frac{n}{2}} \to \mathbb{Z}_2^{\frac{n}{2}} : x, y \to z = x \oplus y \Leftrightarrow z(i) = x(i) \oplus y(i), \quad 0 \le i \le \frac{n}{2} - 1$$

**2. Substitution Box $S$:** $\text{SEA}_{n,b}$ uses the following 3-bit substitution table:

$$S_T := \{0, 5, 6, 7, 4, 3, 1, 2\},$$

in C-like notation. For efficiency purposes, it is applied bitwise to any set of three words of data using the following recursive definition:

$$S : \mathbb{Z}_{2^b}^{n_b} \to \mathbb{Z}_{2^b}^{n_b} : x \to x = S(x) \Leftrightarrow$$

$$x_{3i} = (x_{3i+2} \wedge x_{3i+1}) \oplus x_{3i},$$
$$x_{3i+1} = (x_{3i+2} \wedge x_{3i}) \oplus x_{3i+1},$$
$$x_{3i+2} = (x_{3i} \vee x_{3i+1}) \oplus x_{3i+2}, \quad 0 \le i \le \frac{n_b}{3} - 1,$$

where $\wedge$ and $\vee$ respectively represent the bitwise AND and OR.

**3. Word Rotation $R$:** The word rotation is defined on $n_b$-word vectors:

$$R : \mathbb{Z}_{2^b}^{n_b} \to \mathbb{Z}_{2^b}^{n_b} : x \to y = R(x) \Leftrightarrow \quad y_{i+1} = x_i, \quad 0 \le i \le n_b - 2,$$
$$y_0 = x_{n_b-1}$$

**4. Bit Rotation $r$:** The bit rotation is defined on $n_b$-word vectors:

$$r : \mathbb{Z}_{2^b}^{n_b} \to \mathbb{Z}_{2^b}^{n_b} : x \to y = r(x) \Leftrightarrow \quad y_{3i} = x_{3i} \ggg 1,$$
$$y_{3i+1} = x_{3i+1},$$
$$y_{3i+2} = x_{3i+2} \lll 1, \quad 0 \le i \le \frac{n_b}{3} - 1,$$

where $\ggg$ and $\lll$ represent the cyclic right and left shifts inside a word.

**5. Addition mod$2^b$ $\boxplus$:** The mod $2^b$ addition is defined on $n_b$-word vectors:

$$\boxplus : \mathbb{Z}_{2^b}^{n_b} \times \mathbb{Z}_{2^b}^{n_b} \to \mathbb{Z}_{2^b}^{n_b} : x, y \to z = x \boxplus y \Leftrightarrow z_i = x_i \boxplus y_i, \quad 0 \le i \le n_b - 1$$

## 2.3    The Round and Key Round

Based on the previous definitions, the encrypt round $F_E$, decrypt round $F_D$ and key round $F_K$ are pictured in Figure 1 and defined as the functions $F$ : $\mathbb{Z}_{2^{n/2}}^2 \times \mathbb{Z}_{2^{n/2}} \to \mathbb{Z}_{2^{n/2}}^2$ such that:

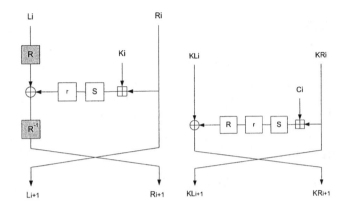

**Fig. 1.** Encrypt/decrypt round and key round

$$[L_{i+1}, R_{i+1}] = F_E(L_i, R_i, K_i) \qquad \Leftrightarrow \qquad R_{i+1} = R(L_i) \oplus r\big(S(R_i \boxplus K_i)\big)$$
$$L_{i+1} = R_i$$

$$[L_{i+1}, R_{i+1}] = F_D(L_i, R_i, K_i) \qquad \Leftrightarrow \qquad R_{i+1} = R^{-1}\Big(L_i \oplus r\big(S(R_i \boxplus K_i)\big)\Big)$$
$$L_{i+1} = R_i$$

$$[KL_{i+1}, KR_{i+1}] = F_K(KL_i, KR_i, C_i) \quad \Leftrightarrow \quad KR_{i+1} = KL_i \oplus R\Big(r\big(S(KR_i \boxplus C_i)\big)\Big)$$
$$KL_{i+1} = KR_i$$

## 2.4    The Complete Cipher

The cipher iterates an odd number $n_r$ of rounds. The following pseudo-C code encrypts a plaintext $P$ under a key $K$ and produces a ciphertext $C$. $P, C$ and $K$ have a parametric bit size $n$. The operations within the cipher are performed considering parametric $b$-bit words.

$C=\textbf{SEA}_{n,b}(P, K)$
{
    % initialization:
        $L_0 \& R_0 = P$;
        $KL_0 \& KR_0 = K$;
    % key scheduling:
        **for** $i$ **in** 1 to $\lfloor \frac{n_r}{2} \rfloor$
            $[KL_i, KR_i] = F_K(KL_{i-1}, KR_{i-1}, C(i))$;
        switch $KL_{\lfloor \frac{n_r}{2} \rfloor}$, $KR_{\lfloor \frac{n_r}{2} \rfloor}$;
        **for** $i$ **in** $\lceil \frac{n_r}{2} \rceil$ to $n_r - 1$

$$[KL_i, KR_i] = F_K(KL_{i-1}, KR_{i-1}, C(r-i));$$
% encryption:
    **for** $i$ **in** 1 **to** $\lceil \frac{n_r}{2} \rceil$
        $[L_i, R_i] = F_E(L_{i-1}, R_{i-1}, KR_{i-1});$
    **for** $i$ **in** $\lceil \frac{n_r}{2} \rceil + 1$ **to** $n_r$
        $[L_i, R_i] = F_E(L_{i-1}, R_{i-1}, KL_{i-1});$
% final:
    $C = R_{n_r} \& L_{n_r};$
    switch $KL_{n_r-1}, KR_{n_r-1};$
},

where $\&$ is the concatenation operator, $KR_{\lfloor \frac{n_r}{2} \rfloor}$ is taken before the switch and $C(i)$ is a $n_b$-word vector of which all the words have value 0 excepted the LSW that equals $i$. Decryption is exactly the same, using the decrypt round $F_D$.

## 3  Security Analysis

### 3.1  Design Properties of the Components

**Substitution Box $S$:**  The substitution box was searched exhaustively in order to meet the following security and efficiency criteria:

- $\lambda$-parameter[1]: $1/2$.
- $\delta$-parameter[2]: $1/4$.
- Maximum nonlinear order, namely 2.
- Recursive definition.
- Minimum number of instructions.

Remark that, if 3-operand instructions are available, the recursive definition allows to perform the substitution box in 2 operations per word of data. As a comparison, the $3 \times 3$ bitwise substitution box used in 3-WAY [15] requires 3. The counterpart of this efficiency is the presence of two fixed points in the table.

**Bit and Word Rotations $r$ and $R$:**  The cyclic rotations were defined in order to provide predictable low-cost diffusion within the cipher, when combined with the bitslice substitution box. It is illustrated in Figure 2 for a single substitution box scheme with parameters $n = 48$, $b = 8$, $n_b = 3$.
    Looking at the figure, it can be seen that $\text{SEA}_{n,b}$ divides its data in $\frac{2n_b}{3}$ blocks of 3 words. The substitution box is applied in parallel to these blocks. Therefore, the diffusion process (starting with one single active bit in the left branch) is divided into two steps[3]:

---

[1] We define the *bias* of a linear approximation that holds with probability $p$ as $\epsilon = |p - 1/2|$. The $\lambda$-*parameter* of a substitution box is equal to 2 times the bias of its best linear approximation.

[2] The $\delta$-parameter equals the probability of the best differential approximation.

[3] For simplicity purposes, we don't consider the additional diffusion provided by the carry propagation in the mod $2^b$ key addition in this discussion.

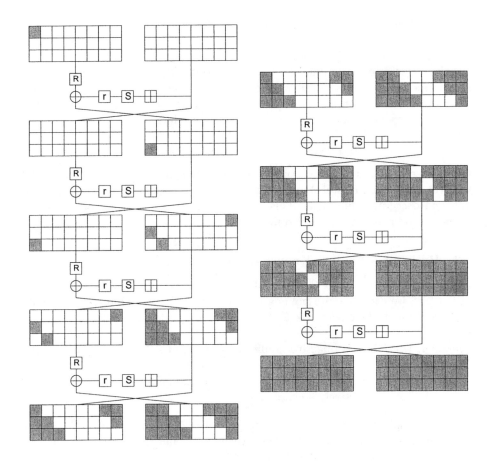

**Fig. 2.** Diffusion process: grey boxes represent active bits

- During an initialization step, the single active bit has to be propagated to all the words of the cipher (*e.g.* to our six words in Figure 2).
- During the second step, the diffusion has to be completed within each block.

The first phase is obtained by the combination of the word rotation $R$ (which is the only transform to provide inter-word diffusion) with the substitution box. It requires at most $n_b$ rounds to be completed (in our example, $n_b = 3$ which yields 3 rounds). Once every word has at least one active bit, the combination of $r$ and $S$ yields six more active bits per block in each round. Therefore, finishing the diffusion of all the blocks requires at most $\lfloor b/2 \rfloor$ rounds. Combining these observations, the diffusion is complete after $n_b + \lfloor b/2 \rfloor$ rounds.

**Addition mod $2^b$ ⊞:** Using a mod $2^b$ key addition in place of a bitwise XOR was motivated by different reasons: (1) improvement of the diffusion process, (2) improvement of the non-linearity, (3) same cost/speed as the bitwise XOR in most processors, (4) necessity to avoid structural attacks (see next section).

**Overall Structure:** The overall structure of the cipher follows the Feistel strategy. However, a few points are specific to SEA$_{n,b}$, namely the key schedule and the position of $R$, $R^{-1}$ in the encrypt/decrypt rounds.

The key schedule is designed such that the master key is encrypted during half the rounds and decrypted during the other half. It allows to obtain a particular structure of the sequence of round keys such that the key expansion is exactly the same in encryption and decryption. Namely, we have:

$$K_0, K_1, K_2, \ldots, K_{\lfloor \frac{r}{2} \rfloor}, K_{\lfloor \frac{r}{2} \rfloor - 1}, \ldots, K_2, K_1, K_0$$

As a consequence of this structure, the encryption/decryption rounds cannot keep the traditional Feistel structure: it would result in having identical encryption and decryption functions. This is the reason of moving the word rotation to the left branch of the Feistel round.

## 3.2   Resistance Against Known Attacks

**Linear and Differential Cryptanalysis.** From the properties of the substitution box, we can compute bounds for the best linear and differential characteristics through the cipher. We first use the following lemma [29]:

*Lemma 1.* Let $f$ be the bijective nonlinear function of a 3-round Feistel cipher. Assuming that the linear parameter of $f$ is smaller than $\lambda$ and its differential parameter is smaller than $\delta$, then the linear, differential parameters of the 3-round cipher $\Delta, \Lambda$ are respectively smaller than $\lambda^2$, $\delta^2$.

Since our nonlinear function $S$ has parameter $\delta = 2^{-2}$ and parameter $\lambda = 2^{-1}$, it implies that 3 rounds of SEA$_{n,b}$ have their linear and differential parameters respectively bounded by $\Delta < 2^{-4}$ and $\Lambda < 2^{-2}$.

However, for a $n$-bit block cipher, it is respectively required that $\Delta \simeq 2^{-n}$ and $\Lambda \simeq 2^{-\frac{n}{2}}$ to resist against differential [4] and linear cryptanalysis [28]. In order to approach these bounds, we require that:

$$\delta^{2n_r/3} = \left(2^{-2}\right)^{2n_r/3} < 2^{-n} \quad \text{and} \quad \lambda^{2n_r/3} = \left(2^{-1}\right)^{2n_r/3} < 2^{-\frac{n}{2}}. \qquad (1)$$

In both cases, the required number of rounds is: $n_r \geq 3n/4$.

We note that we used a hybrid approach, between the provable security against linear and differential attacks that consists in bounding the parameter of the best differential/hull, like in lemma 1, and the usual heuristics to estimate the best linear/differential *characteristic* through a cipher (as in the previous estimation for $n_r$). In fact, the strategy of Equation (1) is similar to the one of *e.g.* the AES Rijndael [17], but we only assume one active s-box per round.

**Extensions of Linear and Differential Cryptanalysis.** Classical extensions of linear and differential cryptanalysis are non-linear approximations of outer rounds [26], bi-linear cryptanalysis [14], differential-linear cryptanalysis [27], multiple linear cryptanalysis [22, 10], boomerang [31] and rectangle [8] attacks,...

However these extensions usually imply only a small improvement compared to the basic attacks. As a matter of fact, non-linear approximations of outer rounds allow to improve the bias of one or two rounds only. Regarding bi-linear cryptanalysis, we quote the author of [14]: *For ciphers similar to DES, based on small substitution boxes, we claim that bi-linear cryptanalysis is very closely related to LC, and we do not expect to find a bi-linear attack much faster than by LC.* It is difficult to evaluate the efficiency of multiple linear cryptanalysis, but it seems more promising for big substitution boxes (as mentioned in [22]). Moreover the improvement on classical cryptanalysis obtained in [10] for the case of DES (which shares with $SEA_{n,b}$ a Feistel structure and a poor diffusion) is limited. Finally, the complexity of differential-linear cryptanalysis and of the boomerang attack and its variants is inherently greater than the one of the basic attacks. As an example, the boomerang (or rectangle) attack allows us to use two short differentials instead of a long one, but using a long differential with probability $pq$ is in general highly preferable to applying a boomerang attack with two short differentials of probability $p$ and $q$. Therefore although these attacks can perform slightly better in specific cases, the expected improvement is never outstanding. The conclusion is that these extensions actually deserve to be considered in the estimation of the number of rounds necessary to achieve security, but that a reasonable multiplicative factor should be enough to take them into account.

**A Dedicated Related-Key Attack Against a Modified Version.** For $x \in \mathbb{Z}_{2^b}^{n_b}$, we denote by $x \lll a$ the left rotation by $a$ bits of each of the $n_b$ words of $x$. The non-linear and diffusion layers have the following properties:

- $S(x \lll a) = S(x) \lll a$
- $r(x \lll a) = r(x) \lll a$
- $R(x \lll a) = R(x) \lll a$

Consider a modified version of our cipher where key addition is performed using $\oplus$ rather than modular addition, and where all round constants $C_i$ are such that $C_i \lll a = C_i$, *e.g.* all $C_i$'s equal 0. As a consequence of the previous observations, the modified round $F'_E$ and the key round $F_K$ satisfy:

$$F'_E(L \lll a, R \lll a, K \lll a) = F'_E(L, R, K) \lll a$$
$$F_K(KL \lll a, KR \lll a, 0) = F_K(KL, KR, 0) \lll a$$

These properties are iterative, in the sense that they also hold for the composition of several block cipher rounds. It is immediate to deduce from them a distinguisher on the modified cipher, which requires 2 chosen encryption queries under 2 related keys $K$ and $K \lll a$.

In the actual $SEA_{n,b}$, the key addition is performed word-wise mod $2^b$. As the property $(X \lll a) \boxplus (K \lll a) = (X \boxplus K) \lll a$ is prevented by certain carry propagations, it only holds with a probability $p$, which depends on $a$ and the word size $b$. For $a = 1$, $p$ rapidly converges to $3/8$ as $b$ grows. It is smaller for $1 < a < b - 1$. Of course, this probability is averaged for all possible $(X, K)$ and certain keys (*e.g.* "*all zeroes*") yield no carry propagation at all. However, the design properties of the key schedule prevent $SEA_{n,b}$ from having such weak keys.

Moreover the round constants $C_i$ are generally not such that $C_i \lll a = C_i$ (because they are generated from a counter). Combined with the diffusion in the key schedule, it implies that the similarity between the round keys derived from $K$ and those derived from $K \lll a$ rapidly vanishes.

These properties avoid this structural distinguisher to be propagated through more than a few rounds of $\text{SEA}_{n,b}$.

**Square Attacks.** We explored square attacks [16] on $\text{SEA}_{48,8}$. More precisely, we considered all possible sets of inputs to one branch of the Feistel structure, where the input to some of the substitution boxes is active (*i.e.* takes all possible input values the same number of times), and the input to the other substitution boxes is constant. The other branch is also constant. Therefore the number of plaintexts considered goes from $2^3$ (when the input to only one substitution box is active) to $2^{21}$ (when the input to 7 substitution boxes is active). Our experiments showed that square attacks do not allow to pass through more rounds than the diffusion pattern illustrated in Figure 2. It is expected that it remains the same when different parameters $n$ and $b$ are considered, which implies that $n_b + \lfloor b/2 \rfloor$ rounds are enough to prevent square attacks. Note that although our observations also hold for $\oplus\text{-SEA}_{n,b}$, the use of addition mod $2^b$ provides better resistance against square attacks.

**Truncated and Impossible Differentials.** As for square attacks, the diffusion analysis illustrated in Figure 2 provides an estimation of the number of rounds required to prevent truncated differential attacks [25]. Impossible differentials [7] are usually built by concatenating two incompatible truncated differentials. As a consequence, we estimate the number of rounds necessary to prevent the construction of an impossible differential distinguisher as $2 \cdot (n_b + \lfloor b/2 \rfloor)$.

**Interpolation Attacks.** The interpolation attack [21] is possible when the whole cipher can be written as a relatively simple algebraic expression. It requires the substitution box to have a compact expression, and the diffusion layer to permit the composition of these expressions. In the case of $\text{SEA}_{n,b}$, there is a priori no such expression, and the bitwise diffusion would make the combination of algebraic expressions difficult anyway.

**Slide Attacks.** The sequence of round keys of $\text{SEA}_{n,b}$ is the same as the one of ICEBERG. Therefore the analysis done in [30] is still valid. Namely, the non-periodicity of the sequence should make slide attacks [11, 12] irrelevant. The particular structure of this sequence also has some similarities with the one of GOST, of which the vulnerability against slide attacks is examined in [12]. None of the attacks presented in [12] seems to be applicable to our cipher.

**Related-Key Attacks.** The first related-key attack has been described in [5]. It is the related-key counterpart of the slide attack. Such an attack is applicable when a round key $K_i$ is computed from the previous round key $K_{i-1}$ using a function $f$ which is always the same: $K_i = f(K_{i-1})$. However in the case of

$SEA_{n,b}$, a round constant that changes for each key round is used, which prevents this attack. Another type of related-key attack is the differential related-key attack [23, 24]. The non-linearity of the $SEA_{n,b}$ key schedule should prevent it. Moreover, note that the improvement of the differential related-key attack over classical differential cryptanalysis usually results from the fact that choosing a given round key difference allows to "counter" the effect of the diffusion layer on the differential characteristic; a typical example is the attack on 3-WAY [24]. As the security of $SEA_{n,b}$ against differential cryptanalysis results from its large number of rounds rather than from its diffusion, this effect is not relevant here.

**Complementation Properties.** The DES has the following complementation property: if $P \xrightarrow{K} C$ denotes the fact that encryption of $P$ under key $K$ gives ciphertext $C$, then: $P \xrightarrow{K} C \iff \overline{P} \xrightarrow{\overline{K}} \overline{C}$. The non-linear key scheduling and the presence of carry propagations in the actual $SEA_{n,b}$ algorithm prevents this property. We are not aware of any other similar structural feature in the design.

**Algebraic Attacks.** Algebraic attacks intend to exploit the simple algebraic structure of a block cipher. For example, certain block ciphers can be written as an overdefined system of quadratic equations. Reference [13] argues that a method called XSL might provide a way to effectively solve this type of equations and recover the key from a few plaintext-ciphertext pairs. Clearly, $SEA_{n,b}$ has a simple algebraic structure, as it is based on a 3-bit substitution box. Therefore, if such an attack practically applies to a cipher like Serpent [1], it is likely applicable to one of the versions of our routines. As the complexity of XSL is supposedly polynomial in the plaintext size and number of rounds, it is specially true when those values increase. However, as the criteria for these techniques to be successful are still being discussed [9], we did consider this latter point as a scope for further research. We note that resistance against algebraic attacks would anyway exclude the use of small substitution boxes and therefore the possibility to build very low cost encryption routines.

### 3.3   Suggested Number of Rounds

From the previous descriptions, the minimum required number of rounds to provide security against known attacks would be $\frac{3n}{4} + 2 \cdot (n_b + \lfloor b/2 \rfloor)$. This roughly corresponds to the number of rounds to resist linear/differential attacks plus twice the number of rounds to obtain complete diffusion (to prevent both structural attacks and outer rounds improvements of statistical attacks). A more conservative approach (applied in most present block ciphers) would be to take a large security margin, e.g. by doubling this number of rounds[4]. $n_r$ has to be odd: we add one if it is even. We also assume a minimum word size $b \geq 8$ bits.

---

[4] Note that the additional non-linearity provided by the modular addition also provides a security margin, under-estimated in our predictions.

## 4   Performance Analysis

$SEA_{n,b}$ is targeted for being implemented on low-cost processors, with little code size and a small instruction set. However, $SEA_{n,b}$'s simple structure makes it easy to implement on any processor. In appendix, we propose a pseudo-assembly code of an encryption/decryption design with "on the fly" key scheduling. The implementation objectives were, in decreasing order of importance: (1) low RAM and registers usage, (2) low code size and (3) speed. It is based on the following (very) reduced instruction set (assuming 2-operand instructions only):

- Arithmetic and logic operators: $\vee, \wedge, \oplus, \boxplus, \ggg, \lll$.
- Branch instructions: goto, subroutine call and return.
- Comparison, load RAM in register, store register in RAM.

According to the code in appendix, the performances can be roughly estimated as follows. First, the combined number of RAM words and registers equals $5n_b + 3$. Then, the code size and implementation time (both in expressed in ops.) is evaluated by summing the values given in appendix. For the code size, it directly yields $31n_b + 36$ ops. For the implementation time, the round and key round respectively require $12n_b + 11$ ops. and $10n_b + 11$ ops. It yields a total of $(n_r - 1) \times (12n_b + 11 + 10n_b + 11 + 7) + (12n_b + 11) + 8n_b + 7$. These values are summarized in Table 1. Remark that, due to the particular structure of the key scheduling, we do not need to keep the master key in memory as, at the end of an encryption/decryption, we have $K_{n_r-1} = K_0$. Remark also that this implementation uses a low number of registers, namely $n_b + 3$. However, if more registers are available, they can be traded for RAM words, which will result in lower code size and faster implementation.

For illustration purposes, we implemented $SEA_{n,b}$ on Atmel AVR ATtiny [3] and ARM [2] microprocessors. The Atmel ATtiny represents a typical target for such a low-cost encryption routine. We chose the ARM platform in order to provide rough comparisons between $SEA_{n,b}$ and the AES Rijndael.

While direct comparisons are made difficult by their high dependencies on the target devices, the following general comments can be made:

- $SEA_{n,b}$ designs combine encryption and decryption more efficiently than most other encryption algorithms. In particular, key agility in decryption is usually not possible (e.g. for the AES Rijndael).
- The combined number of RAM words and registers of $SEA_{n,b}$ implementations (i.e. $5n_b + 3$) is generally lower than for other block ciphers.
- The code size of $SEA_{n,b}$ is generally lower than for other block ciphers implemented on similar platforms.

**Table 1.** Performance evaluation of $SEA_{n,b}$ (encryption + decryption)

|  | # ram | # regs. | code size (ops.) | implementation time (ops.) |
|---|---|---|---|---|
| $SEA_{n,b}$ | $4n_b$ | $n_b + 3$ | $31n_b+36$ | $(n_r - 1) \times (22n_b + 29) + 20n_b + 18$ |

**Table 2.** Comparisons: the code size is expressed in bytes. The results of $SEA_{128,32}$ where obtained by multiplying the code size and number of cycles of $SEA_{192,32}$ by $2/3$, since 128 is not a multiple of 6.

| Algorithm | $E/D$ | Device | # ram | # regs. | code size | # clock cycles | # cycles × code size |
|---|---|---|---|---|---|---|---|
| $SEA_{96,8}$ | yes | Atmel ATtiny | 1 | 32 | 386 | 17 745 | $6849.10^3$ |
| $SEA_{192,32}$ | yes | ARM (risc-32) | 6 | 12 | 420 | 27 059 | $11\ 364.10^3$ |
| Rijndael [19] | no | ARM (risc-32) | 16 | 12 | 1404 | 2889 | $4056.10^3$ |
| $SEA_{128,32}$ | yes | ARM (risc-32) | 6 | 12 | 280 | 18 039 | $5050.10^3$ |

The flexibility of $SEA_{n,b}$ also makes it less sensitive to the choice of a processor than fixed-sized algorithms, although it is obvious that large buses improve efficiency. The drawback of these limited resources is in the number of cycles required for the encryption (*i.e.* $SEA_{n,b}$ trades space for time, which may be relevant due to present processors speeds). Looking at the code size - cycles product, the efficiency of $SEA_{n,b}$ remains similar to the one of Rijndael (encryption only) that is well known for its efficient smart cards implementations.

## 5    Conclusion

$SEA_{n,b}$ is a scalable encryption algorithm targeted for small embedded applications. The plaintext size, key size and processor (or word) size are parameters of the design. The structure of $SEA_{n,b}$ allows a fast evaluation of the cipher efficiency on any RISC machine. Its typical performances (encryption + decryption) for present key sizes and processors (*e.g.* 128-bit key, 1 Mhz 8-bit RISC) are in the range of an encryption/decryption in a few milliseconds, using a few hundreds bytes of ROM. One additional advantage of the design is its extreme simplicity. Based on the pseudo code provided in this paper, it is expected that the implementation of the cipher in assembly can be done within a few hours. We note finally that the design criteria of $SEA_{n,b}$ do not make it a conservative algorithm by nature. Further cryptanalysis efforts are consequently required.

**Acknowledgements.** The authors would like to thank François Koeune for his help and comments about ARM assembly tools and the NSF grant CCR-0122419, Center for Bits and Atoms. François-Xavier Standaert is a post doctoral researcher funded by the FNRS (Funds for National Scientific Research, Belgium).

## References

1. R. Anderson, E. Biham, L. Knudsen, *Serpent: A Flexible Block Cipher With Maximum Assurance*, in the proceedings of The First Advanced Encryption Standard Candidate Conference, Ventura, California, USA, August 1998.
2. ARM, *32-bit RISC microprocessors*, http://www.arm.com/products/CPUs/

3. Atmel, *AVR 8-Bit RISC*, http://www.atmel.com/products/AVR/
4. E. Biham, A. Shamir, *Differential Cryptanalysis of the Data Encryption Standard*, 1993, Springer Verlag.
5. E. Biham, *New types of cryptanalytic attacks using related keys*, Journal of Cryptology, vol 7, num 4, pp 229-246, Fall 1994, Springer Verlag.
6. E. Biham, A. Biryukov, A. Shamir, *Miss-in-the-Middle Attacks on IDEA, Khufu, and Khafre*, in the proceedings of FSE 1999, Lecture Notes in Computer Sciences, vol 1636, pp 124-138, Rome, Italy, March 1999, Springer-Verlag.
7. E. Biham, A. Biryukov, A. Shamir, *Cryptanalysis of Skipjack Reduced to 31 Rounds using Impossible Differentials*, in the proceedings of Eurocrypt 1999, Lecture Notes in Computer Sciences, vol 1592, pp 12-23, Prague, Czech Republic, May 1999, Springer Verlag.
8. E. Biham, O. Dunkelman, N. Keller, *The Rectangle Attack, Rectangling the Serpent*, in the proceedings of Eurocrypt 2001, Lecture Notes in Computer Science, vol 2045, pp 340-357, Innsbruck, Austria, May, 2001 Springer-Verlag.
9. A. Biryukov, C. De Cannière, *Block Ciphers and Systems of Quadratic Equations*, in the proceedings of FSE 2003, Lecture Notes in Computer Science, vol 2887, pp 274-289, Lund, Sweden, February 2003, Springer-Verlag.
10. A. Biryukov, C. De Cannière, M. Quisquater, *On Multiple Linear Approximations*, in the proceedings of Crypto 2004, Lecture Notes in Computer Science, vol 3152, pp 1-22, Santa Barbara, USA, August 2004, Springer-Verlag.
11. A. Biryukov, D. Wagner, *Slide attacks*, in the proceedings of FSE 1999, Lecture Notes in Computer Sciences, vol 1636, pp 245-259, Rome, Italy, March 1999, Springer-Verlag.
12. A. Biryukov, D. Wagner, *Advanced Slide Attacks*, in the proceedings of Eurocrypt 2000, Lecture Notes in Computer Science, vol 1807, pp 589-606, Bruges, Belgium, May 2000, Springer-Verlag.
13. N. Courtois, J. Pieprzyk, *Cryptanalysis of Block Ciphers with Overdefined Systems of Equations*, in the proceedings of Asiacrypt 2002, Lecture Notes in Computer Science, vol 2501 , pp 267-287, Queenstown, New Zealand, December 2002, Springer-Verlag.
14. N. Courtois, *Feistel Schemes and Bi-linear Cryptanalysis*, in the proceedings of Crypto 2004, Lecture Notes in Computer Science, vol 3152, pp 23-40, Santa Barbara, USA, August 2004, Springer-Verlag.
15. J. Daemen, R. Govaerts, J. Vandewalle, *A New Approach Towards Block Cipher Design*, in the proceedings of FSE 1993, Lecture Notes in Computer Science, vol 809, pp 18-32, Cambridge, UK, December 1993, Springer-Verlag.
16. J. Daemen, L. Knudsen, V. Rijmen, *The Block Cipher SQUARE*, in the proceedings of FSE 1997, Lecture Notes in Computer Science, vol 1267, pp 149-165, Haifa, Isreal, January 1997, Springer-Verlag.
17. J. Daemen, V. Rijmen, *The Design of Rijndael,* Springer-Verlag, 2001.
18. FIPS 197, *"Advanced Encryption Standard,"* Federal Information Processing Standard, NIST, U.S. Dept. of Commerce, November 26, 2001.
19. G. Hachez, F. Koeune, J.-J. Quisquater, *cAESar Results: Implementation of Four AES Candidates on Two Smart Cards*, in the proceedings of the Second Advanced Encryption Standard Candidate Conference, pp 95-108, Rome, Italy, March 1999.
20. N. Gershenfeld, R. Krikorian, D. Cohen, *The Internet of Things*, Scientific American, Octobre 2004, pp 76-81.
21. T. Jakobsen, L.R. Knudsen, *The Interpolation Attack on Block Ciphers*, in the proceedings of FSE 1997, Lecture Notes in Computer Science, vol 1267, pp 28-40, Haifa, Israel, January 1997, Springer-Verlag.

22. B.S. Kaliski, M.J.B. Robshaw, *Linear Cryptanalysis using Multiple Approxima-tions*, in the proceedings of Crypto 1994, Lecture Notes in Computer Science, vol 839, pp 26-39, Santa Barbara, California, USA, August 1994, Springer-Verlag.

23. J. Kelsey, B. Schneier, D. Wagner. *Key-Schedule Cryptanalysis of IDEA, G-DES, GOST, SAFER, and Triple-DES*, in the proceedings of Crypto 1996, Lecture Notes in Computer Science, vol 1109, pp 237-251, Santa Barbara, California, USA, August 1996, Springer-Verlag.

24. J. Kelsey, B. Schneier, D. Wagner, *Related-Key Cryptanalysis of 3-WAY, Biham-DES, CAST, DES-X, NewDES, RC2, and TEA*, in the proceedings of ICICS 1997, Lecture Notes in Computer Sciences, vol 1334, pp 233-246, Bejing, China, November 1997, Springer-Verlag.

25. L.R. Knudsen, *Truncated and Higher Order Differentials*, in the proceedings of FSE 1995, Lecture Notes in Computer Sciences, vol 1008, pp 196-211, Leuven, Belgium, 1995, Springer-Verlag.

26. L.R. Knudsen and M.J.B. Robshaw, *Non-Linear Approximations in Linear Crypt-analysis*, in the proceedings of Eurocrypt 1996, Lecture Notes in Computer Science, vol 1070, pp 224-236, Saragossa, Spain, May 1996, Springer-Verlag.

27. S. Langford, M. Hellman, *Differential-Linear Cryptanalysis*, in the proceedings of Crypto 1994, Lecture Notes in Computer Science, vol 839, pp 17-25, Santa Barbara, California, USA, August 1994, Springer-Verlag.

28. M. Matsui, *Linear Cryptanalysis Method for DES Cipher*, in the proceedings of Eurocrypt 1993, Lecture Notes in Computer Science, vol 765, pp 386-397, Lofthus, Norway, May 1993, Springer-Verlag.

29. M. Matsui, *Supporting Document of MISTY1*, Submission to the NESSIE project, available from http://www.cosic.esat.kuleuven.ac.be/nessie/

30. F.-X. Standaert, G. Piret, G. Rouvroy, J.-J. Quisquater, J.-D. Legat, *ICEBERG : an Involutional Cipher Efficient for Block Encryption in Reconfigurable Hardware*, in the proceedings of FSE 2004, Lecture Notes in Computer Science, vol 3017, pp 279-299, New Delhi, India, February 2004, Springer-Verlag.

31. D. Wagner, *The Boomerang Attack*, in the proceedings of FSE 1999, Lecture Notes in Computer Sciences, vol 1636, pp 156-170, Rome, Italy, March 1999, Springer-Verlag.

32. D.J. Wheeler, R. Needham, *TEA, a Tiny Encryption Algorithm*, in the proceedings of FSE 1994, Lecture Notes in Computer Science, vol 1008, pp 363-366, Leuven, Belgium, December 1994, Springer-Verlag.

33. G. Yuval, *Reinventing the Travois: Encryption/MAC in 30 ROM Bytes*, in the proceedings of FSE 1997, Lecture Notes in Computer Science, vol 1267, pp 205-209, Haifa, Israel, January 1997, Springer-Verlag.

| Pseudo-assembly code: | # ram | # regs. | # ops. |
|---|---|---|---|
| **% Init** | | | |
| $L_0, R_0, KL_0, KR_0$ stored in RAM; | $4n_b$ | | |
| Set $i = 1$; | | 1 | |
| Set E/D; | | 1 | |
| | | | |
| **% Subroutines** (including return): | | | |
| $S$: $reg \leftarrow S(reg)$; | | $n_b + 1$ | $3n_b + 1$ |
| $r$: $reg \leftarrow r(reg)$; | | $n_b$ | $n_b + 1$ |
| $sw$: switch $KL_i, KR_i$; | | 2 | $4n_b + 1$ |
| | | | |
| **Round:** | | | |
| $reg \leftarrow R_i$; | | $n_b$ | $n_b$ |
| if $i \leq \lceil n_r/2 \rceil$ | | | 1 |
| goto a: | | | 1 |
| $reg \leftarrow reg \boxplus KL_i$; | | $n_b + 1$ | $2n_b$ |
| goto b: | | | 1 |
| a: $reg \leftarrow reg \boxplus KR_i$; | | $n_b + 1$ | $2n_b$ |
| b: call $S$; | | | 1 |
| call $r$; | | | 1 |
| if E/D=1; | | | 1 |
| goto c: | | | 1 |
| $reg \leftarrow reg \oplus L_i$; | | $n_b + 1$ | $2n_b$ |
| goto d: | | | 1 |
| c: $reg \leftarrow reg \oplus R(L_i)$; | | $n_b + 1$ | $2n_b$ |
| d: $L_{i+1} \leftarrow R_i$; | | 1 | $2n_b$ |
| if E/D=1; | | | 1 |
| goto e: | | | 1 |
| $R_{i+1} \leftarrow R^{-1}(reg)$; | | $n_b$ | $n_b$ |
| goto f: | | | 1 |
| e: $R_{i+1} \leftarrow reg$; | | $n_b$ | $n_b$ |
| f: return; | | | 1 |
| | | | |
| **Key round:** | | | |
| $reg \leftarrow KR_i$; | | $n_b$ | $n_b$ |
| if $i < \lceil n_r/2 \rceil$ | | | 1 |
| goto g: | | | 1 |
| $temp \leftarrow n_r - i$; | | 1 | 2 |
| $reg \leftarrow reg \boxplus temp$; | | $n_b + 1$ | 1 |
| goto h: | | | 1 |
| g: $reg \leftarrow reg \boxplus i$; | | $n_b$ | 1 |
| h: call $S$; | | | 1 |
| call $r$; | | | 1 |
| $reg \leftarrow R(reg) \oplus KL_i$; | | $n_b + 1$ | $2n_b + 1$ |
| $KL_{i+1} \leftarrow KR_i$; | | 1 | $2n_b$ |
| $KR_{i+1} \leftarrow reg$; | | $n_b$ | $n_b$ |
| return; | | | 1 |
| | | | |
| **% Total:** | | | |
| j: call round; | | | 1 |
| if $i \neq \lceil n_r/2 \rceil$ | | | 1 |
| goto k: | | | 1 |
| call $sw$; | | | 1 |
| k: if $i = n_r$ | | | 1 |
| goto end: | | | 1 |
| call key round; | | | 1 |
| $i = i + 1$; | | | 1 |
| goto j: | | | 1 |
| end: call $sw$; | | | 1 |
| switch $L_i, R_i$; | | 2 | $4n_b$ |

# Low-Cost Cryptography for Privacy in RFID Systems

Benoît Calmels, Sébastien Canard, Marc Girault, and Hervé Sibert

France Telecom R&D, 42, rue des Coutures, BP6243, 14066 Caen Cedex 4, France
{benoit.calmels, sebastien.canard, marc.girault,
herve.sibert}@francetelecom.com

**Abstract.** Massively deploying RFID systems while preserving people's privacy and data integrity is a major security challenge of the coming years. Up to now, it was commonly believed that, due to the very limited computational resources of RFID tags, only ad hoc methods could be used to address this problem. Unfortunately, not only those methods generally provide a weak level of security and practicality, but they also require to revise the synopsis of communications between the tag and the reader. In this paper, we give evidence that highly secure solutions can be used in the RFID environment, without substantially impacting the current communication protocols, by adequately choosing and combining low-cost cryptographic algorithms. The main ingredients of our basic scheme are a probabilistic (symmetric or asymmetric) encryption function, e.g. AES, and a coupon-based signature function, e.g. GPS. We also propose a dedicated method allowing the tag to authenticate the reader, which is of independent interest. On the whole, this leads to a privacy-preserving protocol well suited for RFID tags, which is very flexible in the sense that each reader can read and process all and only all the data it is authorized to.

## 1 Introduction

RFID (Radio-Frequency IDentification) technology appeared quite a long time ago. However, it only recently began to spread into a very wide range of applications, because of both technical improvements and dramatic cost decrease. Indeed, the price of the simplest RFID tags is no more than 5 cents per tag. Thus, RFID applications such as stocks management yield cuts in expenses that represent more than the price of *tagging* every item in the stocks.

However, widely spread RFID tags usually broadcast a unique identifier over the air whenever they are powered on. This is the case of Electronic Product Code (EPC) tags with long range used in supply chains, but also that of most short range (ISO 14443/15693) tags regardless of theoretically broader abilities. For instance, the Navigo tags used by commuters in the Paris public transportation system answer readers' requests with a unique identifier. This behavior raises many concerns on privacy, and slows down massive deployment of RFID tags. On the other hand, it is commonly believed that strong cryptographic mechanisms

J. Domingo-Ferrer, J. Posegga, and D. Schreckling (Eds.): CARDIS 2006, LNCS 3928, pp. 237–251, 2006.

cannot be embedded into RFID tags because they require too high computing resources. As a consequence, literature essentially focuses on ad hoc techniques, the security level of which (as well as the practicality) is often questionable.

The purpose of this paper is to reconcile privacy concerns with RFID technology, without restricting the range of applications the tags can be used for. Whereas, in previous work, this was usually done by adding interactions between the tag and the reader, our approach is to implement in the tag some low-cost but secure cryptographic functions. This allows us to achieve a high level of privacy, without requiring any substantial change in the synopsis of communication between the tag and the reader. This also means that the tag broadcasts the same data to any reader which, depending on the authorizations it has been given, will be able to read and process part or all of the said data.

Our paper is organized as follows: we first state the problem we address, i.e. what the privacy issues are, how they are (or not) presently dealt with, and which applications should be concerned. Then, we outline the solution we propose. In section 4, we present our basic tools, namely low cost cryptographic primitives and an authentication protocol of the reader by the tag which is of independent interest. Then we describe our basic protocol, and show in the following section how it can be used in various applications. Finally, we conclude.

## 2  Tags and Privacy

Privacy is a particularly big concern when millions and millions of small devices are expected to be embedded into goods and to send various information over the air about them and their holders. Many popular applications of the RFID tags require these tags to be traced, but how to proceed without threatening the privacy of the people who use or wear it ? Reconciling privacy with RFID tags is therefore a very challenging task for the coming years. To achieve this goal, we first have to define precisely the different uses of these devices and the different needs they generate in terms of privacy.

### 2.1  Different Needs for Different Uses

By making remote identification possible without requiring any visual contact, RFID tags are suitable in many environments where barcodes are not. For instance, RFID technology enables the quick account of the tags surrounding a tag reader, thus providing stores and warehouses with means to manage stocks and inventories more effectively than ever.

However, depending on the context, an application needs or not uniquely identify the tags it issued. While unique identification is useful for a shop that wants not only to count, but also trace its stocks, only knowing the category of the product is for other purposes often sufficient. E.g. in an airport, customs only need to detect and/or count products submitted to restrictions, without having to trace them further. Only the nature of the product, not its serial number, is relevant here. On the other hand, checking authenticity of a product can be of great importance, e.g. in order to thwart counterfeiting. As we can see, needs related to RFID technology deeply depend on the applications they are involved in.

**Detection Needs.** Detection consists, by using a tag reader, in first finding objects that emit signals with sufficient power to reach the reader, whereever they may be hidden, and second getting some information about them. Thus, provided the level of information given by the tags is appropriate, every accounting application can be fulfilled by this procedure (see above the customs example).

However, when the level of information which is publicly available from the tags is too high, privacy concerns arise, as provided data could allow anyone to uniquely (or almost uniquely) identify each tag. Therefore, it becomes necessary to design a general scheme for RFID tags and readers, which allows tags to disclose the nature of the items they are included in, without identifying themselves uniquely to any tag reader.

**Authentication Needs.** Another emerging application of RFID tags is control of authenticity. Manufacturers of the luxury industry have already begun to integrate RFID tags in their products, so that counterfeiting can be detected more easily. Moreover, counterfeiting is becoming more and more usual, and luxury goods are no longer the only products concerned. As a matter of fact, every well-known brand is a potential victim of counterfeiting. Despite these threats, basic RFID tags broadcasting EPC (Electronic Product Code) 64 or 96-bit numbers can be easily duplicated. As a consequence, they do not provide at the time a satisfactory solution to authentication needs.

**Identification Needs.** Identification needs are closely related to traceability, which consumers often consider as a threat to their privacy. This is a reason why, if not the main one, spread of RFID technology is not as fast as expected. However, traceability is required by many applications (shipments, after-sales follow-up...). Thus, in order to protect consumers' privacy, a first step is to prevent tag readers with no special privilege from tracing items.

## 2.2   Previous Work on Privacy in RFID Tags

**Tag Deactivation.** Tag deactivation consists in preventing the tag from communicating once and for all. It can be, for instance, the physical destruction of the link between the tag and its antenna, or some software deactivation function. For long, tag deactivation has been the only means to deal with privacy concerns raised by RFID tags. Deactivation is supposed to take place when the consumer has bought the product containing the tag. However, this solution is not very satisfactory, because it prevents any application that could take place later from using the tag. In case of software deactivation, the tag could be reactivated later, but this raises the problem of managing rights to (de)activate the tag.

**The Blocker Tag.** In [15], Juels, Rivest and Szydlo consider the most widespread tags singulation protocol (i.e., a scheme designed to enable the detection by a reader of all the surrounding tags in its environment, and one-to-one communications between the reader and each tag). This scheme, based on tree walking, is subject to a basic attack. Starting from this attack, the authors yield the design of a privacy-enabling tag, the *blockertag*. This approach is appealing, but it implies that RFID-based architectures are not self-sufficient in order to ensure privacy. Moreover, the attack works when applied to the cheapest, first generation tags, whose "applicative" ID (that is, their serial number, which is unique and constant) is used at the network level for the singulation process. But for instance, among Philips RFID tags from the I-CODE 1 series, several models of probabilistic singulation protocols are designed, for which the blocker tag design loses its efficiency.

**Applicative Privacy.** With privacy in mind, many papers have proposed to include cryptographic mechanisms into RFID tags. In [14], Juels and Pappu propose a re-encryption approach for tagged banknotes designed to protect privacy. However, this approach requires external computation and is hardly adaptable to tags embedded in consumer goods. In [13], Juels describes minimalist cryptographic mechanisms designed to enhance privacy in RFID technologies at a very low cost. Works of Feldhofer *et al.* promote low-cost implementations of standard algorithms, such as AES [7], or challenge-response-type symmetric mechanisms for authentication with extensions to mutual authentication [1].

**Network Layer Privacy.** In [3], Avoine and Oechslin show how important it is to take the network layer exchanges into consideration. Indeed, this is where the singulation protocol takes place, and, as we have seen in Section 2.2, privacy greatly depends on the way singulation is carried out. There are advances at this level, because at this layer the only requirement is that the tag reader gains the ability to distinguish temporarily between all the tags it is surrounded by. Thus, there is no requirement on the signification of the data transmitted at this level, and using secure pseudo-random generators at this level is sufficient to ensure network layer privacy. However, one should note that singulation protocols actually implemented in the tags do not take privacy into account.

## 3   Outline of the General Scheme

As described earlier, several needs (detection, authentication, identification) are not fulfilled with the standard mechanisms. In addition, privacy issues must also be addressed.

The main idea behind our solution is to integrate seamlessly privacy preservation mechanisms into the usual framework of a single response from the RFID tag to the reader. We use lightweight cryptographic tools in order to hide the information necessary for the usual applications of RFID systems. Then, on a single request from the reader, the tag's response can be decoded to different levels of information by different RFID readers, depending on their knowledge.

For **detection** purpose, a way to meet the privacy requirements is to draw a separation line between public and private data in the unique identifier EPC (which is a serial number) of an RFID tag. The public data would consist mainly of digits that identify the product category, and the private data would, for instance, consist of the remaining digits of the serial number. Only the public data would be broadcast with no restriction.

One could be concerned by the public data being the same for two items of the same category, possibly causing collision problems during detection. This is not the case, because we are only dealing with the applicative level, and the singulation protocol at the network layer ensures the distinction between two items of the same category. Of course, in order to prevent tracking by every tag reader at this network level, one has to make sure that the singulation algorithms and responses from the tag are not flawed. This problem is considered, for instance, in [3].

Contrary to public data, private data must be encrypted. It will nevertheless fulfill the **identification** needs, since revealing the complete identifier only to authorized equipments. The main question is whether it is necessary and/or even possible to use an asymmetric or a symmetric encryption algorithm. While authentication can be publicly available, identification must remain very restricted, so here, depending on the applications that are aimed at, symmetric or asymmetric encryption can be chosen. However, for costs concerns, one may prefer to use symmetric encryption, especially if it is completed by some means to check the authenticity of the tag.

A simple way to meet **authentication** needs is to provide the tag with data authentication ability. This mechanism can be either symmetric (MACs) or asymmetric (digital signatures). However, it is necessary to define precisely the data that should be authenticated. In accordance with privacy protection, the signed data should not include constant information sufficient to authenticate uniquely the tag. Moreover, in order to prevent replay attacks, the signed data should include time-variant parameters. For security and practical reasons, asymmetric signatures should be preferred to MACs. Indeed, everyone (and consequently every reader) should be able to check the authenticity of a product, so means to check authenticity have to be publicly available. In case of a signature, certificates can be supplied to the reader by the tag, or can already be stored in the reader if they are available, for instance, in an online database.

## 4   Basic Tools

Before presenting our solution, we first introduce the cryptographic primitives it relies on. Then we propose a new and practical way for a RFID tag to authenticate the RFID reader before interacting with it, which is of independent interest.

### 4.1   Cryptographic Primitives

Our solution, sketched in Section 3, involves several cryptographic primitives: probabilistic encryption, signature and pseudo random number generation. Since a RFID tag is limited in terms of processing power and memory, we need to find out the cryptographic algorithms well suited for the RFID context. In this section, we introduce some possible algorithms for each one of these primitives.

**Encryption.** The result of encrypting a message $M$ is denoted by $\text{Enc}_{K_e}(M)$, where $\text{Enc}$ can be a symmetric or an asymmetric algorithm that is used with the encryption key $K_e$. The result of the decryption step is denoted by $\text{Dec}_{K_d}(C)$ where $K_d$ is the decryption key[1] and C is the ciphertext. Note that we will need the encryption scheme be semantically secure, which (informally) means that the ciphertext does not leak any partial information whatsoever about the plaintext that can be computed in expected polynomial time. As a consequence, the encryption scheme shall be probabilistic.

As a symmetric encryption scheme, we can for example think of the Federal Standard AES (Advanced Encryption Standard [18]). Indeed Feldhofer et al. [7] have presented at CHES'04 a hardware implementation, the gate count of which is estimated to 3595. Furthermore, this implementation is expected to be improved in a near future. In the mean-time, proprietary algorithms can be used but their security is of course much less established.

As an asymmetric encryption scheme, we can think of NTRU [11], since the company NTRU Cryptosystems Inc. claims that it is implemented with around 1000 gates in their product called Genuid.

**Signature.** The signature of a message $M$ will be denoted by $\text{Sign}_{K_s}(M)$ where $K_s$ is the private signature key. The corresponding verification algorithm of the signature $S$ on a message $M$ is noted $\text{Ver}_{K_v}$ and the result $\text{Ver}_{K_v}(S, M)$ ("Yes" or "No"), where $K_v$ is the public verification key. In the sequel, the algorithm considered is asymmetric (namely, we do not consider Message Authentication Code).

At CHES'04, Girault and Lefranc [10] propose a variant of GPS [8, 19] that requires the prover (or the signer) to compute only one on-line addition (in $\mathbb{Z}$). From this result, we can consequently consider that a signature can be processed with less than 2000 gate equivalents using this algorithm.

Low-cost GPS necessitates that the RFID tag stores a set of coupons. A coupon is an integer that is computed beforehand and stored in the RFID tag. This computation is high-cost but can be computed by a powerful computer and sent to the RFID tag. The latter will consequently only have to send a new coupon at each new signature. As a (restrictive) consequence, the number of signatures that a RFID tag can produce is limited by the number of stored coupons, except if it is possible to refill to RFID tag with new ones. This possibility depends on the use of the RFID tag (see Section 6). Nevertheless, it is possible to use hashed values for coupons, so that the hash function needs only to be implemented by the verifier [9]. Within that framework, we can consider that coupons are 32-bit long, so that several tens of coupons fit in the tag at a reasonable memory cost.

---

[1] $K_d = K_e$ if the algorithm is symmetric.

The signature scheme can also be replaced by an authentication scheme. In this case, the proof is not transferable, but this does not impact the applications of our scheme described in Section 6, as we need only convince the reader of the authenticity of the tag. Nevertheless, in the case of the authentication version of GPS, it adds one pass to the general scheme described in Section 5.2.

**PRNG.** The Pseudo Random Number Generator (PRNG) will be denoted by PRNG($l$) where $l$ is the size of the output (for example in bits). This PRNG is used by the encryption scheme to ensure its probabilistic property. It can also be used to (re-)generate, during the signature phase, the random data embedded in the coupons that are used in the GPS signature scheme (see [9] for details).

We can use any PRNG that is suitable for the RFID context, that is, with a minimum of gate equivalents. It is also possible to use a block cipher algorithm (see AES in the previous section) to design a PRNG, by using standard techniques. Note that the anti-clone functions can also be turned into a PRNG. We can consequently have a PRNG in either 3600 gate equivalents or in less than 1000 gate equivalents.

## 4.2  Authentication of the Reader

Most authentication schemes proposed for RFID tags are dedicated to the authentication of a tag by a reader. Nevertheless, the lightweight GPS signature introduced in Section 4.1 implies the use of coupons. Thus, we have to thwart the possible denial of service attack that would consist in forcing the tag to produce many signatures, so that it uses all its coupons. This is the reason why we also propose an (optional) mechanism dedicated to the authentication of the reader. This is not a usual cryptographic authentication scheme, but rather a mechanism to distinguish between legitimate and rogue readers, based on the fact that rogue readers are unlikely to be close to the tag. We want to stress that, if it became possible to use a signature scheme that does not require coupons, then this phase could be left out.

This authentication mechanism is a kind of challenge-response scheme, and works as follows:

1. The RFID tag receives a request from a reader.
2. The RFID tag sends a challenge $c$ to the reader (we describe below the way $c$ is generated).
3. The reader computes $r = g(c)$ (where $g$ is some function defined below), and sends $r$ to the tag,
4. On reception of a value $r'$, the RFID tag checks : $d(r', g(c)) \leq m$, where $d$ is a distance (e.g. the Hamming distance), and $m$ is an acceptance level.
5. The RFID tag accepts the initial request of the reader only if the previous inequality is verified.

The value $m$ can be chosen to be equal to 0 (i.e. the RFID tag checks that $r' = g(c)$) in case data transmission already involves error-correcting codes.

The first, most interesting variant, is dedicated to tags with a short range. This is the case for ISO 14443 (proximity) tags and some ISO 15693 (vicinity) tags with a short range, this range being about a few centimeters. This is one of the most important cases, as these norms are used for contactless payment and ticketing. In this variant, $c$ is either constant or pseudo-randomly generated by using the memory contents of the tag. It can also be picked up from a list of values, and this list can change in a deterministic way, using ideas from [13]. But the main point of this variant is that $g$ can be chosen to be the identity function. In other words, the response is equal (or close) to the challenge ! This is made possible by the asymmetry between the emission range of the tag and the one of the reader. Indeed, an illegitimate reader is very unlikely to be in the emission range of the tag, so that it will not receive the challenge, and will consequently not be able to answer properly.

This should also work when the emission range is about one meter, because it is quite likely that an attacker aiming at making a denial of service on tags will be quite far from its potential victims. Moreover, considering that tags are moving with the persons they are carried by, it is even more unlikely that an attacker will succeed more than once to send a request that will be answered by the tag, because of this mechanism.

However, we have to take into consideration the fact that, in some places (for instance, places where luggage is gathered in an airport), this attack could be effective even if this variant is implemented. In such a case, it is recommended to use this challenge-response protocol in a classical way, i.e. by making $g$ depend on a shared secret key, known only by the tag and authorized readers.

## 5   General Scheme

In this section, we introduce the general scheme of our solution on the tag's side. As outlined in Section 3, it fits seamlessly into the usual synopsis of communication between a tag and a reader. Essentially, the scheme consists in encrypting some data, and signing this ciphertext together with some public plaintext. Thus, the transmitted data do not depend on the identity of the reader.

The scalability of this construction is the essence of our scheme, since it enables privacy protection together with the applications introduced in Section 2.1. Indeed, on a single request from the reader, the tag's response can be decoded to different levels of information depending on the knowledge of the reader, thus enabling (or preventing) each application in a scalable way. We will introduce the relations between the knowledge of the reader and the possible applications/use cases in Section 6.

### 5.1   Data Elements in the RFID Tag

Our solution requires the RFID tag to store some values such as an identifier and, since it also performs some cryptographic operations, to store cryptographic keys. Let us introduce our notations of the data elements stored in the tag.

- $Id_p$: this is the public part of the identifier of the RFID tag. It can be, for example, a part of the EPC number. This public part contains general characteristics of the RFID tag, not precise enough to uniquely identify the item carrying this RFID tag. This part of the identifier has a size denoted by $l_p$.
- $Id_s$: this is the secret part of the identifier of the RFID tag. It is typically the remaining part of the EPC number (64 or 96 bits long). This data element must be considered as sensitive because it is unique and, consequently, fully identifies a particular RFID tag. If not secret, it could be used to trace the user of this RFID tag or to know where it comes from. This identifier part has a size denoted by $l_s$ (and consequently $l_p + l_s$ will typically be the length of the entire EPC number, that is 64 or 96 bits).
- $K_s$: this is the signature private key that permits the RFID tag to use the algorithm Sign in order to sign a message. If we use the GPS algorithm, this key can be of size 160 bits. The corresponding public key $K_v$ that will be used by the reader, is linked (in a way or another) to $Id_p$. The pair ($K_v$, $K_s$) can be either:

  - certified[2] by an authorized certification authority, or
  - written in a secured database (locally saved or not) that is used by the verifier.

  Consequently, all RFID tags that belong to the same group of public identifier $Id_p$ have the same private signature key.
- $K_e$: this is the encryption key used by the RFID tag in the Enc algorithm to encrypt messages. This key can be secret (if the algorithm is symmetric) or public (if the algorithm is asymmetric). Using AES, the size of this key can be equal to 128 bits. Using the anti-clones functions, we need to store 320 bits for this key. Finally, if one wants to use NTRU, the key size depends on the security level : 1000 bits for NTRU-167, 2000 bits for NTRU-263 and 4000 bits for NTRU-503[3]. The corresponding decryption key $K_d$ will be used by the tag reader. Note that the pair ($K_e$, $K_d$) should be the same for a given $Id_p$.

### 5.2    The General Scheme Embedded in the RFID Tag

The general scheme presented in this section is to be embedded into the RFID tag. This general scheme is called each time the RFID tag is requested by a RFID reader, whatever the RFID reader may be. The request from a RFID reader includes a challenge sent to the tag. This challenge can for example be a random value generated by the RFID reader, the date of the request, or simply the request sent at the network layer (see Figure 1 for details). Note that

---

[2] This solution requires the RFID tag to store the certificate, which may conflict with memory limitations due to cost target.

[3] In terms of security, NTRU-503 is claimed to be equivalent to RSA-4096. However, the size of the key would be too high for storage in RFID tags.

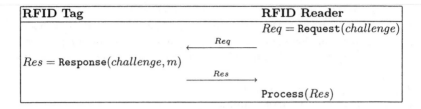

**Fig. 1.** General Scheme: Interactions

this challenge-response protocol is consistent with the communication protocol between a tag reader and an RFID tag[4].

The generation of the response by a RFID tag is then computed as follows:

1. The RFID tag first encrypts its secret identifier $Id_s$ plus some optional extra data $m_s$ with the probabilist encryption scheme.

$$C = \mathtt{Enc}_{K_e}(Id_s \| m_s)$$

where the symbol $a\|b$ denotes the concatenation of $a$ and $b$.

2. The RFID tag then signs a message which consists of the ciphertext $C$, the public identifier $Id_p$, the *challenge* and some optional extra public data $m_p$.

$$S = \mathtt{Sign}_{K_s}(C \| Id_p \| challenge \| m_p).$$

3. The RFID tag finally generates the response formed as $Id_p$, the ciphertext $C$, the signature $S$ and some optional extra data $p$. The data $p$ at least includes the extra public data $m_p$.

$$Res = Id_p \| C \| S \| p.$$

After receiving the response of the RFID tag, the RFID reader has to process it. The way a RFID reader proceeds depends on the cryptographic keys it holds: this leads to various applications that are detailed in the next section.

### 5.3   Security Arguments

The lightness of this security part is due to the fact that our scheme fits into the standard RFID model, in which a tag issues a single response to the request of a reader. The response of the tag, except for the signature part, is the same for every tag, be it legitimate or not. For the signature part, the tag includes in the signed message the challenge sent by the reader, which is a classical technique used to turn signature into interactive proof of knowledge, thus providing authentication. Thus, it turns out that our scheme does not require a particular security model and proof, the security of the scheme being essentially that of the cryptographic primitives used.

---

[4] Since an RFID tag never sends a message without a request.

There may be some security concerns due to the fact that the private signature key should be shared between (possibly very) many tags. A way to improve this is to use group signatures [6, 2] with revocability, since there is the same problem in [5]. This would require a group signature scheme that is low-cost on the side of the signer. Thus, we think that research in this direction is definitely one of the biggest needs to concile security and privacy preservation with the massive deployment of pervasive, low-cost devices.

# 6   Applications

In our paper, we consider that there are various types of RFID readers, depending on the keys (secret or "public") they hold. We will consequently consider three types of RFID readers:

1. The RFID reader which holds no cryptographic key related to our scheme. We call it a "Detection reader".
2. The RFID reader which holds the verification public key that allows to verify a signature produced by a RFID tag. We call it an "Authentication reader".
3. The RFID reader which holds the decryption secret key that allows to decrypt the ciphertext generated by a RFID tag. We call it an "Identification reader".

Let us now study in details these three types of RFID readers.

## 6.1   Detection

An RFID reader that holds no cryptographic functionality related to the scheme described in section 4 can only read the public data sent by the reader without being able to verify them: it can consequently only detect the presence of an RFID tag. This is why we call it a "Detection reader".

**Reader Side.** The only data this kind of reader is able to manage are $Id_p$ and $p$. In particular, the reader is not able to derive any benefit from the signature $S$. The reader is also unable to decrypt the ciphered data $C$, ensuring the privacy of the tag (and of its owner), and preventing traceability.

**Use Case.** Though enjoying no privileges, a "Detection reader" can be useful in different situations:

- it is able to detect hidden items. For instance, it can be used in **theft detection**. In such scenarii, the articles hidden by the robber are tagged. Any reader is then able to detect tags that should not pass through a portal for instance. No authentication of the tag is required for this, and "after purchase" privacy issues are solved since unprivileged reader are not able to trace the tag.

– it can be used to **count** and **control purposes**. In a trusted environment, for instance in a warehouse where the access is controlled (and theft is not considered an issue), a Detection reader is able to count tags for inventory purpose even if it is not able to differentiate two objects[5] with the same public identifier $Id_p$. In an untrusted environment it can be used to detect an overtaking, for instance for customs purpose. If $Id_p$ reveals a type (alcohol) or a brand, customs are able to easily count tags revealing a minimum of the quantity really carried.

– It can be used to **facilitate** the **search** of lost objects, since the technology does not require a visual contact and has a limited range.

## 6.2 Authentication

An RFID reader that holds the verification public key can check the validity of what is sent by the RFID tag. By verifying the signature, this type of RFID reader can authenticate the RFID tag. This is why we call it an "Authentication reader".

**Reader Side.** The reader is able to manage $Id_p$ and $p$, but is also able to verify the signature $S$, certifying the public data. It is unable to understand the ciphered data, ensuring privacy protection w.r.t. this kind of reader.

To check the signature $S$, the reader retrieves the public key $K_v$ from the public identifier $Id_p$. The key can be stored locally in the reader or might be extracted from a database, depending on the use case. The RFID tag can also send the corresponding certificate linked to $Id_p$, which contains the verification public key.

**Use Case.** The cryptographic functionalities of the reader allow it to perform operations requiring trust:

– It can be used for count and **control purposes**, with the guarantee that the final count matches the reality (e.g. for inventory purpose)

– The signature can be used to **prevent counterfeits**: the tags can prove their characteristics such as the brand (for luxury products), or their origin[6] (passport, identification cards), etc.

– Other services such as **traceability services** for mail and delivery can use the signature to ensure the authenticity of the product they are following up[7].

---

[5] As discussed earlier, to do so, the discovering protocol at the network layer must be designed with this requirement in mind. The classical "tree parsing protocol" for instance would not allow the reader to properly count tags with the same $Id_p$.

[6] Such information can be considered as sensitive and private, so the signature could be used to validate ciphered data, and the "Authentication reader" used in conjunction with an "Identification reader".

[7] Again, to be able to identify precisely an item, such a reader should be used in conjunction with an "Identification reader".

## 6.3   Identification

An RFID reader that holds the decryption secret key can decrypt what is sent by the RFID tag, and more particularly the secret identifier $Id_s$ of the RFID tag. This is why we call it an "Identification reader".

**Reader Side.** The reader is able to manage $Id_p$ and $p$, but is also able to decrypt the data $M$ in order to gain access to the secret identity $Id_s$ and $m_s$.

The reader retrieves the secret key $K_d$ thanks to the public identifier. To do so, several methods can be chosen depending on the use case. This key can be locally stored in the tag reader for instance. It can also be stored in a remote database. Then, the reader needs to authenticate itself to the remote server, and ask the required key to the server. The tag reader can also simply relay the messages to the server which will find the right key and perform the decryption.

The problem of retrieving a symmetric key to decrypt the response of a tag was adressed in [4, 17]. In our scheme, each tag having the same public identifier should use the same encryption key, thus retrieving this key is straightforward in this case. However, one may want to diversify encryption keys for security concerns. Then, the tags having the same public identifier should be divided into several subgroups sharing the same encryption key, in order to increase security (and rely less on tamper-resistance of the tags) while keeping low table lookup costs to retrieve the key, using for instance a hash-based approach.

**Use Case.** The encryption ensures the traceability w.r.t. the readers which do not hold the decryption secret. Conversely, being able to decrypt the ciphered data allows the reader to precisely identify a product. This property can then be used to:

- **identify** the owner of a **lost or stolen product**. After the purchase of a product, a database managed by the manufacturer (for instance) can link the $Id_s$ to the identity of the customer. If a lost or stolen product is found, police services can contact the manufacturer and ask him to reveal the secret identity. To do so, the reader can relay the exchanges with the tags to the manufacturer to perform an on-line decryption.
- easily identify a product serial number for **after-sale services**. The manufacturer can get access to the whole identification code in order to know if a product is concerned by e.g. a specific problem. Then a manufacturer can call back a faulty sub-series, after rapidly and cheaply identifying them.

## 7   Conclusion

We have presented a protocol which allows to reconcile privacy with RFID technology. By making an optimal choice of algorithms, the cost of our solution in terms of gate equivalents is less than 5000. As stated by Juels and Weis [16], the total number of gates in supply chain RFID tags is usually between 5000 and 10000. Among these, about 2000 can currently be dedicated to security functions. Moreover, short range tags can include several times this number of gates. As a consequence, our solution suits present (or available in a very near future) hardware abilities, and we think the additional cost of such a solution is justified both by continuously decreasing costs, due to production increases and strengthening market competition, and by the functionalities it provides. In any case, we wish to emphasize that tags need to be equipped with cryptographic functions in order to enhance privacy protections in RFID systems. This should encourage the research activity in (ultra-)low cost cryptography.

# References

1. M. Aigner and M. Feldhofer. Secure symmetric authentication for rfid tags. In *Telecommunication and Mobile Computing – TCMC 2005*, Graz, Austria, March 2005.
2. G. Ateniese, J. Camenisch, M. Joye, and G. Tsudik. A practical and provably secure coalition-resistant group signature scheme. In T. Okamoto, editor, *Advances in Cryptology - Asiacrypt '00*, volume 1976 of *Lecture Notes in Computer Science*, pages 255–270. Springer-Verlag, 2000.
3. G. Avoine and P. Oechslin. RFID Traceability: A Multilayer Problem. In *Financial Cryptography 2005*, Lecture Notes in Computer Science. Springer-Verlag, 2005.
4. Gildas Avoine and Philippe Oechslin. A scalable and provably secure hash based RFID protocol. In *International Workshop on Pervasive Computing and Communication Security – PerSec 2005*, pages 110–114, Kauai Island, Hawaii, USA, March 2005. IEEE, IEEE Computer Society Press.
5. S. Canard and M. Girault. Implementing group signatures schemes with smart cards. In *Smart Card Research and Advanced Applications V - Cardis 2002*. Kluwer, 2002.
6. David Chaum and Eugène van Heyst. Group signatures. In *EUROCRYPT*, pages 257–265, 1991.
7. M. Feldhofer, S. Dominikux, and J. Wolkerstorfer. Strong Authentication for RFID Systems Using the AES Algorithm. In Joye and Quisquater [12], pages 357–370.
8. M. Girault. Self-Certified Public Keys. In D. W. Davies, editor, *Advances in Cryptology - Eurocrypt '91*, volume 547 of *Lecture Notes in Computer Science*, pages 490–497. Springer-Verlag, 1991.
9. M. Girault. Low-Size Coupons for Low-Cost IC Cards. In J. Domingo-Ferrer, D. Chan, and A. Watson, editors, *Cardis 2000*, volume 180 of *IFIP Conference Proceedings*, pages 39–50. Kluwer Academic Publishers, 2000.
10. M. Girault and D. Lefranc. Public Key Authentication with one Single (on-line) Addition. In Joye and Quisquater [12], pages 413–427.
11. J. Hoffstein, J. Pipher, and J. H. Silverman. NTRU: A Ring-Based Public Key Cryptosystem. In *The 3rd International Symposium ANTS-III*, volume 1426 of *Lecture Notes in Computer Science*, pages 267–288, 1998.
12. M. Joye and J. J. Quisquater, editors. *CHES 2004*, volume 3156 of *Lecture Notes in Computer Science*. Springer-Verlag, 2004.
13. A. Juels. Minimalist Cryptography for Low-Cost RFID Tags, 2003.
14. A. Juels and R. Pappu. Squealing Euros: Privacy Protection in RFID-Enabled Banknotes. In R. N. Wright, editor, *Financial Cryptography 2003*, volume 2742 of *Lecture Notes in Computer Science*, pages 103–121. Springer-Verlag, 2003.

15. A. Juels, R. L. Rivest, and M. Szydlo. The blocker tag: selective blocking of RFID tags for consumer privacy. In *10th ACM conference on Computer and communications security*, pages 103–111. ACM Press, 2003.
16. Ari Juels and Stephen Weis. Authenticating pervasive devices with human protocols. In V. Shoup, editor, *Advances in Cryptology - Crypto 05*, Lecture Notes in Computer Science. Springer-Verlag, 2005.
17. David Molnar and David Wagner. Privacy and security in library RFID: Issues, practices, and architectures. In Birgit Pfitzmann and Peng Liu, editors, *Conference on Computer and Communications Security – ACM CCS*, pages 210–219, Washington, DC, USA, October 2004. ACM, ACM Press.
18. National Institute of Standards and Technology (NIST). FIPS-197: Advanced Encryption Standard. November 2001.
19. G. Poupard and J. Stern. Security Analysis of a Practical "on the fly" Authentication and Signature Generation. In K. Nyberg, editor, *Advances in Cryptology - Eurocrypt '98*, volume 1403 of *Lecture Notes in Computer Science*, pages 422–436. Springer-Verlag, 1998.

# Optimal Use of Montgomery Multiplication on Smart Cards

Arnaud Boscher and Robert Naciri

Oberthur Card Systems SA, 71-73, rue des Hautes Pâtures,
92726 Nanterre Cedex, France
{a.boscher, r.naciri}@oberthurcs.com

**Abstract.** Montgomery multiplication is used to speed up modular multiplications involved in public-key cryptosystems. However, it requires conversion of parameters into $N$-residue representation. These additional pre-computations can be costly for low resource devices like smart cards. In this paper, we propose a new, more efficient method, suitable for smart card implementations of most of public-key cryptosystems. Our approach essentially consists in modifying the representation of the key and the algorithm embedded in smart card in order to take advantage of the Montgomery multiplication properties.

**Keywords:** Montgomery Multiplication, Smart Card, RSA, ECDSA, GQ2.

## 1 Introduction

Almost all public-key cryptosystems embedded in low resource devices, such as smart cards and PDAs, require an efficient implementation of modular multiplication.

One of the best methods of modular multiplication is due to P.L. Montgomery [1]. It consists in replacing division by an arbitrary number with division by a fixed-number, which can be chosen to be a power of 2 for efficiency reasons. Montgomery multiplication requires pre-computation of a constant to change the representation of the operands. This pre-computation requires time and memory space and must be performed each time the cryptosystem is computed. We will see how most of the public-key cryptosystems can be implemented on a smart card using Montgomery multiplication without this drawback.

The paper is organized as follows. In Section 2, we recall the basics about Montgomery multiplication. In Sections 3 and 4 we propose a method for RSA and CRT RSA implementations using Montgomery multiplication. In Section 5, we adapt the method to GQ2 algorithm [6] which results in an improvement of up to 50 % in execution time compared to the classical methods. Lastly, we look at ECDSA signature [7] in Section 6.

## 2 Montgomery Multiplication

Throughout the rest of the paper, we use · to denote classical multiplication and ∗ to denote Montgomery multiplication.

J. Domingo-Ferrer, J. Posegga, and D. Schreckling (Eds.): CARDIS 2006, LNCS 3928, pp. 252–262, 2006.
© IFIP International Federation for Information Processing 2006

Let $b$ be the length of the machine word (typically $b = 2^k$ with $k = 8, 16$ or 32). Let $X, Y$ and $N$ be three integers of length $n : X = (x_{n-1}...x_0)_b$, $Y = (y_{n-1}...y_0)_b$. We denote by $R$ the value $b^n$.

For $N$ odd, the Montgomery multiplication of $X$ and $Y$ modulo $N$ is defined by:

$$X * Y \bmod N = X \cdot Y \cdot R^{-1} \bmod N \ .$$

It can be computed by applying the following algorithm shown in [3]:

---

**Algorithm 2.1.** Montgomery multiplication

INPUT: $X, Y, N, R$ and $N' = -N^{-1} \bmod b$
OUTPUT: $X \cdot Y \cdot R^{-1} \bmod N$

---

1. $A \leftarrow 0$
2. For $i$ from 0 to $n - 1$ do
   (a) $u \leftarrow (a_0 + x_i \cdot y_0)N' \bmod b$
   (b) $A \leftarrow (A + x_i \cdot y + u \cdot N)/b$
3. If $A \geq N$ then $A \leftarrow A - N$
4. Return($A$)

---

Let us denote by $*$ the Montgomery exponentiation defined by:

$$X^{*e} \bmod N = X^e \cdot R^{1-e} \bmod N \ . \tag{1}$$

As it can be deduced from Relation (1), classical modular exponentiation can be computed using Montgomery exponentiation. First, we have to change the representation of the operand, then carry out the Montgomery exponentiation and finally correct its output to obtain the expected result. This can be summarized by:

$$X^e \bmod N = [(X * R^2)^{*e}] * 1 \bmod N \ ,$$

or by the following algorithm taken from [3]:

---

**Algorithm 2.2.** Modular Exponentiation using Montgomery Multiplication

INPUT: $X, e, N, R$
OUTPUT: $X^e \bmod N$

---

1. $\tilde{X} \leftarrow X * R^2 \bmod N$
2. $A \leftarrow R \bmod N$
3. For $i$ from $n - 1$ to 1 do
   (a) $A \leftarrow A * A \bmod N$
   (b) If $e_i = 1$ then $A \leftarrow A * \tilde{X} \bmod N$
4. $A \leftarrow A * 1 \bmod N$
5. Return($A$)

---

The value $\tilde{X} = X \cdot R \bmod N = X * R^2 \bmod N$ is called the Montgomery representation of $X$. To obtain this representation, the value $R^2 \bmod N$ must be computed. In order to do this, one can use Montgomery multiplication and the following proposition:

**Proposition 1.** *Let $R$ and $N$ be two integers with $N$ odd, then we have:*

$$R^2 \bmod N = (2 \cdot R)^{*log_2[R]} \bmod N \ .$$

*Proof.*

$$\begin{aligned}
(2 \cdot R)^{*log_2[R]} &= 2^{log_2[R]} \cdot R^{log_2[R]} \cdot R^{1-log_2[R]} \bmod N \\
&= 2^{log_2[R]} \cdot R \bmod N \\
&= R \cdot R \bmod N \\
&= R^2 \bmod N \ .
\end{aligned}$$
□

As a consequence of Proposition 1, the pre-computation of $R^2 \bmod N$ requires $log_2[R]$ Montgomery multiplications. As $R$ equals $h^n$, for public-key cryptosystems using large parameters $n$ (like RSA), this can be a problem in terms of time or memory on low cost devices.

On smart cards for instance, initialization of the parameters can take more time than the Montgomery multiplication itself. One reason is that initialization is made by software, whereas Montgomery multiplication is made by hardware. Another reason is the clock frequency: dedicated hardware for Montgomery multiplication has higher clock frequency than classical CPU.

In the next section, we introduce a new method of computing RSA signatures with Montgomery multiplications without the pre-computation of $R^2 \bmod N$.

## 3   RSA

### 3.1   Classical Method for RSA

The RSA cryptosystem [4] uses a public modulus $N$, product of two large prime numbers $p$ and $q$, a public exponent $e$ co-prime with $\phi(N) = (p-1) \cdot (q-1)$ and a private exponent $d$, inverse of $e$ modulo $\phi(N)$.

To sign a message $M$ using Montgomery multiplication, one can apply the following algorithm:

---
**Algorithm 3.1.**  RSA using Montgomery multiplication
---
INPUT: $M, d, N, R$
OUTPUT: $M^d \bmod N$

---

1. $X \leftarrow R^2 \bmod N$
2. $\tilde{M} \leftarrow M * X \bmod N$
3. $S \leftarrow \tilde{M}^{*d} \bmod N$
4. $S \leftarrow S * 1 \bmod N$
5. Return($S$)

---

## 3.2  Our New Method for RSA

Let us assume that the public exponent $e$ is known (as it is often the case). We give in the following a new way of computing a RSA signature:

---

**Algorithm 3.2.** Optimized RSA using Montgomery multiplication

INPUT: $M, d, e, N$
OUTPUT: $M^d \bmod N$

1. $S \leftarrow 1^{*(e-1)} \bmod N$
2. $S \leftarrow M * S \bmod N$
3. $S \leftarrow S^{*d} \bmod N$
4. Return($S$)

---

Before arguing the correctness of Algorithm 3.2., let us notice that:

$$1^{*(e-1)} \bmod N = 1^{e-1} \cdot R^{1-e+1} \bmod N = R^{2-e} \bmod N \ .$$

So, after the first step of Algorithm 3.2. we have:

$$S = R^{2-e} \bmod N \ .$$

And from the second step, we obtain:

$$\begin{aligned} S = M * S \bmod N &= M * R^{2-e} \bmod N \\ &= M \cdot R^{2-e} \cdot R^{-1} \bmod N \\ &= M \cdot R^{1-e} \bmod N \ . \end{aligned}$$

Finally, using Fermat's little theorem in the last step:

$$\begin{aligned} S = S^{*d} \bmod N &= (M \cdot R^{1-e})^{*d} \bmod N \\ &= M^d \cdot R^{(1-e)d} \cdot R^{1-d} \bmod N \\ &= M^d \cdot R^{1-ed} \bmod N \\ &= M^d \bmod N \ . \end{aligned}$$

Algorithm 3.2. works for every $e$, but is especially interesting when $e$ is small (typically $2^{16} + 1$).

Even if the total of Montgomery multiplications in Algorithm 3.1. and in Algorithm 3.2. is not very different, the execution time of the second one will be faster in a smart card context. Indeed, the initialization step of operands takes more time than the Montgomery multiplication itself. This is a consequence of the smart card architecture, where Montgomery multiplication uses dedicated hardware.

# 4   CRT RSA

## 4.1   Traditional Method for CRT RSA

When the values $p$ and $q$ are available, one usually applies the Chinese Remainder Theorem and the Garner's algorithm [5] to improve performance of RSA signature. In the so-called CRT mode, RSA involves the 5 parameters $p, q, d_p, d_q, A$, where $d_p = d \bmod p - 1, d_q = d \bmod q - 1$ and $A = p^{-1} \bmod q$.

The CRT RSA signature of a message $M$ using Montgomery multiplication is given by:

---
**Algorithm 4.1.**   CRT RSA using Montgomery multiplication

INPUT: $M, p, q, d_p, d_q, A, R$
OUTPUT: $M^d \bmod N$

---

1. $X \leftarrow R^2 \bmod p$
2. $\tilde{M} \leftarrow M * X \bmod p$
3. $\tilde{S}_p \leftarrow \tilde{M}^{*d_p} \bmod p$
4. $S_p \leftarrow \tilde{S}_p * 1 \bmod p$
5. $X \leftarrow R^2 \bmod q$
6. $\tilde{M} \leftarrow M * X \bmod q$
7. $\tilde{S}_q \leftarrow \tilde{M}^{*d_q} \bmod q$
8. $S_q \leftarrow \tilde{S}_q * 1 \bmod q$
9. $X \leftarrow R^2 \bmod p$
10. $\tilde{A} \leftarrow A * X \bmod p$
11. $S \leftarrow [(S_q - S_p) * \tilde{A} \bmod p] \cdot p + S_p$
12. Return($S$)

---

## 4.2   Our New Method for CRT RSA

We assume that the public exponent $e$ is available. Moreover, we recall that every message $M$ can be written $M_1 \cdot R + M_0$.

If we store in the smart card the value $\tilde{A}$, instead of $A$ itself, we obtain an optimized CRT RSA implementation using Montgomery multiplication:

---
**Algorithm 4.2.**   Optimized CRT RSA using Montgomery multiplication

INPUT: $M, p, q, d_p, d_q, \tilde{A}, e$
OUTPUT: $M^d \bmod N$

---

1. $X \leftarrow 1^{*(e-2)} \bmod p$
2. $S_p \leftarrow (M_1 + M_0 * 1) \bmod p$
3. $S_p \leftarrow S_p * X \bmod p$
4. $S_p \leftarrow S_p^{*d_p} \bmod p$
5. $X \leftarrow 1^{*(e-2)} \bmod q$
6. $S_q \leftarrow ((M_1 + M_0 * 1) \bmod q$
7. $S_q \leftarrow S_q * X \bmod q$
8. $S_q \leftarrow S_q^{*d_q} \bmod q$
9. $S \leftarrow [(S_q - S_p) * \tilde{A} \bmod p].p + S_p$
10. Return $S$

---

After the first step of the algorithm, we have:

$$X = 1^{*(e-2)} \bmod p = R^{3-e} \bmod p \ .$$

Then, the second step gives:

$$S_p = M_1 + M_0 * 1 \bmod p = M_1 + M_0 \cdot R^{-1} \bmod p \ .$$

Hence, at the third step we have:

$$\begin{aligned}
S_p * X \bmod p &= S_p * R^{3-e} \bmod p \\
&= (M_1 + M_0 \cdot R^{-1}) \cdot R^{3-e} \cdot R^{-1} \bmod p \\
&= (M_1 + M_0 \cdot R^{-1}) \cdot R^{2-e} \bmod p \\
&= (M_1 \cdot R + M_0) \cdot R^{1-e} \bmod p \\
&= M \cdot R^{1-e} \bmod p \ .
\end{aligned}$$

Thus, Montgomery exponentiation (step 4) gives:

$$\begin{aligned}
S_p^{*d_p} \bmod p &= (M \cdot R^{1-e})^{*d_p} \bmod p \\
&= (M \cdot R^{1-e})^{d_p} \cdot R^{1-d_p} \bmod p \\
&= M^{d_p} \cdot R^{(1-e)d_p} \cdot R^{1-d_p} \bmod p \\
&= M^{d_p} \cdot R^{1-ed_p} \bmod p \\
&= M^{d_p} \bmod p \ .
\end{aligned}$$

For the same reason, we have:

$$S_q^{*d_q} \bmod q = ((M_1 + M_0 * 1) * 1^{(e-2)})^{*d_q} \bmod q.$$

By definition of $\tilde{A}$, we obtain a correct CRT RSA signature.

This CRT RSA implementation using Montgomery multiplication is optimized for smart cards.

## 5    GQ2

### 5.1    Description

GQ2 [6] is a zero-knowledge algorithm whose security is equivalent to the factorization problem. It can be converted to a signature scheme.

Like RSA, GQ2 uses a public modulus $N$, product of two large primes $p$ and $q$. The parameters of the public key are $N$ and two small numbers, $g_1 = 3$ and $g_2 = 5$. The parameters of the private key are two numbers $Q_1$ and $Q_2$ (lower than $N$), verifying the formula: $Q_i^{512} \cdot g_i^2 = 1 \bmod N$ .

Let us recall in the following the GQ2 authentication protocol.

---

**Algorithm 5.1.** GQ2 authentication of a prover by a verifier

INPUT: $N, Q_1, Q_2$
OUTPUT: Success or failure

---

1. The prover generates a random number $r$ and sends the commitment $W = r^{512} \bmod N$ to the verifier.
2. The verifier sends a 2-byte challenge $d = d_1 \| d_2$.
3. The prover computes the response $D = r \cdot Q_1^{d_1} \cdot Q_2^{d_2} \bmod N$.
4. The verifier computes $W' = D^{512} \cdot g_1^{2d_1} \cdot g_2^{2d_2} \bmod N$.
5. The verifier returns "Success" if $W' = W$, "Failure" otherwise.

---

The GQ2 protocol is faster than RSA due to the small length ($2 \times 8$ bits) of the exponents involved in modular exponentiation. That is why, if Montgomery multiplication is used, computation of the value $R^2 \bmod N$ is very inconvenient: a big part of execution time of the algorithm will be employed for this.

## 5.2   Our New Method for GQ2

To optimize GQ2 algorithm, we propose to store the values $\tilde{Q}_1$ and $\tilde{Q}_2$ in the non-volatile memory of the smart card. This can be performed once, during personalization step of the card, in factory.

The modified GQ2 algorithm executed by the card is:

---

**Algorithm 5.2.** GQ2 authentication with Montgomery multiplication

INPUT: $N, \tilde{Q}_1, \tilde{Q}_2$
OUTPUT: Success or failure

---

1. The prover generates a random number $r$ and sends the commitment $W = r^{*512} * 1 \bmod N$ to the verifier.
2. The verifier sends a 2-byte challenge $d = d_1 \| d_2$.
3. The prover computes the response $D = r * \tilde{Q}_1^{*d_1} * \tilde{Q}_2^{*d_2} * 1 \bmod N$.
4. The verifier computes $W' = D^{512} \cdot g_1^{2d_1} \cdot g_2^{2d_2} \bmod N$.
5. The verifier returns "Success" if $W' = W$, "Failure" otherwise.

---

The computed commitment is equal to:

$$W = r^{*512} * 1 \bmod N$$
$$= r^{512} \cdot R^{1-512} * 1 \bmod N$$
$$= r^{512} \cdot R^{1-512} \cdot R^{-1} \bmod N$$
$$= r^{512} \cdot R^{-512} \bmod N$$
$$= (r \cdot R^{-1})^{512} \bmod N \ .$$

So the random used during the rest of the algorithm is $r \cdot R^{-1} \bmod N$.

The computed response is equal to:

$$D = r * \tilde{Q}_1^{*d_1} * \tilde{Q}_2^{*d_2} * 1 \bmod N$$
$$= r \cdot \tilde{Q}_1^{*d_1} \cdot \tilde{Q}_2^{*d_2} \cdot R^{-3} \bmod N$$
$$= r \cdot \tilde{Q}_1^{d_1} \cdot \tilde{Q}_2^{d_2} \cdot R^{-3} \cdot R^{1-d_1+1-d_2} \bmod N$$
$$= r \cdot \tilde{Q}_1^{d_1} \cdot \tilde{Q}_2^{d_2} \cdot R^{-1-d_1-d_2} \bmod N$$
$$= r \cdot (Q_1.R)^{d_1} \cdot (Q_2 \cdot R)^{d_2} \cdot R^{-1-d_1-d_2} \bmod N$$
$$= r \cdot Q_1^{d_1} \cdot R^{d_1} \cdot Q_2^{d_2} \cdot R^{d_2} \cdot R^{-1-d_1-d_2} \bmod N$$
$$= r \cdot Q_1^{d_1} \cdot Q_2^{d_2} \cdot R^{-1} \bmod N$$
$$= r \cdot R^{-1} \cdot Q_1^{d_1} \cdot Q_2^{d_2} \bmod N \ .$$

So the response is valid according to the random used by the card.

This method allows a big improvement compared to the classical method. For example, if the bit-length of the modulus $N$ is 1024, computation of the value $R^2 \bmod N$ requires 10 Montgomery multiplications whereas the computation of $D$ involves between 16 and 32 Montgomery multiplications. So this method for GQ2 algorithm decreases execution time of more than 50% compared to classsical use of Montgomery multiplication.

## 6    ECDSA Signature

### 6.1    Description

Elliptic Curves Digital Signature Algorithm [7] produces short signatures and so, are suitable for smart card. The precedent technique can still be applied in order to improve the time of calculation.

In the following, we only consider the case of elliptic curves over prime fields. Let $(E)$ be the elliptic curve over a finite field of prime characteristic $p$ defined by:

$$y^2 = x^3 + ax + b \ \ with \ a, b \in GF(p) \ .$$

Let $G = (x_G, y_G)$ be a point of $(E)$ of order $n$ prime. The ECDSA private key is an integer $d$ such that $d \in [0, n-1]$. The corresponding public key is the point $Q = (x_Q, y_Q) = d \times G$.

The ECDSA signature algorithm is:

---

**Algorithm 6.1.** ECDSA signature

INPUT: $M, (E), G, d, n$
OUTPUT: $r, s$

---

1. Generate a random number $k$, such that $k \in [1, n-1]$.
2. Compute the elliptic curve point $k \times G = (x_k, y_k)$.
3. Set $r = x_k \bmod n$.
4. Compute $s = k^{-1}(\text{SHA-1}(M) + d \cdot r) \bmod n$.
5. Return$(r, s)$.

---

## 6.2    First Method

ECDSA involves modular computation over $GF(p)$ for computation of the scalar multiplication described in step 2 of algorithm, but computation over $GF(n)$ for the rest of the algorithm. For clarity reasons, when Montgomery multiplications are executed modulo $p$ (resp. $n$), we use notations $*_p$ (resp. $*_n$) and $R_p$ (resp. $R_n$).

Let $(\tilde{E})$ be the image of $(E)$ using Montgomery representation. It is defined by:

$$\tilde{y}^2 = \tilde{x}^3 + (a.R_p) *_p \tilde{x} + (b.R_p) \ .$$

To configure the smart card for ECDSA signature scheme, we need to replace $G = (x_G, y_G)$ by $\tilde{G} = (\tilde{x}_G, \tilde{y}_G) = (x_G.R_p \bmod p, y_G.R_p \bmod p)$ and $d$ by $\tilde{d} = d \cdot R_n \bmod N$ . This rewritten in Montgomery representation is performed once, on a computer, and the modified parameters are stored in the smart card during the personalization phase.

The new ECDSA signature scheme using Montgomery arithmetic is the following:

---

**Algorithm 6.2.**  ECDSA signature using Montgomery multiplication

INPUT: $M, (\tilde{E}), \tilde{G}, \tilde{d}, n$
OUTPUT: $r, s$

---

1. Generate a random number $k$, such that $k \in [1, n-1]$.
2. Compute $k_1 = k *_n 1$.
3. Compute the elliptic curve point $k \times \tilde{G} = (\tilde{x}_k, \tilde{y}_k) = (x_k \cdot R_p \bmod p, y_k \cdot R_p \bmod p)$.
4. Compute $r = \tilde{x}_k *_p 1$.
5. Compute $r = r \bmod n$.
6. Compute $s = k_1^{*(-1)} *_n (\text{SHA-1}(M) + \tilde{d} *_n r) \bmod n$.
7. Return $(r, s)$.

---

This algorithm computes a correct ECDSA signature of message $M$ using only Montgomery multiplications. The correctness of the computation is due to:

$$
\begin{aligned}
s &= k_1^{*(-1)} *_n (\text{SHA-1(M)} + \tilde{d} *_n r) \bmod n \\
&= k_1^{-1} \cdot R_n^2 *_n (\text{SHA-1(M)} + \tilde{d} *_n r) \bmod n \\
&= k_1^{-1} \cdot R_n \cdot (\text{SHA-1(M)} + \tilde{d} *_n r) \bmod n \\
&= (k \cdot R_n)^{-1} \cdot R_n \cdot (\text{SHA-1(M)} + \tilde{d} *_n r) \bmod n \\
&= k^{-1} \cdot (\text{SHA-1(M)} + \tilde{d} *_n r) \bmod n \\
&= k^{-1} \cdot (\text{SHA-1(M)} + \tilde{d} \cdot r \cdot R_n^{-1}) \bmod n \\
&= k^{-1} \cdot (\text{SHA-1(M)} + d \cdot R_n \cdot r \cdot R_n^{-1}) \bmod n \\
&= k^{-1} \cdot (\text{SHA-1(M)} + d \cdot r) \bmod n \ .
\end{aligned}
$$

The value $r$ satisfies the following equalities:

$$r = \tilde{x}_k *_p 1 \bmod p$$
$$= \tilde{x}_k \cdot R_p^{-1} \bmod p$$
$$= x_k \cdot R_p \cdot R_p^{-1} \bmod p$$
$$= x_k .$$

## 6.3 Second Method

Algorithm 6.2. can also be computed by using the notion of Montgomery inverse introduced by B. Kaliski. The Montgomery inverse of an element $a$ is defined by:

$$a \rightarrow \widehat{a}^{-1} = a^{-1} \cdot R_n \bmod n.$$

B. Kaliski proposed an efficient binary algorithm [8] to compute this inverse.

Using this algorithm and the parameters $(\tilde{E}), \tilde{G}$ and $\tilde{d}$, the ECDSA signature scheme can be optimized for Montgomery multiplication in the following way:

---

**Algorithm 6.3.** ECDSA signature using Montgomery multiplication and Kaliski inverse

INPUT: $M, (\tilde{E}), \tilde{G}, \tilde{d}, n$
OUTPUT: $r, s$

---

1. Generate a random number $k$, such that $k \in [1, n-1]$.
2. Compute the elliptic curve point $k \times \tilde{G} = (\tilde{x}_k, \tilde{y}_k) = (x_k \cdot R_p \bmod p, y_k \cdot R_p \bmod p)$.
3. Compute $r = \tilde{x}_k *_p 1$.
4. Compute $r = r \bmod n$.
5. Compute $s = \widehat{k}^{-1} *_n (\text{SHA-1}(M) + \tilde{d} *_n r) \bmod n$.
6. Return$(r, s)$.

---

This algorithm computes a correct ECDSA signature of a message $M$ using only Montgomery multiplications. The correctness of the computation is due to:

$$s = \widehat{k}^{-1} *_n (\text{SHA-1(M)} + \tilde{d} *_n r) \bmod n$$
$$= k^{-1} \cdot R_n *_n (\text{SHA-1(M)} + \tilde{d} *_n r) \bmod n$$
$$= k^{-1} \cdot R_n . R_n^{-1} (\text{SHA-1(M)} + \tilde{d} *_n r) \bmod n$$
$$= k^{-1} (\text{SHA-1(M)} + d \cdot R_n *_n r) \bmod n$$
$$= k^{-1} (\text{SHA-1(M)} + d \cdot R_n \cdot r \cdot R_n^{-1}) \bmod n$$
$$= k^{-1} (\text{SHA-1(M)} + d \cdot r) \bmod n .$$

# 7 Conclusion

We have proposed new ways of using Montgomery multiplication to improve the performance of cryptographic algorithms when they have to be implemented on smart cards.

Our approach comprises two interlocking parts. The first part uses a Montgomery representation to store the private parameters in the smart card. This representation can be computed externally, during the personalization phase of the card, where resource limitations are not a problem. The second part modifies the cryptographic algorithms in order to use a Montgomery representation of the private parameters. This method improves the execution time of the underlying algorithm. For example, a GQ2 authentication is twice as fast compared to the traditional approach. The method is different from those proposed in [9] because the result returned by the card is correct without modifying the protocols. The verifier doesn't need to know how the computation was made.

We have seen that this method can be applied to RSA, GQ2 and ECDSA signature, but it can also be applied for others public-key crypto-systems like ECDSA verification or Feige-Fiat-Shamir [10] for example.

**Acknowledgements.** We would like to thank Emmanuel Prouff for many fruitful comments.

# References

1. P.L. Montgomery. *Modular multiplication without trial division.* Mathematics of computation 44, 1985.
2. D.E. Knuth. *The Art of Computer Programming, vol.2 : Seminumerical Algorithms.* 3rd ed., Addison-Wesley, Reading MA, 1999.
3. A.J. Menezes and P.C. van Oorschot and S.A. Vanstone. *Handbook of Applied Cryptography.* CRC Press, 1997.
4. R. Rivest, A. Shamir, L. Adleman. *A method for obtaining digital signatures and public-key cryptosystems.* Comm. of the ACM 21: 120-126, 1978.
5. C. Couvreur, J-J. Quisquater. *Fast decipherement algorithm for RSA public-key cryptosystem.* Electronic Letters 18(21): 905-907, 1982.
6. L.C. Guillou, M. Ugon, J-J. Quisquater. *Cryptographic authentication protocols for smart card.* Computer Networks: 437-451, 2001.
7. ANSI X9.62. *Public key cryptography for the financial services industry: The Elliptic Curve Digital Signature Algorithm (ECDSA).* 1999.
8. B. Kaliski. *The Montgomery Inverse and its application.* IEEE Transactions on Computers, 44: 1064, 1995.
9. D. Naccache, D. M'Raihi. *Montgomery-Suitable Cryptosystems.* Algebraic Coding 781: 75-81, 1994.
10. U. Feige, A. Fiat, A. Shamir. *Zero-knowledge proofs of identity.* Journal of Cryptology, 1: 77-94, 1988.
11. H. Handschuh, P. Paillier. *Smart Card Crypto-Coprocessors for Public-Key Cryptography.* CryptoBytes 4(1): 6-11, 1998.

# Off-Line Group Signatures with Smart Cards

Jean-Bernard Fischer and Emmanuel Prouff

Oberthur Card Systems,
71-73 rue des Hautes Pâtures 92 726 Nanterre Cedex France
{jb.fischer, e.prouff}@oberthurcs.com

**Abstract.** Group signatures allow a group member to sign messages anonymously on behalf of the group and, if needed, a group authority is able to identify the signer. In most applications, groups are dynamic and the number of arrivals and departures is non-negligible. Group signature schemes must take into account this situation and deal with member revocation. Even if group signature schemes have been intensively investigated during the last decade, few are applicable in low resource context. Among them, the simplest and most efficient has been proposed by Canard and Girault at Cardis 2002 and involves the smart card as security proxy. This solution has many advantages; however, there is a need to be connected to a group authority in order to sign or to verify the signature. Clearly, this is a drawback in embedded security for mobile applications. Based on a re-assessment of the notion of group signature, we propose an improvement of the Canard-Girault scheme allowing to perform signature and verification both off-line. In particular, we introduce the notion of *risk-management* for group signature schemes, which leads us to a novel approach of the member revocation problem.

**Keywords:** Group signature, smart card, dynamic group, revocation, risk management.

## 1 Introduction

In 1991, Chaum and Heijst [17] introduced the concept of group signatures. Unlike ordinary signatures, group signatures provide *anonymity* to the signer. Moreover, in exceptional cases, any group signature can be opened by a designated *revocation manager* to reveal indisputably the identity of the signer. In other words, group signatures also provide *traceability*.

Group signature is a very interesting cryptographic functionality, as it allows individuals to perform signatures on behalf of a group (typically a company). Thanks to anonymity, the individual is protected in the group. This is of particular interest when the need is to link the signature with a function in the company and not with a person in particular. In many applications, there is also a strong need that the signer can be held accountable for his actions inside the group, meaning that his anonymity can be uncovered if for example some fraudulent transactions are discovered. As mentioned in [8], a number of projects

J. Domingo-Ferrer, J. Posegga, and D. Schreckling (Eds.): CARDIS 2006, LNCS 3928, pp. 263–277, 2006.

have emerged nowadays that require the properties of group signatures (see for instance [1, 2, 11]).

In [17], Chaum and Heijst focus on *static groups* in which the number of group members and their identities are fixed and frozen in the setup phase. In real life applications, groups must be considered being *dynamic* as people join and leave the group (*e.g.* the company) all the time. So, since the original paper [17], most schemes have been designed to take into account the dynamicity of the group structure [3, 4, 13, 14, 15, 18, 26]. Adding a member to an existing group is usually quite simple: it consists in allowing him to access the secrets shared by all the group members. The situation is more complex when a member leaves the group. Indeed, he does so with all the knowledge to continue performing signatures. Thus, the so-called LEAVE protocol provided by the group signature scheme must remove the ability to sign for the leaving member in such a way that the signing ability of all the remaining members is unaffected.

Usually, group signature schemes are derived from personal signature schemes. In these cases, the computational cost of both signature and verification is very high. Moreover, providing good *coalition-resistance* and easy member revocation is difficult and adds further complexity. The fact that members have access to a lot of information about the system explains the complexity of the schemes. Indeed, various tricks, such as proofs of knowledge, must be used to verify that signatures have been honestly performed.

If one were to remove all knowledge of the secret group parameters from the members, yet still provide them with a means to perform the signatures, the schemes could be vastly simplified. So, it seems natural to have a trusted third party do the actual computation as a proxy for both the members (ensuring anonymous signature) and the group (ensuring traceability). In Cardis 2002, Canard and Girault [16] investigated this approach by having a tamper-resistant device (typically a smart card) carry out the group signature on behalf of each member. In this setting, the smart card is considered as a honest entity that performs correct signatures even if its possessor is dishonest. This allows new schemes mimicking closely the classic personal signatures with a very low computational cost. Moreover, using smart cards, several standing problems like coalition-resistance become trivial to solve and simple procedures can be used for the LEAVE protocol.

To check that a signature has been produced by a non-revoked member of a group, Canard and Girault propose two solutions. They both have the same drawback: the group membership has to be checked on-line, either by the signer or by the verifier. Clearly, being on-line to perform a signature goes against the fundamental idea that the smart card is a tool to perform security operations in a non-connected situation.

Based on the ideas developed in [16], we propose a new scheme with the following improvement: the group parameters remain constant throughout the lifetime of the group, the smart cards can sign off-line and the verification of a signature can be done off-line. This solution is made possible through a trade-off:

the smart card is allowed to become de-synchronized, and we resolve the membership issue by introducing the concept of *risk management* on the verifier's side.

This paper is organized as follows. In Sect. 2, we provide background on group signature schemes and we point out the remaining problems. In Sect. 3, we focus on group signature schemes using smart cards and we discuss the proposal of Canard and Girault. Based on this analysis, we present in Sect. 4 a new group signature scheme allowing both the signer and the verifier to perform all the operations off-line.

## 2   Group Signature Schemes in the Literature

### 2.1   Introduction to the Notion of Group Signature

Desmedt was the first to notice in [19] that conventional and public key systems (in the sense of Diffie and Hellman [20]) are not adapted when individuals must act on behalf of a group. In particular, he introduced the notion of *group oriented cryptography* and investigated the different kinds of groups and their cryptographic needs. A few years later, group signatures were introduced by Chaum and Heijst [17] to allow individual members to sign messages on behalf of a group. The identity of the signer is secret (anonymity) except that a *group authority* can identify the signer if needed (traceability). Since [17], more security requirements were added to group signatures. Nowadays, such schemes must satisfy the following security properties:

**Correctness :** signatures formed by a group member must be accepted by the verifier.

**Unforgeability :** only group members are able to sign messages on behalf of the group.

**Anonymity [17]:** given a valid signature of one or several message(s), identifying the actual signer is computationally hard for everyone but the revocation manager.

**Unlinkability:** deciding whether two valid signatures were computed by the same group member is computationally hard.

**Exculpability [5]:** neither a group member nor the group authority can sign on behalf of other group members.

**Traceability [17]:** the group authority is always able to open a valid signature and identify the signer.

**Coalition-resistance [5]:** a colluding subset of group members (even if comprised of the entire group) cannot generate a valid signature that the group authority cannot link to at least one of the colluding group members.

### 2.2   Group Signature for Static Groups

In the original paper of Chaum and Heijst [17], the structure of the group is assumed to be *static*. In their setting, the number of group members and their identities are fixed and frozen in the setup phase. A trusted entity chooses not only all the group parameters (including the keys) and an *opening key* for the group authority, but also chooses the signing key of each group member.

Such a scheme requires an uncomfortably and unrealistically high degree of trust in the party performing setup. Indeed, the latter can frame any group member, since he knows the signing keys of all members. A second major drawback concerns the group signature key. In Chaum and Heijst's schemes, its length is at least linear in the size of the group, and therefore the running time of the verification algorithm depends on the number of group members. Moreover, the length of the signature itself and the running time of the signing algorithm depend on the group size.

Improvements or generalizations of the schemes of Chaum and Heijst were later presented by Chen and Pedersen [18], Camenisch [12], Petersen [25] and more recently by Boneh and Shacham [8], but they did not overcome all the disadvantages of Chaum and Heijst's schemes for practical implementations.

## 2.3   Group Signature for Dynamic Groups

Clearly, static groups limit the applicability of group signatures, since they do not allow the addition of members to the group over time. The limitations of the schemes derived from [17] were in fact recognized early in the development of the area, and the practical literature has from the start focused on the case where the group is dynamic. In this setting, neither the number nor the identity of group members are fixed or known in the setup phase, which now consists of the group authority choosing only a group public key and an opening key (for traceability). An entity can join the group and obtain a private signing key at any time by engaging in an appropriate joining protocol with the group authority. Reciprocally, a group member can leave the group at any moment. In this case, he loses his ability to sign on behalf of the group. The following definitions are borrowed from Ateniese *et al.* [3]: a group signature scheme in a dynamic context is a digital signature scheme comprised of the following procedures.

SETUP: an algorithm for generating the initial group public key $pk_G$ and the corresponding private key $sk_G$.

JOIN: a protocol between the group authority (GA) and an user that results in the user becoming a new group member.

G-SIGN: an algorithm whereby a group signature is computed by a group member given a group private key and a message.

G-VERIFY: an algorithm for establishing the validity of a group signature given a group public key and a signed message.

OPEN: an algorithm that, given a signed message and a group private key, allows the revocation manager to determine the identity of the signer.

LEAVE : a protocol between the group authority (GA) and the members of the group that results in the user who leaves the group being no more able to sign as a group member.

Until 1997, dynamic signature schemes were designed as processes involving static group signature schemes together with dynamic group management.

Indeed, in these schemes, the group is re-created each time a member joins or leaves the group. The signature algorithm itself works as if it were intended for a static group. From this point of view, we can consider that the signature is not dedicated to a dynamic context.

Camenisch and Stadler [15] were the first to propose a signature scheme where the lengthes of the public keys and of the signatures are independent of the number of group members, and can therefore be used for large and dynamic groups. Furthermore, Camenisch and Stadler propose a JOIN procedure allowing the group authority to add new members without modification of the group public key. As a result, the identification of the group by its signature public key is now possible. Nowadays, the security of schemes derived from Camenisch and Stadler's solution has become well-established [6, 7], allowing them to be used in various applications such as electronic cash [26] or voting [24]. Moreover, the practical deployment of these schemes is investigated in [22] and different ways of co-operatively forming signatures are proposed. But despite all these efforts, problems still remain, among which the difficulty to achieve coalition-resistance and to deal with member revocation. For these reasons, the properties of these schemes do not match the properties of group signatures given by Ateniese *et al.*

### 2.4   The Problem of Member Revocation in Dynamic Groups

Bresson and Stern in [10] and Bresson in [9] proposed some ways of modifying the schemes of Camenisch and Stadler [15], Camenisch and Michels [14] and Ateniese *et al.* [3] to obtain a signature scheme with a LEAVE protocol. Nowadays, the proposal of Camenisch and Lysyanskaya [13] is preferred to transform the signature schemes [15] and [3] into group signatures schemes (with LEAVE protocols). However, the resulting solutions are still very complex and costly in memory space and computation time. Indeed, each member of the group has access to a part of the group-signature parameters and thus is able to use them for cheating. Numerous asymmetric algorithms (involving costly arithmetic computations) are used to counteract such internal attacks.

The use of a tamper proof device such as the smart card makes it easy to prevent a member from cheating, by letting his trusted device both store secretly the signature keys and control their legitimate usage.

## 3   Group Signature Schemes for Smart Cards

### 3.1   Smart Card Approach: A Step by Step Construction

**General Idea.** The basic idea is to use the smart card as a deputy for signing, since the card is reputed honest. This means that the card will not perform operations out of the context it has been designed for: it will not allow the modification of the secrets, their disclosure or the performance of a computation with wrong data or execution errors. If a computation has been performed by a smart card, then the result can be considered as exactly what is expected:

the honest behaviour of the signer (which is now the smart card) is not to be doubted, and no other proof of correctness is needed. As recalled in this section, this approach enables a simple and generic solution with very straightforward protocols.

**Anonymity.** From the algorithmic point of view, we would start from an ordinary signature scheme (RSA or DSA for instance), with private key $sk_G$ and with public key $pk_G$. The parameter $sk_G$ is stored in a non-volatile memory inside the smart cards of the group members. In that way, any smart card can sign for the group, and a message is signed by two different smart cards in exactly the same way. This is a perfect anonymous signature. In order to ensure that the group authority cannot sign for a group member (and thus to satisfy the unforgeability property), we can distribute $sk_G$ to the smart cards in such a way that the group authority is not able to use it for signing. A very simple way is to have a smart card play the role of the group authority; thus, secrets are perfectly safe and the group authority cannot sign for others since such a functionality is simply not implemented in this card.

**Traceability.** Being totally anonymous, the scheme above does not satisfy yet all the properties of a group signature which have been recalled in Sect. 2.1. To allow traceability, the identity of the signer must be added to the message which is signed. Furthermore, this has to be done such that the anonymity of the signer is still enforced for everyone but the group authority: said identity should be enciphered in such a way that only the group authority can decipher it. Since smart cards are trusted to protect the secrets, the ciphering algorithm can be symmetric. In such a case, all the smart cards of the group members share a symmetric key $K_G$ with the group authority's smart card, which is the only one having the ability to decipher a ciphered identity. To satisfy the unlinkability property, the encryption of the signer identity must be *probabilistic* (in our particular case, we can for instance design such an algorithm by modifying a deterministic encryption algorithm as described in [23], page 306).

**The Scheme.** If Alice wants to sign as a member of the group, she has to hold a smart card containing her unique identifier, the group signature key $sk_G$ and the parameter $K_G$ to encipher her identity, along with the group signature algorithm. These are provided during the JOIN procedure by the group authority, either as a specific dedicated smart card, or as an application running on a multi-applicative smart card.

Let $\text{ENC}(x, K_G)$ denote the probabilistic encryption of a message $x$ with a key $K_G$ and let $\text{DEC}$ denote the corresponding decryption algorithm. Let $\text{SIGN}(x, sk_G)$ denote the signature (RSA or DSA for instance) of a digest of $x$ with an asymmetric private key $sk_G$ and let $\text{VERIFY}$ be the corresponding algorithm for establishing the validity of the signature given a group public key $pk_G$, a message $m$ and its signature $s$. We resume in the following the G-SIGN procedure performed by Alice's smart card:

**Procedure 3.1.** G-SIGN procedure for smart cards

INPUTS: a message $m$, the signer identity $Id_A$, the pair of keys $(sk_G, K_G)$
OUTPUT: a group signature of $m$

1. $c \longleftarrow \text{Enc}(Id_A, K_G)$
2. $s \longleftarrow \text{SIGN}(m||c, sk_G)$
3. Output $(m, c, s)$

The G-VERIFY algorithm associated with Procedure 3.1. is simple. The verifier obtains the message $m$, the cipher $c$ and the signature $s$. Then, he simply verifies with the group public key $pk_G$ that the signature corresponds to the concatenation of $m$ and $c$. If needed, the group authority can apply the OPEN procedure which consists in decrypting $c$ to recover the identity $Id_A$ of the signer.

**Security Analysis.** The algorithm depicted in Procedure 3.1. is very efficient, since a group signature is performed by computing only one encryption and one ordinary signature. Furthermore, if the involved algorithms ENC and SIGN are assumed to be secure, then the properties of a group signature are all provided thanks to the tamper-resistance of the smart card:

- Unforgeability: only group members have $sk_G$ in their smart card and $sk_G$ is never made public to anyone (including the smart card holder), so that no one outside of the group can sign with this key.
- Anonymity: the signature key is the same for all the group members and the identity is ciphered.
- Unlinkability: the cryptosystem is semantically secure.
- Exculpability: the identity of the signer is unique and is added by the smart card, which prevents any fraud.
- Traceability: the card always encrypts the identity of the member in a way that can be recovered by the group authority.
- Coalition-resistance: smart cards being tamper-resistant, group members cannot access to any information about the group keys $sk_G$ and $K_G$ (in that setting, coalition-resistance is equivalent to unforgeability).

The group authority can add new members very easily by loading onto their smart cards a unique identifier $Id$ together with the pair $(sk_G, K_G)$. However, it is not simple to tackle the issue of member revocation: if a member leaves the group with his smart card still empowered with the group signature's service, how can the group authority prevent him from signing for the group?

### 3.2 Group Signature Schemes of Canard and Girault

In [16], Canard and Girault propose a group signature scheme along the lines of what has been described in Sect. 3.1. To provide a revocation process, they suggest two different approaches, either based on an additional group-shared signature key, or based on a *black listing* scheme. We analyze in the following the two approaches and we show that they are impractical in a typical smart-card setting, where transactions are performed off-line and where the participants have no access to central servers.

**First Approach.** It simply consists in generating a second signature on the concatenation of the message and the group signature.

---

**Procedure 3.2.** G-SIGN procedure for smart cards

---

INPUTS: a message $m$, the signer identity $Id_A$, a triplet of keys $(sk_G, K_G, dsk_G)$
OUTPUT: a group signature of $m$

1. $(m, c, s') \longleftarrow$ **Procedure 3.1.** $(m, Id_A, sk_G, K_G)$
2. $s \longleftarrow$ SIGN$(m||s', dsk_G)$
3. Output $(m, c, s, s')$

---

The signature computed with $dsk_G$ at the second step of Procedure 3.2. is dynamic: whenever a member leaves the group, all the smart cards of the remaining members are provided with a new key $dsk_G$. Since the revoked member does not know this new key, he cannot continue to sign as a group member. Let us denote by $dpk_G$ the public key corresponding with $dsk_G$. We recall in the following the verification procedure associated with Procedure 3.2.:

---

**Procedure 3.3.** G-VERIFY procedure for smart cards

---

INPUTS: an uplet $(m, c, s, s')$, a group identity $Id_G$
OUTPUT: ACCEPT or REJECT

1. $(dpk_G, pk_G) \longleftarrow$ Ask for the pair of public keys associated with $Id_G$
2. Check1 $\longleftarrow$ VERIFY$(m||c, s', pk_G)$
3. Check2 $\longleftarrow$ VERIFY$(m||s, dpk_G)$
4. **if** Check1 = ACCEPT **and** Check2 = ACCEPT
   Output ACCEPT
5. **else** output REJECT

---

A group signature scheme involving Procedures 3.2. and 3.3. has several drawbacks.

Firstly, each time a verifier checks a signature, he has to access a list in order to retrieve the corresponding key. This imposes on the verifier to be on-line in order to access such a list. Furthermore, each key in the list has to be associated with a validity period, from the time of distribution to the time of revocation, so that the verifier can decide which key corresponds to the time of the signature. This also implies that the verifier must have a way to know when the signature has been performed.

Secondly, the distribution of the dynamic group keys to the smart cards is problematic. The whole process is cumbersome, since the authors sketch a scheme based on several group authorities sharing a discrete logarithm as a private key. Synchronizing all the smart cards is also going to be difficult: being in essence a portable device, a smart card is more likely to be in the pocket of the member than connected to the group authority. Thus, a member may issue invalid signatures in good faith, simply because the group authority has issued a new key and his smart card is de-synchronized.

Finally, this approach works only if all the smart cards are on-line permanently, or at least have a way to synchronize the group key with the group authority before actually performing the signature. It becomes quickly inefficient when the number of group members is large (distribution) and when revocations occur often (synchronization), as for a thousand employees strong company.

**Second Approach.** It consists in using the so-called *revocation lists*. It is the most convenient of the two solutions proposed by Canard and Girault, since it has the advantage of involving only a static pair of group keys $(sk_G, pk_G)$. The group authority maintains a list of revoked members and, before every signature, the smart card simply looks up the list in order to confirm its own belonging to the group. If the member identity is not on the list, it signs with the fixed group key as described in Procedure 3.1.. Otherwise, the member is revoked: its smart card cancels its group belonging and will not sign for this group anymore.

The obvious drawback of this approach is that the smart card has to be on-line in order to sign, since verification of the revocation list is a prerequisite for signature. This goes against the fundamental idea of the smart card being a mobile device that permits operations off-line.

# 4   Our Proposal

With a personal signature, time is mostly irrelevant. Indeed, a signature, either handwritten or electronic, is proof of a commitment by a physical person; it does not change over time and it is similarly binding whether the signature has been performed yesterday or several years ago (ignoring issues of key ageing or obsolescence). As we argue in the following section, time plays a central role in group signatures, where the membership question must be resolved.

## 4.1   Group Signature: A Question of Timing

A group is an abstract notion, an intellectual construction which partitions entities into two sets, those belonging to the group and those who do not. When it comes to partitioning people, a straightforward and usual way is to give a differentiator to the group members, setting them apart from the others. In the case of group signatures, the group authority gives to the members the means to sign on behalf of the group. In that sense the group can be defined as those who can sign. Thus, the fact that someone can produce a valid signature is often considered in itself as a proof of membership. But, however appealing, this approach precludes from performing the signature off-line. Indeed, the group authority has to be involved to resolve the question of membership.

Let us now re-discuss the membership notion. Clearly, in a dynamic group, membership in essence is a question of time: the period of time during which someone is a member of a group is clearly defined. Consequently, there are two critical moments in the relationship between a physical person and an abstract group: joining the group and leaving the group. So, if the verifier wants to link the signature to the group, two things have to be verified: firstly that the signature is valid, and secondly that the signer was member of the group at the time of signature. When designing a group signature scheme, the main difficulty is to resolve the membership question, and the following two threats must be considered:

**Threat 1:** a member can sign a document ante-dated to a time before him joining the group.

**Threat 2:** a member can sign a document post-dated to a time after he will have left the group. In particular, the revocation issue, when a member leaves the group with the means to sign, can be considered thus.

In any case, the validity of the group signature is in jeopardy if the verifier cannot determine whether the signature has been issued by a member at a time when he was part of the group. Clearly, any group signature should provide an easy way to check that the signer belonged to the group at the instant of signature.

The classical approach to solve the revocation issue is to rebuild the group after each departure, distributing new means to sign to the remaining members. This restores the basic partition between those in the know and the others (including now the leaving member). It amounts to rebuilding a static group each time (as it is done by Canard and Girault in their first approach described in 3.2). This mandates an evidence included in the signature that is clearly visible to the verifier and is not forgeable by a former member of the group. It is usually done by changing the public key of the group each time a member leaves the group. Meaning that, in order for the verifier to know which key has been used at the time of signature, he has to get it from the group authority in an authenticated manner; and the deciding parameter is the time of the signature, which solves postdating. Ante-dating is usually not considered, as it would imply changing the group key also at each joining.

Our idea consists in incorporating in the signature all the relevant elements of date, in such a way that the verifier can easily make an informed decision on the fact that the member belongs to the group at the moment of signing. In that way, we are able to prevent Threats 1 and 2. Implementing this idea in smart cards, we show in the following that we are also able to perform operation with the signer and the verifier being off-line.

## 4.2    Off-Line Group Signatures and Risk Management

Let us assume that, from time to time, Alice's smart card verifies on-line with the group authority that it belongs to the group. Let us denote by $Md_A$ the *Membership date*, which corresponds to the date of the last successful membership test with the group authority. We present our new group signature algorithm in the following:

---

**Procedure 4.1.** New G-SIGN procedure for smart card

INPUTS: a message $m$, the signer's identity $Id_A$, the pair of keys $(sk_G, K_G)$, the signing date $d$ and the membership date $Md_A$
OUTPUT: a group signature of $m$

---

1. $c \longrightarrow \text{ENC}(Id_A, K_G)$
2. $s \longrightarrow \text{SIGN}(m||d||Md_A||c, sk_G)$
3. Output $(m||d||Md_A||c, Id_G, s)$

---

When the verifier gets a message signed by Alice, he first checks the correctness of the classical signature. Then, he follows what we called a *risk management procedure*. It consists in comparing the two dates $d$ and $Md_A$, so that the verifier can decide whether the time interval between the last connection of the card to the group authority and the date of the actual signature is acceptable in view of its security policy. If the verifier deems the dates $d$ and $Md_A$ to be too far apart for him to confidently accept the signature, then the off-line part of the verification procedure rejects the signature. When this occurs, the verifier has two options: to stop the procedure and reject the signature, or to start the on-line part of the verification procedure by connecting to the group authority.

We resume all these operations in the following G-VERIFY procedure, associated with Procedure 4.1.:

---

**Procedure 4.2.** New G-VERIFY procedure for smart card

INPUTS: an uplet $(m||d||Md_A||c, s)$ and a group identifier $Id_G$
OUTPUT: ACCEPT or REJECT

---

1. **if** $\text{VERIFY}(m||d||Md_A||c, s, pk_G) = \text{REJECT}$
       Output REJECT
2. **if** $\text{RISK-MANAGEMENT}(m, d, Md_A, Id_G) = \text{REJECT}$
       **if** $\text{ONLINE-CONFIRM} (m||d||Md_A||c, s, Id_G) = \text{REJECT}$
           Output REJECT
3. Output ACCEPT

---

We give in the following an instance of RISK-MANAGEMENT procedure:

---

**Procedure 4.3.** RISK-MANAGEMENT procedure

INPUTS: an uplet $(m, d, Md_A)$ and a group identifier $Id_G$
OUTPUT: ACCEPT or REJECT

---

1. Compute time difference between $d$ and $Md_A$
2. Make decision according to security policy for the group $Id_G$ and/or ask human verifier
3. Output ACCEPT or REJECT

---

In order to check on-line the belonging of the signer to the group, the verifier has to send the signature information to the group authority. As an example, we used the following protocol in our implementation:

---

**Procedure 4.4.** ONLINE-CONFIRM procedure

INPUTS: a pair $(m||d||Md_A||c, s)$ and a group identifier $Id_G$
OUTPUT: ACCEPT or REJECT

---

1. Connect in authenticated manner to group authority (GA) of group $Id_G$
2. Send $(m||d||Md_A||c, s)$ to GA
3. GA verifies signature and computes $Id_A = \text{DEC}(c, K_G)$
4. if $Id_A$ belonged to the group $Id_G$ at the date $d$
     Output ACCEPT
5. else output REJECT

---

Let us recapitulate the different procedures for our signature protocol.

Setup: the group authority is in possession of a GA smart card. He chooses the group parameter $Id_G$ and provides it to the GA smart card. The smart card generates the signature key set $(sk_G, pk_G)$ and the symmetric key $K_G$ and outputs $pk_G$. The group authority publishes $pk_G$ for all the verifiers to know.

Join: the new member $A$ is issued a smart card personalised with a unique identity $Id_A$. The smart card contacts the group authority and is issued the keys $sk_G$ and $K_G$ in a secure and confidential manner from smart card to smart card. Then, the member card makes a first connection to the group authority to update (actually initialise) the membership date.

G-Sign: see Procedure 4.1.

G-Verify: see Procedure 4.2.

Open: the group authority deciphers $c$ and returns the signer identity.

Leave: if the card connects to the group authority after the user has left the group, it will be issued a command to stop signing on behalf of that group. From there on, the former member will not be able to sign anymore with his card. Otherwise, if the card does never connect again to the group authority, then the value $Md_G$ shall never be updated and the signature will quickly loose any credibility.

*Remark 1.* Whatever the signature scheme, a former member can always sign a document ante-dated to a time when he was part of the group, there is no way to prevent this. However, in our protocol, the window of time in which he can ante-date a signature is restricted to the time between his last membership update and the time of his revocation.

## 4.3 Discussion About the New Proposal

The protocol described in the previous section allows both the signer and the verifier to interact off-line. This is a crucial advantage for the smart card, as it is in essence mobile. Without this feature, the communication between the verifier and the group authority is a major obstacle which completely prevents the completion of the signature process.

This paper does not aim to discuss the details of the risk management procedure. It is up to the verifier to define it in compliance with its security policy. It can for example take into account the security importance of the document, the level of confidence in the signer, the endorsement leeway of the verifier, etc.

In the on-line mode, our protocol is similar to the second approach of Canard and Girault (depicted in Sect. 3.2). The two solutions essentially differ with respect to the entity (signer or verifier) which checks the membership on-line with the group authority. As for hand-written signatures, our protocol has been defined such that the group-membership test is the verifier's responsibility. By involving a risk management process, we give him the means to decide wether or not such an on-line test is necessary.

## 5   Conclusion

In this paper, we recalled why the use of a smart card is natural when we want to design an efficient signature scheme for dynamic groups. After having pointed out the difficulty of dealing with member revocation, we designed a new group signature improving the proposals of Canard and Girault. Our scheme allows to perform signature and verification both off-line, which was not possible with the previous solutions. We succeeded in resolving the membership issue by introducing the concept of risk management on the verifier's side. In this manner, the group signature we propose is very close to a hand-written signature: it is always possible to sign on behalf of the group if one has the means for doing it, and the verifier checks both the signature and some additional information on the signer in order to quantify the risk of a falsified signature.

## References

1. IEEE P1556 working group, VSC project. Dedicated short range communications (DSRC), 2003.
2. Trusted computing group. Trusted Computing Platform Alliance (TCPA) Main Specification, 2003.
3. G. Ateniese, J. Camenisch, M. Joye, and G. Tsudik. A practical and provably secure coalition-resistant group signature scheme. In M. Bellare, editor, *Advances in Cryptology – CRYPTO 2000*, volume 1880 of *Lecture Notes in Computer Science*, pages 255–270. Springer-Verlag, 2000.
4. G. Ateniese, D. X. Song, and G. Tsudik. Quasi-efficient revocation in group signatures. In M. Blaze, editor, *Financial Cryptography 2002*, volume 2357 of *Lecture Notes in Computer Science*, pages 183–197. Springer, 2002.
5. G. Ateniese and G. Tsudik. Some open issues and new directions in group signatures. In Kalisky Jr. [21], pages 196–211.

6. M. Bellare, D. Micciancio, and B. Warinschi. Foundations of group signatures: formal definition, simplified requirements and a construction based on trapdoor permutations. In E. Biham, editor, *Advances in cryptology - EUROCRYPT 2003, proceedings of the internarional conference on the theory and application of cryptographic techniques*, volume 2656 of *Lecture Notes in Computer Science*, pages 614–629, Warsaw, Poland, May 2003. Springer-Verlag.

7. M. Bellare, H. Shi, and C. Zhang. Foundations of group signatures: The case of dynamic groups. Cryptology ePrint Archive, Report 2004/077, 2004. http://eprint.iacr.org/.

8. D. Boneh and H. Shacham. Group signatures with verifier-local revocation. Manuscrit, 2004.

9. E. Bresson. *Protocoles cryptographiques pour l'authentification et l'anonymat dans les groupes*. PhD thesis, École polytechnique, Oct. 2002.

10. E. Bresson and J. Stern. Efficient revocation in group signatures. In K. Kim, editor, *Public Key Cryptography – PKC 2001*, volume 1992 of *Lecture Notes in Computer Science*, pages 190–206. Springer-Verlag, 2001.

11. E. Brickell. An efficient protocol for anonymousy providing assurance of the container of a private key. Submitted to the Trusted Computing Group, april 2003.

12. J. Camenisch. Efficient and generalized group signatures. In W. Fumy, editor, *Advances in Cryptology – EUROCRYPT '97*, volume 1233 of *Lecture Notes in Computer Science*, pages 465–479. Springer-Verlag, 1997.

13. J. Camenisch and A. Lysyanskaya. Dynamic accumulators and application to efficient revocation of anonymous credentials. In M. Yung, editor, *CRYPTO*, volume 2442 of *Lecture Notes in Computer Science*, pages 61–76. Springer-Verlag, 2002.

14. J. Camenisch and M. Michels. A group signature scheme with improved efficiency. In K. Ohta and D. Pei, editors, *ASIACRYPT*, volume 1514 of *Lecture Notes in Computer Science*, pages 160–174. Springer, 1998.

15. J. Camenisch and M. Stadler. Efficient group signature schemes for large groups. In Kalisky Jr. [21], pages 410–424.

16. S. Canard and M. Girault. Implementing group signature schemes with smart cards. In *CARDIS 2002*, pages 1–10. USENIX, 2002.

17. D. Chaum and E. van Heyst. Group signatures. In J. Feigenbaum, editor, *Advances in Cryptology – EUROCRYPT '91*, volume 547 of *Lecture Notes in Computer Science*, pages 257–265. Springer-Verlag, 1991.

18. L. Chen and T. Pedersen. New group signatures schemes. In A. D. Santis, editor, *Advances in Cryptology – EUROCRYPT '94*, volume 950 of *Lecture Notes in Computer Science*, pages 171–181. Springer-Verlag, 1994.

19. Y. Desmedt. Society and group oriented cryptography: A new concept. In C. Pomerance, editor, *CRYPTO'87*, volume 293 of *Lecture Notes in Computer Science*, pages 120–127. Springer, 1987.

20. W. Diffie and M. Hellman. New Directions in Cryptography. *IEEE Transaction on Information Theory*, 22(6):644–654, november 1976.

21. B. Kalisky Jr., editor. *Advances in Cryptology – CRYPTO '97*, volume 1294 of *Lecture Notes in Computer Science*. Springer-Verlag, 1997.

22. G. Maitland and C. Boyd. Co-operatively formed group signatures. In B. Preneel, editor, *CT-RSA*, volume 2271 of *Lecture Notes in Computer Science*, pages 218–235. Springer-Verlag, 2002.

23. A. Menezes, P. van Oorschot, and S. Vanstone. *Handbook of Applied Cryptography*. CRC Press, 1997. Electronic version available at http://www.cacr.math.uwaterloo.ca/hac/.

24. K. Q. Nguyen and J. Traoré. An online public auction protocol protecting bidder privacy. In E. Dawson, A. Clark, and C. Boyd, editors, *ACISP*, volume 1841 of *Lecture Notes in Computer Science*, pages 427–442. Springer, 2000.
25. H. Petersen. How to convert any digital signature scheme into a group signature. In *Security Protocols Workshop*, 1997.
26. J. Traoré. Group signatures and their relevance to privacy-protecting off-line electronic cash systems. In J. Pieprzyk, R. Safavi-Naini, and J. Seberry, editors, *ACISP'99*, volume 1587 of *Lecture Notes in Computer Science*, pages 228–243. Springer, 1999.

# Analysis of Power Constraints for Cryptographic Algorithms in Mid-Cost RFID Tags

Tobias Lohmann, Matthias Schneider, and Christoph Ruland

Institute for Data Communication Systems,
University of Siegen, Hoelderlinstraße 3; D- 57076 Siegen, Germany
{tobias.lohmann, matthias.schneider,
christoph.ruland}@uni-siegen.de

**Abstract.** Radio Frequency Identification (RFID) systems can be found in wide spread applications – from simple theft prevention over multi bit transponders up to complex applications involving contactless smartcards. This paper shows that the security gap between low-cost RFID Tags that only provide simple security features and contactless smartcards can be filled. It is examined how much energy a passive tag can gain from a magnetic field and which amount is needed by basic logic functions. The gate-equivalents of several cryptographic operations are then compared with the available energy and a conclusion is drawn if they are feasible for RFID tags.

## 1 Introduction

Modern automatic identification (Auto-ID) systems have a long technological history and multiple roots. The most widely recognized Auto-ID system is the bar code system developed during the early 1970's [1] but the technology which is more related to the actual one is even older. During the $2^{nd}$ World War, allied planes were equipped with devices that allowed a friend or foe recognition [2]. A civil variant is able to detect friends and foes inside a shop: the well known electronic article surveillance (EAS) system. More sophisticated systems also found their way in public life and people are using ID technology for entering their ski-lift or to disable the immobilizer of their car. In the last couple of years there has been done lot of work to map all those "root-technologies" to one inheritor: Radio Frequency Identification (RFID). Some of them just had to be renamed to the term RFID, others had to be reinvented like the EPC tag (Electronic Product Code) to replace EAN bar codes (Electronic Article Number) [3]. The major task in this sector is to downsize the costs of a tag, so that it is lower than the monetary benefit that the RFID-System is able to gain. This still seems to be hard because the ink which is needed for bar codes is nearly free.

Another fact is that there are rising concerns about the technology that provides information and can be read wirelessly and without notice of its owner. People are afraid (or aware) of the probability that they can loose their privacy [4]. A lot of suggestions have been made to maintain privacy by adding extra functionality to the RFID tags but they all add more circuitry and higher costs. One basic method is to introduce a kill-command that disables a tag [5] – but the question is: who will be authorized to issue such a command? It is clear that this function has to be protected by a key or password. It must be secured. Applying even simple means against unauthorised tag access introduce the problem of key management. It is necessary to find a

J. Domingo-Ferrer, J. Posegga, and D. Schreckling (Eds.): CARDIS 2006, LNCS 3928, pp. 278–288, 2006.

trade-off between the relative gain in security and the costs that come with them. When we talk about costs in this paper we do not only mean increasing chip sizes and increasing monetary costs, in the scope of this paper we especially address the increasing power consumption. 90% to 95% of the RFID devices are passive [7] which implies that they have to be powered by inductive coupling. Chapter 2 will show that increasing power consumption leads to a lowered maximum read range.

Developers of smartcards already had to face and solve most of the questions and problems that occur when adding security functions in embedded systems in the last decade. Smartcards have become very powerful and are able to process various cryptographic protocols such as 3DES and strong asymmetric computations with RSA and on Elliptic Curves (ECC) [6]. They are designed to fulfil high demanding security requirements and are evaluated up to Common Criteria EAL5. Most RFID tags also need electronic circuitry inside. Therefore a tag can be seen as an embedded system with wireless interface. It was just a logic step to add the wireless RF interface to existing smartcard controllers. The result is a very secure RFID tag with state of the art cryptography. The resulting device is also only able to operate close to a reader and the monetary cost for a smartcard is 20 times higher than for a simple tag.

This research was driven by the fact that the authors could not find products that offer good asymmetric cryptography and the full functionality according to ISO15693 "Identification cards – Contactless integrated circuit(s) cards - Vicinity cards" that operate at distances up to a meter.

## 2   Estimation of the Available Energy

Passive RFID tags gain their energy form the alternating magnetic field that is radiated by the antenna of the reader. Formula (1) shows the equation of the magnetic field, given in spherical coordinates [9][10].

$$H = -\frac{Idl}{4\pi}\beta^2 2\cos\theta\left[\frac{1}{(j\beta r)^2}+\frac{1}{(j\beta r)^3}\right]e^{-j\beta r}\vec{e}_r - \frac{Idl}{4\pi}\beta^2\sin\theta\left[\frac{1}{j\beta r}+\frac{1}{(j\beta r)^2}+\frac{1}{(j\beta r)^3}\right]e^{-j\beta r}\vec{e}_\theta \qquad (1)$$

with $\beta = \frac{2\pi}{\lambda}$.

Inductive coupling is only possible in the so called "near field", which dimension is mainly conditioned by the used frequency. The maximum distance is determined by the simplified equation (2).

$$d = \frac{\lambda}{2\pi} \qquad (2)$$

If $\beta r$ is set $<< 1$ (or $r << \lambda/2\pi$) the exponential term of equation (1) will be close to 1 and the magnetic field decreases with $1/r^3$. The complete derivation of those coherences cannot be covered by this paper and can be found in [2].

RFID Systems according to ISO14443 or ISO15693 operate at a frequency of 13.56MHz [8]. The upper bound of the operational radius is therefore 3.5 m.

This chapter provides an estimation of the available energy that can be induced in the coil of the tags antenna. Therefore, a closer look at the supplying magnetic field of the reader has to be taken. The highest strength of the magnetic field can always be found in orthogonal direction to the plane of the coil. We can therefore simplify equation (1) and obtain equation (3) which has been used during our simulations.

$$H(z) = \frac{N_1 I r_R^2}{2(r_R^2 + z^2)^{3/2}} \vec{e}_z \tag{3}$$

The curve is dependent on the current I, the number of windings $N_1$ and the square of the antenna radius $r_R$. Figure 1 shows the MATLAB [16] simulations of the emitted fields that are radiated by antennas with same currents and windings but different diameters.

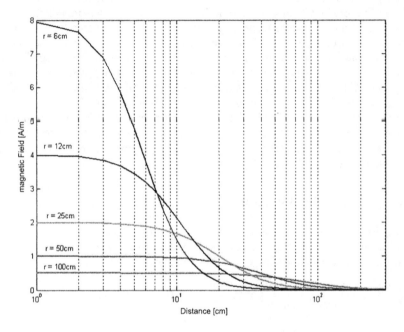

**Fig. 1.** The distribution of the magnetic flux by distance

Figure 1 shows that a smaller diameter of the antenna coil results in a higher initial strength of the magnetic field but an earlier and sharper decline as they occur with bigger loops.

It is not allowed to increase the strength of the magnetic field arbitrarily to achieve the needed distance because the usage of the electromagnetic spectrum is regulated by local authorities. They defined absolute maximum ratings of the power that an antenna may emit. In the European ISO14443 standard the maximum strength of the magnetic field is defined to be 7.5 H/m [8].

RFID Systems can basically be seen as a transformer with a big gap between primary- and secondary side. This implies that the well known electronic equations can be used.

The voltage $V_{tag}$ that is available for the logic of the tag is [7]

$$V_{tag} = \frac{V_{2,1}}{\sqrt{(\omega L_2 / R_L + \omega R_{L_2} C_2)^2 + (1 + R_{L_2} / R_L - \omega^2 L_2 C_2)^2}} \cdot \tag{4}$$

The load $R_L$ has a major effect on the available voltage as it can be seen in equation (4). This formula is converted to formula (5) to show the possible value of the load resistor for a given and needed voltage.

$$R_L = \left( \frac{R_{L_2}}{\left( \frac{V_{2;1}}{V_{tag}} \right)^2 - 1 - \left( \omega R_{L_2} C_2 \right)^2 + 2\omega^2 L_2 C_2 - \left( \omega^2 L_2 C_2 \right)^2} \right)$$

$$\pm \frac{\sqrt{R_{L_2}^2 - \left( \left( R_{L_2}^2 + (\omega L_2)^2 \right) \left( 1 + \left( \omega R_{L_2} C_2 \right)^2 - 2\omega^2 L_2 C_2 + \left( \omega^2 L_2 C_2 \right)^2 - \left( \frac{V_{2;1}}{V_{tag}} \right)^2 \right) \right)}}{1 + \left( \omega R_{L_2} C_2 \right)^2 - 2\omega^2 L_2 C_2 + \left( \omega^2 L_2 C_2 \right)^2 - \left( \frac{V_{2;1}}{V_{tag}} \right)^2}$$

(5)

In the last step, we obtain the available power by applying formula (6).

$$P = \frac{U^2}{R_L}.$$

(6)

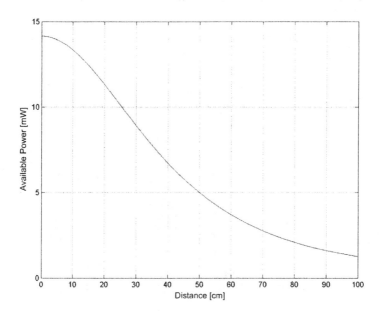

**Fig. 2.** Available tag power in dependence of the range

A more handy representation is obtained in Figure 2 where the absolute power in dependence of the distance is shown. It gives the maximum range of a tag whose power consumption is known. Or in the other direction: the curve defines the upper bound of the power which could be consumed if the tag has to operate at a given distance.

The proof of these results is obtained by comparing the calculated curve with data sheets of several tags. For example, if the average power consumption is given by 2 mW, they should not have a read range greater than 70 cm.

## 3 Estimation of a Tags Power Consumption

The circuitry of most RFID tags is based on CMOS (complementary metal oxide semiconductor) technology. CMOS technology has the great advantage that it is possible to design electronic circuits with only relevant power consumption when the transistors change their operational state.

This chapter investigates the average power consumption needed by basic logic functions. The integrated circuits are simulated with WinSpice [17] which allows a good reproduction of the real hardware behavior. The transistors were designed to provide the needed functionality with the smallest possible geometry. A lot of process dependent parameters were obtained by the databases of the MOSIS service [11]. This allowed comparing the influence of different manufacturing sizes and technologies.

This paper presents an analysis of three basic building blocks often needed by cryptographic operations. These are shift-registers, XOR operations and NAND gates.

### Shift-Register Cell

A shift-register like shown in Figure 3 is built by serialization of two inverters that are clocked by orthogonal signals $clk$ and $\overline{clk}$.

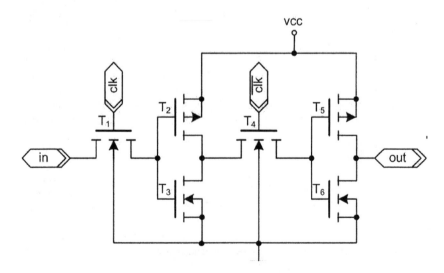

**Fig. 3.** CMOS shift-register [14]

The power of the register cell is supplied by VCC and only has to deliver current when the level of the input signal is changing. This correlation is shown in the following plot where the output curve v(5) is delayed by the clock rate.

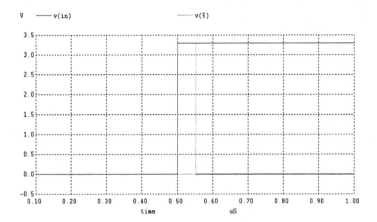

**Fig. 4.** Input and output voltages of a shift register

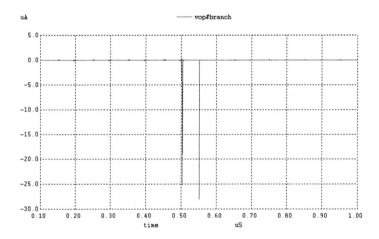

**Fig. 5.** Current consumption of a register cell when changing its state

Static and other currents can be omitted because their amplitudes are negligible. They can be seen in the upper simulation plot as small dips in the current curve vop#branch. Results of the simulation runs are given in table 1. The resulting energy is obtained by multiplying the average of the current with the voltage VCC and the time interval where the current occurred. It is estimated that the transitions between logic "1" and logic "0" are equally distributed and the mean energy will be used for further calculations.

**Table 1.** Energy overview of a shift-register

| Process | VCC [V] | Interval t(0-1) [ns] | Current $I_{mittel}$ (0-1) [µA] | Energy $W_{0-1}$ [fWs] | Interval t(1-0) [ns] | Current $I_{mean}$(1-0) [µA] | Energy $W_{1-0}$ [fWs] | Energy $W_{mean}$ [fWs] |
|---|---|---|---|---|---|---|---|---|
| 0.35 µm TSMC | 3.3 | 4.5 | 7.2716 | 140.18 | 1.1 | 11.8731 | 176.94 | 158.56 |
| | | 1.1 | 8.86937 | | 5 | 8.11171 | | |
| 0.25µm TSMC | 2.5 | 4.5 | 8.84425 | 128.78 | 1.1 | 12.8971 | 142.23 | 135.51 |
| | | 1.1 | 10.6490 | | 5.6 | 7.60818 | | |
| 0.18µm TSMC | 1.8 | 5 | 3.70572 | 42.21 | 1.4 | 7.66053 | 62.96 | 52.59 |
| | | 0.8 | 6.15294 | | 6 | 4.04206 | | |

## XOR

XOR Gates can be implemented in various ways. We examined realisations based on transmission gates, CVSL (Cascode Voltage Switch Logic) and in AOI (And Or Inverter) realisation. Since the CVSL solution had a high dynamic loss and the current peaks of the transmission gate implementation were too short for WinSpice, only the results of our AOI-based XOR simulations are presented.

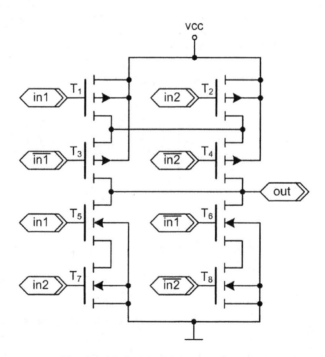

**Fig. 6.** XOR-Gate in AOI realization [14]

Although the other realisations might be more effective, it is estimated that the lower performance should not affect the decision if one cryptographic scheme is practicable or not, because the presented results of chapter 2 are absolute maximum ratings and there should always be a margin to ensure reliable functionality. An XOR gate with two inputs has four different states, each with three possible transitions. The results of those single simulations are shown in the following tables. For presentation purposes we change the notation and write A1 if input "in1" is logic high or B0 for "in2" at low level. A0 and B1 are built respectively.

**Table 2.** CMOS AOI XOR energy consumption

| Technology | A0,B0 → A0,B1 [fWs] | A0,B1 → A0,B0 [fWs] | A0,B0 → A1,B0 [fWs] | A1,B0 → A0,B0 [fWs] | A0,B0 → A1,B1 [fWs] | A1,B1 → A0,B0 [fWs] |
|---|---|---|---|---|---|---|
| 0.35 μm | 158.7 | 160.92 | 73.46 | 70.76 | 52.26 | 32.50 |
| 0.25 μm | 128.82 | 129.06 | 60.56 | 54.28 | 39.48 | 22.12 |
| 0.18 μm | 38,34 | 61.02 | 18.5 | 13.8 | 10.1 | 4.78 |

| Technology | A0,B1 → A1,B0 [fWs] | A1,B0 → A0,B1 [fWs] | A0,B1 → A1,B1 [fWs] | A1,B1 → A0,B1 [fWs] | A1,B0 → A1,B1 [fWs] | A1,B1 → A1,B0 [fWs] | Mittel [fWs] |
|---|---|---|---|---|---|---|---|
| 0.35 μm | 37.74 | 31.44 | 73.66 | 70.76 | 157.94 | 160.18 | 90.03 |
| 0.25 μm | 26.92 | 21.02 | 61.10 | 54.86 | 128.72 | 129.06 | 71.34 |
| 0.18 μm | 7.02 | 9.08 | 18.32 | 13.54 | 37.84 | 35.94 | 22.52 |

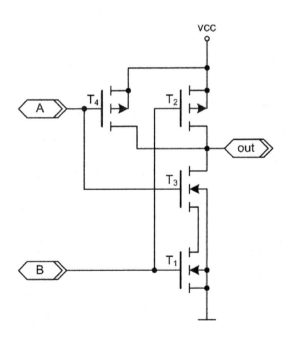

**Fig. 7.** CMOS NAND [14]

## NAND

In order to find an approximation for the power consumption of a certain algorithm, the NAND gate has a special relevance. In the development of highly integrated circuits, there are often used "ready made" VHDL cores. The complexity of these logic components are mainly given by a certain number of gates. A gate in this context is equivalent to one NAND.

An ideal NAND-gate only needs power if its output changes the logic level. Although we do not deal with ideal transistors, other static losses can be neglected.

**Table 3.** CMOS NAND energy consumption

| Technology | A0,B0 → A1,B1 [fWs] | A1,B0 → A1,B1 [fWs] | A0,B1 → A1,B1 [fWs] | A1,B1 → A0,B0 [fWs] | A1,B1 → A1,B0 [fWs] | A1,B1 → A0,B1 [fWs] | Mittel [fWs] |
|---|---|---|---|---|---|---|---|
| 0.35 µm | 15.28 | 20.78 | 22.11 | 65.98 | 78.03 | 53.21 | 42.57 |
| 0.25 µm | 5.71 | 8.96 | 9.87 | 19.85 | 57.95 | 40.9 | 28.87 |
| 0.18 µm | 0.02 | 1.48 | 1.64 | 15.54 | 16.89 | 12.85 | 8.07 |

## 4 Cryptographic Implementations

Since we have not implemented cryptographic algorithms so far, we present some commercial implementations of arithmetic operations and cryptographic schemes. This allows us to obtain the margins of the needed resources. Those implementations are available in IP (Intellectual Property) –cores which are ready made models,

**Table 4.** Cost of basic arithmetic and cryptographic operations

| Arithmetic Operation | Number of gates |
|---|---|
| 32 bit Add/Subtract Unit | 4488 |
| 32 bit Multiply Unit | 12155 |
| 32 bit Divide Unit | 30294 |
| 32 bit Compare Unit | 514 |
| 64 bit Add/Subtract Unit | 9069 |
| 64 bit Multiply Unit | 38568 |
| 64 bit Compare Unit | 1028 |

| Cryptographic scheme | Number of gates |
|---|---|
| DES | 3000 |
| 3DES | 5500 |
| AES encryption | 38000 |
| AES decryption | 50000 |
| RSA 1024 bit | 34000 |
| ECC 163 bit | 3260 |

written in VHDL (Very High Speed Integrated Circuit Hardware Description Language). The modules can be integrated in most development environments for designing ASICs (Application Specific Integrated Circuit), FPGAs (Field Programmable Gate Arrays) or other hardware [12][13].

## 5 Analysis of RFID Cryptography

In order to determine if and which type of cryptographic algorithm can be implemented in RFID tags, this paper takes an approach which implies that the only limiting factor is the straitened power transfer between an RFID reader and the tag. Since the specific implementations were not analysed in detail, the resulting assumptions had to be done from a more "global" point of view. As an indication for the complexity of the desired algorithm, the parameters given in chapter 4 were used. The complexities are given as a certain number of gates because they are basic building blocks in an FPGA design.

The knowledge about available power at a certain distance was obtained in chapter two. Together with the amount of energy needed for switching one NAND gate and the desired clock rate, it is possible to estimate if selected cryptography is possible or not.

For example, if the target application has to operate at a distance of 1 meter, the available power P(d) is 1.2651 mW. If the logic is clocked with 6.78 MHz (half rate of the reader's frequency)

$$E_{clock} = \frac{P(d)}{f_{clock}} \tag{7}$$

the available energy per clock cycle is 186.59 pWs like derived from formula 7. This energy is divided by the consumption of a singe 0.35µm NAND gate.

$$N_{gates} = \frac{E_{clock}}{E_{NAND}} \tag{8}$$

It is therefore enough energy for operating 4383 gates in 0.35µm CMOS technology and should be sufficient for implementing elliptic curve cryptography.

In this calculation, we assume that the whole circuitry is operating the whole time. This might be imprecise but will at least compensate some of the best case assumptions made in chapter 2.

## 6 Conclusion

The amount of power which is available for a tag at a certain distance was given in chapter two. Together with the results of chapter three it was therefore possible to estimate the maximum number of NAND gates that can be driven at a certain clock rate. This value was compared with the complexity of a cryptographic algorithm.

The authors are aware of the fact that tags cannot be designed under the assumption that the position of tag and reader are in such optimum positions like it is done in chapter 2 but it was shown that strong asymmetric should even be possible with a relative coarse semiconductor process of 0.35µm. Furthermore, an RFID specific implementation will probably not only use NAND based circuits when it is possible to perform the specific operation with a custom made design. We therefore also simulated basic building blocks like a shift-register and XOR gates like they are uses in praxis. The actual algorithms should be deeply analysed in further studies in order to obtain better knowledge about their actual hardware utilisation. Unfortunately, we had no further information on the algorithms i.e. how many clock cycles they need for execution or if they already contain the amount of RAM they need. Another fact is that the available power cannot be exclusively used by the cryptographic engine. RFID Tags have to contain other circuitries which handle radio access (anti-collision) and other functions. There are two other important facts that should also be mentioned. It is theoretically possible to obtain as much energy as needed, as long as the tag stays in the supplying magnetic field of the reader. The problem is that it is not possible or payable to store noteworthy amounts of energy in the tag. The second factor is the speed in which the algorithm has to run. If it is possible for the application and the user to wait longer for the tag's response, the clock rate can be reduced and the number of possible gates increases by the same factor.

Anyway, the semiconductor technology is still under rapid development. The authors predict that the capabilities of RFID tags will increase in the same way. If the market for RFID providing public key cryptography is big enough it should be possible to fill the mentioned security gap between AutoID tags and Smartcards.

# References

[1]  S. E. Sarma, S. A. Weis, D. W. Engels. *RFID Systems and Security and Privacy Implications*. Cryptographic Hardware and Embedded Systems - CHES, August 2002.

[2]  K. Fong. *RFID Security*, http://www.cs.siu.edu/~kfong/research/RFID.ppt

[3]  MIT Auto-ID Center. http://www.autoidcenter.org

[4]  CASPIAN. http://www.nocards.org

[5]  Auto-id Center. *Draft protocol specification for a 900 MHz class 0 Radio Frequency Identification Tag*, 23 Feb 2003.

[6]  Infineon technologies. *SLE 66CLX641P Short Product Information*, April 2004.

[7]  K. Finkenzeller. *RFID-Handbuch*, Hanser Verlag 2002.

[8]  ISO/IEC 14443. *Identification cards – Contactless integrated circuit(s) cards – Proximity cards – Part 2: Radio frequency power and signal interface*, July 2001.

[9]  G. Lehner, G. *Elektomagnetische Feldtheorie für Ingenieure und Physiker*, Springer Verlag, 1990

[10]  W.R. Smythe. *Static and Dynamic Electricity, McGraw-Hill Book Company*, 1968

[11]  MOSIS, www.mosis.org

[12]  ASICSws, www.asics.ws

[13]  J. Krasner. *Using Elliptic Curve Cryptography (ECC) for Enhanced Embedded Security*, November 2004.

[14]  R. J. Baker, H. W. Li, D. E. Boyce. *CMOS Circuit Design, Layout, And Simulation*. IEEE Press 1998.

[15]  MATLAB. http://www.mathworks.com

[16]  WinSpice. http://www.winspice.com

# Noisy Tags: A Pretty Good Key Exchange Protocol for RFID Tags

Claude Castelluccia[1] and Gildas Avoine[2]

[1] INRIA, France
Claude.Castelluccia@inria.fr
[2] EPFL, Switzerland
Gildas.Avoine@a3.epfl.ch

**Abstract.** We propose a protocol that can be used between an RFID tag and a reader to exchange a secret without performing any expensive computation. Similarly to the famous blocker tag suggested by Juels, Rivest, and Szydlo, our scheme makes use of special tags that we call *noisy tags*. Noisy tags are owned by the reader's manager and set out within the reader's field. They are regular RFID tags that generate noise on the public channel between the reader and the queried tag, such that an eavesdropper cannot differentiate the messages sent by the queried tag from the ones sent by the noisy tag. Consequently, she is unable to identify the secret bits that are sent to the reader. Afterwards, the secret shared by the reader and the tag can be used to launch a secure channel in order to protect communications against eavesdroppers. It can also be used to securely refresh a tag's identifier by, for example, xoring the new identifier with the exchanged secret key. Refreshing tags' identifiers improves privacy since it prevents tracking tags.

## 1 Motivations

An RFID (Radio-Frequency IDentification) tag is small circuit attached to a small antenna, capable of transmitting data to a distance of several meters to a reader device (reader) in response to a query. Most RFID tags are passive, meaning that they are battery-less, and obtain their power from the query signal. They are already attached to almost anything: clothing, foods, access cards and so on.

Unfortunately, the ubiquity of RFID tags poses many security threats: denial of service, tag impersonation, malicious traceability, and information leakage. We focus in this paper on this latter point that arises when tags send sensitive information, which could be eavesdropped by an adversary. In the framework of a library, for example, the information openly communicated by the tagged book could be its title or author, which may not please some readers. More worryingly, marked pharmaceutical products, as advocated by the US Food and Drug Administration, could reveal a person's pathology. For example, an employer or an insurer could find out which medicines a person is taking and thus work out his state of health. Large scale applications like the next generation of passports

J. Domingo-Ferrer, J. Posegga, and D. Schreckling (Eds.): CARDIS 2006, LNCS 3928, pp. 289–299, 2006.
© IFIP International Federation for Information Processing 2006

are also subject to such an issue. The *e-passports* [8] will be equipped with an RFID chip that will store some kind of biometric information about the bearer (fingerprint and digital picture).

Avoiding eavesdropping can be done by establishing a secure channel between the tag and the reader. This requires the establishment of a session secret key, which is not always an easy task considering the very limited devices' capacities. This difficulty is reinforced by the fact that tags and reader do not share a master key in most of the applications. In the future, implementing a key establishment protocol may become a mandatory feature. For example Californian Bill 682 requires such a technical measure to be implemented in ID-cards deployed in California. Furthermore, as explained in Section 4.2 for the library application, a secret key can be used to improve privacy and prevent tracking by securely refreshing a tag identifier.

This paper describes a novel way of establishing a key through a public channel between an RFID tag and a reader. The paper is structured as follows: Section 1 motivates our work. Section 2 presents the related work. Section 3 describes our 3 proposed key-exchange protocols. Section 4 presents some possible applications of our schemes. Section 5 discusses the relevance of our proposals and their security.

## 2    Related Work

The problem of secure pairing of wireless devices has been tackled by several researchers. The proposed solutions can be classified into the following categories:

*Public-Key Cryptography Based Solutions:* These solutions rely on public-key based key exchange protocols such as Diffie-Hellman or RSA [5, 6, 7]. In Diffie-Hellman based schemes, devices exchange their Diffie-Hellman components and derive a key from them. In RSA-based schemes, one of the devices selects a secret key and encrypts it under the other device's public key. The main problem of these solutions is performance. They require that devices perform CPU-intensive operations such as exponentiation, which are prohibitive for CPU-constrained devices such as RFID tags.

*PIN-Based Schemes:* In Bluetooth, two wireless devices derive a shared key from a public random value, the addresses of each device and a secret PIN. The PIN is provided to each device by the user via an out-of-band channel, such as a keyboard. While this solution is computationally efficient, it requires that *both* devices be equipped with some kind of physical user interface. As a result, this solution cannot be used to pair devices lacking physical interfaces, such as RFID tags.

*Physical Contact or Imprinting:* In [11], Stajano and Anderson propose a solution, called *imprinting*, based on physical contact. Two devices get paired by linking them together with an electrical contact that transfers the bits of a shared secret. No cryptography is involved, since the secret is transmitted in plaintext. Furthermore, the key validation phase is not necessary since there is no ambiguity about the devices that are involved in the binding (i.e., man-in-the-middle attacks are impossible). While this solution is interesting, it requires each device to have some additional hardware to perform the electrical contact.

*Physical Protection:* The simplest solution is to shield the RFID and the reader by a Faraday cage – a container made of metal mesh or foil impenetrable by radio signals – and have the two devices exchange their secret in cleartext. While very simple, this solution is not practical for RFID tags that are embedded in larger objects, such as humans, cars, clothing, that can not easily be placed in containers.

*Shake Them Up!:* Another solution is proposed in [3]. This paper presents a new pairing protocol that allows two CPU-constrained wireless devices $A$ and $B$ to establish a shared secret at a very low cost over an anonymous channel. On an anonymous channel, an eavesdropper can actually read the content of the exchanged packets but cannot identify their source. [3] proposes to implement such a channel by bringing the devices close to each other and shaking them during the key exchange [1]. With the proposed protocol, $A$ can send the secret bit 1 to $B$ by broadcasting an (empty) packet with the source field set to $A$. Similarly, $A$ can send the secret bit 0 to $B$ by broadcasting an (empty) packet with the source field set to $B$. Only $B$ can identify the real source of the packet (since it did not send it, the source is $A$), and can recover the secret bit (1 if the source is set to $A$ or 0 otherwise). An eavesdropper cannot retrieve the secret bit since it cannot figure out whether the packet was actually sent by $A$ or $B$. By randomly generating $n$ such packets $A$ and $B$ can agree on an $n$-bit secret key.

This solution is interesting but requires to shake the tag and the reader, which is not always practical. Also, the security is based on the assumption that it is difficult to identify the packets sent by the two parties. This assumption does not hold in an RFID environment because distinguishing packets sent by a reader from packets sent by a tag is straightforward.

## 3   Noisy Tag Protocol (NTP)

### 3.1   Background

Our protocol is inspired by the tag blocker proposal [9] and a key-exchange scheme developed by some unknown researcher at Bell Telephone Labs during World War II.

The idea of using special device in RFID environment was already proposed by [9] and [12]. [12] proposes to use a special device to simulate RFID tags as a way of spoofing such systems into believing that stolen items are still present in a retail environment. [9] defines the concept of blocker tags that simulate the set of

---

[1] This is to guarantee that an eavesdropper cannot identify the packets sent by $A$ from those sent by $B$ using data from the RSSI (Received Signal Strength Indicator) registers available in commercial wireless cards.

all possible tag identifiers for privacy protection i.e., to prevent a malicious user to trace some tags. Our application is quite different: we use a special RFID tag – *the noisy tag* – to establish secret key on-the-fly between a reader and RFID tags. While the blocker tag is owned and borne by the consumer, the noisy tag is owned by the system.

The crux of the key-exchange scheme proposed by the Bell Telephone Labs is that a receiver can effectively drown out any signal by injecting noise onto a communication channel. An eavesdropper would only hear the noise, but the receiver could subtract the noise and recover the signal.

This idea can easily be extended to establish a key between two parties $A$ and $B$ over a public channel as follows: $B$ starts by generating a sequence of random bits, noise $N(i)$, on the channel. Simultaneously $A$ sends the secret key bits $k(i)$ over the channel. An eavesdropper will see the sequence of bits $s(i) = k(i) + N(i)$ and won't be able to recover the secret bits $k(i)$ while $B$ can subtract the noise $N(i)$ and recover $k(i)$. $A$ and $B$ did then exchange a secret key.

We propose to apply this idea to allow an RFID tag to exchange a secret key with a reader without performing any expensive computation. For that, a noisy tag must be installed in the reader's field. A noisy tag is a regular RFID tag that shares a secret key $K$ with the reader (this key can be pre-configured). It is used to generate the noise bits $N(i)$ as defined previously. The noise bits are generated from a pseudo-random function, the secret shared with the reader and some public nonce. As a result, they can be reconstructed (and subtracted) by the reader. However they look random to an adversary.

To illustrate this approach, we supply three examples of RFID key-exchange protocols based on noisy tags. In the rest of this paper, $R$ denotes the reader, $T$ the tag and $NT$ the noisy tag. We also assume that $T$ wants to exchange a $n$-bit long secret, $s$, with $R$.

## 3.2   Bit-Based Protocol, Version 1

This protocol assumes that collisions are allowed and therefore several tags can reply simultaneously to a reader. When several tags replies simultaneously, it is assumed that the amplitude (i.e. voltage) of the different bits get added. Assuming this property, a tag $T$ can send a sequence of secret bits $b$ to the reader $R$ using the protocol described in this section. This protocol is composed of two phases:

*Exchange Phase:*

(1) $R$ broadcasts a random nonce $N$.
(2) Both $NT$ and $T$ reply simultaneously with one bit (one bit per time slot) until the reader halts the protocol. The $i$th bit sent by $NT$ is the $i$th bit of $h(K, N)$, where $h(.)$ is a pseudo-random function such as a hash function. The $i$th bit sent by $T$ is random.
(3) Since the reader can predict the sequence of bits sent by the noisy tag, it can easily filtered them out, and recover the bits sent by $T$.

If, for example, $T$ sends the bit 1, implemented by a pulse of $x$mV, and $NT$ the bit 0, implemented by a pulse of 0mV, $R$ will receive the bit 1. Since it can compute that the bit sent by $NT$ was 0, it can retrieve the bit sent by $T$, i.e. 1. Note however that this protocol does not work if both $T$ and $NT$ reply with the same bit. In fact, if both $T$ and $NT$ send simultaneously the bit 1, a pulse of $2.x$mV will be generated on the channel. In that case, an adversary knows that both $T$ and $NT$ sent the bit 1. Similarly if both $T$ and $NT$ send the bit 0, a pulse of $0mV$ will be generated on the channel and the adversary knows that both $T$ and $NT$ sent the bit 0. This is what we refer to as the "same-bit" problem. When $T$ and $NT$ send the same bit in a given time slot, this bit should not be used to generate the secret key. Hence, the reader halts the exchange phase when at least $n$ time slots contain different bits. On average, the reader halts the protocol after $2n$ time slots. The reconciliation phase consists for the reader to inform the tag which bits should be used to generate the secret key.

*Reconciliation Phase:*

(4) $R$ sends to $T$ the relevant time slots' numbers. $T$ uses this information to recover the secret bits that should be used to compute the shared secret.

The security relies on the fact that an adversary is not able to separate $T$'s signal from $NT$'s signal. This implies that $T$ and $NT$ are close enough otherwise an adversary may be able to determine which bit comes from $T$ and which one comes from $NT$ using specific material, e.g., directed antennas. This also implies that $T$ and $NT$ use the same standard, i.e. frequency and transmission power. Because one may think that an adversary would be able to separate a few bits, it may be preferable to generate a secret longer than the expected secret key, and then hash it.

### 3.3   Bit-Based Protocol, Version 2

In the previous protocol, $T$ and $NT$ must reply simultaneously and their bits get added. This requires that the tag $T$ and the noisy tag $NT$ be perfectly synchronized. This might not always be practical or even possible. In this section, we present a solution that removes this assumption. Like in the previous version, this protocol assumes that collisions are allowed.

*Exchange Phase:*

The exchange phase contains several rounds. Each round is composed of 2 consecutive time slots: $slot_0$ and $slot_1$. In a given round, $T$ sends the bit 1 by setting $slot_1$ to 1. It sends the bit 0 by setting $slot_0$ to 1.

The protocol operates as follows:

(1) $R$ broadcasts a random nonce $N$.
(2) $NT$ computes a sequence of pseudo-random bits, $c$, from the nonce $N$, the secret $K$ it shares with $R$ and a pseudo-random function $h(.)$, i.e. $c = h(K, N)$.

(3) At round $i$, $T$ picks a random bit $b_i$ and sets the slot number $b_i$ to 1. Similarly $NT$ sets the slot number $c_i$ to 1. When $R$ receives the 2 slots, it can identify the slot set by the $NT$ and retrieve the secret bit send by $T$.

Note however that this protocol suffers also from the "same-bit" problem: if $T$ and $NT$ select the same slot, the secret bit can be retrieved by an adversary. In fact, if both $T$ and $NT$ select the slot 1 (resp. 0), an eavesdropper can conclude that the secret bit sent by $T$ was 1 (resp. 0). As a result, such rounds must be ignored and the reader halts the exchange phase when at least $n$ rounds have both slots set to 1. On average, the reader halts the protocol after $2n$ time slots. The reconciliation phase consists for the reader to inform the tag which bits should be used to generate the secret key.

*Reconciliation Phase:*

(4) $R$ sends to $T$ the relevant round numbers. $T$ uses this information to identify the secret bits to be used in the shared secret.

## 3.4  Code-Based Protocol

The two previous protocols suffer from the "same-bit" problem. As a result, on average, $2 \times n$ rounds are required to agree on a $n$-bit long key, $s$.

A solution to this problem consists of having the tag and noisy tag send codes (as in the CDMA protocol) instead of individual bits. If the code is large enough (we use $n$-bit long codes), the probability of code collision is very small and the number of rounds can be reduced to $n$. As we will see it later in this section, using codes instead of bits has several other important benefits.

As in the previous schemes, we assume that the reader shares a secret key, $K$, with the noisy tag. This key is used by the noisy tag together with a pseudo-random function to generate its codes.

The code-based protocol is composed of $n$ rounds. Round $i$ is described as follows:

- **step1:** The reader broadcasts a random nonce, $N_i$.
- **step2.1:** The noisy tag, $NT$, replies with a noisy code, $ncode_i$, which is generated from a pseudo-random function, the nonce $N_i$ and the secret key, $K$. For example, $ncode_i = h(K||N_i)$. This code looks random to an eavesdropper, but can easily be recomputed by the reader.
- **step2.2:** The tag replies with a *random* code, $code_i$. Note that the order of step2.1 and step2.2 must be random at each round otherwise an eavesdropper could easily identify the code coming from the noisy tag from the code coming from the tag. This could be implemented as in the CSMA (Carrier Sense Multiple Access) protocol: upon reception of $N_i$, the tag and the noisy tag set a timer with a random value $\in [0; t]$, where $t$ is the duration of a round. The tag whose timer expires first, sends its reply first.
- **step3:** Upon reception of $ncode_i$ and $code_i$, the reader filters out $ncode_i$ (by computing $h(K||N_i)$) and retrieve the code sent by the tag $code_i$. For an

eavesdropper, both $code_i$ and $ncode_i$ look random and she, therefore, cannot retrieve the code sent by the tag.

At the end of the $n$ rounds, the reader and the tag share $n$ codes. They can then generate a secret key, $s$, as follows: $s = code_1 \oplus code_2 \oplus \cdots code_n$.

This protocol has several benefits compared to the previous scheme:

1. It prevents the "same bit" problem, since the probability of the tag and the noisy tag selecting the same code is very small, and therefore reduces the number of rounds to $n$.
2. The tag and the noisy tag can potentially send several codes per rounds (unlike the previous solution which requires the tag and noisy tag to send one bit per slot). This makes the adversary's analysis more difficult.
3. The noisy tag functionality can be *distributed* over several tags, i.e. several noisy tags can be used. In this case, the reader shares a different secret key, $K_i$, with each of the noisy tag. When the reader broadcasts a random nonce $N$, all the noisy tags (or a random subset of the noisy tags- this is only possible because the reader can identify the participating noisy tags from the ncodes) compute their corresponding ncodes, $ncode_i = h(K_i, N)$, and send them back to the reader. As in the basic scheme, the tag replies with a random code. The reader can then filter out the codes sent by the noisy tags and recover the one sent by the legitimate tag. Using several noisy tags increases the noisy codes diversity (power, frequency,...). It is therefore more difficult for the adversary to identify the *codes* from the *ncodes* using, for example, power or energy measures. Also, as described in the following section, using several noisy tags, can reduce the number of necessary rounds for the same level of security.

Since the adversary does not know the secret key, $K$, shared by the noisy tag and the reader, she cannot differentiate the codes sent by the tag from the codes sent by the noisy tag. As a result, at each round, the probability of selecting the correct code is $\frac{1}{2}$. After $n$ rounds, the probability for the adversary of selecting the $n$ correct codes, and therefore computing the secret key $k$, is $\frac{1}{2^n}$. Therefore 80 rounds are required in order to obtain a level of security of $2^{80}$.

If several noisy tags are used, the probability of selecting the correct code, at each round, becomes $\frac{1}{Q+1}$, where $Q$ is the number of noisy tags replying per round. After $n$ rounds, the probability for the adversary of computing the secret key $k$, is then $\frac{1}{2^{n.log_2(Q+1)}}$. Therefore if $Q = 15$, only 20 rounds are needed to obtain a level of security of $2^{80}$.

## 4    Applications

### 4.1    E-Passports

NTP can be used in many applications to establish a secret channel between a reader and an RFID tag. The key is established opportunistically, i.e., it does not authenticate the end-points of the secure channel. This authentication has to be provided by another mean.

For example, NTP can be used to establish a key between an e-passport and a reader. The next-generation passport, called *e-passport*, will contain an RFID chip, capable of storing and transmitting over the air biometric data together with standard information such as the name, date of birth, nationality of the bearer. This technology creates many security and privacy problems [8]. If no encryption and access control mechanisms are provided, it becomes trivial for anyone to skim e-passports and retrieve their information. In order to mitigate this problem, it is expected that the covers of the e-passports will contain RF blocking material. As a result, once closed it becomes impossible to skim an e-passport. A user can then authorize the reading of his e-passport (for example at a custom) by physically opening it. This simple solution improves the security considerably but does not prevent an eavesdropper from snooping on a legitimate reading. Encryption, and therefore a key-exchange protocol, is required to solve this problem. One proposed solution takes advantage of the fact that passports carry optically readable information. The idea is then to have the reader scan the e-passport and use the scanned information to generate an encryption key. This solution has at least two limitations. Firstly, it requires optical contact, which somehow alleviates the benefits of using RFID. Secondly, since the optically readable information is constant, the same key will be used by all readers. Consequently, it can leak.

NTP can be used to establish a temporary and fresh key between an e-passport and its reader as follows: the user opens its e-passport in front of the legitimate reader. The NTP is then executed between the reader and the e-passport to exchange a key. We assume that the reader has deployed one or several noisy tags. The e-passport can then send its encryption data to the reader.

The use of NTP is not limited to e-passports. It can be used in any applications where the link between a tag and reader need to be secret.

## 4.2   Libraries

In the e-passport application, the threat was the leakage of sensitive information on the backward channel, i.e., the channel from tags to readers. The problem is even worse when considering the forward channel, i.e., the channel from readers to tags, because the data sent can be eavesdropped at a much longer distance, e.g., one hundred meters.

In the famous paper [10], Molnar and Wagner suggested a protocol that mitigates the privacy problem in libraries. Their protocol roughly consists in refreshing the book's random identifier each time it is borrowed. Although the adversary can still track the book borrowed by Mister X, she cannot determine that this book is the same than the one previously borrowed by Mister Y.

More precisely, in [10], on each check-out the reader reads the data $D$ contained in the tag (e.g., title, author, etc.), picks a random identifier $N$, stores the pair $(N, D)$ in the system's database, erases $D$ from the tag, and finally writes $N$ in the tag. On check-in, the reader obtains the identifier $N$ from the tag, looks for $(N, D)$ in the system's database, erases $N$ from the tag, and writes $D$ instead.

However, eavesdropping the forward channel smashes the purpose of the protocol. Consequently, reducing the risk of malicious traceability by avoiding the adversary to eavesdrop the forward channel is important. This can be done by using a secure channel, which requires a key agreement protocol. Note that preventing passive attacks does not required authentication. Ensuring both authentication and privacy using only symmetric cryptography is actually a hard problem in practice because this involves in large scale applications a heavy key management, as explained in [1, 10].

When dealing with very low-cost tags, using a hash function or a symmetric cipher is still unrealistic today, even if a few lightweight implementations of symmetric cryptographic functions have been proposed [4, 13]. However, NTP is suited to such tags because NTP can be used to refresh the identifier of the tagged book without involving symmetric cryptographic functions on the tag's side (a symmetric cryptographic function must be implemented in the noisy tags but not in the books' tags). Indeed, since the identifier of the tag is random, reader and tag can agree on a common identifier instead of a secret key used to secure the channel. Thus, no symmetric cipher is required because we no longer use a secure channel, and moreover the privacy amplification phase, which requires a hash function, is not mandatory. Note that this is possible because the identifier is random, but NTP cannot be used to exchange a chosen information without establishing a secure channel, since reader and tag does not know, *a priori*, which bits will be withdrawn during the information reconciliation phase.

## 5   Discussion and Security Analysis

### 5.1   NTP Purpose

The primal purpose of this work is to provide a key agreement protocol between a reader and a tag that is resistant in presence of *passive* adversaries. NTP focuses only on passive adversaries because it does not ensure authentication. Clearly, dealing with passive adversaries instead of active ones is sometimes irrelevant. However, NTP is relevant in many environments, as explained below.

Active attacks require the adversary being able to stay close to the tag or reader in order to carry out her attack. Certain environments do not allow an adversary to be close enough to the tag or reader, e.g., in private areas (house, building, etc.). Furthermore, it is much easier to perform a passive attack, in particular on the forward channel, which can be eavesdropped from long distance.

Very low-cost tags are not able to use symmetric cryptography. That is the case for example with the tags used in libraries as described by Molnar and Wagner in [10]. In their protocol (and in most of the protocols used in libraries today – probably all of them), no security features are implemented, neither on the forward channel, nor on the backward channel. In that case, NTP is an interesting security measure, because it can be implemented cheaply.

In some cases, the authentication that could protect the tag against active adversaries, could be provided through another channel. For example, with the electronic passports, the officer swipes the data page through an optical reader and thus obtains information (name, date of birth, etc.), which can be used to authenticate the radio frequency channel. As explained above, the great interest of the noisy tag is to generate a fresh random session key, while the ICAO (International Civil Aviation Organization) recommends to generate a key directly from static data available on the passport.

## 5.2   NTP Security

Assuming that (1) the bits sent by the tag are uniformly distributed; (2) the bits sent by the noisy tag are uniformly distributed as well; (3) the adversary is not able to determine (with a probability better than $1/2$) which signal comes from the tag and which one comes from the noisy tag; then NTP is perfectly secure, meaning that the adversary learns nothing about the shared secret key.

Assuming that tags are able to generate random bits is a common assumption in RFID. For example, [2] shows that privacy cannot be ensured if tags do not possess a cryptographically secure pseudo-random number generator. Indeed, such a generator is mandatory in the communication layer to avoid an adversary tracking tags because of the collision-avoidance protocol.

The assumption on the noisy tag's side is stronger. The generated bits should be indistinguishable from random bits, but the reader must be capable of generating itself the same series. This can be achieved using a pseudo-random function. In practice, a hash function can be used. Note that synchronization is not required between the reader and the noisy tag because bits are generated from the secret key (shared by the reader and the noisy tag) and a nonce broadcast by the reader.

The third assumptions relies on the difficulty for an eavesdropper to differentiate the information sent by the noisy tags from the information sent by the legitimate tag. Note that the popular tag blocker scheme relies on a rather similar assumption. As admitted in [9], it is conceivable that a well-equipped attacker might actually be able to use the signals' characteristics (fingerprints) to identify the source of each message and filter out the tag blockers or noisy tags. However, such an attack is hard to be put into practice and requires very specialized material. Moreover, if we assume that an attacker is able to recognize tags' fingerprints then protecting privacy, in particular avoiding malicious traceability of the tags, is unsolvable. Last but not least, the adversary should not be able to distinguish the legitimate tag's signal from the noisy tag's signal according to the geographical position. This implies that the legitimate tag should be close to the noisy tag. Possibly, several noisy tags can be used simultaneously to render more difficult the adversary's job. Furthermore, shaking the tag during the key exchange protocol, as suggested in [3], might randomize the power of its transmitted bits and might also be another way to increases security.

# References

1. Gildas Avoine, Etienne Dysli, and Philippe Oechslin. Reducing time complexity in RFID systems. In Bart Preneel and Stafford Tavares, editors, *Selected Areas in Cryptography – SAC 2005*, Lecture Notes in Computer Science, Kingston, Canada, August 2005. Springer-Verlag.

2. Gildas Avoine and Philippe Oechslin. RFID traceability: A multilayer problem. In Andrew Patrick and Moti Yung, editors, *Financial Cryptography – FC'05*, volume 3570 of *Lecture Notes in Computer Science*, pages 125–140, Roseau, The Commonwealth Of Dominica, February–March 2005. IFCA, Springer-Verlag.

3. Claude Castelluccia and Pars Mutaf. Shake Them Up! In *ACM/Usenix Mobisys*, June 2005.

4. Martin Feldhofer, Sandra Dominikus, and Johannes Wolkerstorfer. Strong authentication for RFID systems using the AES algorithm. In Marc Joye and Jean-Jacques Quisquater, editors, *Workshop on Cryptographic Hardware and Embedded Systems – CHES 2004*, volume 3156 of *Lecture Notes in Computer Science*, pages 357–370, Boston, Massachusetts, USA, August 2004. IACR, Springer-Verlag.

5. Christian Gehrmann and Kaisa Nyberg. Enhancements to bluetooth baseband security. In *Nordsec'01*, Copenhagen, Denmark, November 2001.

6. Jaap-Henk Hoepman. Ephemeral pairing in anonymous networks. Available at: http://www.cs.kun.nl/~jhh/publications/anon-pairing.pdf.

7. Jaap-Henk Hoepman. The ephemeral pairing problem. In *Financial Cryptography – FC'04*, LNCS, pages 212–226, Key West, Florida, February 2004. IFCA, Springer-Verlag.

8. Ari Juels, David Molnar, and David Wagner. Security and privacy issues in e-passports. In *Conference on Security and Privacy for Emerging Areas in Communication Networks – SecureComm 2005*, Athens, Greece, September 2005. IEEE.

9. Ari Juels, Ronald Rivest, and Michael Szydlo. The blocker tag: Selective blocking of RFID tags for consumer privacy. In Vijay Atluri, editor, *Conference on Computer and Communications Security – CCS'03*, pages 103–111, Washington, DC, USA, October 2003. ACM, ACM Press.

10. David Molnar and David Wagner. Privacy and security in library RFID: Issues, practices, and architectures. In Birgit Pfitzmann and Peng Liu, editors, *Conference on Computer and Communications Security – CCS'04*, pages 210–219, Washington, DC, USA, October 2004. ACM, ACM Press.

11. Frank Stajano and Ross Anderson. The resurrecting duckling: Security issues for ad-hoc wireless networks. In *International Workshop on Security Protocols*, pages 172–194, 1999.

12. Stephen Weis. Security and privacy in radio-frequency identification devices. Master thesis, Massachusetts Institute of Technology (MIT), Massachusetts, USA, May 2003.

13. Kaan Yüksel. Universal hashing for ultra-low-power cryptographic hardware applications. Master thesis, Worcester Polytechnic Institute, Worcester, Massachusetts, USA, April 2004.

# MARP: Mobile Agent for RFID Privacy Protection

Soo-Cheol Kim, Sang-Soo Yeo, and Sung Kwon Kim

Chung-Ang University,
221 Huk-Suk-dong, Dong-Jak-gu, Seoul, Korea
{sckim, ssyeo}@alg.cse.cau.ac.kr
skkim@cau.ac.kr

**Abstract.** Recently many researchers in various fields has noticed RFID system. RFID system has many advantages more than other automatic identification system. However, it has some consumer privacy problems, such as location tracking and disclosure of personal information. Most of related works have focused on the cryptographic scheme for the RFID tag and the reader. In this paper, a proxy agent scheme using personal mobile device for the privacy protection. Our MARP, mobile agent for RFID privacy protection, has strong cryptographic modules with a powerful CPU and battery system and guarantees more high-level security than other protection schemes. MARP acquires a tag's secrete information partially and becomes the proxy agent of the tag which is in its sleep mode. All readers can communicate with MARP instead of the tag and can attempt authentication with MARP. Since the tag should have only one hash module in the environment of MARP, we can use the existing tag hardware with slight modification for protection consumer's privacy in RFID system.

## 1 Introduction

RFID(Radio Frequency Identification) system, which uses radio frequency for contactless communications, is considered as an extended one of smart card system. RFID system differs form smart card system in manufacturing cost, application field and transmission distance. Generally a smart card has security key, biometrics, financial account information or traffic ticket values and its cost may be several dollars [1]. On the other hand, an RFID tag is embedded in every good in a market and it costs a few dimes. Moreover, an RFID tag can be recognized omnidirectionally by interrogators in a few meters.

In this paper, we address RFID system and its privacy problems. As we mentioned above, RFID is a technology that automatically identifies an object by reading the information stored in an RFID tag in a contactless method using radio frequency. The information is stored in an RFID tag, composed of an antenna and an IC chip, which is then attached to the object to be identified. The information is recognized through an RFID reader. It is expected that RFID system will replace the barcode system in the near future and help in drastic innovation of logistics and distribution industries [1, 2, 3, 4].

J. Domingo-Ferrer, J. Posegga, and D. Schreckling (Eds.): CARDIS 2006, LNCS 3928, pp. 300–312, 2006.

However, the fact that the RFID system allows the wireless data communication without physical contact raises a new issue. Currently, an RFID tag responds to any reader. That means anyone with a reader can read the information in the tag, potentially violating the privacy of the owner of the object with the RFID tag [5]. The privacy violation problem can be viewed in terms of information leak and location tracking.

First, information leakage deals with the fact that the direct identification information of the unique ID of the tag can be transmitted to anyone and everyone with the reader. Since a personal object can reflect the owner's life style, income level, consumption inclination and physical condition, violation of privacy due to tag information leakage should be considered significant [6].

Second, the location tracking is the problem caused by the tags always sending the same information. That can be used by the adversary with illicit purpose to track the location of the specific tag owner. It is like embedding a cheap positioning system to a tag. Of course, tracking the location or moving path of the tag owner without the approval would be serious privacy violation [7].

There have been many studies of the schemes to protect the privacy. The most simple and definite method is the *Kill command* [8]. Other methods include reader authentication using hash functions and protection of the user privacy using the *blocker tag* [9, 10]. *RFID Guardian* method using a specific device is similar to MARP in concept [11, 12]. However, all of the above mentioned method cannot completely protect the privacy [13].

We propose a new method that ensures high level privacy protection using a special mobile agent device. The concept of MARP is for a special mobile device to manage the tags and gather some of the information embedded in the tag to substitute its role. MARP can provide the high level cryptographic services that are unable in the low price tags.

The rest of the paper is organized as follows. Section 2 describes a few well-known RFID privacy protection methods. Section 3 describes the brief introduction of the RFID system and the required assumptions for the proposed scheme. Section 4 describes MARP in details, separated into the initial setup phase, the privacy protection phase and the authentication phase. And the main scheme using MARP is also explained. Section 5 describes the analysis for the proposed scheme. Section 6 presents the conclusions.

## 2    Related Work

The most extreme way to protect the privacy in RFID system is to destroy the RFID tag attached to an object or disable its functionality using the *Kill command*. The *Kill command* is a basic function included in all EPC tags [4, 7, 8]. The tag function is removed by entering a special secret code value (PIN) to prevent tag information leakage and tracking. Although it is the simplest and surest way to protect the privacy, it is not a recommended approach since it also loses all the potential advantages for using the RFID system.

Weis proposed the hash based metaID method [7]. Tag can be either in locked or unlocked mode, and only the authenticated reader can unlock a tag. When a tag is in the locked mode, all functions except transmission of the metaID of the tag are disabled. The metaID based method allows identification of a unique ID only by the authenticated reader. However, it does not solve the problem of location tracking since a tag in locked mode always transmits the same metaID value. Weis proposed another scheme, "Randomize hash-lock" in [7]. In this scheme, the tag has a hash function and a PRNG(pseudo-random number generator). This scheme satisfies indistinguishability, but has some security holes in reader-tag communication and very heavy load in the back-end server [13, 14].

Juels proposed the "blocker tag" method [9, 10]. The blocker tag method uses a type of defense shield to protect the tag. The blocker tag always responds in both 0 and 1 to the reader inquiry. Therefore it hides its existence and forces the reader to give up trying to recognize the tag. The privacy is protected by preventing the reader to recognize the tag ID through a type of interference. However, the blocker tag presents the risk of being misused, and selective blocking is not possible.

Collo proposed a scheme using re encryption [15]. In this scheme, the Reader and the tag have to compute ElGamal public key cipher. And the tag must be re-encrypted very Frequently. However, this scheme can be attacked through various security vulnerability.

There are other methods of arbitrating the communication between the reader and tag using the mobile device [11, 12, 16, 17]. This device protects the privacy with high capacity memory and calculation capability. The device mainly has four functions: 1) monitoring of the new tag or reader, 2) managing the key on behalf of the tag, 3) controlling the access by the tag or reader, and 4) authenticating if the reader is legitimate on behalf of the tag.

## 3   The RFID System for MARP

An RFID system generally consists of RFID tag, RFID reader and back-end server. For the proposed system in this paper, there is additional personal privacy protection agent (MARP) that arbitrates the communication between the reader and tag, and the trusted public key management center. Fig.1 shows that the RFID system for MARP.

- **RFID Tag** *Transponder* — A tag is attached to a certain object with its unique identification. In general, it consists of the IC chip and antenna. When the reader sends an inquiry, the tag responds with its own internal data or the result of calculation using the data. An RFID tag can be either an active tag or passive tag. The passive tag, which has not own battery for reducing the manufacturing cost, receivers reader's query through radio signal and sends its answer to reader using harvested energy from the electromagnetic field of the reader's radio signal. The system proposed in this study assumes a hash enabled passive tag.
- **RFID Reader** *Transceiver*— A reader is the device that transmits RF signal to the tag and receive the response from the tag. Its role is to send an inquiry

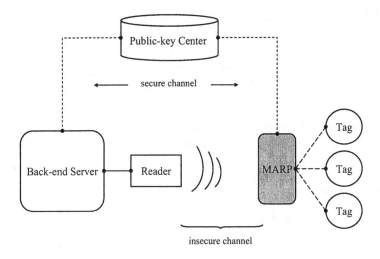

**Fig. 1.** The RFID system for MARP

to the tag, receive the data from the tag and then identifies it using its own subsystem or external back-end system. For this study, the readers are assumed to be in a certain group [18] and contain the group ID as well as the group individual key and public key. In the proposed scheme, the access authority to the tags is classified by the group ID.

- **Reader Subsystem** — The data processing subsystem is attached to the reader and retrieves appropriate information from its own database or external database server according to the data obtained by the reader. Generally, the data processing subsystem is considered as a pard of reader.
- **Back-end Server** — The back-end server is a server system that processes the tag related data sent by the reader. The back-end server has the tag related information in a database. The answer of the tag is transmitted securely to the back-end server through authenticated reader and it is used to identify the tag. The back-end server must be trusted and must have the capability to process every query from a lot of readers concurrently.
- **MARP** *(Mobile Agent for RFID Privacy Protection)* — This is the key part of the proposed scheme. MARP is a compact battery-powered mobile device, such as Personal Digital Assistants (PDA) or cellular phones. It has the role of gathering the secret information of tag and functioning on behalf of the tag. In this study, each MARP has the individual key and public key. It is also assumed that the reader can easily differentiate tag from MARP.
- **Trusted Public-key Center** — MARP scheme utilizes authentication using the public key. Since each reader group and MARP has the public key pair, a trusted third party public key distribution center is needed to manage them.

# 4   Mobile Agent for RFID Privacy Protection

This section describes MARP scheme proposed in this study. MARP is a mobile device with high performance capability, memory and high calculation capability. An RFID user will carry around MARP to register the tags to MARP and then use it to represent the tags.

The key to MARP is to secure some of the tag's secret information and use it to authenticate the tag. MARP registers all user tags, record them in the database and perform the mutual authentication to provide the tag information appropriate for the reader class.

## 4.1   Term Definition

- $h()$ : the one-way hash function algorithm.

- $Uid_t$ : the unique identifier of the tag $t$.

- $Key_t$ : the secrete value of the tag $t$.

- $PIN_t$ : mode change key of the tag $t$.

- $Rid_g$ : identifier of reader group $g$.

- $K_d^g$ : private key of reader group $g$.

- $K_e^g$ : public key of reader group $g$ .

- $K_d^m$ : private key of MARP $m$.

- $K_e^m$ : public key of MARP $m$.

- $\|$ : concatenation.

- $\oplus$ : exclusive-OR.

## 4.2   Initial Setup Phase

Before performing MARP scheme, there is certain preparation needed. Each tag must contain the $PIN_t$. Only those MARP having the key can register the tag and toggles it between sleep and wake modes. If a store has the tagged items for sale, the store DB will contain $PIN_t$ of each tagged item. After the item is sold, $PIN_t$ will be transferred to MARP of the buyer who registers the item.

A reader is assigned with a specific group ID. It has the authority to read the tag only with the group ID. It is a type of classification. For an example, when scanning the tags for the purpose of advertising similar to spam mail, the

**Table 1.** Data states in the RFID system for MARP

| Back-end Server | Reader | MARP | Tag |
|---|---|---|---|
| $Uid_t$ | $Rid_g$ | $K_d^m$ | $Uid_t$ |
| $Key_t$ | $K_d^g$ | $K_e^m$ | $Key_t$ |
| $Rid_g$ | $K_e^g$ | $Rid_g$ | $PIN_t$ |
| $K_d^g$ | | $K_e^g$ | |
| $K_e^m$ | | $Uid_t$ | |
| | | $h(Key_t)$ | |
| | | $PIN_t$ | |

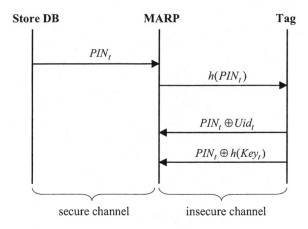

**Fig. 2.** Initial setup phase

legal regulation may force the reader to have the group ID such as SPAM. Then the users who do not want the spam scan will prevent access by the SPAM group readers. With the group ID and the group public key, readers can also be authenticated for their legitimacy.

For secure communication, MARP also has the individual ID and public key. Therefore, a trusted public key distribution center is needed to manage the public keys. Each MARP contains the reader group ID's it manages and can attain the reader group public key through the public key distribution center.

In terms of the data for each RFID system component, the server contains the tag related information (tag ID, secret data, and $PIN_t$) and reader group related information (reader group ID and reader group public key). It can also attain MARP public key through the trusted public key authentication center. The reader must contain its own group ID, public key and individual key. MARP contains its own information (public key and individual key) as well as the information of the reader group (ID and public key) with the access authority. It must also contain the information (ID, hashed secret data and $PIN_t$) of the tags it controls. The tag contains its own ID, secret data and $PIN_t$. Table 1 shows that the data states in proposed RFID system MARP fist needs to gather tag's secret data before it represents a tag. When a tagged item is purchased at a store, the $PIN_t$ of the tag will be transferred to MARP which gathers the tag data and puts the tag in sleep mode using the $PIN_t$. Collecting the secret data of the tag is simple. The hashed $PIN_t$ is sent to the tag in a short distance. (It is assumed that the tag can be registered only within a short distance for security purpose.) The tag confirms validity of the information and then sends its secret data (ID and hashed secret key) by first XORing with $PIN_t$. The data transmission is secure since wiretapping the data alone cannot decode the secret tag information. Fig.2 shows that the tag registration protocol in the proposed system.

**Detailed Protocol.**

1. Store DB send $PIN_t$ to MARP.
   - Store DB $\longrightarrow$ MARP : $PIN_t$.
2. The hashed $PIN_t$ is sent to the tag in as short distance.
   - MARP $\longrightarrow$ Tag : $h(PIN_t)$.
3. The tag confirms validity of the information and then sends its secret data (ID and hashed secret key) by first XORing with $PIN_t$.
   - Tag : computes $PIN_t$ from received $h(PIN_t)$.
   - Tag : authenticates MARP.
   - Tag $\longrightarrow$ MARP: $PIN_t \oplus Uid_t$ , $PIN_t \oplus h(Key_t)$.

### 4.3   Privacy Protect Phase(Tag Sleep Mode)

Once the secret information of the tag is stored in MARP, the tag is put into sleep mode. This mode allows MARP to act on behalf of the tag and is the most typical mode of the proposed scheme. In this mode, data communication occurs only between MARP and the reader. The mutual authentication process consists of 5 steps, and the procedure and communication protocol of each step is as follows(Fig.3):

**Detailed Protocol.**

1. The reader sends an inquiry along with the group ID and a random number which are signed by the reader group individual key to MARP.
   - Reader $\longrightarrow$ MARP : $Query \parallel E_{K_d^g}(Rid_g \parallel R_r)$.

2. MARP checks the signature to identify the reader group ID before generating another random number. Both random numbers are signed with its own individual key and encrypted with the reader group public key then securely sent to the reader.
   - MARP : checks the signature to identify the reader group ID.
   - MARP : generate random number. $R_m$.
   - MARP $\longrightarrow$ Reader : $a_1 = E_{K_e^m}(E_{K_d^g}(R_r \parallel R_m))$.

Back-end Server          Reader                    MARP

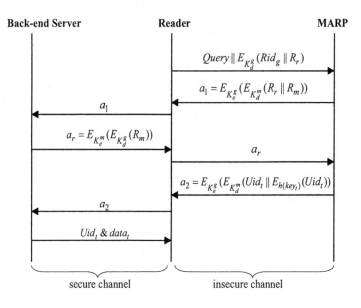

**Fig. 3.** Privacy protection phase

3. The reader transmits the received information to the server. The server checks the signature to attain MARP ID. After that, the server signs the random number sent by MARP with its own individual key, encrypts it with MARP public key and re-sends it.
   - Reader $\longrightarrow$ Server : $a_1$.
   - Server : checks the signature to attain MARP ID and $R_m$.
   - Server $\rightarrow$ Reader $\rightarrow$ MARP : $a_r = E_{K_e^m}(E_{K_d^g}(R_m))$.
4. Once MARP receives the information from the reader and confirms it, the mutual authentication is completed. After that, MARP only transfers the approved tag data using the keys on the device.
   - MARP : confirms information, the mutual authentication is completed.
   - MARP $\rightarrow$ Reader $\rightarrow$ Server : $a_2 = E_{K_e^g}(E_{K_d^m}(Uid_t \parallel E_{h(key_t)}(Uid_t)))$.
5. The server decrypts the received information and transfers the concerned information to the reader.
   - Server : decrypts the received information.
   - Server $\longrightarrow$ Reader: $Uid_t$ & $data_t$.

### 4.4   Authentication Phase(Tag Wake Mode)

This mode is used for the certain cases which require inspection of the illicitly altered tag by MARP. If the tag is to transfer the raw secret data to MARP, its counterfeiting or alteration can be done very easily. A canceled tag may act as if it has the secret information or sends the information of another tag. Therefore, the data is hashed with a simple scheme. To verify the tag, the tag authentication using the tag's secret data all it's needed. The tag validation protocol consists of three steps as follows(Fig.4):

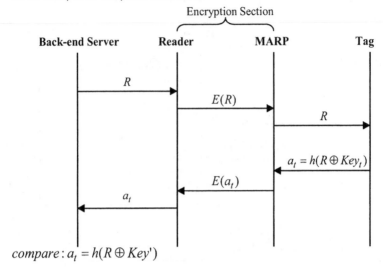

**Fig. 4.** Authentication phase

## Detailed Protocol.

1. The server generates a random number and sends it to MARP which puts the tag in wake mode and sends the random number to it using $PIN_t$.
   - Server : generates a random number.
   - Server $\rightarrow$ Reader $\rightarrow$ MARP: $E_{K_d^g}(R)$.
   - MARP : puts the tag in wake mode to it using $PIN_t$.
   - Tag $\longrightarrow$ MARP : $R$.
2. Awaken tag XOR's the received random number with its own secret data, hashes it and sends it to MARP. MARP transfers the received data to the server.
   - Tag $\rightarrow$ MARP $\rightarrow$ Reader $\rightarrow$ Server : $a_t = h(R \oplus Key_t)$.
3. The server compares the information from the tag with its own and authenticates the tag if they are in agreement.
   - Server : compares $a_t = h(R \oplus Key')$.
   - Server : authenticates Tag.

### 4.5   Main Scheme

Authentication between the tag and MARP, between MARP and reader, and between the server and tag are separately described above. It is now needed to consider each step collectively. The main scheme is not MARP acting on behalf of the tag using the sleep or wake mode. It is carried out in the shape of the tags being depended upon MARP. If the sleep mode of the tag is used, MARP can alter the tag at any time. Therefore, authentication step is needed time to time. However, what if the authentication step is carried out in each operation?

First of all, the tag should not react to any scan by the readers once it is affiliated with MARP. It may only communicate with MARP that know its

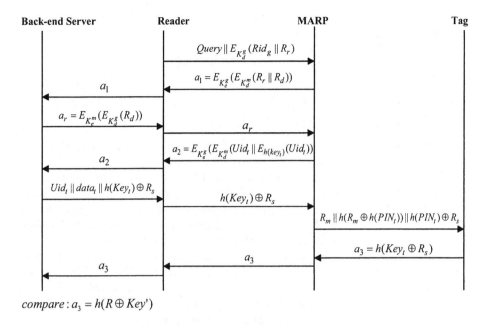

Back-end Server          Reader              MARP                    Tag

$$Query \| E_{K_d^g}(Rid_g \| R_r)$$

$$a_1 = E_{K_e^g}(E_{K_d^m}(R_r \| R_d))$$

$$a_1$$

$$a_r = E_{K_e^m}(E_{K_d^g}(R_d))$$

$$a_r$$

$$a_2 = E_{K_e^g}(E_{K_d^m}(Uid_t \| E_{h(key_t)}(Uid_t)))$$

$$a_2$$

$$Uid_t \| data_t \| h(Key_t) \oplus R_s$$

$$h(Key_t) \oplus R_s$$

$$R_m \| h(R_m \oplus h(PIN_t)) \| h(PIN_t) \oplus R_s$$

$$a_3 = h(Key_t \oplus R_s)$$

$$a_3$$

$$a_3$$

$$compare: a_3 = h(R \oplus Key')$$

**Fig. 5.** Main scheme using MARP

$PIN_t$. It's a type of master-slave relation. Since the tag will not respond to an inquiry unless an accurate $PIN_t$ is provided, it will not be recognized by any readers with the $PIN_t$. Employing that, authentication using the secret data can be requested to the tag for each communication.

There is some change as the authentication protocol is added at the later part of the above mentioned scheme. The server can calculate the tag ID and the related data by analyzing the data sent by MARP and send the information to the reader. Fig.5 shows the main scheme using MARP.

**Detailed Protocol.**

1. At the same time, the hashed secret data is XOR'ed with the random number $R_s$ and sent.
   - Server $\longrightarrow$ Reader : $Uid_t \| data_t \| (Key_t) \oplus R_s$.
   - Reader $\longrightarrow$ MARP : $h(Key_t) \oplus R_s$.
2. MARP calculates $R_s$ received from the server. It then XOR's the hashed $PIN_t$ with $R_s$ and sends it to the tag. It also sends the key that verifies that it is the tag master. For example, the tag's secret data can be hashed, XOR'ed and sent.
   - MARP : calculates $R_s$ and generate new $R_m$.
   - MARP $\longrightarrow$ Tag: $R_m \| h(R_m \oplus h(PIN_t)) \| h(PIN_t) \oplus R_s$.
3. The tag analyzes the information sent by MARP. It responds only after confirming that MARP is its master. If it is, the secret data is added to R

and hashed before being sent to MARP. The server calculates the received response and authenticates the tag.

- Tag : authenticates MARP.
- Tag → MARP → Reader → Server: $h(Key_t \oplus R_s)$.
- Server : authenticates Tag.

### 4.6  Overall Scenario Using MARP

This scenario presents how MARP can be used in real situation.

- When a good with an RFID tag arrives at a shop, the master of the shop stores the PIN of the RFID tag in the shop's DB.
- When a consumer purchases the good, the PIN of the RFID tag of the good transmitted to the consumer's MARP. There are some feasible methods that sends the PIN information to MARP. One method is that the DB system of the shop prints the PIN on receipt and gives it to the consumer. Another method is that the DB system of the shop communicates the PIN to the consumer's MARP using a secure channel, such like bluetooth or direct cable.
- The consumer register the tag and its PIN in his MARP. The MARP acquires some of the tag's secret information through authentication using the tag's PIN. After the consumer register the tag, he can change the PIN for keeping security. These steps constitutes the initial setup phase.
- After the initial setup phase, the tag is subordinate to the MARP, and ignores any unauthenticated requests. This is master/slave state and only the MARP can read the tag.
- A reader have to communicate with the MARP instead of the tag. In the communication between the reader and the MARP, public key cryptosystem would be used for high level security. Each of them can acquire the other's public key form the public key distribution center. These steps constitutes the main scheme. And in the main scheme, the reader or the back-end server can be assured of the tag's reality through verifying the tag's secret information using the tag involved protocol. This scheme should prevent the MARP from forging the tag.
- During the consumer has the good with the tag at home, he can make the tag normal state and/or can communicate with the MARP.
- If the consumer transfer the good to another user, he have to sends the PIN information of the good to another user. After the new user registers the tag, he must change the PIN of the tag. This prevent the old user from accessing the tag illegally.

## 5  Analysis

We analyze the proposed scheme in this section. Our scheme is designed for a secure RFID system with low-cost tags. A tag uses its PIN or its hashed PIN as an encryption key in every session for secure communication with a MARP. Since we use hash functions and random numbers in the communication between a back-end server and a MARP, an attacker cannot know the secret information of the tag. And since only authenticated readers and tags can joined to our communication protocols, our scheme is secure. It is impossible for the attacker to trace the location of the specific tag which sends indistinguishable answers in every query by him.

In MARP scheme, a tag has two phase protocols that are the initial setup phase and main scheme phase. In the initial setup phase, the tag sends only some of its secret information to the MARP. If the tag has already hashed PIN and hashed Key in its memory, it computes only exclusive-OR operation twice. In the main scheme phase, the tag computes two hash operations and two exclusive-OR operations. Eventually, in our MARP scheme, a tag needs to have one hash module and one exclusive-OR module.

In REP scheme of Juels[17], which is a mobile agent scheme using a re-encryption method, a tag must send all of its secret information to the agent. This causes an important security problem that the mobile agent can counterfeit or masquerade after returning or transferring of the item with the tag. On the contrary, in our scheme, MARP obtain only some of secret information of the tag and we have authentication protocol that confirm the reality of the tag. These features should reduce the possibility of forging the tag.

## 6   Conclusions

This study deals with protection of the privacy for the RFID system. Since the low cost RFID tags have only hundreds bits of memory and thousands of logical gates, the existing privacy protection method typically used in the mobile communication system cannot be used in RFID system. Therefore, many proposals have been made to protect the privacy under the limited resources. We have mentioned those RFID privacy protection schemes and pointed out their weakness.

We proposed MARP as a concept using the external proxy agent device for the privacy protection. MARP attains a part of the secret information of the tags to act on behalf of them. Once the secret information is attained, it communicates with the authenticated reader groups with high level security. The proposed scheme is a unique one that overcomes the built-in limitation of the tags.

Since MARP is an external device, it can be applied without much change to the currently existing RFID system. Furthermore, it has the added benefit of requiring minimum hardware capability in the tag since the privacy protection protocol is processed by the external device. We think that it is feasible to implement MARP on the current mobile devices, since an ordinary cellular phone has some cryptographic modules and a common PDA has almost perfect cryptographic modules except RF communication ability. Now we are implementing MARP on a PDA with Java platform for simulating the our scheme.

## Acknowledgement

This work was supported by grant No. R01-2005-000-10568-0 from the Basic Research Program of the Korea Science & Engineering Foundation.

# References

1. K. Finkenzeller, *RFID handbook*, John Wiley & Sons, 1999.
2. D. Brock, "The Electronic Product Code - A Naming Scheme for physical Objects", *Auto-ID White Paper*, http://www.autoidlabs.com/whitepapers/MIT-AUTOID-WH-002.pdf , January 2001.
3. H. Knospe and H. Pobl, "RFID Security", *Infomation Security Technical Report*, vol. 9, no. 4, pp. 39-50, Elsevier, 2004.
4. S. Sarma, S. Weis, and D. Engels, "Radio-Frequency Identification: Security Risks and Challenges", *Cryptobytes*, vol. 6 no. 1, pp. 2-9, RSA Laboratories, Spring 2003.
5. G. Avoine and P. Oechslin, "RFID Traceability: A Multilayer Problem", *Financial Cryptography - FC'05*, vol. 3570 of LNCS, pp. 125-140, February 2005.
6. R. Anderson and M. Kuhn, "Low Cost Attacks on Tamper Resistant Devices", *International Workshop on Security Protocols - IWSP*, vol. 1361 of LNCS, pp. 125-135, April 1997.
7. S. Weis, S. Sarma, R. Rivest, and D. Engels, "Security and Privacy Aspects of Low-cost Radio Frequency Identification Systems", *Security in Pervasive Computing - SPC 2003*, vol. 2802 of LNCS, pp. 454-469, March 2003.
8. S. Sarma, S. Weis, and D. Engels, "RFID Systems and Security and Privacy Implications", *Cryptographic Hardware and Embedded Systems - CHES 2002*, vol. 2523 of LNCS, pp. 454-469, August 2002.
9. A. Juels, R. Rivest, and M. Szydlo, "The Blocker Tag : Selective Blocking of RFID Tags for Consumer Privacy", *Computer and Communications Security - ACM CCS 2003*, pp. 27-30, October 2003.
10. A. Juels, J. Brainard, "Soft Blocking : Flexible Blocker Tags on the Cheap", *Workshop on Privacy in the Electronic Society - WPES 2004*, pp. 1-7, October 2004
11. M. Rieback, B. Crispo, and A. Tanenbaum, "RFID Guardian: A Battery-powered Mobile Device for RFID Privacy Management", *Australasian Conference on informaiton Security and Privacy - ACISP 2005*, vol. 3574 of LNCS, pp. 184-194, July 2005.
12. A. Tanenbaum, G. Gaydadjiev, B. Crispo, M. Rieback, D. Stafylarakis, and C. Zhang, "The RFID Guardian Project.", http://www.cs.vu.nl/~melanie/rfid_guardian/people.html
13. G. Avoine, "Adversarial Model for Radio Frequency Identification", *Cryptology ePrint Archive*, Report 2005/049, http://eprint.iacr.org, 2005.
14. J. Saito, J.C. Ryou and K. Sakurai, "Engancing Privacy of Universal Re-Encryption Scheme for RFID Tags", *Embedded and Ubiquitous Computing - EUC '04*, vol. 3207 of LNCS, pp. 879-890, August 2004.
15. P. Golle, M. Jakobsson, A. Juels, and P. Syverson, "Universal Re-Encryption for Mixnets", *Track on the RSA Conference – CT-RSA '04*, vol. 2964 of LNCS, pp. 163-178, February 2004.
16. S. Konomi, "Personal Privacy Assistants for RFID Users", *International Workshop Series on RFID 2004*, November 2004.
17. A. Juels, P. Syverson, and D. Bailey, "High-Power Proxies for Enhancing RFID Privacy and Utility", *Center for High Assurance Computer Systems - CHACS 2005*, August 2005.
18. X. Gao , Z. Xiang , G. Wang , J. Shen , J. Huang , and S. Song, "An Approach to Security and Privacy of RFID System for Supply Chain", *Conference on E-Commerce Technology for Dynamic E-Business – CEC-East'04*, pp. 164-168, September 2005.

# Certifying Native Java Card API by Formal Refinement

Quang-Huy Nguyen and Boutheina Chetali

Axalto, Smart Cards Research,
34-36 rue de la Princesse, 78431 Louveciennes Cedex, France
{qnguyen, bchetali}@axalto.com

**Abstract.** This paper describes a refinement-based approach to show that a native Java Card API function fulfills its specification. We refine a native function from its informal specification (by Sun) through several intermediate models into a low-level model which is very close to its C implementations. We formally prove the correctness of the refinement steps between two adjacent levels. The low-level model is sufficiently detailed such that its correspondence to the C implementation can be informally checked. This work provides a framework to enforce the security of the native code by formal analysis and can be generalized to verify a complete implementation of the Java Card platform.

## 1 Introduction

Native API methods are usually written in C and are considered as part of the Java Card platform. On the contrary, non-native methods are written in Java Card and can be seen as applications running on the Java Card platform. Formal analysis of Java Card API methods has been done in several previous works (*i.e.,* [1, 2, 3]) using languages and tools dedicated to Java such as JML [4] (and its associated tools) and JACK [5]. On the contrary, in our knowledge, native methods have never been addressed. The main obstacle is related to their C implementation which is yet to be well handled by formal analysis.

*Refinement* is one of the cornerstones of formal approaches for software engineering: the process of developing a more detailed design or implementation from an abstract specification through a sequence of mathematically-based steps that maintain correctness *w.r.t.* the original specification. In the formal tools like B-Method or Esterel, the informal specification can be modelled, refined and then automatically translated into C code. However, in both of these systems, the generated code is not sufficiently efficient (in terms of performance and resource consuming) to fit into smart cards. Some attempts (*e.g.,* [6]) have been done to optimize the generated code but these optimizations are usually complex and may jeopardize the rigour provided by formal tools. Furthermore, in the industry, we often need to directly deal with an already developed product rather than starting from its informal specification.

In this work, we aim at certifying an existing implementation of the native methods that are already embedded on smart cards. To this end, we build a

J. Domingo-Ferrer, J. Posegga, and D. Schreckling (Eds.): CARDIS 2006, LNCS 3928, pp. 313–328, 2006.
© IFIP International Federation for Information Processing 2006

low-level model of the JCVM (Java Card Virtual Machine) which is sufficiently close to its C implementation such that the correspondence between them can be informally checked. We also build two intermediate models in order to refine the informal specification of the native methods to the low-level model. Both of the models are built using the Coq proof assistant [7] which allows us to formally prove the correctness of each refinement step.

The rest of this paper is organized as follows. Section 2 describes several refining models of the native API methods. In Section 3, we provide their low-level model basing on a concrete JCVM implementation. Section 4 presents the correctness of refinement steps and its proof. Section 5 shows the relation between the low-level model and the concrete implementation. We discuss the related work in Section 6 and give some concluding remarks in Section 7.

## 2   Refining Informal Specification

The model of a native method must be built upon a model of the whole JCVM. In this paper, the JCVM is always modelled as a state machine. A *state* is a snapshot of all components of the JCVM: installed CAP files, heap, frame stack, static fields image, JCRE elements, etc. A *primitive operation* is a basic access service to one of these component (*e.g.,* popping and pushing a frame onto the frame stack, getting and setting an object in the heap). A primitive operation takes a state and its parameters and yields a new state and (possibly) a value. Any JCVM function (*e.g.,* a bytecode or a native function) can be seen as a sequence of primitive operations. The execution of a JCVM function transforms an (initial) state into a (final) state and (possibly) returns a value. If an exception is raised during this execution, then the returned value is the address of this exception which allows the JCVM to lookup for the exception handler.

The informal specification of a native method is refined by the following intermediate models (see a resume in Figure 1):

**FSP** is the Functional SPecification of the native function and is built upon the FIVM (Formal Internal Virtual Machine) state machine. In this model, a native function is specified by its expected input and output which are respectively defined by a pre-condition and a post-condition following Hoare logic [8]. These input and output are described in the informal specification and hence, the FSP model is completely independent of any concrete implementation.

| Model | State Machine | Data structures | Primitive operations | Implementation dependency ? | Specification of native methods |
|-------|---------------|-----------------|----------------------|------------------------------|---------------------------------|
| FSP | FIVM | abstract | Coq relations | no | expected input and output |
| HLD | FIVM | abstract | Coq functions | no | abstract algorithm |
| LLD | CVM | refined | Coq functions | yes | refined algorithm |

**Fig. 1.** Resume of intermediate models

**HLD** is the High-Level Description of the native function which is also built upon the FIVM state machine. However, in this model, the native function is specified by its algorithm *i.e.,* a function taking its input and returning its output. This function is written by a sequence of primitive operations. Because the data structures and the primitive operations are kept abstract in FIVM, the HLD model is also independent of any concrete implementation.

**LLD** is the Low-Level Description of the native function built upon the CVM (Concrete Virtual Machine) state machine. Like the HLD model, the LLD model of a native function specifies its algorithm as a sequence of primitive operations. However, all CVM data structures and primitive operations are fully defined basing on a concrete JCVM implementation (by Axalto). Therefore, the LLD model is also strongly related to this concrete implementation.

### 2.1   Functional Specification Model

**FIVM States.** In FIVM, the card memory is seen as a set of memory cells. Each cell is associated to an address which will be used to access to this cell. The `addr_null` address represents to the null pointer. A FIVM state (`fivm_state`) is a snapshot of the card memory and is composed of the following components:

1. *Installed packages* stores the list of already installed packages (CAP files).
2. *Heap* stores the heap elements which are either an object or an array. An object is represented by a header structure as follows: Record *fivm_object_header*

   : *Set* := {
       *fivm_object_status* : *object_context*;
       *fivm_object_transient_mode* : *transience*;
       *fivm_object_remote_mode* : *bool*;
       *fivm_object_class* : *address*
   }.

   This structure contains the security context of the applet that owns the object, a flag indicating its memory mode (persistent, `CLEAR_ON_RESET` or `CLEAR_ON_DESELECT` transient), a boolean flag indicating its remote mode, and the address of its `class_info` structure (which defines its class) in the installed packages. Similarly, an array is represented by its header structure which contains the type of its elements, its length, its security context and its memory mode.

3. *Frame stack* stores the stack of frames and is the core data structure needed for method interpretation [9]. In FIVM, the execution of a method is done inside a frame which is defined as follows:

   Record *fivm_frame_info* : *Set* := {
       *ifrm_pc* : *address*;
       *ifrm_context* : *frame_context*;
       *ifrm_max_locals* : *nat*;
       *ifrm_max_stack* : *nat* }.

where `ifrm_pc` is the program counter and points to the next bytecode to be executed; `ifrm_context` is the currently active context in which the method is being executed; `ifrm_max_locals` is the number of local variables of the method including its parameters; `ifrm_max_stack` is the number of FIVM words allocated to the operand stack where the intermediate results are pushed in and popped out during the execution of the method.

4. *Static fields image* stores the static fields of the installed packages.
5. *JCRE* stores the information used by the JCRE (Java Card Runtime Environment).

**Primitive Operations.** The FSP primitive operations are defined as Coq predicates *i.e.*, relations between the input and the output of the operations in order to ease the modelling of the pre- and post-conditions. The FSP primitive operations are abstract *i.e.*, only their signature is given as Coq parameters. We briefly draw the primitive operations on different FIVM components in the following:

1. *Installed packages*: FIVM provides primitive operations to check if a given package has been correctly installed on the card, and to access to all components of the installed packages.
2. *Heap*: FIVM provides primitive operations to access to all heap elements *i.e.*, object and array headers, object instance fields and array elements. For example, the access to an object header pointed by an address is done via the predicate `heap_object_header`:
   Parameter *heap_object_header: fivm_state → address → fivm_object_header → Prop*.
3. *Frame stack elements*: FIVM provides primitive operations to pop the top frame, and to push a new frame onto the frame stack.
4. *Static fields*: FIVM provides read and write services for static fields.
5. *JCRE*: FIVM provides primitive operations to access to all JCRE information. For example, the currently active applet is accessed by `fivm_selected_applet`:
   Parameter *fivm_selected_applet: fivm_state → applet_ident → Prop*.

**Firewall Control.** The firewall mechanism (Chapter 6 of [10]) ensures that the access to a JCVM element (*e.g.*, objects, arrays, static fields) is allowed if and only if the currently active context (*i.e.*, the context of the currently active applet) is the security context of the element. Exceptionally, the JCRE has a global privileged context and can access to all JCVM elements. All firewall conditions can be modelled using the primitive operations described above.

**Native Methods.** The pre-condition defines the constraints on the input which is composed of the initial FIVM state and the list of parameters encoded as FIVM words (`iword`). The post-condition defines the constraints on the output which is composed of the final FIVM state and a (possibly) returned value encoded as a FIVM word. This optional returned value is encoded in Coq by the type (`option iword`) which covers two cases: (`Some v`) means that a value v of type `iword` is returned and (`None iword`) means that no value is returned (void return).

*Example 1.* This example describes the model of the native method `export` of the class `javacard.framework.service.CardRemoteObject`. This method allows an on-card (remote) object to be (remotely) accessed by the card reader. The method `export` has only one parameter which is the address of the object to be exported. This constraint is modelled by the following pre-condition:

Definition *export_pre* (*ctxt:frame_context*)(*args : list iword*)
: *Prop* := ∃ *theObj:address, args* = (*address2iword theObj*)::*nil.*
where `address2iword` transforms the parameter `theObj` (which is an address) into a FIVM word. The output of `export` depends on its parameter, on the initial FIVM state (`fin`) and on the firewall condition[1]:

- **if** the parameter points to an allocated object in the heap[2] and the firewall condition is satisfied, **then** the remote mode of the object is set to **true** and `export` returns void. By changing the remote mode of the object, a new machine state (`fout`) is created from `fin`.
- **else**, `export` throws a security exception and the FIVM state is not modified.

Definition *export_post* (*args: list iword*)
(*fin fout*: *fivm_state*) (*result: option iword*): *Prop* :=
∃ *theObj: address, args* = (*address2iword theObj*)::*nil* ∧
∃ *hdr: fivm_object_header, heap_object_header fin theObj hdr* ∧
∃ *selapp: applet_ident, fivm_selected_applet fin selapp* ∧
    IF (*obj_jcre_or_same_owner* (*selected_applet_context selapp*)
                                        (*fivm_object_status hdr*))
    THEN
        let *newhdr* := *Fivm_Object_Header obj_status*
                          (*fivm_object_transient_mode hdr*) *true*
                          (*fivm_object_class hdr*)
        in (*heap_object_header fout theObj newhdr*) ∧ *result*=(*None iword*)
    ELSE *fin*=*fout* ∧ *result*=(*Some* (*address2iword SecurityException*)).
where the predicate (*obj_jcre_or_same_owner* ...) checks if the security context of the currently active applet (`selapp`) is either the (global) JCRE context or the security context of the object (to be exported) whose the header structure is `hdr`.

## 2.2 High-Level Model

The HLD model is also built upon the FIVM state machine. The JCVM functions are specified in the HLD model by their algorithm *i.e.,* by a function taking their input and returning their output. In this context, the HLD primitive operations must also be specified by Coq (abstract) functions instead of Coq predicates as in the FSP model.

---

[1] For `export`, the currently active context must be either the JCRE context or the security context of the object to be exported (*cf.* Section 6.1.4 of [10]).

[2] Actually, this condition is ensured by the Java compiler and if it does not hold, then there is an inconsistency in the card memory.

**Primitive Operations.** In the FSP model, the primitive operations are expressed as *partial* functions and defined as *relations*. A function $f$ having parameters of type $A_1, \ldots, A_n$ and yielding a value of type $B$ is generally represented as a relation $R_f$ on $S \times A_1 \times \ldots \times A_n \times B$, where $S$ represents some FIVM state. For functions that modify the content of the memory, their return also includes a new FIVM state. On the other hand, the HLD functions must be defined as *total* computable functions in Coq to ensure the termination of its computations.

In order to transform partial FSP functions into HLD total functions, a new constant (FivmaFatalError) is introduced to lift their co-domain. That is, a partial function is set to return FivmaFatalError when its output is not defined:

Inductive *fivma_fatal_error* : *Set* := *FivmaFatalError* : *fivma_fatal_error*.
Inductive *exc* (*V E* : *Set*) : *Set* :=
| *Value* : *V* → *exc V E*
| *Error* : *E* → *exc V E*.
Definition *fivma_val* (*A* : *Set*) := *exc A fivma_fatal_error*.

Notice that FivmaFatalError represents a model-level error and is not related to any Java Card runtime error or exception. All HLD functions will now return a value of type (fivma_val A) where A is its return type in the normal case. For example, the function fivma_set_remote _object_header updates the (boolean) remote mode flag of an object pointed by an address is specified as follows:

Parameter *fivma_set_remote_object_header*: *fivm_state* → *address* → *bool* → (*fivma_val fivm_state*).

This function returns a new FIVM state (because the memory content has been modified) and is abstract (like all other HLD primitive operations), that is, its specification consists only of its signature.

**Error Handling.** The error case makes the usage of functions more complex because there is now one more case to consider in each function call. For smoothly handling this case, a new construct is defined:

Definition *try_with* (*C* : *Set*) (*e* : *exc V1 E1*) (*f* : *V1* → *C*) (*g* : *E1* → *C*):
    *C* := *match e with*
    | *Value x* ⇒ *f x*
    | *Error y* ⇒ *g y*
    *end*.

Actually, try_with allows one to handle both cases of a total function. In the error case, the error (y) is handled by the function g. In the normal case, the returned value of the function (x) is used in the rest of the model (f). A new syntactic sugar try1 is also defined such that (try1 w=(F e) in H with err => G) compiles to (G err) if (F e) returns the error err, and to (H val) if it returns the value val. In particular, if err and G are omitted, then any error will be handled by a default procedure which consists in transferring the error to the higher level (*e.g.*, the invoking function).

**Native Methods.** The algorithm of a native method is defined as a sequence of the HLD primitive operations. The input of a native method is composed of the initial FIVM state and the list of parameters encoded as FIVM words. A native method may return a value or throws an exception by returning its address. In any case, the output of the method is composed of the final FIVM state and the (possibly) returned value encoded by the type (`option iword`).

*Example 2.* The algorithm of `export` (see Example 1) is described as follows:

1. **if** the list of arguments is empty, **then** a fatal error is raised, **else,**
2. convert the first argument into an object address using `iword2address`;
3. extract the object header pointed by this address using `fivma_get_object_header`;
4. check if the currently active context is either the global JCRE context (using `fivma_test_jcre_context`), or the security context of the object (using `fivma_test_obj_same_owner`) (the firewall condition);
5. **if** the firewall condition is satisfied, **then** return void and the final state (which has been updated by `fivma_set_remote_object_header`), **else** return the address of the security exception and the initial state.

Definition *fivma_export* (*args: list iword*) (*fin : fivm_state*)
 : (*option iword*) × *fivm_state* :=
   *match args with*
   | *fst* :: _ ⇒ *let obj := iword2address fst in*
      *try1 hdr := fivma_get_object_header fin obj in*
      *try1 selapp := fivma_selected_applet fin in*
      *IF* (*fivma_test_jcre_context* (*selected_applet_context selapp*))||
         (*fivma_test_obj_same_owner* (*selected_applet_context selapp*)
                                        (*fivm_object_status hdr*))
      *THEN*
         *try1 fout := fivma_set_remote_object_header fin obj true in*
            ((*None iword*), *fout*)
      *ELSE* ((*Some* (*address2iword SecurityException*)), *fin*)
   | _ ⇒ *raise FivmaFatalError*
   *end.*

## 3  Low-Level Model of a JCVM Implementation

The LLD model specifies a real JCVM implementation on a new state machine called CVM (Concrete Virtual Machine). All the components of this state machine are defined as concrete data structures. Therefore, all CVM primitive operations can now be defined as concrete algorithms. The algorithm of a native method are then refined to be close to its C implementation. In this section, for space reason, we only concentrate on the frame stack as well as on the invoking and the returning process of a (Java Card or native) method.

## 3.1   Frame Stack

A CVM frame is composed of the following elements:

- an operand stack is a stack of 16-bits words (`cvm_word`).
- a table of local variables, each of them being a 16-bits word.
- a security information representing the currently active context.
- a program counter pointing to the next bytecode to be executed.

As in FIVM state machine, the frame stack is part of the CVM state and is defined as follows:

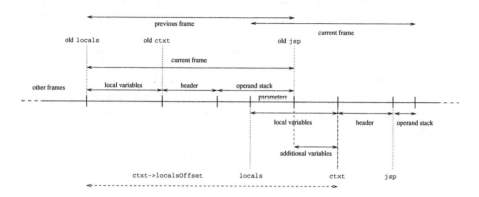

**Fig. 2.** The storage of the CVM frame stack

Record *cvm_state* : *Set* := {
  *cvm_frame_stack* : *c_memory_segment*;
  *jsp* : *c_address*;
  *locals* : *c_address*;
  *ctxt* : *c_address*; ... }.

- The contiguous memory segment `cvm_frame_stack` stores successively the frame stack itself. For each frame, firstly appears the local variable table, then its header, and finally its operand stack (see Figure 2).
- `jsp` is a pointer to the top of the operand stack of the current frame (*i.e.,* the top frame).
- `locals` points to the beginning of the local variable table of the current frame.
- `ctxt` points to the header of the current frame. This header is composed of:
  - `localsOffset`: a byte representing the offset from the header of the current frame (current `ctxt`) to the first item of the local variable table of the previous frame. This information is needed to recover the previous frame upon return from the current method *i.e.,* to recover the old value of `locals`.
  - `contextInfo`: a byte containing the currently active context.

- **nextpc**: a program counter pointing to the location where the virtual machine resumes upon return from the current method.
- **prev**: a pointer to the header of the previous frame (old **ctxt**).

### 3.2    Java Card **Methods**

*Invocation.* When a Java Card method is invoked, a new frame is pushed onto the frame stack. The local variable table (**locals**) of the new frame is set to the first parameter of the invoked method which have been pushed onto the operand stack of the previous frame by the invoking method (see Figure 2). This is an optimization in the JCVM implementation to avoid copying these parameters and to reduce memory consumption. The header of the invoked method is stored after the new local variable table whose the length is determined by its **method_info** structure stored in its CAP file. Then the global variables are updates according to the new current frame:

- **jsp** points to the operand stack of the new frame *i.e.,* just after its header.
- **locals** points to the first item of the new local variable table.
- **ctxt** points to the header of the new frame.

*Return.* The returning process consists in popping the top frame by restoring the values of the global variables as follows:

1. **jsp** is assigned to the value of **locals**, that is all parameters must have been popped from the operand stack during executing the invoked method.
2. **locals** is assigned to the current value of **ctxt** minus the value of the **localsOffset** field of the header of the current frame. This indeed points to the local variable table of the previous frame.
3. **ctxt** is assigned to the value of the **prev** field of the header of the current frame.

### 3.3    Native Methods

When a native method is invoked, its parameters are also pushed into the operand stack (of the current frame) as it is done when invoking a Java Card method. However, the native function is executed in the same frame of the invoking method and no new frame is created on the frame stack. After the execution of the native function, a returned type, which is of type short, is pushed on the top of the operand stack. If this type is 1 or 2, then there is a returned value which has been pushed onto the operand stack just under the returned type. Otherwise, the method returns void. The CVM retrieves the returned value if there is any, pops out the parameters and moves the program counter to the next bytecode to be executed.

In the LLD model, a native method is defined as a total function using the CVM primitive operations. These primitive operations, which are abstract in the HLD model, are fully defined as Coq functions in the LLD model. The input of a native method is composed of the initial CVM state and the list of parameters encoded as CVM words (cvm_word). The output of the method is only composed of the final CVM state because the (possibly) returned value and its type are already pushed onto the operand stack of the current frame.

*Example 3.* The following LLD model of export is very similar to the HLD model presented in Example 2 except for the returning process: in the LLD model, the (possibly) returned value and its type are explicitly pushed onto the operand stack (by cvm_frame_push).

Definition $cvm\_export$ (*args*: *list cvm_word*) (*cin*: *cvm_state*): *cvm_state* :=
    *match args with*
      | *fst* :: _ $\Rightarrow$ *let obj* := *cvm_word2address fst in*
        *try1 hdr* := *cvm_get_object_header cin obj in*
        *try1 selapp* := *cvm_selected_applet cin in*
        *IF* (*fivma_test_jcre_context* (*selected_applet_context selapp*))||
            (*fivma_test_obj_same_owner* (*selected_applet_context selapp*)
                            (*cvm_object_status hdr*))
      *THEN*
        *cvm_frame_push* (*cvm_set_remote_object_header cin obj true*) *szero*
      *ELSE*
        *cvm_frame_push*
        (*cvm_frame_push cin* (*address2cvm_word SecurityException*)) *stwo*
      | _ $\Rightarrow$ *raise CvmFatalError*
  *end.*

## 4    Correctness of Refinement

Informally, the refinement from a model to another model is correct if there is a correspondence between the executions of a native method in these two model.

**Theorem 1 (Correctness of refinement).** *Let* $\mathcal{M}_1$ *be a model of a native function and* $\mathcal{M}_2$ *be a refined model of* $\mathcal{M}_1$. *Let* $\mathcal{R}_1$ *be a relation between the states of* $\mathcal{M}_1, \mathcal{M}_2$ *and* $\mathcal{R}_2$ *be a relation between the data of* $\mathcal{M}_1, \mathcal{M}_2$. *Suppose that the two initial states of the native method are related by* $\mathcal{R}_1$, *and their corresponding parameters are related by* $\mathcal{R}_2$. *The refinement from* $\mathcal{M}_1$ *to* $\mathcal{M}_2$ *is said to be correct if:*

1. *the two final machine states are related by* $\mathcal{R}_1$, *and*
2. *the two returned values of the method, if there is any, are related by* $\mathcal{R}_2$.

### 4.1    FSP to HLD Refinement

This refinement step is correct if the algorithm defined in the HLD model fulfills its specification defined in the FSP model. In Hoare logic, a function $f$ fulfills its pre-condition $Pre_f$ and post-condition $Post_f$ if:

$$\forall xy : y = f(x) \rightarrow Pre_f(x) \rightarrow Post_f(y)$$

where $x, y$ respectively represent the input and the output of $f$. This statement is translated in Coq for the method export as follows:

Theorem *fivma_export_proof*:
$\forall$ (*args*: *list iword*)(*fin fout*: *fivm_state*)(*result*: *option iword*),
(*fivma_export args fin*) = (*result, fout*) $\rightarrow$
(*export_pre args fin*) $\rightarrow$ (*export_post args fin fout result*).

It is not difficult to see that this theorem is a special case of Theorem 1 where both $\mathcal{R}_1$ and $\mathcal{R}_2$ are the identity relation because both FSP and HLD models are built upon the state machine FIVM.

## 4.2  HLD to LLD Refinement

For any native method, this refinement step is correct if the returning process from the method produce a similar effect in the FIVM and CVM state machines. In the HLD model, because the frame stack is abstract, the (possibly) returned value is pushed onto the operand stack and then, be popped by the invoking method in an opaque way. In the LLD model (see Section 3.3), the frame stack is detailed and all pop and push operations are explicitly performed on the operand stack. We need to chow that the two returning process produce the corresponding final states and returned values, providing that the initial states and the method parameters are respectively related by `cvm_fivm_link_state` (which abstractly relates CVM states to FIVM states) and `cvm_word2iword` (which abstractly converts CVM words into FIVM words).

Therefore, the correctness of the refinement must be stated for all two execution scenarios of a native method: (1) it returns a value or the address of an exception, and (2) it returns void. For example, the two theorems to be proved for `export` are described as follows:

1. `export` returns a value or the address of an exception:

> Theorem *cvm_export_value_proof*: $\forall$ *cst1 cst2 fst1 args cst' cst" typ val*,
> (*cvm_fivm_link_state cst1 fst1*) $\rightarrow$
> (*cvm_export args cst1*) = *cst'* $\rightarrow$
> (*cvm_frame_pop cst'*) = (*typ,cst"*) $\rightarrow$
> (*andb* (*Zle_bool typ stwo*) (*Zge_bool typ sone*)) = *true* $\rightarrow$
> (*cvm_frame_pop cst"*) = (*val,cst2*) $\rightarrow$
> $\exists$ *fst2*: *fivm_state*, (*cvm_fivm_link_state cst2 fst2*) $\land$
> (*fivma_export* (*map cvm_word2iword args*) *fst1*) = ((*cvm_word2iword val*), *fst2*).

where the primitive operation `cvm_frame_pop` pops a short value from the operand stack of the current frame and returns a new machine state; `Zle_bool` represents the less-or-equal operator on short values; `andb` represents the conjunctive operator on boolean values.

This theorem states that in the LLD model, after executing `export` on the initial state `cst1` and on the list of parameters `args`, if we pop a short value (`typ`) from the top of the operand stack and this value is 1 or 2, then popping the next short value from the stack yields the returned value (`val`) of `export` and the final CVM state `cst2`. Now if we execute export in the HLD model on the corresponding FIVM state fst1 (because (cvm_fivm_link_state cst1 fst1) holds), and on the corresponding parameters (map cvm_word2iword args), then we obtain the final FIVM state fst2 which corresponds to cst2. Moreover the LLD-returned value val also corresponds to the HLD-returned value (cvm_word2iword val).

2. export returns void:

Theorem *cvm_export_void_proof*: ∀ *cst1 cst2 fst1 args cst' typ*,
(*cvm_fivm_link_state cst1 fst1*) →
(*cvm_export args cst1*) = *cst'* →
(*cvm_frame_pop cst'*) = (*typ,cst2*) →
(*andb* (*Zle_bool typ stwo*) (*Zge_bool typ sone*)) = *false* →
∃ *fst2*: *fivm_state*, (*cvm_fivm_link_state cst2 fst2*) ∧
(*fivma_export* (*map cvm_word2iword args*) *fst1*)=((*None iword*), *fst2*).

In the LLD model, the short value at the top of stack is neither 1 nor 2 and there is no returned value. In this case, the HLD model of export must return void. Furthermore, the two final states (fst2 and cst2) must also be related by cvm_fivm_link_state.

These two theorems are a special case of Theorem 1 where $\mathcal{R}_1$ is the relation cvm_fivm_link_state and $\mathcal{R}_2$ is the function cvm_word2iword.

## 4.3 General Proof Scheme

The general structure of a native function can be seen as a tree whose leaves are primitive operations. The internal nodes of this tree are Coq constructs used for defining the native function. The general proof scheme for the refinement on the native function between two adjacent models is described as follows:

1. Decompose the native function into more simple operations in both models until the primitive operations are reached.
2. Prove the correctness for each decomposition step: because the definitions of the native function in both models follow the same structure, this proof is feasible.
3. Apply the appropriate refinement hypotheses (see Section 4.4) to conclude the correctness for the primitive operations.

This proof scheme is closely related to the structure of the native function. For example, if it is a recursive function, then for proving the correctness of the decomposition steps over it, an proof by induction is needed. Furthermore, because a native function needs to cover all possible error cases, the proof must be done on all of its execution paths. In many cases, this leads to huge and unreadable proof. In order to ease the proof readability and maintenance, we have modularized and factorized the proofs by defining numerous common tactics and lemmas.

### 4.4   Refinement Hypotheses

Because the HLD primitive operations are abstract, the correctness of their refinement from the FSP model must be supposed as hypotheses of the FSP-to-HLD refinement proof. Actually, those hypotheses express the internal consistency of the FIVM state machine.

On the other hand, the LLD primitive operations are fully defined and the correctness of their refinement from the HLD model must also be supposed as hypotheses of the HLD-to-LLD refinement proof. Actually, those hypotheses are part of the abstract relation between the FIVM and CVM state machines. This relation is also expressed by the abstract relations between FIVM states and CVM states (`cvm_fivma_link_state`), and between FIVM data and CVM data (*e.g.*, `cvm_word2iword`).

*Example 4.* Let us consider the primitive operation that yields the header structure of an object. In the FSP model, this operation is modelled by the predicate `head_object_header` and in the HLD and LLD models by the functions `fivma_get_object_header` and `cvm_get_object_header`. The refinements from the FSP model to HLD model and from the HLD model to LLD model are respectively supposed in Coq by the hypotheses `fivma_get_object_header_proof` and `fivma_get_object_header_refinement`:

Hypothesis *fivma_get_object_header_refinement*:
$\forall$ (*fst*: *fivm_state*) (*addr*: *address*) (*hdr*: *fivm_object_header*),
(*fivma_get_object_header fst addr*)=*hdr* $\rightarrow$ (*heap_object_header fst addr hdr*).

Hypothesis *fivma_get_object_header_refinement*:
$\forall$ (*cst*: *cvm_state*) (*fst*: *fivm_state*) (*addr*: *address*),
(*cvm_fivma_link_state cst fst*) $\rightarrow$
(*cvm_get_object_header cst addr*) = (*fivma_get_object_header fst addr*).

## 5   C Implementation vs. Coq Low-Level Model

The conformance of the Axalto implementation *w.r.t.* the LLD model is informally checked by a hypertext document which relates the C code to the Coq model. This is the only informal step in the refinement chain from the informal specification to the implementation of a native function. However, the fact that the LLD model has been refined basing on the C implementation makes the their conformance much more evident.

*Example 5.* The C implementation of `export` is quoted as follows.

```
void CARDREMOTEOBJECT_export()
{
    PEOBJECTHANDLE  pHandle;
    u1              isExport;
    pHandle = soft_check_ref(pass_byteword_0());
```

```
    if(!isHandleRemote(pHandle)) {
    _VM_WriteU2((GEN_ADDRESS)(&pHandle->datalength),
    (u2)(pHandle->datalength | HANDLE_REMOTE)); }
}
```

In the heap, an object header is represented by a bit vector that contains the remote mode flag. Accessing to different fields of the object header is done via macros like `isHandleRemote`, which check the value of the corresponding bits. In the C code of a native function, the macro `pass_byteword_n` is used to pop its $n^{th}$ parameter from the operand stack of the current frame. For `export`, `pass_byteword_0` pops the address of the remote object. The `soft_check_ref` function checks the firewall condition on this object and raises a security exception if it is violated. Otherwise, the function checks if the object has been already exported before setting the remote flag of the object header (`pHandle`) using the `HANDLE_REMOTE` mask. This check is an optimization of the implementation because writing on $E^2PROM$ is costly. In the LLD model, the flag is updated without this check (by `cvm_set_remote_object_header`) because the model is not executable and hence, we are not really concerned by the performance.

## 6   Related Work

Numerous researchers have worked on the formal analysis of the Java Card platform. However, most of them concentrate on ensuring some high-level security properties of the Java Card applets such as well-typedness [11, 12], confidentiality, noninterference, information-flow security [13, 14, 15].

While Java Card API can be formally analyzed as for Java Card applets [1, 2, 3, 16], verifying native functions requires us to work on the C code. Currently, the application of formal methods to the verification of the C code is still at its very early stage. Indeed, the semantics of C is not strictly defined and varies between different compilers[3]. C is however largely used in the embedded software industry thanks to its efficiency. There are currently two approaches for formally handling C code: in the bottom-up approach, the formal model is built using the C code while in the top-down approach, the informal specification is formalized and refined to an C implementation.

The top-down approach is used in several works [6] using B-Method to automatically generate C code from a formal model. The bottom-up approach is used, for example, in [17] to generate Coq model of C code using tools like Caduceus and Why. The method presented in this paper can be seen as a mixed approach because the low-level model is designed by refining the higher-level models and by abstracting the C code to be certified.

While formal verification of C code is still not straightforward, many researchers have focused on the static analysis of information flow [18] (and/or abstract interpretation) as a feasible means to improve the security of C code.

---

[3] Actually, part of the C memory management is not built in the language but is intentionally left to programmers for efficiency reason.

In this direction, the research has given rise to several industrial tools such as CAVEAT [19] or PolySpace.

## 7   Concluding Remarks

We described a refinement-based approach to verify the conformance of a Java Card native function *w.r.t.* their specification. The main idea is to use three intermediate models: the FSP model describes the expected input and output of the function (basing on the informal specification), the HLD model defines the algorithm of the function on an abstract JCVM, and the LLD model refines this algorithm on a concrete JCVM implementation. The refinement steps between two adjacent models are formally proved in Coq. This approach can be applied as well to the bytecode interpretation because a native function is actually a programmer-customized extension to the Java Card instruction set.

The two state machines (FIVM and CVM) used in this work were built during the French-funded FORMAVIE research project to fulfill the Common Criteria requirements [20] on the JCVM development. Using these models, we showed the conformance of the Java Card interpreter and linker developed in Axalto *w.r.t.* the JCVM specification (by Sun). The verification of the native API methods is an extension of this project and is an ongoing work. Actually, the set of native API methods varies between different implementations (this set is not precisely defined in the API specification) but for many methods, only a native implementation can be satisfactory in terms of performance and/or security (*e.g.*, the update operation on arrays or the PIN operations). We based on the Axalto implementation to built the LLD model. On the contrary, the higher-level FSP and HLD models are abstract and can be used for checking other implementations. Furthermore, both of these models can be used to reason on the high-level security properties of the native functions and of the JCVM platform.

## References

1. J. van der Berg, B. Jacobs, and E. Poll. Specification of the JavaCard API in JML. In J. Domingo-Ferrer, D. Chan, and A. Watson, editors, *Proc. of CARDIS'00*, pages 135–154. Kluwer Academic Publishers, 2000.
2. H. Meijer and E. Poll. Towards a Full Specification of the Java Card API. In I. Attali and T. Jensen, editors, *Smart Card Programming and Security*, volume 2140 of *Lecture Notes in Computer Science*, pages 165–178. Springer-Verlag, September 2001.
3. L. Burdy, J-L. Lanet, and A. Requet. Java Applet Correctness: A Developer-Oriented Approach. In K. Araki, S. Gnesi, and D. Mandrioli, editors, *Proc. of FME'03*, volume 2805 of *Lecture Notes in Computer Science*, pages 422–439. Springer-Verlag, September 2003.
4. The Java Modeling Language (JML) homepage. http://www.cs.iastate.edu/~leavens/JML/
5. L. Burdy and A. Requet. Jack : Java Applet Correctness Kit, 2002. Available at http://www.gemplus.com/smart/rd/publications/pdf/BR02jack.pdf.

6. D. Bert, S. Boulm, M-L. Potet, A. Requet, and L. Voisin. Adaptable Translator of B Specifications to Embedded C Programs. In K. Araki, S. Gnesi, and D. Mandrioli, editors, *Proc. of FME 2003*, volume 2805 of *Lecture Notes in Computer Science*, pages 94–113. Springer-Verlag, 2003.

7. The Coq Development Team. *The Coq Proof Assistant*. http://coq.inria.fr/.

8. C. A. R. Hoare. An axiomatic basis for computer programming. *Communications of the ACM*, 12(10):576–580, 1969.

9. B. Venners. *Inside the Java Virtual Machine, 1st edition*. McGraw-Hill Professional, 1999.

10. Sun Microsystems. *Java Card 2.2 Runtime Environment Specification*, 2002. http://www.javasoft.com/products/javacard.

11. G. Barthe, P. Courtieu, G. Dufay, and S. M. de Sousa. Tool-Assisted Specification and Verification of the JavaCard Platform. In H. Kirchner and C. Ringeissen, editors, *Proc. of AMAST'2002*, volume 2422 of *Lecture Notes in Computer Science*, pages 41–59. Springer-Verlag, 2002.

12. G. Barthe and G. Dufay. A Tool-Assisted Framework for Certified Bytecode Verification. In M. Wermelinger and T. Margaria-Steffen, editors, *Proceedings of FASE'04*, volume 2984 of *Lecture Notes in Computer Science*, pages 99–113. Springer-Verlag, 2004.

13. J. Andronick, B. Chetali, and O. Ly. Using Coq to Verify Java Card Applet Isolation Properties. In David A. Basin and Burkhart Wolff, editors, *Proc. of TPHOLs'03*, volume 2758 of *Lecture Notes in Computer Science*, pages 335–351. Springer-Verlag, September 2003.

14. G. Barthe and T. Rezk. Non-interference for a JVM-like language. In Manuel Fähndrich, editor, *Proceedings of TLDI'05*, pages 103–112. ACM Press, 2005.

15. M. Eluard and T. Jensen. Secure object flow analysis for java card. In P. Honeyman, editor, *Proc. of CARDIS'02*. IFIP/USENIX, 2002.

16. M. Pavlova, G. Barthe, L. Burdy, M. Huisman, and J.-L. Lanet. Enforcing high-level security properties for applets. In P. Paradinas and J.-J. Quisquater, editors, *Proceedings of CARDIS'04*. Kluwer Academic Publishers, August 2004.

17. J. Andronick, B. Chetali, and C. Paulin-Mohring. Formal verification of security properties of smart card embedded source code. In J. Fitzgerald, I. J. Hayes, and A. Tarlecki, editors, *Proc. of FM'05*, volume 3582 of *Lecture Notes in Computer Science*, pages 302–317. Springer-Verlag, 2005.

18. A. Sabelfeld and A. C. Myers. Language-based information-flow security. *IEEE J. Selected Areas in Communications*, 21(1):5–19, January 2003.

19. The Caveat Project. http://www-drt.cea.fr/Pages/List/lse/LSL/Caveat/index.html/

20. Common Criteria. http://www.commoncriteria.org/.

# A Low-Footprint Java-to-Native Compilation Scheme Using Formal Methods

Alexandre Courbot[1], Mariela Pavlova[2], Gilles Grimaud[1],
and Jean-Jacques Vandewalle[3]

[1] IRCICA/LIFL, Univ. Lille 1, INRIA futurs, POPS Research Group, France
{Alexandre.Courbot, Gilles.Grimaud}@lifl.fr
[2] INRIA Sophia-Antipolis, Everest Research Group, France
Mariela.Pavlova@sophia.inria.fr
[3] Gemplus Systems Research Labs, La Ciotat, France
Jean-Jacques.Vandewalle@research.gemplus.com

**Abstract.** Ahead-of-Time and Just-in-Time compilation are common ways to improve runtime performances of restrained systems like Java Card by turning critical Java methods into native code. However, native code is much bigger than Java bytecode, which severely limits or even forbids these practices for devices with memory constraints.

In this paper, we describe and evaluate a method for reducing natively-compiled code by suppressing runtime exception check sites, which are emitted when compiling bytecodes that may potentially throw runtime exceptions. This is made possible by completing the Java program with JML annotations, and using a theorem prover in order to formally prove that the compiled methods never throw runtime exceptions. Runtime exception check sites can then safely be removed from the generated native code, as it is proved they will never be entered.

We have experimented our approach on several card-range and embedded Java applications, and were able to remove almost all the exception check sites. Results show memory footprints for native code that are up to 70% smaller than the non-optimized version, and sometimes as low than 115% the size of the Java bytecode when compiled for ARM thumb.

## 1 Introduction

Enabling Java on embedded and restrained systems is an important challenge for today's industry and research groups [1]. Java brings features like execution safety and low-footprint program code that make this technology appealing for embedded devices which have obvious memory restrictions, as the success of Java Card witnesses. However, the memory footprint and safety features of Java come at the price of a slower program execution, which can be a problem when the host device already has a limited processing power. As of today, the interest of Java for smart cards is still growing, with next generation operating systems for smart cards that are closer to standard Java systems [2, 3], but runtime performance in still an issue. To improve the runtime performance of Java systems, a common practice is to translate some parts of the program bytecode into native code.

J. Domingo-Ferrer, J. Posegga, and D. Schreckling (Eds.): CARDIS 2006, LNCS 3928, pp. 329–344, 2006.
© IFIP International Federation for Information Processing 2006

Doing so removes the interpretation layer and improves the execution speed, but also greatly increases the memory footprint of the program: it is expected that native code is about three to four times the size of its Java counterpart, depending on the target architecture. This is explained by the less-compact form of native instructions, but also by the fact that many safety-checks that are implemented by the virtual machine must be reproduced in the native code. For instance, before dereferencing a pointer, the virtual machine checks whether it is null and, if it is, throws a NullPointerException. Every time a bytecode that implements such safety behaviors is compiled into native code, these behaviors must be reproduced as well, leading to an explosion of the code size. Indeed, a large part of the Java bytecode implement these safety mechanisms.

Although the runtime checks are necessary to the safety of the Java virtual machine, they are most of the time used as a protection mechanism against programming errors or malicious code: A runtime exception should be the result of an exceptional, unexpected program behavior and is rarely thrown when executing sane code - doing so is considered poor programming practice. The safety checks are therefore without effect most of the time, and, in the case of native code, uselessly bloat the code.

Several studies proposed to factorize these checks or in some case to eliminate them, but none proposed a complete elimination without hazarding the system security. In this paper, we use formal proofs to ensure that run-time checks can never be true into a program, which allows us to completely and safely eliminate them from the generated native code. The programs to optimize are JML-annotated against runtime exceptions and verified by the Java Applet Correctness Kit (JACK [4]). We have been able to remove almost all of the runtime checks on tested programs, and obtained native ARM thumb code which size was comparable to the original bytecode.

The remainder of this paper is organized as follows. In section 2, we overview the methods used for compiling Java bytecode into native code, and evaluate the previous work aiming at optimizing runtime exceptions in the native code. Then, section 3 describes our method for removing runtime exceptions on the basis of formal proofs. We experimentally evaluate this method in section 4, discuss its limitations in 5 and conclude in 6.

## 2    Java and Ahead-of-Time Compilation

Compiling Java into native code is a common practice in the embedded domain. This section gives an overview of the different compilation techniques of Java programs, and points out the issue of runtime exceptions. We are then looking at how existing solutions address this issue.

### 2.1    Ahead-of-Time and Just-in-Time Compilation

Ahead-of-Time (AOT) compilation is a common way to improve the efficiency of Java programs. It is related to Just-in-Time (JIT) compilation by the fact that both processes take Java bytecode as input and produce native code that the architecture running the virtual machine can directly execute. AOT and JIT compilation differ by the time at which the compilation occurs. JIT compilation is done, as its name states, just-in-time by the virtual machine, and must therefore be performed within a short period of time which leaves little room for optimizations. The output of JIT compilation is machine-language. On the contrary, AOT compilation compiles the Java bytecode way before the program is run, and links the native code with the virtual machine. In other words, it translates non-native methods into native methods (usually C code) prior to the whole system execution. AOT compilers either compile the Java program entirely, resulting in a 100% native program without a Java interpreter, or can just compile a few important methods. In the latter case, the native code is usually linked with the virtual machine. AOT compilation has no or few time constraints, and can generate optimized code. Moreover, the generated code can take advantage of the C compiler's own optimizations.

JIT compilation in interesting by several points. For instance, there is no prior choice about which methods must be compiled: the virtual machine compiles a method when it appears that doing so is beneficial, e.g. because the method is called often. However, JIT compilation requires embedding a compiler within the virtual machine, which needs resources to work and writable memory to store the compiled methods. Moreover, the compiled methods are present twice in memory: once in bytecode form, and another time in compiled form. While this scheme is efficient for decently-powerful embedded devices such as PDAs, it is inapplicable to very restrained devices like smartcards or sensors. For them, ahead-of-time compilation is usually preferred because it does not require a particular support from the embedded virtual machine outside of the ability to run native methods, and avoids method duplication. AOT compilation has some constraints, too: the compiled methods must be known in advance, and dynamically-loading new native methods is forbidden, or at least very unsafe.

Both JIT and AOT compilers must produce code that exactly mimics the behavior of the Java virtual machine. In particular, the safety checks performed on some bytecodes must also be performed in the generated code.

## 2.2   Java Runtime Exceptions

The JVM (Java Virtual Machine) [5] specifies a safe execution environment for Java programs. Contrary to native execution, which does not automatically control the safety of the program's operations, the Java virtual machine ensures that every instruction operates safely. The Java environment may throw predefined runtime exceptions at runtime, like the following ones:

NullPointerException This exception is thrown when the program tries to dereference a null pointer. Among the instructions that may throw this exceptions are: getfield, putfield, invokevirtual, invokespecial, and the set of *type*astore instructions[1].

---

[1] The JVM instructions are parametrized, thus we denote by *type*astore the set of array store instructions, which includes iastore, sastore, lastore, ...

**ArrayIndexOutOfBoundsException** If an array is accessed out of its bounds, this exception is thrown to prevent the program from accessing an illegal memory location. According to the Java Virtual Machine specification, the instructions of the family *type*astore and *type*aload may throw such an exception.

**ArithmeticException** This exception is thrown when exceptional arithmetic conditions are met. Actually, there is only one such case that may occur during runtime, namely the division of an integer by zero, which may be done by idiv, irem, ldiv and lrem.

**NegativeArraySizeException** Thrown when trying to allocate an array of negative size. newarray, anewarray and multianewarray may throw this exception.

**ArrayStoreException** Thrown when an object is attempted to be stored into an array of incompatible type. This exception may be thrown by the aastore instruction.

**ClassCastException** Thrown when attempting to cast an object to an incompatible type. The checkcast instruction may throw this exception.

**IllegalMonitorStateException** Thrown when the current thread is not the owner of a released monitor, typically by monitorexit.

If the JVM detects that executing the next instruction would result in an inconsistency or an illegal memory access, it throws a runtime exception, that may be caught by the current method or by other methods on the current stack. If the exception is not caught, the virtual machine exits. This safe execution mode implies that many checks are made during runtime to detect potential inconsistencies. For instance, the aastore bytecode, which stores an object reference into an array, may throw three different exceptions: NullPointerException, ArrayIndexOutOfBoundsException, and ArrayStoreException.

Of the 202 bytecodes defined by the Java virtual machine specification, we noticed that 43 require at least one runtime exception check before being executed. While these checks are implicitly performed by the bytecode interpreter in the case of interpreted code, they must explicitly be issued every time such a bytecode is compiled into native code, which leads to a code size explosion. Ishizaki et al. measured that bytecodes requiring runtime checks are frequent in Java programs: for instance, the natively-compiled version of the SPECjvm98 compress benchmark has 2964 exception check sites for a size of 23598 bytes. As for the mpegaudio benchmark, it weights 38204 bytes and includes 6838 exception sites [6]. The exception check sites therefore make a non-neglectable part of the compiled code.

Figure 1 shows an example of Java bytecode that requires a runtime check to be issued when being compiled into native code.

It is, however, possible to eliminate these checks from the native code if the execution context of the bytecode shows that the exceptional case never happens. In the program of figure 1, the lines 2 and 3 could have been omitted if we were sure that for all possible program paths, j can never be equal to zero at this point. This allows to generate less code and thus to save memory. Removing

| Java version: | | C version: |
|---|---|---|
| iload i | 1 | int i, j; |
| iload j | 2 | if (j == 0) |
| idiv | 3 | THROW(ArithmeticException); |
| ireturn | 4 | RETURN_INT(i / j); |

**Fig. 1.** A Java bytecode program and its (simplified) C-compiled version. The behavior of the division operator in Java must be entirely reproduced by the C program, which leads to the generation of a runtime exception check site.

exception check sites is a topic that has largely been studied in the domain of JIT and AOT compilation.

## 2.3 Related Work

Toba [7] is a Java-to-C compiler that transforms a whole Java program into a native one. Harissa [8] is a Java environment that includes a Java-to-C compiler as well as a virtual machine, and therefore supports mixed execution. While both environments implement some optimizations, they are not able to detect and remove unused runtime checks during ahead-of-time compilation. The "Java? C!" (JC$^2$) Virtual Machine [9] is a Java virtual machine implementation that converts class files into C code using the Soot [10] framework, and runs their compiled version. It supports redundant exceptions checks removal, and is tuned for runtime performance, by using operating system signals in order to detect exceptional conditions like null pointer dereferencing. This allows to automatically remove most of the `NullPointerException`-related checks.

In [11] and [12], Hummel et al. use a Java compiler that annotates bytecodes with higher-level information known during compile-time in order to improve the efficiency of generated native code. [6] proposes methods for optimizing exceptions handling in the case of JIT compiled native code. These works rely on knowledge that can be statically inferred either by the Java compiler or by the JIT compiler. In doing so, they manage to efficiently factorize runtime checks, or in some cases to remove them. However, they are still limited to the context of the compiled method, and do not take the whole program into account. Indeed, knowing properties about a the parameters of a method can help removing further checks.

We propose to go further than these approaches, by giving more precise directives as to how the program behaves in the form of JML annotations. These annotations are then used to get formal behavioral proofs of the program, which guarantee that runtime checks can safely be eliminated for ahead-of-time compilation.

---

[2] In the remainder of this paper, the *JC* abbreviation is always used to refer to the *"Java? C!"* virtual machine, and never to *JavaCard*.

# 3    Optimizing Ahead-of-Time Compiled Java Code

For verifying the bytecode that will be compiled into native code, we use the JACK verification framework (short for Java Applet Correctness Kit). JACK is designed as a plugin for the Eclipse interface development environment. It supports both the Java Modeling Language (JML [13]) and the ByteCode Specification Language (BCSL [14]), respectively at source and bytecode level, and also supplies a compiler from JML to BCSL. The tool supports only the sequential subset of the Java and Java bytecode languages, but this is sufficient for the purpose of the present paper. Thus, from a Java program annotated with JML or a bytecode program annotated with BCSL, JACK generates proof obligations at the source or bytecode level respectively. JACK can then translate the resulting verification conditions for several theorem provers: Coq, Simplify, Atelier B.

Verifying that a bytecode program does not throw Runtime exceptions using JACK involves several stages:

1. Writing the JML specification at the source level of the application, which expresses that no runtime exceptions are thrown.
2. Compiling the Java sources and their JML specification[3].
3. Generating the verification conditions over the bytecode and its BCSL specification, and proving the verification conditions. During the calculation process of the verification conditions, they are indexed with the index of the instruction in the bytecode array they refer to and the type of specification they prove (e.g. that the proof obligation refers to the exceptional postcondition in case an exception of type Exc is thrown when executing the instruction at index i in the array of bytecode instructions of a given method). Once the verifications are proved, information about which instructions can be compiled without runtime checks is inserted in user defined attributes of the class file.
4. Using these class file attributes in order to optimize the generated native code. When a bytecode that has one or more runtime checks in its semantics is being compiled, the bytecode attribute is queried in order to make sure that the checks are necessary. If it indicates that the exceptional condition has been proved to never happen, then the runtime check is not generated.

Our approach benefits from the accurateness of the JML specification and from the bytecode verification condition generator. Performing the verification over the bytecode allows to easily establish a relationship between the proof obligations generated over the bytecode and the bytecode instructions to optimize.

In the rest of this section, we explain in detail all the stages of the optimization procedure.

---

[3] The BCSL specification is inserted in user defined attributes in the class file and so does not violate the class file format.

## 3.1   JML Annotations

JML is a rich behavioral interface specification language, similar to Java and designed for it, that follows the design by contract paradigm [15]. Among the features that JML supports and which we use in this study are:

**Method preconditions.** The method precondition states what must hold when the method is called, i.e. the precondition must hold at every method call site.

**Method postconditions.** JML allows to specify both the exceptional and normal terminations of a method. One can express which property should hold if a method terminates normally and which property should hold if a method terminates by throwing an exception. The exceptional and normal postconditions state what the method guarantees after its execution and are verified when establishing the correctness of the method implementation.

**Class invariants.** These properties must be established at every visible program state. In particular, the property must hold before and after every method call. The class invariant is not required to hold before calling the class constructor, but must hold once the constructor returns.

**Loop invariants and loop frame conditions.** A loop invariant is a predicate that must hold every time the corresponding loop entry is reached. The loop frame condition states which locations are modified by the loop.

## 3.2   Methodology for Writing a Specification Against Runtime Exceptions

We now illustrate with an example which annotations must be generated in order to check if a method may throw an exception. Figure 2[4] shows a Java method annotated with a JML specification. The method `clear` declared in class `Code_Table` receives an integer parameter `size` and assigns 0 to all the elements in the array field `tab` whose indexes are smaller than the value of the parameter `size`. The specification of the method guarantees that if every caller respects the method precondition and if every execution of the method guarantees its postcondition then the method `clear` never throws an exception of type or subtype `java.lang.Exception`[5]. This is expressed by the class and method specification contracts. First, a class invariant is declared which states that once an instance of type `Code_Table` is created, its array field `tab` is not null. The class invariant guarantees that no method will throw a `NullPointerException` when dereferencing (directly or indirectly) `tab`.

The method precondition requires the `size` parameter to be smaller than the length of `tab`. The normal postcondition, introduced by the keyword `ensures`, basically says that the method will always terminate normally, by declaring that the set of final states in case of normal termination includes all the possible final states, i.e. that the predicate `true` holds after the method's normal

---

[4] Although the analysis that we describe is on bytecode level, for the sake of readability, the examples are also given on source level.

[5] Note that every Java runtime exception is a subclass of `java.lang.Exception`.

```
final class Code_Table {
  private/*@spec_public */short tab[];

  //@invariant tab != null;

  ...

  //@requires size <= tab.length;
  //@ensures true;
  //@exsures (Exception) false;
  public void clear(int size) {
1   int code;
2   //@loop_modifies code, tab[*];
3   //@loop_invariant code <= size && code >= 0;
4   for (code = 0; code < size; code++) {
5     tab[code] = 0;
    }
  }
}
```

**Fig. 2.** A JML-annotated method

execution[6]. On the other hand, the exceptional postcondition for the exception java.lang.Exception says that the method will not throw any exception of type java.lang.Exception (which includes all runtime exceptions). This is done by declaring that the set of final states in the exceptional termination case is empty, i.e. the predicate false holds if an exception caused the termination of the method. The loop invariant says that the array accesses are between index 0 and index size - 1 of the array tab, which guarantees that no loop iteration will cause an ArrayIndexOutOfBoundsException since the precondition requires that size <= tab.length.

### 3.3   Compiling JML Annotations into BCSL Specifications

Once the source code is completed by the JML specification, the Java source is compiled using a normal non-optimizing Java compiler that generates debug information like *LineNumberTable* and *LocalVariableTable*, needed for compiling the JML annotations. From the resulting class file and the specified source file, the JML annotations are compiled into BCSL and inserted into user-defined attributes of the class file. Figure 3 gives the bytecode version of the clear method shown earlier and its BSCL specification. In the example, lv[0] stands for the this instance and lv[1] stands for the first parameter that the method receives. A detailed description of the JML compiler can be found in [14].

---

[6] Actually, after terminating execution the method guarantees that the first size elements of the array tab will be equal to 0, but as this information is not relevant to proving that the method will not throw runtime exceptions we omit it.

```
//@invariant tab(lv[0]) != null;

...

//@requires lv[1] <= length(tab(lv[0]));
//@ensures true;
//@exsures (Exception) false;

method clear

 0 iconst_0
 1 istore_2
 2 goto 15
 5 aload_0
 6 getfield tab
 9 iload_2
10 iconst_0
11 sastore
12 iinc 2 by 1
15 iload_2
16 iload_1
17 if_icmplt 5
20 return
```

**Fig. 3.** The specified bytecode of method `clear`

### 3.4   Generation of the Verification Conditions

In order to generate the verification conditions, we use a bytecode verification condition generator (vcGen) based on a bytecode weakest precondition calculus [14]. The weakest precondition function $wp$ returns, for every instruction ins, normal postcondition $\psi$, and exceptional function $\psi^{exc}$ the weakest predicate $wp(\text{ins}, \psi, \psi^{exc})$ such that if it holds in the pre-state of the instruction ins and if the instruction terminates normally, then the normal postcondition $\psi$ holds in the poststate and if ins terminates on an exception Exc, then the predicate $\psi^{exc}(\text{Exc})$ holds. From the annotated bytecode the vcGen calculates a set of verification conditions for every method of the application. The verification conditions for a method are generated by tracing all the execution paths in it starting at every return, athrow and loop end instruction up to reaching the method entry point. During the process of generation of the verification conditions, for every instruction that may throw a runtime exception a new verification condition is generated.

In figure 4, we show the weakest precondition rule for the getfield instruction. As the virtual machine is stack-based, the rule mentions the stack stack and the stack counter cntr, thus the stack top element is referred as stack(cntr). If the top stack element stack(cntr) is not null, getfield pops stack(cntr) which is an object reference and pushes the value of the referenced field onto the operand stack in stack(cntr). If the stack top element is null, the

$$wp(ind : \texttt{getfield Cl.f}, \ \psi, \ \psi^{exc}) =$$
$$\texttt{stack(cntr)} \neq \texttt{null} \Rightarrow$$
$$\psi\,[\texttt{stack(cntr)} \leftarrow \texttt{Cl.f(stack( cntr))}]$$
$$\left( \begin{array}{l} \wedge \\ ind : \texttt{stack(cntr)} = \texttt{null} \Rightarrow \\ \quad \psi^{exc}(\texttt{NullPointerException}) \begin{array}{l} [\texttt{cntr} \leftarrow 0] \\ [\texttt{stack(0)} \leftarrow \texttt{ref}_{\texttt{NullPointer}}] \end{array} \end{array} \right)$$

**Fig. 4.** The weakest precondition rule for the `putfield` instruction

Java Virtual Machine specification says that the `getfield` instruction throws a `NullPointerException`.

When the verification condition generator works over a method, it labels the formula related to the exceptional termination of every instruction with the index of the instruction in the bytecode array of the method. For example, if a `getField` instruction is met in the bytecode of a method, a conjunction is generated and the conjunct related to the exception is labeled as shown by figure 4. Finally, indexing the verification conditions allows to identify later in the proof phase which instructions can be optimized.

Another important point is that the underlying vcGen is proved to be correct [14], thus our methodology also correctly performs optimizations.

### 3.5   From Program Proofs to Program Optimizations

In this phase, the bytecode instructions that can safely be executed without runtime checks are identified. Depending on the complexity of the verification conditions, Jack can discharge them to the fully automatic prover Simplify, or to the Coq and AtelierB interactive theorem prover assistants.

There are several conditions to be met for a bytecode instruction to be optimized safely – the precondition of the method the instruction belongs to must hold every time the method is invoked, and the verification condition related to the exceptional termination must also hold. In order to give a flavor of the

$$\begin{array}{l} \ldots \\ \texttt{length(tab(lv[0])}) \leq \texttt{lv[2]}_{15} \vee \texttt{lv[2]}_{15} < 0 \\ \wedge \\ \texttt{lv[2]}_{15} \geq 0 \\ \wedge \\ \texttt{lv[2]}_{15} < \texttt{lv[1]} \\ \wedge \\ \texttt{lv[1]} \leq \texttt{length(tab(lv[0]))} \end{array} \qquad \Rightarrow false$$

**Fig. 5.** The verification condition for the `ArrayIndexOutOfBoundException` check related to the `sastore` instruction of figure 3

verification conditions we deal with, figure 5 shows part of the verification condition related to the possible `ArrayIndexOutOfBounds` exceptional termination of instruction `11 sastore` in figure 3, which is actually provable.

Once identified, proved instructions can be marked in user-defined attributes of the class file so that the compiler can find them.

### 3.6   More Precise Optimizations

As we discussed earlier, in order to optimize an instruction in a method body, the method precondition must be established at every call site and the method implementation must be proved not to throw an exception under the assumption that the method precondition holds. This means that if there is one call site where the method precondition is broken then no instruction in the method body will be optimized.

Actually, the analysis may be less conservative and therefore more precise. We illustrate with an example how one can achieve more precise results.

Consider the example of figure 6. On the left side of the figure, we show source code for method `setTo0` which sets the `buff` array element at index k to 0. On the right side, we show the bytecode of the same method. The `iastore` instruction at index 3 may throw two different runtime exceptions: `NullPointerException`, or `ArrayIndexOutOfBoundException`. For the method execution to be safe (i.e. no runtime exception is thrown), the method requires some conditions to be fulfilled by its callers. Thus, the method's precondition states that the `buff` array parameter must not be null and that the k parameter must be inside the bounds of `buff`. If at all call sites we can establish that the `buff` parameter is always different from null, but there are sites at which an unsafe parameter k is passed, the optimization for `NullPointerException` is still safe although the optimization for `ArrayIndexOutOfBoundException` is not possible. In order to obtain this kind of preciseness, a solution is to classify the preconditions of a method with respect to what kind of runtime exception they protect the code from. For our example, this classification consists of two groups of preconditions. The first is related to `NullPointerException`, i.e. `buff != null` and the second consists of preconditions related to `ArrayIndexOutOfBoundException`, i.e.

. . .

```
//@requires buff != null;
//@requires k >= 0 ;                    0 aload_2
//@requires k <= buff.length;          1 iload_1
//@ensures true;                        2 iconst_0
//@exsures (Exception) false;          3 iastore
public void setTo0(int k,int[] buff)   4 return
{
  buff[k] = 0;
}
```

**Fig. 6.** The source code and bytecode of a method that may throw several exceptions

`k >= 0 && k <= buff.length`. Thus, if the preconditions of one group are established at all call sites, the optimizations concerning the respective exception can be performed even if the preconditions concerning other exceptions are not satisfied.

# 4    Experimental Results

This section presents an application and evaluation of our method on various Java programs.

## 4.1    Methodology

We have measured the efficiency of our method on two kinds of programs, that implement features commonly met in restrained and embedded devices. `crypt` and `banking` are two smartcard-range applications. `crypt` is a cryptography benchmark from the Java Grande benchmarks suite, and `banking` is a little banking application with full JML annotations used in [4]. `scheduler` and `tcpip` are two embeddable system components written in Java, which are actually used in the JITS [16] platform. `scheduler` implements a threads scheduling mechanism, where scheduling policies are Java classes. `tcpip` is a TCP/IP stack entirely written in Java, that implements the TCP, UDP, IP, SLIP and ICMP protocols. These two components are written with low-footprint in mind ; however, the overall system performance would greatly benefit from having them available in native form, provided the memory footprint cost is not too important.

For every program, we have followed the methodology described in section 3 in order to prove that runtime exceptions are not thrown in these programs. We look at both the number of runtime exception check sites that we are able to remove from the native code, and the impact on the memory footprint of the natively-compiled methods with respect to the unoptimized native version and the original bytecode. The memory footprint measurements were obtained by compiling the C source file generated by the JITS ahead-of-time (AOT) compiler using GCC 4.0.0 with optimization option -Os, for the ARM platform in thumb mode. The native methods sizes are obtained by inspecting the .o file with `nm`, and getting the size for the symbol corresponding to the native method.

Regarding the number of eliminated exception check sites, we also compare our results with the ones obtained using the JCk virtual machine mentioned in 2.3, version 1.4.6. The results were obtained by running the `jcgen` program on the benchmark classes, and counting the number of explicit exception check sites in the generated C code. We are not comparing the memory footprints obtained with the JITS and JC AOT compilers, for this result would not be relevant. Indeed, JC and JITS have very different ways to generate native code. JITS targets low memory footprint, and JC runtime performance. As a consequence, a runtime exception check site in JC is heavier than one in JITS, which would falsify the experiments. Suffices to say that our approach could be applied on any AOT compiler, and that the most relevant measurement is the number of runtime exception check sites that remains in the final binary - our measurements on the native code memory footprint are just here to evaluate the size impact of exception check sites.

## 4.2 Results

Table 1 shows the results obtained on the four tested programs. The three first columns indicate the number of check sites present in the bytecode, the number of explicit check sites emitted by JC, and the number of check sites that we were unable to prove useless and that must be present in our optimized AOT code. The last columns give the memory footprints of the bytecode, unoptimized native code, and native code from which all proved exception check sites are removed.

**Table 1.** Number of exception check sites and memory footprints when compiled for ARM thumb

| Program | # of exception check sites | | | Memory footprint (bytes) | | |
|---------|----------|-----|-----------|----------|-----------|-----------|
|         | Bytecode | JC  | Proven AOT | Bytecode | Naive AOT | Proven AOT |
| crypt     | 190  | 79  | 1 | 1256  | 5330  | 1592  |
| banking   | 170  | 12  | 0 | 2320  | 5634  | 3582  |
| scheduler | 215  | 25  | 0 | 2208  | 5416  | 2504  |
| tcpip     | 1893 | 288 | 0 | 15497 | 41540 | 18064 |

On all the tested programs, we were able to prove that all but one exception check site could be removed. The only site that we were unable to prove from crypt is linked to a division, which divisor is a computed value that we were unable to prove not equal to zero. JC has to retain 16% of all the exception check sites, with a particular mention for crypt, which is mainly made of array accessed and has more remaining check sites.

The memory footprints obtained clearly show the heavy overhead induced by exception check sites. Despite of the fact that the exception throwing convention has deliberately been simplified for our experiments, optimized native code is less than half the size of the non-optimized native code. The native code of crypt, which heavily uses arrays, is actually made of exception checking code at 70%.

Comparing the size of the optimized native versions with the bytecode reveals that proved native code is just slightly bigger than bytecode. The native code of crypt is 27% bigger than its bytecode version. Native scheduler only weights 13.5% more that its bytecode, tcpip 16.5%, while banking is 54% heavier. This last result is explained by the fact that, being an application and not a system componant, banking includes many native-to-java method invocations for calling system services. The native-to-java calling convention is costly in JITS, which artificially increases the result.

Finally, table 2 details the human work required to obtain the proofs on the benchmark programs, by comparing the amount of JML code with respect to

**Table 2.** Human work on the tested programs

| Program | Source code size (bytes) | | Proved lemmas | |
|---|---|---|---|---|
| | Code | JML | Automatically | Manually |
| crypt | 4113 | 1882 | 227 | 77 |
| banking | 11845 | 15775 | 379 | 159 |
| scheduler | 12539 | 3399 | 226 | 49 |
| tcpip | 83017 | 15379 | 2233 | 2191 |

the comments-free source code of the programs. It also details how many lemmas had to be manually proved.

On the three programs that are annotated for the unique purpose of our study, the JML overhead is about 30% of the code size. The banking program was annotated in order to prove other properties, and because of this is made of more JML annotations than actual code. Most of the lemmas could be proved by Simplify, but a non-neglectable part needed human-assistance with Coq. The most demanding application was the TCP/IP stack. Because of its complexity, nearly half of the lemmas could not be proved automatically.

The gain in terms of memory footprint obtained using our approach is therefore real. One may also wonder whether the runtime performance of such optimized methods would be increased. We did the measurements, and only noticed a very slight, almost undetectable, improvement of the execution speed of the programs. This is explained by the fact that the exception check sites conditions are always false when evaluated, and therefore the amount of supplementary code executed is very low. The bodies of the proved runtime exception check sites are, actually, dead code that is never executed.

## 5   Limitations

Our approach suffers from some limitations and usage restrictions, regarding its application on multi-threaded programs and in combination with dynamic code loading.

### 5.1   Multi-threaded Programs

As we said in section 3, JACK only supports the sequential subset of Java. Because of this, we are unable to prove check sites related to monitor state checking, that typically throws an IllegalMonitorStateException. However, they can be simplified if it is known that the system will never run more than one thread simultaneously. It should be noted, that Java Card does not make use of multi-threading and thus doesn't suffer from this limitation.

### 5.2   Dynamic Code Loading

Our removal of runtime exception check sites is based on the assumption that a method's preconditions are always respected at all its call sites. For closed systems, it is easy to verify this property, but in the case of open systems which may load and execute any kind of code, the property could not always be ensured. In the case where the set of applications that will run on the system is not statically known, our approach could not be safely applied on public methods since dynamically-loaded code may call them without respecting their preconditions.

### 5.3 Implications Regarding Security

In addition to the two limitations mentioned above, one should also be aware that our method doesn't protect the system from errors injections in the code through hardware attacks. Suppressing dynamic checking on systems that are subject to such attacks would potentially open a security breach.

## 6 Conclusion

The main contribution of the present article is a new Java-to-native code optimization technique based on static program verification using formal methods. The methodology gives more precise and therefore better results than other existing solutions in the field and allows us to remove almost all the exception check sites in the native code, as we show in section 4. The memory footprints of natively-compiled methods thus become comparable with the ones of the original bytecode when compiled in ARM thumb.

Although we applied this work to the ahead-of-time compilation of Java methods, the bytecode annotations could also be interpreted by JIT compilers, which would then also be able to completely get rid of a considerable part of runtime exceptions.

## Acknowledgments

The authors would like to thank Jean-Louis Lanet for kindly providing us with the JML-annotated sources of the banking, scheduler and tcpip programs evaluated in this paper.

## References

1. D. Mulchandani, "Java for embedded systems," *Internet Computing, IEEE*, vol. 2, no. 3, pp. 30 – 39, 1998.
2. L. Lagosanto, "Next-generation embedded java operating system for smart cards," in *4th Gemplus Developer Conference*, 2002.
3. G. Grimaud and J.-J. Vandewalle, "Introducing research issues for next generation Java-based smart card platforms," in *Proc. Smart Objects Conference (sOc'2003)*, (Grenoble, France), 2003.
4. L. Burdy, A. Requet, and J.-L. Lanet, "Java applet correctness: A developer-oriented approach," in *FME 2003: Formal Methods: International Symposium of Formal Methods Europe* (K. Araki, S. Gnesi, and D. Mandrioli, eds.), vol. 2805, pp. 422–439, 2003.

5. T. Lindholm and F. Yellin, *Java Virtual Machine Specification*. Addison-Wesley Longman Publishing Co., Inc., 1999.
6. K. Ishizaki, M. Kawahito, T. Yasue, M. Takeuchi, T. Ogasawara, T. Suganuma, T. Onodera, H. Komatsu, and T. Nakatani, "Design, implementation, and evaluation of optimizations in a just-in-time compiler," in *JAVA '99: Proceedings of the ACM 1999 conference on Java Grande*, (New York, NY, USA), pp. 119–128, ACM Press, 1999.
7. T. A. Proebsting, G. Townsend, P. Bridges, J. H. Hartman, T. Newsham, and S. A. Watterson, "Toba: Java for applications: A way ahead of time (wat) compiler," in *Third USENIX Conference on Object-Oriented Technologies (COOTS)*, (Portland, Oregon), University of Arizona, June 1997.
8. G. Muller, B. Moura, F. Bellard, and C. Consel, "Harissa: a flexible and efficient java environment mixing bytecode and compiled code," in *Third USENIX Conference on Object-Oriented Technologies (COOTS)*, Portland, Oregon: USENIX, June 1997.
9. "JC Virtual Machine." http://jcvm.sourceforge.net/.
10. R. Vallée-Rai, L. Hendren, V. Sundaresan, P. Lam, E. Gagnon, and P. Co, "Soot - a java optimization framework," in *Proceedings of CASCON 1999*, pp. 125–135, 1999.
11. J. Hummel, A. Azevedo, D. Kolson, and A. Nicolau, "Annotating the Java bytecodes in support of optimization," *Concurrency: Practice and Experience*, vol. 9, no. 11, pp. 1003–1016, 1997.
12. A. Azevedo, A. Nicolau, and J. Hummel, "Java annotation-aware just-in-time (ajit) complilation system," in *JAVA '99: Proceedings of the ACM 1999 conference on Java Grande*, (New York, NY, USA), pp. 142–151, ACM Press, 1999.
13. G. T. Leavens, E. Poll, C. Clifton, Y. Cheon, C. Ruby, D. Cok, P. Mller, and J. Kiniry, *JML Reference Manual*, July 2005.
14. M. Pavlova, "Java bytecode logic and specification," tech. rep., INRIA, Sophia-Antipolis, 2005. Draft version.
15. B.Meyer, *Object-Oriented Software Construction*. Prentice Hall, 2 revised ed., 1997.
16. "Java In The Small." http://www.lifl.fr/RD2P/JITS/.

# Automatic Test Generation on a (U)SIM Smart Card

Céline Bigot[1], Alain Faivre[2], Christophe Gaston[2], and Julien Simon[1]

[1] Oberthur Card Systems, R&D – EMC, 71-73 rue des Hautes-Pâtures,
92726 Nanterre Cedex, France
{c.bigot, j.simon}@oberthurcs.com
[2] CEA/LIST, Saclay, F-91191 Gif sur Yvette Cedex, France
{alain.faivre, christophe.gaston}@cea.fr

**Abstract.** Usually, testing smart card software is carried-out by specialized engineers in a proprietary language. Testing represents generally half of smart card development effort. With the increasing use of semi-formal and formal modeling languages, such as UML, and the emergence of automatic test generators in the industry, we have studied a way to adapt these techniques for smart card. In this article, we present an automatic test generator, named AGATHA, and its architecture, which can handle UML specifications. Then, we suggest a way to model (U)SIM smart card functionalities in UML. We use the test generator on our (U)SIM smart card UML models and automatically produce our first test cases.

## 1 Introduction

It's not necessary to remind that in any industry, the later a bug is discovered in a development process, the more it costs to correct it. Today, in the smart card industry, half of the effort of the development activity is devoted to testing. Testing includes:

- unit testing, carried out during the programming activity by programmers, which ensures that each elementary item has a correct behaviour and rules out basic programming errors,
- α-testing, carried out after the programming activity by α-testers, which ensures that smart cards have a correct behaviour compared with the functionalities described in the specifications,
- β-testing, carried out after α-tests by β-testers, which ensures that smart cards in mobile phones, in payment machines or in any other devices also comply with the specifications.

In the context of this long and complex process, handwritten by programmers and testers, we would like to study the possible automatic generation of a part of these tests. Our first idea, described in this article, consists in taking into account the α-test activity. By automatic test generation, we expect to increase the coverage and the quality of the tests in order to ensure a complete validation of the specification.

Moreover, with the increase of system complexity, it's difficult between two versions of a project to know which tests evolve, which ones are obsolete, etc. It's also difficult for a non-tester to understand produced tests. Thus, our idea is to combine automatic test generation with a simple formalism to represent test specifications and their evolution.

J. Domingo-Ferrer, J. Posegga, and D. Schreckling (Eds.): CARDIS 2006, LNCS 3928, pp. 345–358, 2006.

Methods and tools required for validation are not recent, and a lot of researches has been done to try to fill the deficiency. For test generation, we can take as examples [11], [19], [2] and [32]. Semi-formal and formal methods, such as UML [30], B [1] or SDL [20], allow an abstract design for a behavioural specification of the system under test. Thanks to simple, expressive and abstract notations, textual or graphical, we can easily use these types of formalisms to design smart cards. Moreover, these formalisms allow the use of existing validation tools.

The last few years, several studies were conducted on design and validation of smart card software. For example, [8] represents results on the CEPS standard, [3] shows validation results on the GSM 11.11 standard [12], [31] used automated test generation on the WAP Identity Module, [5] describes techniques which can be apply at different levels of smart card software, [6] represents an automatic test generation with the LEIRIOS tool [26] from B specifications, [29] presents a method to automatically generate test for Java card applets and [7] offers a semi formal model of Java Card applications in UML.

In our context, we would like to use a more simple and graphical formalism, which can be used by any engineer. With the emergence of UML in industry and the multiple types of diagrams offered, this formalism represents a good alternative. In the panel of automatic test generators (see [33] for examples of automatic test generators), we were interested by the symbolic approach of the AGATHA[1] tool [17], [25], [34], [4], [28] and [14], developed at the CEA[2]-List.

Therefore, the article is organized as follows. First, we present the AGATHA tool and the automatic test generation. Second, after presenting how we can model a part of smart card in UML, we describe the use of AGATHA on our semi-formal models and present our first results on a PIN command. We finally conclude and explain our future actions.

## 2  AGATHA, an Automatic Test Generator

There exists several ways to validate system specifications. A first one consists in theorem proving and model checking [9]. These kinds of techniques have successfully proved their use for the validation of critical systems. But two major drawbacks of these techniques remain: for model checking, the combinatorial explosion due to variable domains, and, for theorem proving, the need of high-level skills from the developer, who must be aware of formal method foundations.

Automatic test generation is another way to tackle the problem of system validation. Compliance testing is the most well known part of this domain, which consists in verifying that a system matches its specification. Our first purpose is to validate a system specification, and generate tests in order to execute them on the specification and possibly on the system itself.

Most validation tools use enumerative techniques and are therefore limited by the combinatorial explosion problem when trying to exhaustively identify the numerical

---

[1]  AGATHA : "Atelier de Génération Automatique de Test Holistiques à partir d'Automates" – Automatic holistic tests generation framework for automates.

[2]  CEA: "Commissariat à l'Energie Atomique" – French atomic energy reseach center.

behaviours of a system. Several validation tools focus on verification on particular aspects: test purpose [15], temporal properties [36], etc.

The solution proposed by AGATHA is exhaustive symbolic path coverage. Test generation allows detecting specification deadlocks, unreachable transitions, losses of messages, etc. Moreover, the AGATHA toolset is designed to be as transparent as possible in order to reduce the effort of detection and comprehension of errors. In that context, it is not necessary to be an expert in formal methods, as for model checkers or theorem provers, to interpret AGATHA results and to correct specifications or implementations.

The following subsections present the AGATHA architecture and an overview of the different academic techniques used in order to reach minimal exhaustive path coverage.

## 2.1 General Principles

The AGATHA approach intends to help conception and validation of formal specifications modelled with communicant automata systems. Thus, with symbolic execution techniques, AGATHA computes the exhaustive symbolic behaviour graph of the specification. Then, from this graph, it generates test cases used to debug the specification or to validate the implementation, along with an incremental conception process.

Figure 1 details the AGATHA general architecture.

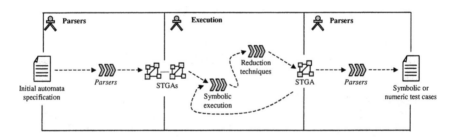

**Fig. 1.** AGATHA general architecture

The tool treats automata specifications and translates it into its internal language, called STGA (Symbolic Transition Graph with Assignment) [27]. This translation allows the symbolic execution of the specification as defined in [18]. Thus, it allows obtaining an exhaustive behaviour graph of the specification. Thanks to reduction techniques defined in [25] and in [34], with the help of the rewriting tool Brute [21], the graph is reduced in a particular STGA. On this particular STGA, AGATHA uses a constraint solver Omega [23] providing for each path of the graph corresponding to a symbolic behaviour, one or more numerical test cases.

## 2.2 Main Principle: Symbolic Execution

At the beginning, symbolic execution has been proposed in [24] and in [10] to construct structural tests for sequential programs. The main idea of symbolic execution consists to use symbols as entry data of the program, denoting any entry data, instead of numerical values and to interpret the entry language in a way that allows manipulating symbolic expressions instead of numerical ones. AGATHA uses an adaptation of symbolic execution to generate tests from specifications based on automata.

The input language of AGATHA is based on the STGA formalism [27], which is a symbolic transition graph. Like graph formalisms, a STGA includes states and transitions. This type of graph allows representing in an abstract manner all behaviours of a specification. Transitions represent events that allow the evolution of the system: events can be received or emitted. Triggering a transition can be conditioned by a logical expression and system variables can evolve.

*STGA Example.* Figure 2 presents a STGA example of an elevator system. It contains four states and seven transitions. The initial state is $Q_0$.

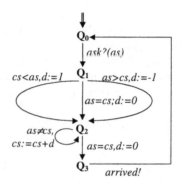

**Fig. 2.** STGA sample of an elevator system

To trigger the output transition of $Q_0$, the elevator system awaits the reception of the message *ask*, denoted *ask?(as)*, which represents a call to a stage by the user in the cabin which is stored in the *as* variable. After the triggering of the transition, the system is in the state $Q_1$. $Q_1$ has three output transitions towards $Q_2$. The left one is conditioned by the logical expression: *cs<as* meaning the asked stage *as* is over (< sign) the current stage represented by the *cs* variable. The right one is conditioned by: *cs>as* meaning the asked stage is under the current stage. The middle one is conditioned by: *cs=as* meaning the asked stage is equal to the current one. In the first case, the elevator moves up the cabin, which is materialized by the operation *d:=1* (d represents the direction), while in the second case, the elevator moves down the cabin, which is materialized by *d:=-1*. In the third one, the elevator leaves the cabin at its current stage, which is materialized by *d:=0*. $Q_2$ has two outgoing transitions: one with $Q_2$ for target and one with $Q_3$. The transition with $Q_2$ for target is conditioned by the logical expression: *as≠cs* and increases the current stage *cs* with the direction *d*, materialized by the operation *cs:=cs+d*. This transition means that as long as the current stage is different from the asked stage, the cabin has to continue to move up or down. The second transition is conditioned by: *as=cs* and initializes the direction *d* to 0. This transition means that if the current stage is equal to the asked stage, the cabin is stopped. The $Q_3$ outgoing transition allows to come back to $Q_0$ and tells the user in the cabin that the elevator has reached the asked stage, which is represented by the emission of the message *arrived*, denoted *arrived!*.                                    ◊

In the AGATHA context, [25] redefines symbolic execution for STGA using the approach defined in [19]. Thus, symbolic execution simulates the behaviour of a STGA specification in assigning symbolic values to variables instead of numerical ones. Then, the specification is executed according to the semantics of each instruction and communication.

The general principle of symbolic execution consists in computing symbolic states of a system, each of them being denoted by a couple *(guard, symbolic memory)*, where:

  - *guard* is the condition needed to reach this symbolic state,
  - *symbolic memory* is a function which associates to each variable of the system an expression based on symbolic input values.

The expression associated to a variable in a symbolic state corresponding to an execution path, from the initial state of the system, is computed by interpreting one by one instructions met all along this execution path. The associated guard is composed of the conjunction of all the execution conditions (denoted by constraints on symbolic input values) met all along the considered execution path. This guard is called a path condition or PC. To simplify this type of expression, AGATHA uses the simplifier Brute [21] extracted from CafeOBJ tool of JAIST[3]. This is a rewriting tool, which transforms terms in normal forms with the help of a set of rewriting rules and evaluation strategies defined by the AGATHA user.

The result of a symbolic execution is a symbolic execution tree where each path represents the symbolic evolution of all variables according to initial symbolic values. Each path is a particular behaviour of the STGA specification.

*Symbolic Execution Example.* In our example of the elevator system presented in Figure 2, an extract of the symbolic execution tree computed by the AGATHA symbolic execution is presented in Figure 3.

At the initialization, the STGA specification obtained by symbolic execution is in a state corresponding to the initial state $Q_0$ of the elevator system. The elevator specification manipulates the variables: *as, cs* and *d* on which there are no initial constraints. A symbolic constant is assigned to each variable: $a_0$, $b_0$ and $c_0$ (resp.) on which there are no initial constraints, denoted by the condition true. The elevator system can evolve if it receives the ask message with a value. This value is stored in the variable *as* and is supposed to have the symbolic value $a_1$. $a_1$ is assigned to the as variable. As the trigger of the transition is not conditioned, the condition to reach this second symbolic state is always true (true ∧ true = true).

To leave the state $Q_1$, there are three transitions. So to leave the symbolic state $Q_1$, there are also three transitions.

As the first transition is conditioned by the expression: *cs<as*, and, as $cs = b_0$ and $as = a_1$ in this state, the condition to reach the symbolic state $Q_2$ corresponds to $b_0 < a_1$. On this transition, 1 is also assigned to *d*, which is reflected in the symbolic state.

---

[3] JAIST: Japan Advanced Institute Technology.

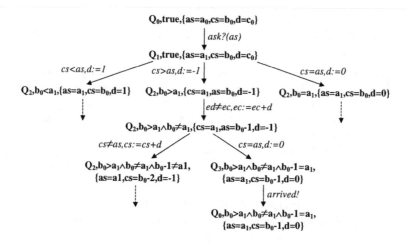

**Fig. 3.** Extract of the symbolic execution of the elevator system

As the second transition is conditioned by the expression: $cs>as$, the condition to reach the symbolic state $Q_2$ corresponds to $b_0>a_1$ and $-1$ is assigned to $d$.

As the third transition is conditioned by the expression: $cs=as$, the condition to reach the symbolic state $Q_2$ corresponds to $b_0=a_1$ and $0$ is assigned to $d$.

To leave the symbolic state $Q_2$ where $d=-1$, two transitions have to be considered. The first one is conditioned by: $as=cs$ and the second one by: $as\neq cs$. However, as $b_0>a_1$, predictably $as\neq cs$ and only the second transition can be triggered. The output transition of the symbolic state $Q_2$ where $d=-1$ leads to another symbolic state $Q_2$ reached if the condition: $b_0>a1$ and $as\neq cs$ is verified and such as $as=a_1$, $cs=b_0-1$ and $d=-1$. In this state, we can also trigger the two same transitions. As the symbolic value of $cs$ evolves, the two transitions can be triggered. The first one leads to the symbolic state $Q_3$ and the second one to another symbolic state $Q_2$. The trigger of the first transition implies that the condition to verify to reach the symbolic state $Q_3$ is: $b_0>a1$ and $as\neq cs$ and $a_1=b_0-1$ and $as=a_1$, $cs=b_0-1$ and $d=0$. To leave this state the only transition is conditioned by the emission of the message *arrived* and allows the system to come back to state $Q_1$.

The other steps of the computation are based on the same principle.                    ◊

## 2.3  Further Techniques

As the symbolic execution tree represents all behaviours of a specification, its construction is subordinated to reduction procedures in order to eliminate as many redundant paths as possible. There exists different tactics such as:

- use a classical graph coverage, as for example a transition coverage (the symbolic execution stops when all the transitions are triggered once if possible), a state coverage, a path coverage, etc,
- cut "empty" path conditions when detected both from a Boolean criteria or polyhedral criteria. AGATHA uses the Omega constraint solver, based on Presburger theory [23] to achieve that,

- avoid computation of a path deductible from another modulo an interleaving detection less sophisticated than in [35]: an internal transition without any temporal constraint with other transitions,
- compute comparison procedures between symbolic nodes and, if necessary for the current calculated nodes, refer to an already existing symbolic node.

These procedures are necessary to avoid the state explosion problem.

AGATHA uses several heuristics to compute comparison procedures for each symbolic node:

- an equality procedure: two symbolic nodes are considered as equivalent if the corresponding control nodes are the same and the symbolic guards are syntactically equal,
- an inclusion procedure: two symbolic nodes are considered as equivalent if the corresponding control nodes are the same and if the polyhedron induced by variable domains defined by the guard of one is included in the other polyhedron,
- an equivalence procedure: two symbolic nodes are considered as equivalent if the corresponding control nodes are the same and if polyhedrons induced by variable domains defined by guards are equal.

As symbolic expressions of variables may also quickly grow, a last simplification procedure must be applied "on-the-fly" in order to shorten expression and to detect useless paths [16]. We use the simplifier Brute, based on rewriting techniques. These rewriting rules actually composed of more than three hundred rules, allow both to maintain symbolic expressions within a reasonable size range and to obtain normal forms of expressions, easing the comparison between expressions needed by algorithms such as comparison procedures.

Other tactics and reduction techniques have been introduced in [34] and in [33]. Generally, a mix of the different tactics is used to obtain the minimal result required to guarantee the entire coverage of the specification.

## 2.4  Test Extraction

Symbolic test cases are extracted from the symbolic execution tree. As each path of the tree represents a symbolic behaviour of the specification, a test case is extracted from each leaf of this symbolic tree. From each symbolic test case, one or more numerical test cases may be produced with the help of constraint resolution techniques used on the path condition associated to the tree leaves. The constraint solver is used to extract the symbolic value of each variable with the associated path condition and to generate numerical values, which respect the path condition. The choice of the constraint solver connected to AGATHA depends on the applicative context. For example, we can use the Omega tool [23].

*Test Extraction Example.* With the symbolic execution of the elevator system, Figure 3, we identify the path: $Q_0Q_1Q_2Q_2Q_3Q_0$, which represents the symbolic test case such as the asked stage, is under the current stage of one stage. To generate a numerical test case corresponding to this symbolic test case, we have to find numerical values for: $a_0, a_1, b_0$ and $c_0$ which verify the path condition: $b_0 > a_1 \land b_0 \neq a_1 \land b_0 - 1 = a_1$.

For example, we can choose: $a_0 = 2$, $a_1 = 3$, $b_0 = 2$ and $c_0 = 0$.

Any other series of numerical values verifying the path condition is valid and forms a possible numerical test case. Techniques used by AGATHA allow considering that every numerical test case contained in a symbolic one are equivalent. So, only one numerical test case by each symbolic one is required to cover all the specification.

Moreover, note that the size of our elevator, which is not defined, doesn't step in the symbolic computation. Thus, our specification allows representing an elevator with two, three or more stages.    ◊

These test cases can be simulated either on industrial tools that allow generating specifications or on implementations. It often requires an adjustment to the adequate formats.

## 3    Application to (U)SIM Smart Card

The aim of this article is to study the utility of the AGATHA tool in the smart card environment. To begin our experience, we shall limit our domain to (U)SIM smart cards. For (U)SIM smart cards, there are different standards, which describe a lot of card features. Function specifications are described in the 3GPP 11.11 standard [12] and tests on these functions are described in the 3GPP 11.17 standard [13]. For Oberthur Card Systems, a test case is a sequence of instructions in a proprietary language, using hexadecimal codes.

In this section, we propose a UML representation for test cases of (U)SIM smart card behaviours. Then, we present results obtained by the application of AGATHA on these UML models.

### 3.1   A UML Representation for (U)SIM Smart Card Tests

As smart card tests consist in sequences of instructions and as we would like to represent smart card tests and smart card behaviours, we propose to use UML state diagrams. For the moment, we only use this type of diagram. It is very intuitive and can be learned very quickly even by a UML uninitiated: it's a sort of automata language, with states and transitions. The trigger of a transition can be conditioned by a message reception, a message emission, a logical expression, etc. For our work, we only use a sub-part and not the entire power of state diagram notations.

Suppose that we would like to represent a test case from the 3GPP 11.17 standard. As for a function, the test is a sequence of instructions. Our corresponding UML state diagram reflects this sequence. In some instances, we can identify sub-parts in a test case and represent these sub-parts in the UML state diagram, as described in the following example.

*The CHANGE CHV[4] Function Example: UML representation for test cases.* Above all, we recall the CHANGE CHV specification extracted of the 3GPP 11.11 standard ([12] p.34):

---

[4]   chv: Card holder verification information; access condition used by the SIM for the verification of the identity of the user.

The CHANGE CHV function assigns a new value to the relevant CHV subject to the following conditions being fulfilled: CHV is not disabled; CHV is not blocked.

The old and new CHV will be presented.

1) If the old CHV presented is correct, the number of remaining CHV attempts for that CHV will be reset to its initial value 3 and the new value for the CHV becomes valid.

2) If the old CHV presented is false, the number of remaining CHV attempts for that CHV will be decremented and the value of the CHV remains unchanged. After 3 consecutive false CHV presentations, not necessarily in the same card session, the respective CHV is blocked and the access condition can never be fulfilled until the UNBLOCK CHV function has been performed successfully on the respective CHV.

Input: indication CHV1, old CHV1, new CHV1.

Output: none.

The test case of the CHANGE CHV function, extracted from the 3GPP 11.17 standard (see [13] pp.65-67), is composed of:

1) An incorrect CHANGE CHV, steady of a status verification: how much attempts remained, a correct CHANGE CHV and a status verification,

2) Two incorrect CHANGE CHV, steady of a reset, an incorrect CHANGE CHV, a reset, an incorrect CHANGE CHV and a correct UNBLOCK CHV,

3) A correct DISABLE CHV, an incorrect CHANGE CHV and a correct ENABLE CHV.

A correct function is characterized by a returned status 90 00 and an incorrect one is characterized by a returned status 98 04 or 98 40, this one meaning that the smart card is blocked. Status verification is done by comparison of expected data and effective data.

The corresponding state diagram is presented in Figure 4. The initial state is •. We suppose that the output transition from the initial state to state A contains data for initializing smart card such as the personalization. A holds two output transitions.

The right one to C is conditioned by the reception of the message *disable_chv(chv1_ref, used_chv1)* which represents the DISABLE CHV function. This transition is also conditioned by the logical expression *used_chv1 = chv1*, which represents the fact that the chv used by DISABLE CHV, is equal to the chv of the card. The expected status for this reception is 90 00. Next transitions represent the sub-case 3 of the CHANGE CHV test.

The left one to B is conditioned by the reception of the message *change_chv(chv1_ref, used_chv1, new_chv1)*, which represents the CHANVE CHV function. This transition is also conditioned by the logical expression *used_chv1 != chv1* which represents the fact that the chv used by CHANGE CHV is not equal to the chv of the card. The expected status for this reception is 98 04. C

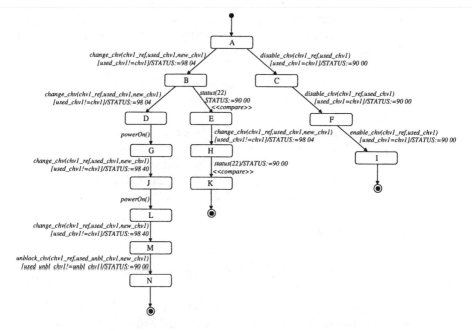

**Fig. 4.** The 3GPP 11.17 test of the CHANGE CHV function

holds two output transitions. The right path represents the sub-case 1 of the CHANGE CHV test and the left one the sub-case 2.

A status verification is represented by a transition conditioned by the reception of message *status(n)* where *n* represents the size of the data to verify, in byte, 22 for our example. The expected status for this reception is 90 00. The data to compare are given in the *<<compare>>* stereotype. For example, on the transition from B to E, the *<<compare>>* stereotype contains: *xxxx xxxx xxxx xx xxxxxx xx xx xx xx xx xx xx xx 83 xxxxxx* which means the 19th byte is 83 and other bytes are any value, denoted x.                                                                                  ◊

## 3.2  A UML Representation for Smart Card Specification

With a UML state diagram, we can also represent a function specification. This diagram contains all the behaviours of a function in the same way as for a test. This abstract vision allows representing a function specification exhaustively. For example, on the CHANGE CHV function, this diagram has to represent a case with a direct correct CHANGE CHV, which is not considered in Figure 4.

*The CHANGE CHV Function Example: UML Representation for Specification.* To represent the CHANGE CHV specification exhaustively, we consider the 3GPP 11.11 standard given before. The corresponding state diagram is presented in Figure 5.

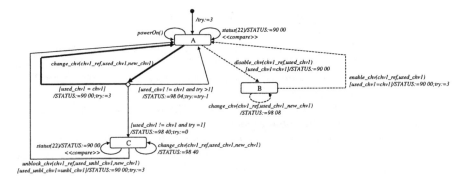

**Fig. 5.** Example of an abstract state-transition diagram for the CHANGE CHV functionalities

As we abstract the behaviour of the function, we introduce a counter *try*, which represents the number of attempts to change a chv. The initial state is •. The output transition of the initial state is improved with the initialization of the *try* variable to 3 as mentioned in the specification.

The sub-case 1 of the specification is represented with bold lines: a *change_chv(chv1_ref, used_chv1, new_chv1)* message is received. The *used_chv1* is equal to *chv1* so the expected status is 90 00, the *chv1* is changed to *new_chv1* and we can verify the status by the transition form A to A with the *status* message. As this diagram is an abstraction of the specification, the *<<compare>>* stereotype contains: *xxxx xxxx xxxx xx xxxxxx xx xx xx xx xx xx xx xx (80+try) xxxxxx*.

The sub-case 2 of the specification is represented with normal lines: a *change_chv* is received. The *used_chv1* is not equal to *chv1* so the expected status is 94 04 if *try* is different from 1 and is 98 40 if *try* is equal to 1. If status is 94 04, the transition goes in A and we can verify the status or reset the session card, which has no impact on the variable *try* and so on the remaining number of attempts to change. If the status is 98 40, the card is blocked and the transition goes in C where we can verify the status and receive *change_chv* messages. As the card is blocked, nothing appends. Except if an *unblock_chv(chv1_ref, used_unblock_chv1, new_chv1)* message is received with *used_unblock_chv1* equal to *unblock_chv1*.

We improved the specification with a behaviour described in the 3GPP 11.17 test but missing in the 3GPP 11.11 specification: the use of a correct DISABLE CHV before a CHANGE CHV. This behaviour is designed with dashed lines.                    ◊

### 3.3  Automatic Test Generation for UML Smart Card Model

In part 2.2, we present how the AGATHA tool can generate automatically test cases. We applied this tool to our UML diagrams.

Firstly, as our representation of smart card test is very sequential, we use a coverage of transitions to compute a set of symbolic test cases. In that case in our example, AGATHA computes three paths. AGATHA extracts three numerical test cases. For a card that validates the 3GPP 11.17 tests, it also validates these automatically generated tests.

Secondly, for our representation of smart card specification, we use a more complicated criterion, the inclusion one to cover all the symbolic behaviours. In that case in our example, AGATHA computes more than two hundred paths, each of them corresponding to a symbolic behaviour. On a card that validates the 3GPP 11.17 tests, it has also to validate these automatically generated tests. It could be impressive to pass two hundred tests for a simple function but we test all possible behaviours of the CHANGE CHV function. Current works on AGATHA will certainly permit to reduce this number of tests with some optimization associated to the inclusion criteria. But in our case this reduction will not be very important due to the fact that the number of distinct symbolic behaviours associated to our example remains very close to the present one calculated by AGATHA: this is the price of exhaustiveness.

## 4  Related Work and Conclusion

In this article, we have summarized a solution to automatically generate tests for smart card functions. Assuming the validity of our approach, we have presented an automatic test generator, AGATHA based on symbolic execution techniques. We have also presented a way to design smart card functions with UML state diagram. We have used AGATHA on our UML diagrams and exposed obtained results. This first experience shows that it is possible to generate tests for smart card functions in an automatic way. Surely, and this is our first objective, our approach has to be used in a real context and in a complete development cycle of a smart card to completely improve its efficiency. We could reasonably hope an increase of the coverage and quality of test for each function taken separately.

Our approach is closed to the one developed in STG [22]. However, in STG, the test purposes must be defined by an expert. In that case, we may obtain « clever » test purposes but we have no way to measure the specification coverage. On the contrary, AGATHA suggests a limited number of predefined test purposes linked to structural or semantical coverage criteria. In that case, the set of generated tests allows to control with a great confidence the level of specification coverage.

LTG, the LEIRIOS test generator [26], uses classical structural coverage criteria which limit the combinatory of generated test cases. AGATHA also proposes criteria based on the analysis of the specification behaviours. Such criteria may be more accurate when generating test cases but can also be more subject to combinatory explosion. To avoid this problem, we are currently introducing some heuristics which allows to reasonably limit the number of generated test cases.

The use of UML state diagrams to design smart card behaviours allows us to consider more global behaviours that mix different smart card functions. Then we test the card rigorously and monitor the results. We also could consider atypical (or negative) tests that allow verifying smart card reactions outside of the admissible input domain defined by the specification. In this context, we could ensure a complete validation of a smart card.

Last point, as AGATHA is not only a test generator, we consider validating smart card properties corresponding to a security policy as defined for example in common criteria. In this context, we could ensure security properties of smart cards.

# Acknowledgements

The authors would like to thanks Clément Simon for his precious help during the development of this project. They also would like to thanks the CARDIS'06 reviewers and David Montouroy for their proofreading and their constructive remarks.

# References

[1]  J.R. Abrial, *The B-Book, Assigning programs to meanings*, Cambridge University Press, 1996

[2]  S. Behnia, H. Waeselynck, *Test criteria definition for B models*, in procs. of the World Congress on Formal Methods (FM'99), vol.1708 of LNCS, pp.509-529, Toulouse (France), 1999

[3]  E. Bernard, B. Legeard, X. Luck, F. Peureux, *Generation of test sequences from formal specifications: GSM 11.11 standard case-study*, The Journal of Software Practice and Experience, vol.34.10 pp.915-948, 2004

[4]  C. Bigot, A. Faivre, J.P. Gallois, A. Lapitre, D. Lugato, J.Y. Pierron, N. Rapin, *Automatic test generation with AGATHA*, TACAS, 7-11 April 2003

[5]  F. Bouquet, F. Peureux, *Generation of functional test sequences from B formal specifications – Presentation and industrial case-study*, in procs. of the 16th International Conference on Automated Software Engineering (ASE'01), pp.377-381, San Diego (USA), November 2003

[6]  F. Bouquet, B. Legeard, F. Peureux, E. Torreborre, *Mastering Test Generation from Smartcard Software Formal Models*, in Procs of the International Workshop on Construction and Analysis of Safe, secure and Interoperable Smart devices (CASSIS'04), vol.3362 of LNCS, pp.70-85, Marseille (France), March 2004

[7]  O. Carre, H. Martin, J.J. Vandewalle, *A semi formal model of Java Card 2.1 in UML*, in 1st Gemplus Developer Conference, Paris, France, June 21-22, 1999

[8]  D. Clarke, T. Jéron, V. Rusu, E. Zinovieva, *Automated test and oracle generation for smart-card applications*, in procs. of the International Conference on Research in Smartcards (e-Smart'01), vol.2140 of LNCS, pp.58-70, Cannes (France), September 2001

[9]  E.M. Clarke, O. Grumberg, D.A. Peled, *Model Cheking*, The MIT press, 1999

[10]  L.A. Clarke, *A System to Generate Test Data and Symbolically Execute Programs*, IEEE Transactions on Software Engineering, vol.SE-4 n.3, PP.178-187, September 1976

[11]  J. Dick, A. Faivre, *Automating the generation and sequencing of test cases from model-based specifications*, in procs. of the International Conference on Formal Methods Europe (FME'93), vol.670 of LNCS, pp.268-284, April 1993

[12]  European Telecommunications Standards Institute, F-06921 Sophia Antipolis (France), *GSM 11.11 v7.2.0 Technical Specification*, 1999

[13]  European Telecommunications Standards Institute, F-06921 Sophia Antipolis (France), *GSM 11.17 v8.1.0 Technical Specification*, 1999

[14]  A. Faivre, C. Gaston, *Test generation methodology based on symbolic execution for the Common Criteria higher levels*, in MoDeVa workshop, Montego Bay (Jamaica), October 2005

[15]  J.C. Fernandez, C. Jard, T. Jéron, C. Viho, *Using on the fly verification techniques for the generation of test suites*, Proceedings of CAV'96, LNCS 1102, Springer, New Brunswick, n.46, pp.145-150, 1997

[16]  J.P. Gallois, A. Lanusse, *Le test structurel pour la vérification de spécifications de systèmes industriels*, Génie logiciel n.46 pp.145-150, 1997

[17]  J.P. Gallois, A. Lapitre, P. Lé, *Analyse de spécifications industrielles et génération auto-matique de tests*, ICSSEA'99, CNAM-Paris, France, 8-10 décembre, 1999

[18]  M. Hennessy, H. Lin, *Symbolic bisimulations*, Theorical Computer Science, Vol.138 pp.353-389, Elsevier, 1995

[19]  R. Hierons, *Testing from Z specification*, The journal of Software Testing, Verification and Reliability, vol.7 pp.19-33, 1997

[20]  International Union of Telecommunications, *Langage de programmation – Langage de Description et de Spécification du CCITT – Norme 34*, Recommandation UIT T Z.100, March 1993

[21]  M. Ishisone, T. Sawada, *Brute: brute force rewriting engine*, GAIST, http://www.theta. theta.ro/ cafeobj, January 2001

[22]  B. Jeannet, T. Jéron, V. Rusu, E. Zinovieva, *Symbolic Test Selection Based on Approxi-mate Analysis*, pp. 349-364, TACAS'05, Edinburgh (UK), April 2005

[23]  W. Kelly, V. Maslov, W. Pugh, E. Rosser, T. Shpeisman, D. Wonnacott, *The Omega Li-brary version 1.1.0*, University of Maryland, http://www.cs.umd.edu/projects/omega, November 1996

[24]  J.C .King, *Symbolic Execution and Program Testing*, communications de l'ACM, vol.19 n.7, pp.385-394, July 1976

[25]  A. Lapitre, *Procédure de réduction pour les systèmes à base d'automates communicants : formalisation et mise en oeuvre*, Phd Thesis, University of Paris XI, in collaboration with the CEA, December 2002

[26]  *LEIRIOS tool*, http://www.leirios.com/index.php

[27]  H. Lin, *Symbolic Transition Graph with Assignment*, CONCUR'96, Springer-Verlag, LNCS, Pise (Italie), August 1996

[28]  D. Lugato, C. Bigot, Y. Valot, *Validation and automatic test generation on UML models: the AGATHA approach*, STTT (Software Tools for Technology Transfer), vol.5 n.2 pp.124-139, March 2004, Springer

[29]  H. Martin, L. du Bousquet, *Automatic test generation for Java-Card applets*, in Java card Workshop, Cannes (France), September 2000

[30]  OMG, *Unified Modelling Language 2.0*, OMG, Rapport formel/2003-04-01, January 2003

[31]  J. Philipps, A. Pretschner, O. Slotosch, E. Aiglestorfer, S. Kriebel, K.Scholl, *Model-based test case generation for smartcards*, in procs. of the 8th International Workshop on Formal Methods for Industrial Critical Systems (FMICS'03), vol.80 of ENTCS, Trond-heim (Norway), June 2003

[32]  J.Y. Pierron, J.-P. Gallois, E. Fievet, A. Lapitre, D. Lugato, V*alidation de systèmes in-dustriels par le test symbolique sur spécification STATEMATE*, ICSSEA'00, CNAM-Paris, France, December 5-8, 2000

[33]  J.Y. Pierron, *Définition de critères de sélection de tests fonctionnels pour la validation des systèmes électroniques embarqués*, Phd Thesis, University of Evry, France, in colla-boration with the CEA and PSA, April 2003

[34]  N. Rapin, *Validation de spécification à base d'automates par des techniques de déplia-ges et d'exécution symbolique*, Phd Thesis, University of Evry (France), in collaboration with the CEA and Ligeron S.A., July 2004

[35]  P. Wolper, P.Godefroid, *Partial-Order Methods for Temporal Verification*, procs. of CONCNUR'93, pp.233-246, Hildesheim (Belgium), August 1993

[36]  S. Yovine, *Kronos: A verification tool for real time systems*, Springer International Jour-nal of Software Tools for Technology Transfer, vol. 1 n.1/2, October 1997

# Author Index

# Lecture Notes in Computer Science

For information about Vols. 1–3823

please contact your bookseller or Springer

Vol. 3928: J. Domingo-Ferrer, J. Posegga, D. Schreckling (Eds.), Smart Card Research and Advanced Applications. XI, 359 pages. 2006.

Vol. 3927: J. Hespanha, A. Tiwari (Eds.), Hybrid Systems: Computation and Control. XII, 584 pages. 2006.

Vol. 3925: A. Valmari (Ed.), Model Checking Software. X, 307 pages. 2006.

Vol. 3924: P. Sestoft (Ed.), Programming Languages and Systems. XII, 343 pages. 2006.

Vol. 3923: A. Mycroft, A. Zeller (Eds.), Compiler Construction. XIII, 277 pages. 2006.

Vol. 3922: L. Baresi, R. Heckel (Eds.), Fundamental Approaches to Software Engineering. XIII, 427 pages. 2006.

Vol. 3921: L. Aceto, A. Ingólfsdóttir (Eds.), Foundations of Software Science and Computation Structures. XV, 447 pages. 2006.

Vol. 3920: H. Hermanns, J. Palsberg (Eds.), Tools and Algorithms for the Construction and Analysis of Systems. XIV, 506 pages. 2006.

Vol. 3916: J. Li, Q. Yang, A.-H. Tan (Eds.), Data Mining for Biomedical Applications. VIII, 155 pages. 2006. (Sublibrary LNBI).

Vol. 3915: R. Nayak, M.J. Zaki (Eds.), Knowledge Discovery from XML Documents. VIII, 105 pages. 2006.

Vol. 3907: F. Rothlauf, J. Branke, S. Cagnoni, E. Costa, C. Cotta, R. Drechsler, E. Lutton, P. Machado, J.H. Moore, J. Romero, G.D. Smith, G. Squillero, H. Takagi (Eds.), Applications of Evolutionary Computing. XXIV, 813 pages. 2006.

Vol. 3906: J. Gottlieb, G.R. Raidl (Eds.), Evolutionary Computation in Combinatorial Optimization. XI, 293 pages. 2006.

Vol. 3905: P. Collet, M. Tomassini, M. Ebner, S. Gustafson, A. Ekárt (Eds.), Genetic Programming. XI, 361 pages. 2006.

Vol. 3904: M. Baldoni, U. Endriss, A. Omicini, P. Torroni (Eds.), Declarative Agent Languages and Technologies III. XII, 245 pages. 2006. (Sublibrary LNAI).

Vol. 3903: K. Chen, R. Deng, X. Lai, J. Zhou (Eds.), Information Security Practice and Experience. XIV, 392 pages. 2006.

Vol. 3901: P.M. Hill (Ed.), Logic Based Program Synthesis and Transformation. X, 179 pages. 2006.

Vol. 3899: S. Frintrop, VOCUS: A Visual Attention System for Object Detection and Goal-Directed Search. XIV, 216 pages. 2006. (Sublibrary LNAI).

Vol. 3897: B. Preneel, S. Tavares (Eds.), Selected Areas in Cryptography. XI, 371 pages. 2006.

Vol. 3896: Y. Ioannidis, M.H. Scholl, J.W. Schmidt, F. Matthes, M. Hatzopoulos, K. Boehm, A. Kemper, T. Grust, C. Boehm (Eds.), Advances in Database Technology - EDBT 2006. XIV, 1208 pages. 2006.

Vol. 3895: O. Goldreich, A.L. Rosenberg, A.L. Selman (Eds.), Theoretical Computer Science. XII, 399 pages. 2006.

Vol. 3894: W. Grass, B. Sick, K. Waldschmidt (Eds.), Architecture of Computing Systems - ARCS 2006. XII, 496 pages. 2006.

Vol. 3890: S.G. Thompson, R. Ghanea-Hercock (Eds.), Defence Applications of Multi-Agent Systems. XII, 141 pages. 2006. (Sublibrary LNAI).

Vol. 3889: J. Rosca, D. Erdogmus, J.C. Príncipe, S. Haykin (Eds.), Independent Component Analysis and Blind Signal Separation. XXI, 980 pages. 2006.

Vol. 3888: D. Draheim, G. Weber (Eds.), Trends in Enterprise Application Architecture. IX, 145 pages. 2006.

Vol. 3887: J.R. Correa, A. Hevia, M. Kiwi (Eds.), LATIN 2006: Theoretical Informatics. XVI, 814 pages. 2006.

Vol. 3886: E.G. Bremer, J. Hakenberg, E.-H.(S.) Han, D. Berrar, W. Dubitzky (Eds.), Knowledge Discovery in Life Science Literature. XIV, 147 pages. 2006. (Sublibrary LNBI).

Vol. 3885: V. Torra, Y. Narukawa, A. Valls, J. Domingo-Ferrer (Eds.), Modeling Decisions for Artificial Intelligence. XII, 374 pages. 2006. (Sublibrary LNAI).

Vol. 3884: B. Durand, W. Thomas (Eds.), STACS 2006. XIV, 714 pages. 2006.

Vol. 3881: S. Gibet, N. Courty, J.-F. Kamp (Eds.), Gesture in Human-Computer Interaction and Simulation. XIII, 344 pages. 2006. (Sublibrary LNAI).

Vol. 3880: A. Rashid, M. Aksit (Eds.), Transactions on Aspect-Oriented Software Development I. IX, 335 pages. 2006.

Vol. 3879: T. Erlebach, G. Persinao (Eds.), Approximation and Online Algorithms. X, 349 pages. 2006.

Vol. 3878: A. Gelbukh (Ed.), Computational Linguistics and Intelligent Text Processing. XVII, 589 pages. 2006.

Vol. 3877: M. Detyniecki, J.M. Jose, A. Nürnberger, C. J. '. van Rijsbergen (Eds.), Adaptive Multimedia Retrieval: User, Context, and Feedback. XI, 279 pages. 2006.

Vol. 3876: S. Halevi, T. Rabin (Eds.), Theory of Cryptography. XI, 617 pages. 2006.

Vol. 3875: S. Ur, E. Bin, Y. Wolfsthal (Eds.), Hardware and Software, Verification and Testing. X, 265 pages. 2006.

Vol. 3874: R. Missaoui, J. Schmidt (Eds.), Formal Concept Analysis. X, 309 pages. 2006. (Sublibrary LNAI).

Vol. 3873: L. Maicher, J. Park (Eds.), Charting the Topic Maps Research and Applications Landscape. VIII, 281 pages. 2006. (Sublibrary LNAI).

Vol. 3872: H. Bunke, A. L. Spitz (Eds.), Document Analysis Systems VII. XIII, 630 pages. 2006.

Vol. 3870: S. Spaccapietra, P. Atzeni, W.W. Chu, T. Catarci, K.P. Sycara (Eds.), Journal on Data Semantics V. XIII, 237 pages. 2006.

Vol. 3869: S. Renals, S. Bengio (Eds.), Machine Learning for Multimodal Interaction. XIII, 490 pages. 2006.

Vol. 3868: K. Römer, H. Karl, F. Mattern (Eds.), Wireless Sensor Networks. XI, 342 pages. 2006.

Vol. 3866: T. Dimitrakos, F. Martinelli, P.Y.A. Ryan, S. Schneider (Eds.), Formal Aspects in Security and Trust. X, 259 pages. 2006.

Vol. 3865: W. Shen, K.-M. Chao, Z. Lin, J.-P.A. Barthès, A. James (Eds.), Computer Supported Cooperative Work in Design II. XII, 659 pages. 2006.

Vol. 3863: M. Kohlhase (Ed.), Mathematical Knowledge Management. XI, 405 pages. 2006. (Sublibrary LNAI).

Vol. 3862: R.H. Bordini, M. Dastani, J. Dix, A.E.F. Seghrouchni (Eds.), Programming Multi-Agent Systems. XIV, 267 pages. 2006. (Sublibrary LNAI).

Vol. 3861: J. Dix, S.J. Hegner (Eds.), Foundations of Information and Knowledge Systems. X, 331 pages. 2006.

Vol. 3860: D. Pointcheval (Ed.), Topics in Cryptology – CT-RSA 2006. XI, 365 pages. 2006.

Vol. 3858: A. Valdes, D. Zamboni (Eds.), Recent Advances in Intrusion Detection. X, 351 pages. 2006.

Vol. 3857: M.P.C. Fossorier, H. Imai, S. Lin, A. Poli (Eds.), Applied Algebra, Algebraic Algorithms and Error-Correcting Codes. XI, 350 pages. 2006.

Vol. 3855: E. A. Emerson, K.S. Namjoshi (Eds.), Verification, Model Checking, and Abstract Interpretation. XI, 443 pages. 2005.

Vol. 3854: I. Stavrakakis, M. Smirnov (Eds.), Autonomic Communication. XIII, 303 pages. 2006.

Vol. 3853: A.J. Ijspeert, T. Masuzawa, S. Kusumoto (Eds.), Biologically Inspired Approaches to Advanced Information Technology. XIV, 388 pages. 2006.

Vol. 3852: P.J. Narayanan, S.K. Nayar, H.-Y. Shum (Eds.), Computer Vision – ACCV 2006, Part II. XXXI, 977 pages. 2006.

Vol. 3851: P.J. Narayanan, S.K. Nayar, H.-Y. Shum (Eds.), Computer Vision – ACCV 2006, Part I. XXXI, 973 pages. 2006.

Vol. 3850: R. Freund, G. Păun, G. Rozenberg, A. Salomaa (Eds.), Membrane Computing. IX, 371 pages. 2006.

Vol. 3849: I. Bloch, A. Petrosino, A.G.B. Tettamanzi (Eds.), Fuzzy Logic and Applications. XIV, 438 pages. 2006. (Sublibrary LNAI).

Vol. 3848: J.-F. Boulicaut, L. De Raedt, H. Mannila (Eds.), Constraint-Based Mining and Inductive Databases. X, 401 pages. 2006. (Sublibrary LNAI).

Vol. 3847: K.P. Jantke, A. Lunzer, N. Spyratos, Y. Tanaka (Eds.), Federation over the Web. X, 215 pages. 2006. (Sublibrary LNAI).

Vol. 3846: H. J. van den Herik, Y. Björnsson, N.S. Netanyahu (Eds.), Computers and Games. XIV, 333 pages. 2006.

Vol. 3845: J. Farré, I. Litovsky, S. Schmitz (Eds.), Implementation and Application of Automata. XIII, 360 pages. 2006.

Vol. 3844: J.-M. Bruel (Ed.), Satellite Events at the MoDELS 2005 Conference. XIII, 360 pages. 2006.

Vol. 3843: P. Healy, N.S. Nikolov (Eds.), Graph Drawing. XVII, 536 pages. 2006.

Vol. 3842: H.T. Shen, J. Li, M. Li, J. Ni, W. Wang (Eds.), Advanced Web and Network Technologies, and Applications. XXVII, 1057 pages. 2006.

Vol. 3841: X. Zhou, J. Li, H.T. Shen, M. Kitsuregawa, Y. Zhang (Eds.), Frontiers of WWW Research and Development - APWeb 2006. XXIV, 1223 pages. 2006.

Vol. 3840: M. Li, B. Boehm, L.J. Osterweil (Eds.), Unifying the Software Process Spectrum. XVI, 522 pages. 2006.

Vol. 3839: J.-C. Filliâtre, C. Paulin-Mohring, B. Werner (Eds.), Types for Proofs and Programs. VIII, 275 pages. 2006.

Vol. 3838: A. Middeldorp, V. van Oostrom, F. van Raamsdonk, R. de Vrijer (Eds.), Processes, Terms and Cycles: Steps on the Road to Infinity. XVIII, 639 pages. 2005.

Vol. 3837: K. Cho, P. Jacquet (Eds.), Technologies for Advanced Heterogeneous Networks. IX, 307 pages. 2005.

Vol. 3836: J.-M. Pierson (Ed.), Data Management in Grids. X, 143 pages. 2006.

Vol. 3835: G. Sutcliffe, A. Voronkov (Eds.), Logic for Programming, Artificial Intelligence, and Reasoning. XIV, 744 pages. 2005. (Sublibrary LNAI).

Vol. 3834: D.G. Feitelson, E. Frachtenberg, L. Rudolph, U. Schwiegelshohn (Eds.), Job Scheduling Strategies for Parallel Processing. VIII, 283 pages. 2005.

Vol. 3833: K.-J. Li, C. Vangenot (Eds.), Web and Wireless Geographical Information Systems. XI, 309 pages. 2005.

Vol. 3832: D. Zhang, A.K. Jain (Eds.), Advances in Biometrics. XX, 796 pages. 2005.

Vol. 3831: J. Wiedermann, G. Tel, J. Pokorný, M. Bieliková, J. Štuller (Eds.), SOFSEM 2006: Theory and Practice of Computer Science. XV, 576 pages. 2006.

Vol. 3830: D. Weyns, H. V.D. Parunak, F. Michel (Eds.), Environments for Multi-Agent Systems II. VIII, 291 pages. 2006. (Sublibrary LNAI).

Vol. 3829: P. Pettersson, W. Yi (Eds.), Formal Modeling and Analysis of Timed Systems. IX, 305 pages. 2005.

Vol. 3828: X. Deng, Y. Ye (Eds.), Internet and Network Economics. XVII, 1106 pages. 2005.

Vol. 3827: X. Deng, D.-Z. Du (Eds.), Algorithms and Computation. XX, 1190 pages. 2005.

Vol. 3826: B. Benatallah, F. Casati, P. Traverso (Eds.), Service-Oriented Computing - ICSOC 2005. XVIII, 597 pages. 2005.

Vol. 3824: L.T. Yang, M. Amamiya, Z. Liu, M. Guo, F.J. Rammig (Eds.), Embedded and Ubiquitous Computing – EUC 2005. XXIII, 1204 pages. 2005.